Jim —

thanks for considering
our Library of Congress exhibit
for Sir Winston

your pal,

Jack Kemp

(old #15)

A Connoisseur's Guide
to the Books of

Sir Winston Churchill

Also by Richard M. Langworth

Buick Buyer's Guide
Cadillac Buyer's Guide
Camaro
Cars of the Fifties
Cars of the Forties
Cars of the Sixties
Cars That Never Were
Chrysler: The Postwar Years
Chrysler Buyer's Guide
Collector Car Price Guide
Corvette Collector's Guide
Dodge Buyer's Guide
Encyclopaedia of American Cars
High-Performance Chevrolet
Hudson: The Postwar Years
Kaiser-Frazer: Last Onslaught on Detroit

Mercedes-Benz: The First Hundred Years
Mustang Collector's Guide
Oldsmobile Buyer's Guide
Packard Buyer's Guide
Personal Luxury
Porsche: A Tradition of Greatness
Portrait of a Legend
Standard of Excellence
Studebaker Buyer's Guide
Studebaker: The Postwar Years
The American Sports Car
The Complete Book of Corvette
The Complete Book of Ford
The Great American Convertible
Tiger, Alpine, Rapier

Co-Author:

Chevrolet 1911-1985, *with Jan Norbye*
Chrysler: A History, *with Jan Norbye*
Collectible Cars, *with Graham Robson*
General Motors, *with Jan Norbye*

Oldsmobile, *with Beverly Rae Kimes*
Packard: A History, *with 20 others*
Triumph Cars, *with Graham Robson*

Editor & Publisher:

Chevy V-8s, *by Terry Boyce*
India, *by Winston Churchill*
Proceedings of the Churchill Societies

Chartwell Bulletins, *by Winston Churchill*
The Hot One, *by Pat Chappell*
The Studebaker Century, *by Asa Hall*

A Connoisseur's Guide
to the Books of

Sir Winston Churchill

Richard M. Langworth
In association with
The Churchill Center, Washington, D.C.

BRASSEY'S

London • Washington

First English Edition 1998
Revised Edition 2000

A member of the Chrysalis Group plc

UK editorial offices: Brassey's, 9 Blenheim Court, Brewery Road, London N7 9NT
UK orders: Littlehampton Book Services, Faraday Close, Durrington, Worthing,West
Sussex BN13 3RB

North American orders: Brassey's, Inc., 22841 Quicksilver Drive, Dulles, VA 20166,
USA

Richard Langworth has asserted his moral right to be identified as the author of this
work.

Library of Congress Cataloguing in Publication Data
available

British Library Cataloguing in Publication Data
A catalogue record for this book is available from the British Library

ISBN 1 85753 246 5 Hardcover

Typeset by Hedgehog
Printed in Great Britain by Redwood Books Ltd, Trowbridge, Wiltshire

CONTENTS

Foreword by James Muller   vii
Acknowledgements   ix

1.   Introduction   1
2.   The Story of the Malakand Field Force, 1897   11
3.   The River War   27
4.   Savrola   38
5.   London to Ladysmith via Pretoria   51
6.   Ian Hamilton's March   58
7.   The Boer War   63
8.   Mr. Brodrick's Army   65
9.   Lord Randolph Churchill   68
10.   For Free Trade   77
11.   My African Journey   80
12.   Liberalism and the Social Problem   90
13.   The People's Rights   96
14.   The World Crisis   101
15.   My Early Life / A Roving Commission   129
16.   India   148
17.   Thoughts and Adventures / Amid these Storms   154
18.   Marlborough: His Life and Times   164
19.   Great Contemporaries   176
20.   Arms and the Covenant   190
21.   Step by Step 1936–1939   196
22.   Into Battle / Blood, Sweat and Tears   202
23.   The Unrelenting Struggle   212
24.   The End of the Beginning   217
25.   Onwards to Victory   222
26.   The Dawn of Liberation   227
27.   Victory   232
28.   Foreign Translations of War Speech Volumes   237
29.   War Speeches 1940–1945   241
30.   War Speeches Published as Books   243
31.   Secret Session Speeches   247
32.   The Second World War   254
33.   The Sinews of Peace   283
34.   Painting as a Pastime   287
35.   Europe Unite   294
36.   Taler I Danmark   298
37.   In the Balance   300
38.   The War Speeches   303
39.   Stemming the Tide   308
40.   A History of the English-Speaking Peoples   312
41.   The Unwritten Alliance   337
42.   Frontiers and Wars   340
43.   Young Winston's Wars   343
44.   If I Lived My Life Again   347
45.   Winston S. Churchill / His Complete Speeches 1897–1963   349
46.   The Collected Essays of Sir Winston Churchill   353
47.   The Dream   356
48.   The Chartwell Bulletins 1935   360
49.   The Great Republic   361

APPENDICES
Appendix 1:
   The Collected Works   362
   The Major Works   369
Appendix 2:
   The Churchill Center   371
   Recent Discoveries   372

To the memory of

Harriet H. Langworth 1908–1996

FOREWORD

Winston Churchill's prodigious career as a writer has been eclipsed by his better-known achievements as a statesman, yet – as his 1953 Nobel Prize for Literature reminds us – not altogether forgotten. Throughout the English-speaking world, and in many other countries as well, copies of Churchill's books abound, in his native tongue or in translation, in libraries and in millions of private collections. For more than a decade, men and women have come of age who were born after Churchill's death in 1965 and have no personal recollection of his public life. Many recall, however, that his *Second World War* or his *History of the English-Speaking Peoples* had a place on their parents' bookshelves.

With the gradual passing of Churchill's contemporaries, his books have begun to replace personal remembrance of his wartime role in introducing him to younger people. That was Churchill's own idea as early as 1930, when he dedicated his autobiography to 'a new generation'. As the twentieth century draws to a close, younger people discover Churchill by reading a biography by Martin Gilbert or William Manchester, by hearing stories that still circulate about Churchill's wit, by an encounter with one of his books, or occasionally – but not often enough – by some talk of him in class. Thousands are still fascinated by the life and thought of a man who began his public career a hundred years ago.

If you visit a good library, used bookshop or private collection in search of Churchill, you may be astonished by the shelfful of books that he wrote. Some still confuse him with the homonymous American novelist and sometime politician from New Hampshire, once so much better known that Winston *Spencer* Churchill promised to use his middle name so as not to benefit from the American's fame. And readers still marvel, when they open his books, at his wide-ranging vocabulary, his exact diction, his broad experience, his deep understanding of politics and history, his ironic humour, his vivid descriptions and his vigorous English prose. Once they start reading, they find it hard to stop.

Collectors and readers of Churchill's books will soon find that this new book by Richard Langworth is invaluable. It is not the first book on Churchill's writings. Its predecessors include the bibliography compiled by Frederick Woods and academic studies by Keith Alldritt, Maurice Ashley, Manfred Weidhorn, Michael Wolff and the same Frederick Woods, among others. These earlier works have their merits, but none has the same purpose as *The Connoisseur's Guide*: to tell you what exactly it is that you have in your hand.

Mr Langworth accomplishes this purpose in several different ways. First, he describes the book, briefly but tellingly, setting aside in a few words many ingrained scholarly misimpressions. His lucid epitomes of each of Churchill's books make this work an important secondary source for scholars and also a useful reference for lay readers. Second, he offers excerpts from contemporary reviews or academic treatments of the book by others, carefully seeking out judgments at variance with his own. Many of these excerpts are obscure and all but unknown today; some, like the idiosyncratic but often penetrating remarks of Henry Fearon, have never been published before. Third, he meticulously describes the full range of different editions of each of Churchill's books, beginning with those in English but not neglecting translations. He offers the reader and collector an abundance of information that has never been published before.

Though he wrote this book with his usual celerity, Richard Langworth has really been working on it for almost three decades, ever since he founded the International Churchill Society in 1968. As president of that worldwide association, and more recently of The Churchill Center, founded to encourage the study of Churchill, he has been at the forefront of efforts to keep Churchill's example before laymen and scholars alike for more than a generation. It is thanks to him that unbound volumes of Churchill's collected works were rescued from a bindery in Cornwall and made available to hundreds of readers; thanks to him that an appeal was made to publish the remaining companion volumes of the official Churchill biography – which had ceased just as they had reached the Second World War – now appearing thanks to a generous benefaction from Wendy Reves; thanks to him that many Churchill books have reappeared in print; thanks to him for making possible new studies on Churchill; and thanks to him, as editor of the quarterly journal *Finest Hour*, that these developments have been brought to the notice of those interested in Winston Churchill.

At the same time, as a bookseller and an avid reader, Mr Langworth has spent decades handling and studying books by Churchill. No-one can offer his particular combination of knowledge both of the content of Churchill's books and their value to collectors or bibliophiles. Perhaps one day we will have a complete collection of Churchill's writings and speeches on a single compact disc. In the interim, we have relied on the generosity of the man who has been for decades a living compact disc, answering questions from scholars, the press and the public about all things related to Churchill. Now the carefully gathered knowledge that sallies forth from him in conversation is recorded between the covers of this book.

James W. Muller
Professor of Political Science
University of Alaska Anchorage, May 1998

ACKNOWLEDGEMENTS

I am grateful to Winston S. Churchill and the Churchill Literary Estate for permission to quote brief excerpts from the Churchill volumes, the late Fred Woods for permission to quote from his excellent *Artillery of Words,* and Professor Manfred Weidhorn for permission to quote from the most scholarly book on Churchill's writings published to date, *Sword and Pen.* I am thankful as well to Ronald I. Cohen and the late Fred Woods for permission to quote their Bibliographic numbers.

The mistakes, as they say, are mine, all mine, but this book contains as few mistakes as it does because of four people. Chief among these is my friend, bookseller colleague and partner, Mark Weber of London, the consummate scouter of Churchill volumes from Bombay to Reykjavik, who has painstakingly reviewed the text against his own encyclopedic knowledge and massive library. Mark is the only collector I know who has set himself the task of acquiring not only every edition of Churchill's books in every language, but most of the impressions and variants as well. He promises that upon his distant death his library will not be donated to some obscure archive but will be unleashed upon the world, turning the market upside down and allowing any survivors finally to get that elusive odd volume they've heard about herein, but have never seen. I am so very grateful to Mark for his help and expertise over the years, and to his wife Avril for putting up with the two of us.

Curt Zoller, of Mission Viejo, California, began by pointing out all the grammatical mistakes and ended by furnishing me with scores of reviews of Churchill's books from his collection of over 600, many of them for books I didn't even know were reviewed. It was especially instructive to learn, from an obscure review of the Collected Works provided by Curt, to what considerable extent those volumes were not only reset, but reedited. I had no idea they had been so altered until I read it; had I known, I would certainly have tried to convince Leo Cooper to offprint his outstanding 1989-90 new editions (*Malakand*, etc.) from some other text more accessible to researchers.

James W. Muller, Professor of Political Science at the University of Alaska Anchorage, is at work on his own unique contribution to our knowledge of Churchill as author: *The Education of Winston Churchill*, a book not about Churchill's education, but the education he offers us as a historian, politician and philosopher. The introductions which begin each of my entries were carefully reviewed by Professor Muller, who made many vital corrections and critical judgments. The result is a more balanced view of each title in which I hope I have equally represented its strong points and its flaws.

For fifteen years now, Ronald I.Cohen of Ottawa, Ontario, has been labouring on the ultimate Bibliography of Winston Churchill, which the collector of Sir Winston's books will find, ipso facto, indispensable. In view of Ron's work I took care to avoid the detailed bibliographic descriptions he will ultimately present, while he in turn has granted me permission to quote his numbers from his 'Section A,' works entirely by Churchill. He has also reviewed most of my text, always sending me urgent warnings: 'Careful of *Taler I Danmark*, remember that it does not contain war speeches, but is a stand-alone text.' As Sir Martin Gilbert, Churchill's official biographer, said to William Manchester, Churchill's most lyrical biographer: 'our work moves along on parallel tracks.'

Two notable Churchill authors have especially influenced my understanding of our author. William Manchester, author of that wonderful piece of historical literature, *The Last Lion* (Vol. I, 1983, Vol. II, 1988, Vol. III, I hope, not far away) allowed me to quote from his superb introduction to a new edition of *My Early Life*, and I referred to his indexes on almost every other title Churchill wrote. Professor Manfred Weidhorn of Yeshiva College, New York City, wrote the standard work on Churchill's writings, *Sword and Pen* (1974) and allowed me to quote liberally from it. Without his penetrating and critical insights, the title introductions herein would be much less than they are. The friendship and encouragement of these two fine authors over many years has been, moreover, a spur: massive contributions to Churchill studies comprised ever-present inspiration to complete this minor one.

I cannot possibly thank all the people who have aided me with observations, comments and corrections, or allowed me to quote them. The list below does not by any means preclude the rest. New York bookseller Glenn Horowitz has probably forgotten more than any of us know about bibliography, and he is quoted liberally throughout, notably with regard to states of the *Malakand*. Brad Nilsson discovered an odd Edition of the *Malakand* which utterly altered my words on that title. Stanley Smith and Jack Nixon wrote in *Finest Hour* their appreciations, respectively, of *London to Ladysmith* and *The People's Rights*, which I have quoted under those topics. Gordon Cohen made me realize that the Odhams *World Crisis* was not an abridgement but a complete text and, therefore, a bargain. Donald Hurt assisted with a description of an American *Blood, Sweat, and Tears* that I had never seen and didn't know existed. Jean Broome, formerly Administrator of Chartwell, allowed me to visit on a 'closed day,' when I was allowed the run of the bookshelves. Michael Wybrow, longtime Churchill specialist bookseller, accompanied me to Chartwell that day, and has helped me understand the true breadth of Churchill's literary contribution by repeatedly turning me loose in his own substantial library in Sussex.

Algis Valiunas wrote a wonderful appreciation of *The World Crisis* ('A Ground War for All Time:* Churchill's Forgotten Masterpiece') in the *American Spectator* for April 1991, to which I am grateful for permission to quote. The late Harold Mortlake, London bookseller, published a catalogue in 1969 that was instrumental in guiding us through the maze of trade and book club editions of *The Second World War*. The late Henry Fearon wrote about his own Churchill collection in an unpublished catalogue purchased after his death by Mark Weber, who provided me with a copy from which I have quoted; his wise observations are especially instructive on *The World Crisis* and Churchill's wartime and postwar speech volumes, notably the last of them, *The Unwritten Alliance*.

I have worked with many publishers, but few with the diligence and dedication of Brassey's, and I would like to thank in particular Polly Willis, a skilled and sensitive editor and book designer, for so ably fine-tuning the final product, saving me from myself on countless occasions; and Mark Sherwood for eliminating inconsistences and dealing with the problems created by "two nations divided by a common language". I am equally grateful to my proofreaders here in America: Gail Greenly, Barbara Langworth and Mark Weber.

Finally, this work has been produced with the utmost respect, admiration and affection for the Man of the Century, Sir Winston Spencer Churchill, K.G., O.M., C.H., etc. etc. etc., and his gracious daughter, who inspires all who labour to comprehend her father's massive record, champions and critics alike.

Putney House
Hopkinton, New Hampshire
April 1998

Note on the Second Edition

This new edition contains all the additions and corrections I have compiled to date through readers of the First Edition and colleagues around the world. Thanks in particular for his diligent review of the text to my friend, colleague and partner Mark Weber, the Churchill Book Specialist.

Although the reader may regard most of these as trivial, they represent a painstaking effort to correct every mistake discovered. Owners of First Editions wishing to make corrections to their copies will find all corrections posted on my website: www.churchillbooks.com.

Further corrections are most welcome.

Richard M. Langworth
rml@churchillbooks.com

INTRODUCTION

Winston Spencer Churchill begins his essay *Painting as a Pastime* by considering the value of a hobby. The mind is not capable of assimilating our day-to-day activities, he says, without rest periods when it can be focused on something entirely different. Since he was himself a voracious reader, it is not surprising that Churchill suggests books as a diversion: 'As you browse about, taking down book after book from the shelves and contemplating the vast, infinitely varied store of knowledge and wisdom which the human race has accumulated and preserved, pride, even in its most innocent forms, is chased from the heart by feelings of awe not untinged with sadness. As one surveys the mighty array of sages, saints, historians, scientists, poets and philosophers whose treasures one will never be able to admire– still less enjoy–the brief tenure of our existence here dominates mind and spirit.

'"What shall I do with all my books?" was the question; and the answer, "Read them," sobered the questioner. But if you cannot read them, at any rate handle them and, as it were, fondle them. Peer into them. Let them fall open where they will. Read on from the first sentence that arrests the eye. Then turn to another. Make a voyage of discovery, taking soundings of uncharted seas. Set them back on their shelves with your own hands. Arrange them on your own plan, so that if you do not know what is in them, you at least know where they are. If they cannot be your friends, let them at any rate be your acquaintances. If they cannot enter the circle of your life, do not deny them at least a nod of recognition.'

This is very good advice when applied to Churchill's own books. It is certainly a mistake to read too many of them at once–or too soon in life. 'The first impression is the one that counts', he wrote; 'and if it is a slight one, it may be all that can be hoped for. A later and second perusal may recoil from a surface already hardened by premature contact. Young people should be careful in their reading, as old people in eating their food. They should not eat too much. They should chew it well.'

Why read Churchill? I always answer that question by citing Sir Winston's description of his encounter with Franklin Roosevelt at Argentia Bay in 1941: 'Meeting Roosevelt', he said, was 'like opening your first bottle of Champagne.' It is a curious coincidence–or perhaps Churchill had it in mind when he made that statement– that Harold Nicolson likened his friend Winston's autobiography *My Early Life* to 'a beaker of Champagne'.

Too much Champagne perforce can leave you comatose. It is best enjoyed in moderation (and no matter what you hear, Churchill was always a moderate drinker). But let us turn to another authority on the joy of reading Churchill: Robert Pilpel, in his fine book *Churchill in America*. Pilpel's first encounter came at the same time as my own, and over the same set of books: *The Second World War*.

'I took the plunge and cracked the binding of *The Gathering Storm*. Five thousand pages later I was hungry for more. How can I describe this first encounter with Churchill and Churchill's style? First of all and most striking was the feeling of warm communion that enveloped me as I started to read, an almost immediate sensation of fraternal intimacy, of being taken into confidence as a fellow member of the English-speaking tribe. Then there was the wonderful Britishness of expression: the robust roast-beef-and-pewter phrases, rolling cadences, portentous Latinate locutions–alien yet eerily familiar, the echo of a racial memory. Before long I caught sparkles of irrepressible humour percolating through the majestic narrative façade, as though Puck had escaped from *A Midsummer Night's Dream* and infiltrated *Paradise Lost*. Long before I turned the last page of *Triumph and Tragedy* my impression of Churchill had crystallised: so forcefully had his personality come through in his writing that he emerged more alive to me than all contemporary statesmen put together ... I felt I knew him. To be sure, I did not know him quite as well as I presumed, but that was unimportant. What really mattered was not how much I knew, but that all I knew I liked ... It seemed to me that his 90 years had been almost incredibly full and rich: wife, children, books, glory, power, worldwide adulation, and a peaceful old age–all the gifts that could be bestowed by a prodigal and beneficent fate. Had I been older I might have realised that such bounty is by no means proof against the rigors of the human condition, but my ignorance served me well at the time, for I felt compelled to learn more about this phenomenally perfect life, and more about the man who had lived it.'

Recently I've been reading the most popular book of 1938 and the least popular book of 1939: Stuart Hodgson's *The Man Who Made the Peace: The Story of Neville Chamberlain*. Published three weeks after Munich, it is an unadulterated paean of praise. Five months later Hitler's Reich absorbed the rump of Czechoslovakia, and Hodgson's book vanished from the bookstalls.

I do not cite this to be disrespectful of Mr Chamberlain. He tried his best, 'according to his lights' as Churchill put it, and we condemn the practitioners of another time only on the strength of hindsight. Indeed Sheila Lawlor's outstanding *Churchill and Politics of War* (1994) emphatically dispels the notion that Chamberlain did not support Churchill's policy of all-out war after the fall of France. I mention Hodgson's biography because it represents a watershed in the long history of Churchill's writings, and writings about him: for 1939 marks the point at which people stopped being curious about Neville Chamberlain and began seriously to read or write about Winston Churchill.

The Churchill Center checklist, *Churchill Bibliographic Data,* lists 17 works specifically about Churchill published prior to 1939. Now that's not bad for a person of 64: Lady Thatcher has yet to achieve that many, and she is older! But from 1939 forward came over 600 more works about Churchill, and as I write, 50 more are in the pipeline.

Churchill himself, in 1939, had been writing books for 40 years. Up to his death in 1965 he had produced 40 titles in over 60 volumes–published in about equal number before and after 1939. But in sheer quantity of editions, issues, states, impressions and translations, the post-1939 publications outweigh the pre-1939 by ten or fifteen to one. It is that canon–admittedly only the tip of the Churchill bibliographic iceberg–that is the subject of this book, whose mission is to tell you what you are holding in your hand.

The first thing to say about this book is that it is not a bibliography. That is also the second and the third thing. I was helping Frederick Woods plan the revision of his famous bibliography before his premature death in February 1995. For 15 years I have admired and aided the research of Ronald Cohen, who is completing a massive new bibliography. This book omits material that bibliographers consider essential, and contains material that will not be found in bibliographies.

A bibliography provides details relating to circumstances of publication, contractual arrangements, royalty arrangements, and so on, which will not be found here. Indeed I have worked very hard to complement and not to rival Mr Cohen's and Mr Woods's works. There certainly are occasions when I dip into bibliographic description–colours, bindings, dust jackets, etc.–these descriptions may not match Mr Cohen's exactly but overall we think the match will not mislead.

This book is an entirely different concept, a 'connoisseur's guide'. Thus there is a summary of each book with an appraisal of our author's arguments and the way he makes them; excerpts from reviews, hostile and complimentary, old and new; a smörgåsbord of the best current thought on the books from such authorities as William Manchester and Manfred Weidhorn; descriptions of the individual editions, issues and impressions, with details of how to identify first editions; aesthetic judgments as to the merit of each edition; and their 1998 current retail value. These are things I am always asked by Churchill book collectors. The aim of all this is to tell you what you're holding in your hand.

Almost everyone, for example, owns a set of *The Second World War*; but what about the English Chartwell Edition of 1956, or the American Chartwell Edition of 1983, both of which are often encountered by readers who can find no published guidance about them. Are they worth your while? (The answers for these two are 'yes' and 'perhaps'. The English Chartwell Edition is the finest trade edition of *The Second World War* ever published, and includes all of Churchill's final revisions to the text; the American Chartwell Edition is nicely bound in half leather; but the text is photographically reproduced from the First Edition, making it considerably less significant. And, since it was produced mainly for the Book-of-the-Month Club, there is a huge difference in value between the BOMC and the Trade Edition.) This is the kind of information you will find herein.

The bibliographers' tasks are different, and more specific. They are concerned not only with Churchill's books, but his pamphlets, contributions to other books, periodical contributions, or works containing his letters and speeches. We are concerned only with the titles we can legitimately call his books, a book being something larger than a pamphlet and usually hardbound, or at least known to exist hardbound. It is, of course, in his books that most people encounter the 'roast-beef-and-pewter' writings of Winston Churchill.

One purpose of this book is self-defence. It certainly will eliminate a vast number of queries I receive from people asking, 'What exactly am I holding in my hand?' I am perhaps qualified to tell them, since I along with Mark Weber have probably held more of Churchill's books in our hands than anyone since 1982, when Dalton Newfield died. Dal, who served as President of the International Churchill Society and editor of their journal *Finest Hour* from 1970 to 1975, was my friend and Churchill book supplier. To get the volumes I didn't have after he passed away I bought collections. Soon I had duplicates, more than I knew what to do with. So I put the duplicates up for sale. Then people called and said, 'Can you get this or that?' and before I knew it, I was a bookseller. My shop, Churchillbooks, now processes 600 orders, 2,000 titles and 5,000 or more volumes annually.

In the process of handling so many books one becomes curious about the differences between them, often minute, often found in purportedly the selfsame editions, and by comparing and communicating, one learns from others. Passing that knowledge along is my goal.

The interest in Churchill book collecting is rampant worldwide. He is one of the most popular of modern authors in Japan and Korea. The Scandinavians and Swiss, and indeed the Germans, are among the most enthusiastic collectors and readers of Churchill. He is increasingly popular in what used to be called the Soviet empire.

A prime concern of Churchill bibliophiles is what constitutes a first edition, but the sheer variety of desirable later editions is daunting, exciting. This book will examine them all, but I should try to explain at the outset why people lay so much value on first editions, which are and ever will be the most desirable and expensive. The reason is simple: a first edition represents the closest portrayal of the author himself. It is the first form in which, as Churchill said, he submitted his work 'to the judgment or clemency of the public'. The first edition contains all the mistakes, typos and embarrassing misstatements which authors correct in later editions (if they have the chance—and Churchill had countless chances, of which he took full opportunity).

TECHNICALITIES

This book explains precisely how to tell a first edition—and a first edition dust jacket—from later editions, states, impressions and issues. Dust jackets or wrappers are critically important, because they increase the value of Churchill's books by factors of two or more. Yet, either unscrupulously or by accident, first editions are sometimes wrapped in later edition dust jackets. Serious collectors, and perhaps even the curious but unserious, must be aware of the differences. Jackets provide important clues as to how Churchill, his publishers, his reviewers and readers saw him at the time.

The establishment and evolution of a text is the primary responsibility of bibliographers. I have traced such evolution, but formal bibliographic descriptions are omitted. Although I have provided approximate sizes there are no precise measurements of page thicknesses or technical descriptions of bindings, signatures and the like; these are properly the sphere of the bibliographer. Nor have I thought it essential to provide production quantities for more recent editions.

SIZE

I began expecting to list the height, width and thickness of each individual volume, and soon found this a hopeless task. Books vary–especially old books–and I was soon finding variations between identical editions. Also, I found to my astonishment that my measurements often bore no resemblance to the Woods Bibliography. For example, Woods says the First Edition *Malakand Field Force* measures 7½ x 4⅞in. My own copy and several others on the shelf measure 7⅞ x 5¼in. Furthermore, in 15 years of buying and selling Churchill books, not once have I nor anyone else I know referenced Woods's dimensions.

Except where distinct size differences help identify various editions or impressions of the same title, one from another, I've chosen to describe books by the traditional cataloguer's terms, which provide a rough and ready size guide and nothing more:

Folio (Fo.): Very large format, now commonly known as 'coffee table' size; among Churchill folio works is the Time–Life two-volume *Second World War*, measuring 14 x 12in (365 x 305mm) which deserves this description.

Quarto (4to): Normally lying between folio and octavo in size, though varying considerably in this respect. A telephone directory is quarto; but so is *The Island Race*, A138(c), which measures 12¼ x 9¾in (310 x 248mm), although Woods calls it 'octavo' and says it measures 12 x 9½in! Other quarto volumes are the Danish and Norwegian translations of *The Great War*, which measure 11½ x 8½in.

Octavo (8vo): The commonest size of book since the early seventeenth century. A large (demy) octavo is about the size of *Frontiers and Wars*, A142/1, which measures 9½ x 6⅜in (232 x 162mm). A small (crown) octavo is about the size of the English *Young Winston's Wars*, A143(a), which measures 8¾ x 5⅝in (222 x 143mm), although Woods calls it '16mo' and says it measures 8½ x 5½in! (You see the problem ...)

Duodecimo (12mo, commonly called 'twelvemo'): A bit smaller than 8vo but taller than 16mo: the size of a conventional paperback, say 6⅞ x 4¼in (175 x 107mm).

Sextodecimo (16mo, usually pronounced 'sixteenmo'): The smallest size of book covered herein, shorter but perhaps wider than a paperback, for example the 1915 edition of *Savrola*, which measures 6⅝ x 4½in (168 x 114mm).

My only other reference to size will be when an obvious difference can be ascertained between related editions or issues: I thought it useful to mention, for example, that the first edition *Malakand* bulks about 1½in, while the first Colonial issue bulks only about 1¼in; or that there's about half an inch difference between the first impression Macmillan *Aftermath* and the later impressions. Even here, the key word is 'about', since old books swell or shrink depending on storage conditions, and many were not uniform to begin with.

TERMINOLOGY

I have tried to follow John Carter's *ABC for Book Collectors* (New York: Alfred Knopf, eighth printing 1985), which provides generally accepted definitions of the following commonly used terms in this book:

Edition: 'All copies of a book printed at any time or times from one setting-up of type without substantial change, including copies printed from sterotype, electrotype [Carter should now add 'computer scanning'] or similar plates made from that setting of type.'

Impression: 'The whole number of copies of that edition printed at one time, that is, without the type or plates being removed from the press.' A particular conundrum was posed by the discovery that the stated third impression of the Colonial *Malakand Field Force* (pressed November 1898) carried the same extensive textual corrections of the Silver Library Edition (pressed at the same time–indeed both these books used the same sheets). How then to classify the third Colonial? It is clearly not a new impression. My solution was to make it part of a new entry, not cited by Woods, the 'Second Edition', along with the Silver Library Edition.

State: 'When alterations, corrections, additions or excisions are effected in a book during the process of manufacture, so that copies exhibiting variations go on sale on publication day indiscriminately, these variant copies are conveniently classified as belonging to different states of the edition.' Example: the two states of the first English *My Early Life*.

Issue: 'An exception [to the above] is the regular use of issue for variant title pages, usually in respect of the publisher's imprint ... [also] when similar variations can be clearly shown to have originated in some action taken after the book was published, two [or more] issues are distinguished.' Example: the two issues of *The People's Rights*, one with an index and appendix, the other with two appendices and no index.

I occasionally sidestep Carter's strict definitions for clarity. With the *Savrola*, for example, Woods states that the first English 'edition' was produced from a set of electroplates made up in Boston, a duplicate set to the First American Edition. The English 'edition' might therefore be called an 'issue', but I did not do so because no one else does, including Woods, and because it is quite distinct in appearance.

Offprints: Carter defines this as 'a separate printing of a section of a larger publication', which is not exactly how I or modern publishers use it. To us an offprint is a reprint, sometimes reduced but sometimes same-size, of all the pages of an earlier printing (for example the five Canadian offprints of American war speech volumes from *The Unrelenting Struggle* through *Victory*). In earlier years offprinting was accomplished by using plates from the original (like the Canadian issue of *My African Journey*) or by reproducing the type on negatives (like the Australian issue of *Secret Session Speeches*). In the latter case, the offprint usually exhibits heavy-looking type, not as finely printed as the original. Offprints are not usually considered separate editions, but a contretemps arises with modern reprints of long out-of-print works made by photo-reproduction (off-printing), such as my own recent edition of *India* or the Ayer editions of *Amid These Storms* and *While England Slept*. The *India*, which includes new material, undoubtedly qualifies as a separate edition, but books like the Ayer volumes are merely issues, being page-for-page reprints.

Foreign translations: In listing these I have attempted to supply most of the accent marks, particularly the Scandinavian, which are within the capacity of my word processing programme; my apologies to readers for those I have failed to reproduce. In the case of certain French and Spanish titles I have had to use a lower-case letter properly to convey the accent mark.

Proof copies: From *The World Crisis* on, proof copies bound in paper wrappers are occasionally encountered. I have not thought it my duty to describe these, which is a task best left to the bibliographer, except to say that in general they tend to lack illustrations, maps and plans that appear in the published volumes. Although not widely collected, proofs do usually command high prices when they are offered for sale.

DUST JACKETS = DUST WRAPPERS
I generally use the term 'dust jacket' to refer to what English bibliophiles usually call a 'dust wrapper', and I hope they will forgive me. The two terms are interchangeable, though words that describe the parts of the dust jacket, aside from 'spine', are common to both countries. These are as follows:

Flap: The parts of the jacket that fold in around the edge of the boards, front and rear.

Face: The front or back panel of the jacket that you see with the book lying flat in front of you.

FOREIGN TRANSLATIONS
Collectors of editions in foreign languages are enjoying a little-known but rewarding branch of Churchill bibliophilia, not the least for the sometimes magnificent bindings of these works (leading examples: the Monaco edition of *Savrola*, Scandinavian

editions of *The Great War* and the Belgian French edition of *The Second World War*). Foreign translations also often differ importantly from the English editions, depending on what Churchill wished to emphasize or de-emphasize. For example, Sir Martin Gilbert's official biography records that the Dutch, through Churchill's foreign language impresario Emery Reves, were offended by no mention in *The Grand Alliance* of the activities of Dutch submarines in the Allied cause. Churchill replied that he would make no alteration in his English text but had no objection to an amplifying footnote on this subject in the Dutch edition, which was duly entered. (*Winston S. Churchill*, Vol. VIII, 'Never Despair' London: Heinemann, 1988, page 549). While I have not gone into great descriptive detail, I have indicated the broad reach of Churchill's foreign translations in all the editions and impressions I could find.

MAJOR WORKS CITED

Three works are commonly referred to in this book, and I want to mention them prominently.

'Woods' is shorthand for *A Bibliography of the Works of Sir Winston Churchill, KG, OM, CH* by the late Frederick Woods, the Second Revised Edition, second issue (Godalming, Surrey: St Paul's Bibliographies 1975). The late Fred Woods recognised that his work badly needed updating, and was beginning work on the update before his untimely death in 1994.

Fred Woods was the pioneer bibliographer of Sir Winston, who published his first edition in 1963, astonishing not only bibliophiles but the Churchill family with the number of items he uncovered. Dissatisfaction with the completeness and accuracy of his work was inevitable as time passed, and Fred, to whom many of us passed our corrections and suggestions, characteristically recognised this. He was hoping to rectify the situation before his death. He can truly be said to have inspired everyone who has researched or seriously collected the works of Churchill. May his kind and gentle soul rest in peace.

'Cohen' is the new Ronald Cohen Bibliography, to be published by Cassell, a product of at least fifteen years' labour by the author, aided and abetted by scores of bibliophiles and through the pages of *Finest Hour*, journal of The Churchill Center. Both Fred Woods, before he died, and Ronald Cohen, kindly gave me permission to quote their bibliographic numbers as a cross reference.

'ICS' refers to a publication of the International Churchill Societies, *Churchill Bibliographic Data*, Part 1 ('Works by Churchill'). Pending release of the update which he did not succeed in publishing, Mr Woods also permitted the International Churchill Society to publish an 'Amplified list' based on his numbers, but with more detailed sub-designations to pinpoint the various editions and issues. For example, *The World Crisis* was assigned three 'Woods' numbers: A31(a) to A31(c). The ICS 'Amplified Woods list' runs from A31a to A31k (in order to distinguish certain deservedly distinct editions and issues. Except for deleting the parentheses, in no case did ICS alter any basic Woods numbers. For example, even *Blenheim*, which undeservedly holds Woods number A40(c)–it is only an excerpt, and probably should not be among the 'A' titles at all–is retained by ICS. Thus 'ICS' numbers are merely an extension of Woods numbers.

VALUES

After much thought I decided to include current value ranges in the description of most editions. What good is a collector guide without some indication of what to pay for the objects? The argument that assigning values raises the price is, I believe, specious; the book trade is well aware of the value of Churchill first editions. If anything, they are too aware. When I see booksellers offering routine jacketed copies of *The Second World War* or *A History of the English-Speaking Peoples* at book fairs for $500/£300, I become even more convinced that some value statements are necessary. On the other hand, they are sometimes too pessimistic, especially toward non-first editions, some of which are hotly sought after and worth much more than many booksellers ask.

The decision to include values will undoubtedly please most collectors, enrage some of my fellow dealers, and cause some booksellers to ask more. Bookfair prices will hardly be affected; they are already mainly high. I do not mean to condemn Bookfairs; it costs big money nowadays to rent a booth at a major fair, let alone the hotel space and transportation involved; one should expect to pay more for books at fairs–which tend to bring out knowledgeable dealers with exceptional stock. Conversely, one should expect often to pay less than the prices I quote in a general-subject bookshop. General booksellers cannot be expected to be aware of all the price nuances in any one author, and with much larger stock than specialists, they have to keep it moving. But a speciality dealer ought to know the true value of his author, and where Churchill is concerned, I am sure I do.

The value ranges I quote are purposely broad and when I name a figure I often say 'up to ... '; there are a hundred different reasons why an outwardly 'very good' *River War* first edition is offered at $1,950 by one dealer and $3,875 by another. Condition is everything, goes the saying; but the cost to the bookseller is almost everything. The seller may have acquired Volume I for $250, and had to pay $1,500 at auction for Volume II. Remember also that the values stated are retail, not wholesale. Mark-ups in the secondhand booktrade are often 100 per cent or more, not all of it profit. The cost of advertising, catalogues, mailing, shipping, telephone and supplies continues to rise, after all.

I hope that the values herein will not be taken too literally, and that both sellers and buyers will treat them as a rough guide, not a hard and fast rule. All collectors should patronize general-subject bookshops, particularly those with lots of books on offer. Thus you may acquire quite a nice first edition of *The Second World War* for $75 or £50, even though I know for sure that it's worth at least double that. You may even have the 14-carat luck of a friend of mine, who bought a fine jacketed *Arms and the Covenant* off a street vendor on London's Bayswater Road for the grand total of £3 after beating him down from £5.

LEATHER BINDINGS: A CAVEAT

A collector once asked me to take his complete Churchill collection on consignment. At great expense over the years, he had rebound each first edition, many of which were fine originals, in full morocco leather. The bindings were beautiful. He was astonished when I said that for me, these books were virtually unsalable. All I could recommend was that he consign them to an auction house or a big city dealer specialising in fine bindings–and pray a lot.

Finely rebound Churchill volumes are marginally more valuable in England than America, and that is the place to sell them. A scruffy first edition with nice clean internals is a candidate for a fine leather binding. Nothing else is. For Americans and Canadians, who dominate the Churchill collecting field at present, 'original cloth' is what's wanted–unless of course a book was bound in leather by the publisher, like the 100 limited editions of *The Second World War*. Somebody may be more interested in fancy bindings than I; somebody is certainly paying the staggering prices I see for them occasionally at certain auctions.

If you wish to display rows of Churchill works in fine leather spines, consider having your original editions boxed. My late friend Dalton Newfield, the world's first Churchill-only bookseller, once sold a collection in which each original volume was handsomely rebound by Sangorski & Sutcliffe in beautiful half morocco boxes with raised bands and gilt spines. On the shelf, they looked like rows of fine bindings. Inside each box was a pristine original, usually in its dust jacket. 'Boxes', wrote Newfield, 'solve the problem many collectors face by having a book rebound, a process which reduces the value of a book by reducing the percentage of collectors who will buy it. Boxing upgrades the appearance of the book immensely, protects it far more than rebinding, but preserves the original condition of the book and, therefore, the value.'

COMMENTS WELCOME!

A book such as this one is obsolete the week after it is published as more variants are discovered and new editions published. I welcome additions and corrections, and will attempt to maintain a complete list, available through *Finest Hour* and the *Churchill Home Page* (http://www.winstonchurchill.org). Please send your comments to me at PO Box 385, Hopkinton, New Hampshire 03229 USA, or by e-mail to: Malakand@aol.com.

THE STORY OF THE MALAKAND FIELD FORCE, 1897
AN EPISODE OF FRONTIER WAR

COHEN A1, WOODS A1

Churchill's first book is a true-life adventure story, comprising his experiences when attached to Sir Bindon Blood's punitive expedition on the Northwest Frontier of India in 1897. His willingness, as a young lieutenant, to criticise the leading generals of the day typified his precocious approach to speech and writing and alienated some of the generals, including Lord Kitchener, who would later try to prevent Churchill from joining his expedition to reconquer the Sudan (see *The River War*). As Churchill's first book, it has always been desirable; yet, until the publication of a modern edition in 1990, there had been no edition in print in the English language since 1916. (The only edition in any language between 1916 and modern times was issued in 1944 by Churchill's erstwhile Swedish publisher, Skoglunds, which remains the only foreign translation.) Recently, thanks in part to the efforts of the International Churchill Society, the *Malakand* was republished both in hardback and paperback, and is now in good supply at all price levels. Much of this work first appeared in newspaper despatches, setting a precedent for many of the author's works to come.

FROM THE REVIEWS

'There's not an awkward passage in Churchill's first book. He sets the exotic stage as he moves us into the action ... Churchill elbowed his way into the Malakand Field Force seeking military, not literary, distinction. He was a twenty-two-year-old subaltern in the 4th Hussars, a regiment stationed in Bangalore, far to the south. He was poor [and] restless in the peacetime cavalry. When the frontier tribes attacked, he wired the Malakand Field Force commander, Sir Bindon Blood, whom he had met socially, proposing to spend his leave at war. Sir Bindon, who had filled all his slots for junior officers, allowed Winston to come along as a war correspondent.

'The pattern of the campaign was dictated by the region's melodramatic topography. Churchill describes the Bengal Lancers, under fire, trying to swim their horses through a gorge of the swift-flowing Swat River, and he also describes the artillerymen walking their mules over a swinging bridge across the Panjkora River while the current below battered the bodies of dead camels against the rocks. The tribes fought for fun, for loot, and for Islam; one mullah had promised that they would be invulnerable to the bullets of the infidel, and another that they would go to heaven if they were killed. Since they didn't coordinate a strategy, the frontier campaign was a series of separate actions, some consecutive, others simultaneous. Churchill sees to it that the reader is never confused; we will always know where a particular brigade is and what it is trying to do. Though Churchill the writer was at least as green as Churchill the soldier, he knew that it was best to describe little things (for example, that a bullet missing you makes 'a curious sucking noise' in the air) and let the reader discover the big things–the steadiness of the outnumbered imperial forces, the cultural misunderstandings that pervaded the frontier–for himself.'

Naomi Bliven in *The New Yorker*, 26 March 1990

First Edition, Home Issue: Woods A1a
Publisher: Longmans, Green, and Co., London, 1898

Apple green cloth stamped gilt on spine, blind and gilt on front cover. 8vo, usually bulks 1½in (38 cm). 352 pages numbered (i)–(xvi), 1–336, with or without 32-page rear catalogue supplement printed on cheap stock; frontispiece photograph, illustrations and maps. Bylines on both spine and title page contain the initial 'L'. Title page lists Longmans offices in London, New York and Bombay. Published 14 March 1898 at 7s. 6d. ($1.85). According to Woods, some copies exported for sale by Longmans, Green in New York. US price $2.50.

QUANTITIES

A total of 1,954 copies was published, with 1,600 bound in March 1898 and 354 in June. Ronald I. Cohen (*Finest Hour* #54, pages 14–15) reported on his examination of the publisher's records that there were not (per Woods) similar quantities of the Home and Colonial Issues, but in fact 2,000 Home and 3,000 Colonial. From the Home Issue's 2,000, 46 sets of sheets were transferred for use in Colonial Issues in October 1898, leaving the 1,954, disposed of as follows: 1,675 sold in Britain; 200 sent to New York for the American market; and 79 'presentation copies'.

STATES AND IMPRESSIONS

No 'states' can reliably be assigned. (See 'Variants'.) One impression, with several binding and internal variations.

DUST JACKETS

Though a jacket is presumed to have existed, no examples have been found.

VARIANTS

Boards: in addition to the smooth apple green cloth most often encountered, there is a distinctive, brighter, more grainy or blotchy green cloth, which may very well indicate the June 1898 binding. Some pages 231 read '23¹'.

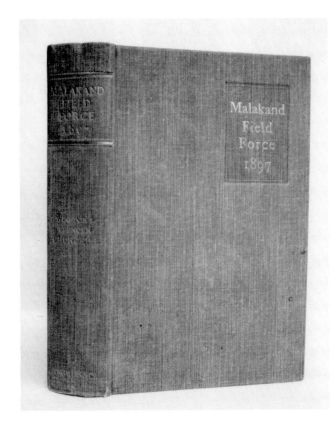

A sparkling first edition of the *Malakand* in mottled apple green cloth, today almost a priceless commodity.

Errata slips: Copies appear with and without a 13-entry errata slip (see illustration: on some slips, the line 'CHURCHILL'S Malakand Field Force' ranged at lower left is trimmed). A longer, 16-entry slip also exists, but has to date been found only in Colonial Issues (see A1ab). Contrary to Woods, errata slips can appear in various positions (usually before or after the folding map opposite page 1). In his article on quantities produced in *Finest Hour*, Ronald Cohen deduced that 3,300 *Malakands* had left the publishers before the first errata slip was printed; therefore, about 1,700 (of the combined Home/Colonial Issues) were available for insertion of errata slips.

Rear catalogues: printed on cheap paper, this 32-page supplement advertising other Longmans titles is dated either '12/97' or '3/98' on its last page. Since the catalogue describes books for sale in London, it is believed that the 200 copies of the *Malakand* sold in America lack catalogues, but many copies sold in England also lack catalogues.

Protective Tissues: All copies are likely to have contained protective tissue over the frontispiece, although some have since lost it and traces of the original tissue may be hard to find. Woods mentions tissues over the folding maps at pages 1 and 146; these are rare and do not appear uniformly.

'States': Variants of this edition are sometimes called 'states', depending on which catalogue they contain or the size or presence of an errata slip. 'First states' are represented as containing the '12/97' dated rear catalogue and no errata slip (the first slips were printed 19 April, not soon enough for the initial binding in March). Copies with '3/98' catalogues and/or errata slips are said to be later states. But these distinctions are not always borne out by the books themselves:

The problem is that sheets were printed in one place, catalogues were bound in somewhere else, errata slips were printed in one or perhaps two other locations and inserted in still different places. This leaves much room for inconsistencies, which are very apparent when examining numerous copies.

Writing in *Finest Hour* #70, bookseller Glenn Horowitz noted that Churchill didn't even post his manuscript from India to London until 29 December 1897, so Longmans must have had a supply of '12/97' catalogues when they began binding the book in March. Yet not all copies contain catalogues. No one knows when the '12/97' catalogues ran out and were replaced with the '3/98' catalogues, or whether and how long an interval (or intervals) occurred when no catalogue of any kind was inserted. Likewise, although errata slips could not have been inserted before they were printed on 19 April 1898, they were often omitted later as well: I have seen copies containing the '3/98' catalogue but no errata slip. This leads to the question: what 'state' is a copy lacking both a rear catalogue and an errata slip? It is impossible to say.

Mr Horowitz concluded: 'copies of the Home Issue exist with a catalogue in the rear dated either "12/97" or "3/98", except in cases where there is no catalogue at all ... some copies have an errata sheet tipped in at various places amongst the first dozen pages; some do not; those with an errata were "distributed" later than 19 April 1898, the day 1,700 errratas were printed. From that evidence no state of issuance can, or should, be ascertained.'

COMMENTS

The First Edition is easily distinguished by its apple green cloth binding, which is uniform in style with the (red) binding of *Ian Hamilton's March*. Inside is a plethora of grammatical errors committed by Churchill's uncle, Moreton Frewen, who handled final proofing (much to the consternation of Churchill when he saw the result). Frewehn's errors begin early, with a host of unnecessary commas in the dedication on page (v). Notable is the byline 'Winston L. Spencer Churchill', which is the only reference to the author's middle name (Leonard) among all his books. (He retained the 'Spencer' to distinguish his work from that of the American novelist Winston Churchill, who regretted, in a charming exchange between them published in *My Early Life*, that he had no middle name to distinguish himself.) With the Second Edition in late 1898, Churchill deleted the 'L.', but it had a life of its own, returning again to grace the 1901 impressions. The 'L.' was finally abandoned in Churchill's second book and never reappeared, although he retained 'Spencer', or at least 'S'.

APPRAISAL

This is a key edition and, as the author's first book, one of the most desirable. Though it is not outstandingly beautiful, it is eminently worth owning. Truly fine copies are extreme rarities, and even those with routine wear and tear are difficult to find. Prices in 1997 were exceeding $5,000/£3,000 for truly fine copies, and virtually any copy in original cloth retails for well over $1,000/£600. The typical 'very good copy' sells for $3,000/£1,800 and up. Condition, not catalogues or errata slips, governs the value of this edition, one of the scarcest and most desirable Churchill works.

First Edition, Colonial Issue: ICS A1ab

Publisher: Longmans, Green, and Co., London & Bombay, 1898

Grey cloth blocked pictorially in the 'Longman's Colonial Library' design in navy blue on cover; spine stamped gilt. 8vo, usually bulks 1¼in, occasionally 1½in. Also published softbound in navy printed light greyish green wrappers in Longmans Green uniform design. 336 pages, printed on thinner paper than the Home Issue; frontispiece photograph, illustrations and maps. Though produced simultaneously with the Home Issue, publication dates would have been later, occurring when copies arrived at their various colonial markets (chiefly India). Title page (and cover of wrapper copies) omits New York from the Longmans offices, states at top, 'Longman's Colonial Library' and at bottom, 'This Edition is intended for circulation only in India and the British Colonies'.

QUANTITIES

A total of 2,796 copies was published. Three thousand sets of sheets were printed (concurrent with the 2,000 Home Issues), from which 250 sets of sheets were extracted for the Canadian Issue, A1ac while 46 sets of sheets were added from the Home Issue. Wrapper copies exceeded clothbound copies by a ratio of about 5:3.

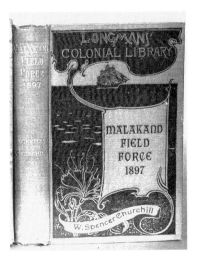

Two Colonial Issues, the first (top, ICS A1ab) and the second (below, ICS A1ba). Note that the second edition omits the initial 'L' from the byline.

IMPRESSIONS

According to Ronald Cohen, who researched the publisher's records (*Finest Hour* #47, page 14), 3,000 sheets of this issue were run off in March 1898; a 'Bibliographical Note' in later editions confirms the March 1898 reprint, so the 3,000 were apparently produced in two pressings. I am not sure there is any way to tell the impressions apart; I have never seen a copy marked 'second impression'.

DUST JACKETS

None are known to exist. The pictorial cover suggests the possibility that no jacket was used on cloth copies in the relatively heavy-duty Colonial market.

VARIANTS

This issue is subject to the same variations of protective tissues as the Home Issue. Colonial Issues do not, however, contain the 32-page advertising supplement.

Errata slips: On Colonial Issues, two distinctive errata slips have been encountered: the 13-entry type described under the Home Issue, and a 16-entry

ERRATA.

Page 30, line last, *for* "Chitral wall," *read* "Chitral road".
,, 31, ,, 19, ,, "Bajans," *read* "Bajaur".
,, 61, ,, 15-19, *read instead:* "Meanwhile the cavalry had been ordered to push on, if possible, to Chakdara and reinforce the garrison at that place. The task was one of considerable . . .".
,, 80, ,, 29, *for* "Senate of," *read* "Senate and".
,, 105, ,, 15, ,, "Royal Lancers," *read* "Bengal Lancers".
,, 165, ,, 15, ,, "invisible," *read* "visible".
,, 169, ,, 13, ,, "Mamunds," *read* "Mohmands".
,, 203, ,, 16, ,, "fulcrums," *read* "fulcra".
,, 225, ,, 32, ,, "to Paradise; yet they," *read* "to Paradise yet. They . . .".
,, 237, ,, 19, ,, "Babri," *read* "Babu".
,, 273, ,, 21, ,, "thirty-three," *read* "thirty-one".
,, 280, ,, 23, ,, "Battije," *read* "Battye".
,, 290, ,, 10, ,, "husk," *read* "thick".

ERRATA.

The attention of the reader is directed to the following errata :—

Page 16 line 10			*for* guides'	*read* Guides'
,, 30	,,	last	,, Chitral wall	,, Chitral road.
,, 31	,,	19	,, Bajans	,, Bajaur.
,, 61	,,	15	,, *lines* 15-19	,, Meanwhile the Cavalry had been ordered to push on if possible to Chakdara and reinforce the garrison of that place. The task was one of considerable. . .
,, 105	,,	15	,, Royal	,, Bengal.
,, 165	,,	15	,, invisible	,, visible.
,, 168	,,	7	,, villages	,, valleys.
,, 169	,,	13	,, Mamunds	, Mohmands.
,, 203	,,	16	,, fulcrums	,, fulcra
,, 225	,,	32	,, to Paradise; yet they	,, to Paradise yet. They
,, 237	,,	19	,, Babri	,, Babu.
,, 238	,,	23	,, primitive	,, punitive.
,, 239	,,	24	,, an offending	,, unoffending.
,, 273	,,	21	,, thirty-three	,, thirty-one.
,, 280	,,	23	,, Battij	,, Battye.
,, 290	,,	10	,, husk	,, thick.

The two known errata slips from the *Malakand*. Top: the more common 13-entry slip, found in Home and Colonial Issues. Bottom: the 16-entry slip found to date only in Colonials.

version in a different typeface. The latter has been found only on Colonial Issues. It is not impossible that Churchill, finding three more errors, caused the longer slip to be printed and inserted in Colonial Issues after the books arrived in India, which is where most of them were sold.

COMMENTS

Although more wrapper copies than cloth copies were produced, the former are now rare: only a few are known to this writer. The clothbound version, though hardly common, exists in a handful of libraries and is occasionally seen in sophisticated book catalogues. The dearth of wrapper copies lies in their greater likelihood of being thrown away. The contents of this edition are distinctively different from Colonials of the Second Edition, A1(ba), which was pressed from extensively altered plates.

APPRAISAL

At least as desirable as the Home Issue, the clothbound Colonial is a Victorian

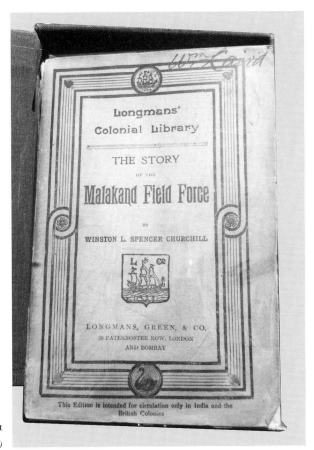

Although most Colonial *Malakand* were paperbacks, few have survived. Wrappers were printed dark blue on light blue paper. *(Photo: Curt Zoller)*

period piece, with its Longmans' trademark Colonial Library pictorial binding (a nice mate to the Colonial *Savrola*). The wrapper version, while much rarer today, is not as aesthetically delectable. In the American book trade, Colonial Firsts may command a slight premium over Home Firsts, all other conditions being equal (which they never are); the British market gives a similar edge to the Home Issue. Although both issues were printed simultaneously, it obviously took more time for the Colonials to reach retail shops.

First Edition, Canadian Issue: ICS A1ac
Publisher: Copp Clark, Toronto, 1898

Olive grey pictorial cloth stamped gilt on spine, navy blue on top board. 8vo, usually bulks 1¼in 336 pages, printed on thinner paper than the Home Issue. Frontispiece photograph, illustrations and maps. Published March or April 1898 with cancel title for Longmans' export agent in Canada, actual appearance delayed until stocks arrived in Canada. The title page cancel differs from the Colonial Issue in its publisher notation, which reads: 'TORONTO | THE COPP CLARK, CO., LIMITED | LONDON | LONGMANS, GREEN, AND CO. | 1898'. Copp Clark's name also appears on spine.

QUANTITIES AND IMPRESSIONS
One issue of 250; taken from stocks of the Colonial Issue, with a cancel title denoting the Canadian Copp Clark Company.

DUST JACKETS AND VARIATIONS
None known to exist and none may have been supplied by the publisher. See A1(ab). This issue is unlikely to contain errata slips, since it was part of the initial press of 3,000 sheets in March 1898.

COMMENTS
Only two examples of this Issue have come to my attention; in appearance it is described as exactly like the normal Colonial Issue, with the Copp Clark imprints noted above. Copp Clark was also responsible for Canadian Issues of at least three later Churchill works (see A3, A4, A5).

APPRAISAL
A real prize for the collector of obscure variations, the Canadian Issue is the rarest of the three First Edition *Malakands*, and everything said under this heading for the Colonial Issue applies to it as well. Its value is on a par with the Colonial Issue.

Second Edition, Colonial Issue: ICS A1ba

Publisher: Longmans, Green and Co., London and Bombay, 1898

Grey cloth blocked pictorially in the 'Longman's Colonial Library' design in navy blue on cover; spine stamped gilt. 8vo, usually bulks 1¼in. Also published softbound in navy printed grey wrappers in Longmans Green uniform design. 336 pages, printed on thinner paper than the Home Issue. Frontispiece photograph, illustrations and maps. Printed November 1898 but published later.

QUANTITIES AND IMPRESSIONS

A total of 1,060 copies was produced: a first impression of 500 (November 1898), 60 sets of sheets transferred from the Silver Library Issue (on or after June 1900), and a second impression of 500 (February 1901). There is a distinct difference in title pages of the two impressions:

First impression: title page differs from the First Colonial in two points: the words 'NEW EDITION' appear above the publisher's name; and the byline omits the initial 'L.', reading 'WINSTON SPENCER CHURCHILL'.

Second impression: 'NEW EDITION' is replaced by 'NEW IMPRESSION', the 'L.' returns to the byline, thus: 'WINSTON L. SPENCER CHURCHILL', and the date '1898' changes to '1901'.

DUST JACKETS

None are known to exist and none may have been supplied by the publisher.

VARIANTS

A cloth copy, originally sold in New Zealand, has surfaced with a title page conforming to neither description above. Instead, the title page is an exact copy of the First Colonial Issue of March 1898 (including the 1898 date and byline initial 'L.') while the cover and spine byline omit the 'L.'. (This is the second Colonial *Malakand* binding I have seen with the 'L.' missing from the cover and spine.) The title page is integral with the subsequent pages, which are otherwise consistent with the Second Edition (Silver Library text).

The most logical conclusion is that this is one of the 60 Colonials made up from sheets transferred from the Silver Library on or after June 1900 to relieve a small shortage. Since these 60 were created well before the 1901 second impression, I believe Longmans utilised a First Edition plate for the title page, while managing to remove the 'L.' from the spine and byline. This copy is also unique among Colonial *Malakands* for its repeat pattern Longmans logos ('ship and swan') on the endpapers, identical to endpapers of the Silver Library, but printed blue-grey to match the Colonial binding rather than the brown of the Silver Library. (These blue-grey endpapers also occur on the Colonial *Savrola*.)

COMMENTS

In November 1898, Churchill was finally able to engineer plate corrections to the many errors which so upset him in the First Edition. Evidently, the colonial market was most in need, because according to the 'Bibliographical Note' on the title page verso, the Colonial 'New Edition' was published two months before the Silver Library Issue (January 1899), which also contained corrected pages.

With the exception of slight colour variation and one byline alteration (see above), these books were bound in the style of the First Colonial, A1(ab). That their contents differed dramatically is the discovery of Brad Nilsson, who recorded his find in *Finest Hour* #73, pages 25–27. Since this issue preceded the Silver Library by about two months, this is the first appearance of the *Malakand* as Winston Churchill wished it to read.

APPRAISAL

Because of its importance in conveying a significantly revised text, this is an important issue, but alas rare. The only copy examined, by Mr Nilsson, is in the Hoover Library at Stanford University, and unfortunately has been rebound in library cloth. It would be wonderful to know that other examples exist. The variant copy mentioned above was recently offered at $1,800/£1,100.

Second Edition, Silver Library Issue: ICS A1bb
Publisher: Longmans, Green and Co., London, 1899

Reddish brown cloth stamped gilt on spine, gilt or blind rules on front cover. 8vo, usually bulks 1¼in 340 pages, the last three blank; frontispiece photograph, illustrations and maps. Contains a new 'Preface to the Second Edition' at page (xi). First printed in November 1898 but official publishing date is January 1899. Some copies contain 32-page catalogues of other Longmans titles. Endpapers, like all Longmans Silver Library titles, are printed brown with a design of swans and ships between ivy leaves. Woods A1(b).

QUANTITIES

A total of 2,500 copies was published: 1,500 printed November 1898 and 1,000 printed February 1901. Writing in *Finest Hour* #54, Ronald Cohen disclosed that through 1912 1,668 had been sold in Britain, 65 in the USA, 60 had been transferred to the Colonial issue, three used as presentation copies, leaving 663 in stock and 41 unaccounted for.

IMPRESSIONS

Title pages of the two impressions are distinctly different:

First impression title page contains the Silver Library ship logo, byline 'WINSTON SPENCER CHURCHILL', the words 'NEW EDITION' and the date '1899' (despite a

Title page of the second edition, first Silver Library issue, labelled 'New Edition' and omitting the initial 'L.' from the byline.

'Bibliographical Note' on the verso stating January 1900 as the publication date).

Second impression title page omits the Silver Library ship logo (which is transferred in larger format to the first free endpaper), adds the byline letter 'L.', states 'NEW IMPRESSION', and contains the date '1901'. The title page verso contains a revised 'Bibliographical Note' containing the reprint date (February 1901) and a boxed advert for Churchill's four subsequent books.

See Woods for the revised arrangement of preliminaries on the February 1901 impression. Rear catalogues are found in both impressions and bear various dates. The existence of a catalogue dated '5/03' in a 1901 impression suggests that not all sheets were bound after the second printing in February 1901, but kept in stock and bound as required. This accounts for the several variant bindings encountered (see below).

DUST JACKETS
Jackets are not known but are assumed to have existed.

VARIATIONS
On the top board, the border rule has been found gilt on both impressions, but also found blind on some 1901 impressions.

Title page of the second Colonial Issue, 1901 second impression, stating 'NEW IMPRESSION' instead of 'NEW EDITION'.

THE STORY
OF THE
MALAKAND FIELD FORCE
AN EPISODE OF FRONTIER WAR

BY
WINSTON SPENCER CHURCHILL
Lieutenant, 4th Queen's Own Hussars

" They (Frontier Wars) are but the surf that marks the edge and the advance of the wave of civilisation."
LORD SALISBURY, Guildhall, 1892

WITH MAPS, PLANS, ETC.

NEW EDITION

LONGMANS, GREEN, AND CO.
39 PATERNOSTER ROW, LONDON
NEW YORK AND BOMBAY
1899

Longmans' Colonial Library

THE STORY
OF THE
MALAKAND FIELD FORCE

AN EPISODE OF FRONTIER WAR

BY
WINSTON L. SPENCER CHURCHILL
Lieutenant, the 4th Queen's Own Hussars

" They (Frontier Wars) are but the surf that marks the edge and the advance of the wave of civilisation "
LORD SALISBURY, Guildhall, 1892

WITH MAPS, PLANS, ETC.

NEW IMPRESSION

LONGMANS, GREEN, AND CO.
39 PATERNOSTER ROW, LONDON
AND BOMBAY
1901
This Edition is intended for circulation only in India and the British Colonies

Bibliographical notes from title page versos of Silver Library Editions (above) provide us with the dates of issue of Silver and Colonial issues. By February 1901, Longmans were able to announce cumulative sales of Churchill's other books (left).

The 1901 impressions exist with a much smoother medium red plain cloth, no blocking on back board, a blind border of the same dimensions as the normal binding, although it now fills the area completely as the boards have about 4mm less width than normal. The spine has the Silver Library ship logo, but the shape of the ship is slightly different, the date '1724' is on one line and spine type is a different font. The spine letter 'E' has been changed from middle English style to a block capital. The pages are trimmed slightly smaller and there is no catalogue in the two copies examined. This variant has also been encountered with the spine blocked black instead of gilt.

Several other variations of the spine logo have been noted, bearing the two-line dates '17 | 24' and '17 | 25'. The following summary is provided by Mark Weber:

Cloth colour	Date published	Letter 'E' on spine	Under '1897' on spine	Year	Rear catalogue
brown	1899	rounded	leaf	17 over 25	10/99
brown	1899	rounded	leaf	17 over 25	none
brown	1901	rounded	leaf	17 over 24	5/03
brown	1901	rounded	leaf	17 next to 24	7/05
smooth red	1901	straight	rule	17 over 24	none
smooth red	1901	straight	rule	17 next to 24	none

COMMENTS

We collect first editions to get as close as possible to the author's original expression; in the case of Churchill's first book, the First Edition was irrevocably altered by Moreton Frewen's proofreading. It is the Second Edition which conveys the text as Churchill wished it to read from the start. This is at once apparent through the dearth of commas in the dedication, and Churchill's added Preface to the Second Edition, dated 'London, 15th October, 1898'. (He also adds a sentence to his original Preface: 'On general grounds I deprecate prefaces.')

Debate surrounds the question of how many hours the plate corrections to the Second Edition required. Woods states that 'corrections on the first edition [I presume he means the November 1898 printing] necessitated 122 hours' work by the printer', and that the second (1901?) 'needed 196 hours' work by the printer'. Comments Glenn Horowitz: 'This is very confusing and also extraordinary: surely they could copy-edit *The World Crisis* and *Marlborough* in less time than that!' (*Finest Hour* #73, page 26). But a lot of correction went on over fifty changes, for example, in the first ten pages between the First and Silver Library editions.

Presumably, the 122 hours apply to the extensive plate changes in November 1898 for the greatly revised Second Edition–but what about the 196 hours Woods mentions as being needed later? He could only refer to the final, February 1901 printing–but could that have required 196 more hours? I cannot think so. In those days, plates were heavy metal objects which had to be altered laboriously by hand. In a time of 50-hour weeks, it might require 122 man-hours to make Winston's November 1898 alterations. Perhaps the later figure of 196 hours is cumulative, meaning that another 74 hours were put in on the 1901 impression. I would be pleased if some dedicated collector would do a page-by-page check of a 1901 and 1898/1899 issue, to discover exactly how many textual variations exist.

Some small corrections to Woods: he states that in the New Impression of 1901 'the initial L. has been deleted from the author's name on the spine'. This is incorrect; it was deleted on the New Edition of 1898/1899. Woods also says the 'Preface to the Second Edition' is exclusive to the Silver Library Issue (it is also found in the Second Colonial); and that all copies should possess a rear catalogue and tissues over the folding maps (not necessarily).

APPRAISAL

The Silver Library is a serviceable and readily obtained issue, though given to page yellowing. Its chief value is that it contains Churchill's text as he wished it. It has the advantage of being uniform with other Longman titles in the Silver Library series. This allows the fastidious restorer to replace missing endpapers with identical endpapers from other Silver Library titles, a nice plus. The minus is that, inevitably, every cache of Silver Library titles I find has already been relieved of its copy of the *Malakand!* Fine examples of the first impression are rare, but the 1901 impression is rarer in any condition; in ten years' experience I have encountered just three. A truly fine Silver Library first impression may sell for $750/£470, but lesser copies can be had for considerably less.

Shilling Library Edition: ICS A1c
Publisher: Thomas Nelson & Sons, Ltd., London, 1916

Medium blue cloth stamped gilt or black on spine, plain boards, border rule on front board stamped blind. 16mo, 384 pages, frontispiece photograph, maps and plans. Published at 1 shilling (25c). Decorative endpapers printed light blue. Woods A1(c).

QUANTITIES AND IMPRESSIONS
One impression was produced, but subsequent bindings of remaining unbound sheets are likely (see 'Variations').

DUST JACKETS
Publisher's standard jacket for the series, printed black on light blue, showing an author's photo and decorative border on front face, other Nelson titles on flaps and rear face.

VARIATIONS
Books are known with and without gilt top page edges, and a very few exist with black rather than gilt spine blocking. Black lettered copies have not been encountered with gilt top page edges, and a bookplate in one identifying it as a June 1920 school prize suggests that it may represent a remainder binding of leftover sheets.

COMMENTS
Described as 'Cheap Edition April 1916' on its title-page verso, the Nelson Edition appeared as part of an extensive series of little, low-priced books. Among these it was the second and final Churchill title (Nelson had published *The River War* the year before). This was the last *Malakand* to see print for 74 years, and many copies were taken by soldiers to the front during the Great War, or to India (accounting for the many owner inscriptions naming famous regiments). The Nelson Edition contains Churchill's approved text as published in the Second Edition, and quite good maps for its size and price. Being cheap, it tended to be treated carelessly, and most copies are well-worn or display gutter breaks. Jacketed copies are extremely rare.

APPRAISAL
Until the advent of modern reprints this was the only inexpensive alternative to the early editions, but availability of new editions has reduced the price of run-of-the-mill Nelson Editions. Still, a fine one can sell for $150/£90. The variations are scarce and worth looking for, as is, of course, the very rare 'period' dust jacket, which would at least double the price of a copy so equipped.

The New Edition, 1989

A milestone for admirers of our author was the resurrection of his first book in 1989 for the first edition in 74 years. Features common to all issues of this edition are as follows: text photographically reproduced from the *Collected Works*, Volume III (see appendix), which itself was reset from the Silver Library text approved by Churchill; new foreword by Tom Hartmann (in addition to the author's original Preface); appendix on the International Churchill Societies; 236 pages; maps and plans from the *Collected Works* (redrawn) pages. Not in Woods.

All New Editions are essentially the same, nicely if economically produced. According to Leo Cooper, sales of English issues were 'disastrous', but the Norton issue had a long and happy run in the United States, and was then reprinted by the mail order booksellers Barnes & Noble. These are the editions for readers, and for collectors wishing to read the text without wear and tear on valuable early editions. Used copies are readily available at modest prices.

First New Edition: ICS A1da
Publisher: Leo Cooper, London, 1990

Black cloth stamped gilt on spine, plain boards. 8vo, sold at £14.95. Black dust jacket printed white and red, photo of author in dress uniform on front face. One impression, no known variations.

New American Issue: ICS A1db
Publisher: W. W. Norton & Co., New York, 1990

Dark blue cloth stamped silver on spine, plain boards. 8vo, sold at $18.95. White dust jacket printed blue, gold and black, photo of author in dress uniform on front face. One impression, no known variations.

New Paperback Issue: ICS A1dc
Publisher: Mandarin Books, London, 1991

Pictorial colour boards. 8vo, sold at £4.99. One impression, no known variations.

Second American Issue: ICS A1dd
Publisher: Barnes & Noble Inc., New York, 1993

A remainder reprint with similar physical characteristics but with Barnes & Noble replacing Norton as publisher on title page, spine and jacket. One impression, published September 1993.

FOREIGN TRANSLATIONS

Swedish: STRIDEN OM MALAKAND
Published by Skoglunds Bokforlag, Stockholm 1944 in hardback and wrappers. The softbound is the most physically attractive *Malakand* since its wrappers bear multicolour artwork of British cavalry on front face. 8vo, 232 pages; the wrapper version sold for 14.50 kroner, the blue cloth hardback 19.50 kroner. No dust wrapper has been found but Swedish practice suggests that one exists with a design similar to the wrapper version. Appraisal: the best-looking edition of all *Malakands*, and the best produced: large format, high-quality paper, clear large maps. Hardbound copies are rarely encountered outside Sweden.

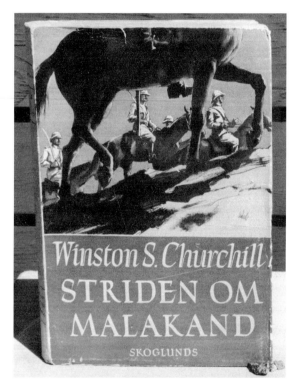

The attractive wrapper of the Swedish edition, the only foreign translation of the *Malakand*, published by Skoglund in 1944.

THE RIVER WAR
AN HISTORICAL ACCOUNT OF THE
RECONQUEST OF THE SUDAN

COHEN A2, WOODS A2

Arguably the most aesthetically beautiful of original trade editions of Churchill's books, *The River War* is a brilliant history of British involvement in the Sudan and the campaign for its reconquest: arresting, insightful, with tremendous narrative and descriptive power. Though published nearly 100 years ago, it is uniquely relevant to our times: combined with Churchill's personal adventure, there are passages of deep reflection about the requirements of a civilised government of ordered liberty.

Far from accepting uncritically the superiority of British civilisation, Churchill shows his appreciation for the longing for liberty among the indigenous inhabitants of the Sudan; but he finds their native regime defective in its inadequate legal and customary protection for the liberty of subjects. On the other hand, he criticises the British army, and in particular its commander Lord Kitchener, for departing in its campaign from the kind of civilised respect for the liberty and humanity of adversaries that alone could justify British civilisation and imperial rule over the Sudan.

In 1885 the Sudan had been overrun by the Dervish tribesmen under their religious leader, the Mahdi, culminating in the death of the British envoy, General Gordon, at the capital of Khartoum. Fourteen years later, London sent Lord Kitchener at the head of a combined British and Egyptian force (including a brash war reporter, Lt. Churchill) to re-establish Anglo-Egyptian sovereignty. Notwithstanding the superiority of British weaponry and tactics to those of the enemy, the obstacles presented by the Nile, the desert, the climate, cholera and a brave, fanatical Dervish army led by the 'Mahdi of Allah' were formidable.

All these features of that now distant campaign Churchill impressively captures in precise detail and exciting narrative, including his own role in the last great cavalry charge of British History. Finely written chapters trace the history of the Sudan, the rise of the Mahdi, the martyr's death of Gordon and, apparently not much exaggerated, the author's adventures. Young Churchill did not hesitate to criticise the actions of the victorious Kitchener, whose treatment of the dead Mahdi was certainly barbaric and whose disdain for the fallen foe after the Battle of Omdurman was shameful.

Later, the author thought it best to be more judicious. For a one-volume edition published in 1902, Churchill excised vast quantities of narrative, including most criticisms of Lord Kitchener. By then he had entered Parliament, and was less sanguine about burning bridges. He also added a chapter, and made additions here and there, making later editions important in their own right. There are therefore two separate texts: the 1902 abridgement survived unchanged through modern paperbacks, while the original two-volume unabridged version, with Angus McNeill's beautiful line drawings, saw only 3,000 copies and was sold out by the early 1900s. The latter is the out-of-print Churchill book most in need of reprinting; a campaign to do just that was recently launched by the International Churchill Society. To be truly complete, a new edition of the original text should add the new material from 1902, and a tabulation of the 1902 excisions.

From a collector standpoint, all editions are important including paperbacks, which are the cheapest way to come to grips at least with the abridged text. *The River War* is one of a handful of titles most likely to be included in numerous variations in advanced Churchill libraries, many of which contain a dozen or more editions. Collectors content to own only one copy of Churchill's other books often make the acquisition of every edition and impression of *The River War*, including foreign language editions, a lifetime quest. And that is a hunt which may very well require a lifetime.

FROM THE REVIEWS

'The salient features of the "river war" are clearly brought out ... A brief sketch of the rebellion of the Mahdi, Gordon's part in it, the history of the Dervish Empire and the preparations for its overthrow, is followed by an account, in greater or lesser detail, of every important step in the advance of the Anglo-Egyptian army.

'Our author is not at his best when describing the campaign in which he took part. Not unnaturally he dwells at too great length on the incidents, sometimes trivial, of which he was an eye-witness. His account of the battle of Omdurman, especially, suffers for this reason. [Today, because of Churchill's subsequent career, the campaign in which he took a part, and Omdurman in particular, are considered among the highlights of the book. –RML]

'The impression of the Sirdar [Kitchener] left by the narrative is forcible and not marred by too indiscriminate praise. He appears throughout a stern, unsympathetic man, unmoved in threatened disaster or in brilliant success, fertile in resources, with eye keen to observe the smallest details in every department; a martinet but not a slave to red tape ...

'The history appropriately ends with a tribute to one whose name seldom appears in its pages, but to whom possibly even more than to the Sirdar, belongs the chief credit of a great achievement. In developing and civilizing the Sudan, Churchill says, "To persevere and trust Lord Cromer is the watchword of the Englishman in Egypt."'

The Nation, New York, 15 February 1900.

First Edition: Woods A2(a)

Publisher: Longmans, Green, and Co., London, 1899

Dark blue-green cloth stamped gilt on spine and front cover. Demy 8vo, two volumes, 488 pages numbered (i)–(xxiv), (1)–462, (2) and 516 pages numbered (2), (i)–(xiv), (1)–499, (1) respectively, printed on high quality thick coated paper, with or without 32-page rear catalogue supplement printed on cheap stock; illustrations by Angus McNeill of the Seaforth Highlanders; frontispiece and other portraits; maps and plans. (The two volumes contain 20 beautiful folding maps in colour.) Published 6 November 1899 at 36s. ($9), a towering price in an age when £1 per week was a living wage. US copies sold for $10.

QUANTITIES AND IMPRESSIONS

Three thousand copies were published in three impressions with press orders for 2,000, 500 (January 1900) and 500 (June 1900). Later impressions are so labelled on title pages and dated 1900 instead of 1899. Half title versos: are blank in first impressions; advertise *Malakand* and *Savrola* in second impressions; and add *London to Ladysmith* to some but not all copies of the third impression.

DUST JACKETS

Printed black on off-white stock, duplicating the style of the boards, with the Nile gunboat and author signature on the front face and the title, byline, Mahdi's tomb artwork and publisher in the usual places on the spine face; the flaps and rear face are blank. There is no difference in jacket design among the three impressions.

Left & centre: An immaculate first edition *River War*, one of the volumes wrapped in a colour photocopy of the extremely rare dust jacket. Right: the 1902 one-volume edition, bound like the firsts but in red cloth. A variant of the 1902 edition lacks the usual blind rule on top board.

VARIANTS

The only variation reported is the absence or presence of the rear catalogue. Again, as in the case of the *Malakand*, it is likely that copies sold in the USA were without the catalogue, but this does not constitute proof of a distinctly 'American' issue, since some books which have spent their entire life in England also lack catalogues.

COMMENTS

Some describe the binding as blue, others green; most first-time viewers I have shown copies to say it is 'blue-green'. The first edition is physically beautiful, perhaps the most luxurious of all Churchill trade editions. The rich and evocative cover and spine artwork is complemented by Angus McNeill's wonderful line drawings, elegant fold-out maps in full colour, and thick, creamy page stock, which is usually still in magnificent condition after nearly a century. Dust jackets are virtually extinct; I know of only one pair. The rear catalogue in Volume I, not mentioned by Woods, appears in about half the copies encountered. Catalogue dates are 12/99 for the second impression and 7/00 for the third impression.

APPRAISAL

The first edition *River War* is not as scarce as the first edition *Malakand*, but the supply of both has tightened up considerably of late, and truly fine copies are hardly ever seen. The heavy pages put a lot of strain on the binding, and many copies are found with hinge or gutter breaks; it is a hard choice either to make repairs (which usually require new replica endpapers) or to preserve originality. If you choose originality, be extremely careful when using the volumes.

From both literary and collectibility standpoints, this is one of the gems of any Churchill library. Second and third impressions are worth about 40–60 per cent of first impressions in comparable condition, and the prices of all are high. Genuinely fine firsts have sold recently for as much as $7,500/£4,700; in the original dust jackets they could certainly command over $10,000/£6,000. As usually seen, 'very good' with minor flaws and the odd gutterbreak, they sell for between $2,000/£1,200 and $4000/£2,500. The cheapest first edition I've seen was on offer in 1997 at only $750/£470; it had clean boards and readable internals, marred by heavy warping of the pages from some long-ago dampness.

Second Edition (Abridged): Woods A2(b)

Publisher: Longmans, Green, and Co., London, 1902

Red cloth stamped gilt on spine and front cover; 8vo, 384 pages with or without 40-page rear catalogue supplement printed on cheap stock; frontispiece and other illustrations, maps and plans. Published 15 October 1902 at 10s. 6d ($3.75); some copies exported for sale at $4 by Longmans, Green in New York, where it was published on 13 December. Note: While Woods correctly describes this edition, 'bound as the 1899 edition, but with the volume number deleted', he should add that it is in red not blue-green cloth and usually (but not always) carries a blind rule around the edge of the front board.

QUANTITIES AND IMPRESSIONS
The first impression of 1,000 copies was followed by a second impression (not noted by Woods). The second impression is so labelled on the title page, and on the verso of its half-title is a boxed advert for other works. Second impressions encountered to date contain the typical Longmans catalogue of other books in the back. The second impression could not have been numerous, but I have no figure on quantity.

DUST JACKETS
None have been reported. Presumably they resemble the known jackets for the first edition, but without volume numbers.

VARIANTS
A variant binding of the first impression exists in rough red cloth, without the usual blind rule on top boards. Because these copies omit the London publisher's rear catalogue, it has been speculated that this was a binding for copies sold by Longmans in New York; however, some otherwise normal copies which were sold new by London bookshops also omit the rear catalogue.

COMMENTS
The primary bibliographic importance of this work is its new material: a new Preface by the author and a new chapter describing the destruction of the Khalifa and the end of the war. Significant historically is that Churchill excised about one-quarter of his original text (notably his attacks on Kitchener) in creating this first one-volume edition, the text of which has been used by every reprint to date. 'What has been jettisoned', he writes, 'consists mainly of personal impressions and opinions, often controversial in character, which, however just, were not essential.' Having been elected to Parliament, Churchill could be said to be trimming his sails for political expediency. On the other hand, his abundance of opinions had been criticised long before he entered Parliament, so he could also be said to have responded to those criticisms. Alas, many detailed appendices and all drawings, as well as nine of the exquisite fold-out colour maps, were also deleted. Eleven folding maps remain, appearing in this edition for the last time.

APPRAISAL
For its important additions and deletions, this book or one of its successors belongs on the shelf alongside the First Edition. Copies are rather scarcer even than the first edition, and are rarely encountered in fine condition; the heavy paper is prone to

edition, and are rarely encountered in fine condition; the heavy paper is prone to gutter breaks and spotting. The binding retains all the Victorian period splendour of the First Edition, however, and the 1902 remains one of the most desirable *River Wars* among bibliophiles. Most copies sell for roughly half the price of fine First Editions in comparable condition. Above average examples are usually offered for between $1,000/£600 and $2,000/£1,200

Shilling Library Edition: Woods A2(c)
Publisher: Thomas Nelson & Sons, Ltd., London, 1915

Medium blue cloth stamped gilt, border rule on front board stamped blind. 16mo, 458 pages plus a 22-page catalogue of other Nelson titles, frontispiece photograph, maps and plans. Published 4 August 1915 at 1 shilling (25c). Decorative endpapers printed light blue on white.

QUANTITIES AND IMPRESSIONS
Quantity unknown. One impression, but remainders are possible.

DUST JACKETS
Publisher's standard jacket for the series, printed black on light blue, showing the author's photo and decorative border on front face, other Nelson titles on flaps and rear face.

VARIATIONS
Books are known with and without gilt top page edges. Black-lettered spines (like the Nelson *Malakand*) have not been encountered by the writer.

Nelson Shilling Library editions. Left to right: *Malakands* with the gilt and variant black letter spines, the former with gilt top page edges; *River Wars* with plain and gilt top page edges, the second bearing a photocopy of the rare dust jacket.

COMMENTS

The first of two Churchill titles in the Nelson series of little, low-priced books, this volume was followed in 1916 by the Nelson *Malakand*. Unlike the latter, it does not contain the label 'cheap edition'. Its existence was ignored by Eyre & Spottiswoode, who in 1933 published what they called the 'first cheap edition' (see following entry). The Nelson Edition contains the 1902 text (reset) including both appendices, but no index. Being cheap, it tended to be treated carelessly, and most copies are well-worn or display gutter breaks.

APPRAISAL

Not often seen, the Nelson is desirable chiefly for collectors wishing to round out their holdings but has no intrinsic advantages; its small size and resultant small-scale maps are uninviting to the eye. Jacketed copies are extremely rare and would command at least $300/£180; unjacketed fine copies, about $150/£90; indifferent copies half that.

Second Cheap Edition, 1933: Woods A2(d)

Seventeen years after the Nelson *River War* (which its publishers forgot altogether when they labelled this book the 'First Cheap Edition') came a long-lived one-volume edition in standard 8vo size, made up from plates of the 1902 edition and carrying the original pagination and index. This is important bibliographically for Churchill's new Introduction, in which he expresses happiness that *The River War* is having a new lease on life, hoping that his countrymen 'may learn from it how much harder it is to build up and acquire, than to squander and cast away'. He was obviously referring to the India Bill, which in 1933 he was vainly opposing. For this new Introduction alone, the work is significant.

Home Issue: Eyre & Spottiswoode, London, 1933: ICS A2da

Lilac cloth stamped black on spine (1933–1941); yellow-tan cloth stamped gilt (1949–1951); grey cloth stamped gilt (1965 remainder binding). Plain boards, 8vo. First published January 1933 at 10s. 6d. ($2.65). Woods A2(d).

QUANTITIES AND IMPRESSIONS

First impression, January 1933 ('First Cheap Edition' on title page verso): 3,000 copies
Second impression, March 1933 ('Second Cheap Edition'): 1,000 copies
Third impression, 1941 ('1940 Third Cheap Edition'): 1,250 copies.* The boards on this impression are noticeably thinner and limper than the other impressions.
Fourth impression, June 1949 (states 'Third Edition'): 3,000 copies
Fifth impression, May 1951 (states 'Third Edition'): 2,600 copies
Remainder binding, 1965 (from 1951 sheets, but grey cloth, jacket advertises

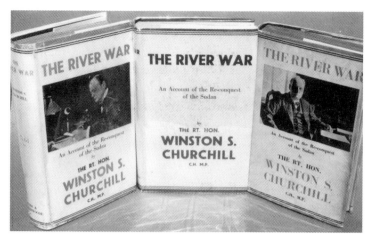

Eyre & Spottiswoode editions of *The River War*. Left to right: the 1933 first and second impressions and the 1941 ("1940") impression, which is by far the rarest.

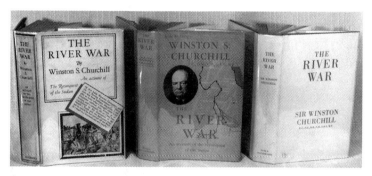

River War reprints. Left to right: Scribners' 1933, Eyre & Spottiswoode's 1949 impression (tan cloth) and their c.1965 remainder binding (grey cloth) with unillustrated red-on-yellow dust jacket.

1965 books)

Total press run: 10,850.

*Woods says the Third impression was printed in 1941 and sold at 15s.; it was printed on 25 February 1941, not 1940 as stated on title page verso, and sold for 10s. 6d.

DUST JACKETS

First impression, 1933: black and light blue on white, side view of Churchill at his desk. Rear face: adverts for a Metternich biography and Liddell Hart's *Foch*. Spine price '7s. 6d.'. This dust jacket is commonly found on later impressions, and may have been interchanged by the publisher.

Second impression, 1933: black on off-white, unillustrated, title/subtitle/byline on front face, back face blank, spine price '7s. 6d. net'. (This impression has been found in a jacket identical to the first impression, adding 'net' to the spine price, indicating possible issuance of remainder copies, or the issuance of remainder copies with the newer style jacket sometime between 1933 and 1940.)

Third impression, 1941 ("1940"): black and light blue on white in the 1933 style but photo shows Churchill facing the camera; back face is blank, flap price is 10s. 6d. but the price is not repeated on the spine. (Some third impressions carry first impression dust jackets.)

Fourth impression, 1949: printed red, navy and tan with a contemporary photo of Churchill and map of the upper Nile, back face advert for *The War in Malaya*, flap price 15s.

Fifth impression, 1951: As 1949, back face advert for *A History of Europe*, flap price 21s.

Remainder binding, 1965: red on yellow, unillustrated, title/byline on front face; back face adverts for *Frontiers and Wars* and Violet Bonham Carter's *Winston Churchill as I Knew Him*.

VARIANTS

Copies of the 1933 first impression and the 1941 ("1940") impression are known to exist in mauve cloth, and I have seen a copy (impression unknown) in blue-grey cloth. A copy of the 1949 impression exists blocked dark brown instead of gilt.

COMMENTS

The six different versions of this work are easily identified; the text is uniform throughout.

APPRAISAL

Jacketed copies, especially 1933–1941 ("1940"), are extremely rare and highly desirable; jacketed postwar copies are more readily available but even they usually command prices exceeding $150/£90; unjacketed copies are presently quite common, especially the first 1933 impression and the postwar impressions. Readers interested in sound hardbound reading copies of *The River War* should make their choice from among these volumes; the more recent, the more likely they are to be in good condition.

American Issue: ICS A2db

Publisher: Charles Scribners Sons, New York, 1933

Lilac cloth stamped black on spine, plain boards. Published 1933 at $2.75. This issue is labelled 'Printed in Great Britain' on the title-page verso and in effect constitutes the first separate American Issue. Binding was probably also done in England, using English sheets and a Scribners title page cancel, since copies are 8vo, bound in the identical lilac cloth, and contain the same signature marks of the

Eyre & Spottiswoode copies. The dust jacket is unique, bearing R. C. Woodville's dramatic illustration of the Charge of the 21st Lancers (see early copies of *My Early Life*) and is especially attractive. This is a highly desirable variant, known to few, and not in Woods. Expect to pay a premium for it, and up to $500/£300 for a fine copy in dust jacket.

Four Square Edition: ICS A2e
Publisher: Landsborough Publications Ltd., London, 1960

The first paperback edition, Four Square no. 195, was released at 3s. 6d. (49c). The cover is a Karsh photo-based painting of Churchill c. Second World War superimposed on a group of lancers observing the approaching Dervish Army. Second impression 1964. Both impressions have 352 pages, but the second uses photographically reduced type and the pagination is different. Not in Woods.

Note: 'Sphere Edition' (formerly ICS A2f)
Woods mentions a Sphere paperback. No copies have ever been encountered by anyone I have consulted, and I believe he was referring to the Four Square Edition.

Award Edition: ICS A2g
Publisher: Universal Publishing & Distributing Corp., New York, 1964

The first American paperback was published in December 1964 at 75¢, and incorrectly labelled, 'never before published in paperback'. The cover bears a Karsh photo of Churchill with Dervishes and Lancers on horseback. It is number KA123S in the Award Books Military Library. 352 pages. Second impression 1965. Not in Woods.

New English Library Edition: ICS A2h
Publisher: N.E.L. Division, Times Mirror Books, Ltd., London, 1973

Published December 1973 at 50p ($1.40) with cover artwork of a patrol of Lancers in the desert. 352 pages. The second impression, issued April 1985 by the N.E.L. under management of Hodder & Stoughton at Sevenoaks, Kent, cost £2.75 and carried a new cover lettered gold on blue. Not in Woods.

Sceptre Edition, ICS A2i
Publisher: Hodder & Stoughton, Sevenoaks, Kent, 1987

Published 1987 by H&S's Sceptre Books Division at £6.95, with a new introduction by Sir John Colville, retaining the Woodville painting from the N.E.L. paperback on a tan cover printed black, red and blue; one impression. An oversize paperback, 7¾ x 5in, 368 pages. Not in Woods.

River War paperbacks. Left to right: Award (1964), Four Square (1960) and New English Library (1973 and 1985). Lying flat: Sceptre edition (1987).

Prion Edition, ICS A2j

Publisher: Prion, London, 1997

Completely reset and published at £9.99 in the Prion 'Lost Treasures' series, this edition carries a new foreword by Winston Churchill, our author's grandson. Unfortunately, its text is not from any previous edition of *The River War*. Instead it is taken from *Frontiers and Wars* (see page 340), a severely truncated sampler of Churchill's first four war books, in which Churchill's 1902–1987 *The River War* abridgement was chopped by about 40 per cent. Oddly, the title page is lifted from a first edition of *The River War*, announcing illustrations and two volumes, which are not present. The Lost Treasure remains lost.

Combined Issue from the *Collected Works*

Sheets leftover from Volume III of the 1974–1975 *Collected Works* have been bound in black cloth blocked gilt, with the Nile gunboat design from the first edition reproduced on the cover.

FOREIGN TRANSLATIONS

Swedish: KRIGET VID FLODEN
Published by Skoglunds Bokforlag, Stockholm, 1938 at 9.5 kr, 8vo, 398 pages, issued both clothbound and in grey card wraps printed black and red-orange. There is no mention of a bound copy; normal practice seems to indicate that a bound version came later.

SAVROLA

A TALE OF THE
REVOLUTION IN LAURANIA

COHEN A3, WOODS A3

Churchill's only novel has traditionally been dismissed as a fluke: a 'Ruritanian romance' of the Emile Zola genre, spun off in an idle and idealistic moment, a book that would have been forgotten had the author not been who he was. In different ways, most reviewers have dismissed it as an insignificant mimic of better novels by Haggard, Hope, Disraeli, Bulwer Lytton and even Conrad. Writing in *Finest Hour* #74, Patrick Powers argues to the contrary, that *Savrola* is really Churchill's 'premier literary effort, [giving] dramatic voice to Churchill's mature philosophical reflections about his fundamental political and ethical principles at the very moment when he settled on them for the rest of his life'. Though *Savrola* was Churchill's third published book, Powers notes, it was composed prior even to the *Malakand*. (It was serialised in *Macmillan's Magazine* before appearing in book form in England.) 'At minimum', Powers continues, it 'ought to be recognised as Churchill's first substantial literary composition.' The great English historian A. L. Rowse, reviewing the 1956 edition, makes much the same point, adding that despite Sir Winston's oft-expressed modesty about it, *Savrola* 'holds one's attention for its own sake'.

The novel is set in a mythical Mediterranean republic whose President, ambitious and unscrupulous, is rapidly developing into a despot. Savrola is the popular leader of the reform party. The President has rigorously and brutally repressed a threatened riot by promptly shooting down the people in the street and Savrola, who had hoped to mend matters by constitutional means, sees that he is bent on a military takeover, and that the time has come to yield to the importunities of his more fiery supporters and resort to force. In the revolutionary maelstrom, Savrola's leadership is temporarily eclipsed by a man named Karl who believes 'in the equality of incomes'–a thinly veiled reference to Marx, which Churchill would vigorously oppose all his later life. In the end, however, Savrola is vindicated, returning from a temporary exile to lead his city-state back to peace and prosperity.

There is no doubt that Savrola is Churchill, and with much the same moral dilemmas. An appreciator of beauty, well able to enjoy luxury, he cannot live 'in dreamy quiet and philosophic calm in some beautiful garden, far from the noise of men' while the life of his nation is at stake. '"Vehement, high and daring", was his cast of mind. The life he lived was the only one he could ever live; he must go on to the end.' Forty years later the author of *Savrola* would exhort his countrymen, 'We shall go on to the end ... We shall never surrender.'

Whether they deem it a key indication of Churchill's innermost philosophy and political morality or just a yarn, *Savrola* continues to exert a grip on devotees of the canon. Thanks to a recent reprint and good supplies of some earlier editions, the book is within the reach of almost everyone who wishes it.

FROM THE REVIEWS

'It is not a Disraelian novel, but rather one of the school that Mr George Meredith founded and Mr Anthony Hope has taken over and carried on so successfully, only that it is less romantic, more realistic than stories of that school are apt to be, comes to closer grip with the actual problems of modern life, and has a high seriousness of its own.

'A man of lofty ideals, a humanitarian, a scornfully incorruptible politician, Savrola is also an eloquent orator who can play upon the sentiments and passions of an audience as skillfully as a musician can upon his instrument; he is an autocratic, not a passionate lover; he is cool and diplomatic enough always to hold his enthusiasms in leash, but he can be heroic and reckless when there is nothing more to be gained by caution. I share the general impression that Savrola is the shadow of his creator, that Mr. Churchill has endowed him with the doubts, the dreams, the aspirations and something of the philosophy that are in reality his own. He has lived his life as if he believed in the commonsense gospel that Savrola propounds ... "Remember that we pay for every pleasure and every triumph we have in this world ... and for all the good things in life men pay in advance."'

'The Reader' in *The Bookman*, London, July, 1908

First Edition: Woods A3(a)
Publisher: Longmans, Green and Co., New York, 1899

Navy blue cloth blocked gilt on cover and spine, cover title and byline framed by rules, title, byline and publisher name on spine, blank endpapers. Crown 8vo, 356 pages, numbered (i)–(x), 1–345 (1), plus a 24-page catalogue of American titles of the publisher. Published at $1.25.

QUANTITIES AND IMPRESSIONS
Two impressions were produced. Woods states that 4,000 copies were first published on 3 February 1900 but this date is certainly incorrect, since a second impression, not mentioned by Woods, dated 'January 1900' on its title-page verso, dates the first impression as 'November 1899'. While it is possible that copies did not reach retail shops until 1900 (the first impression is dated 1900 on its title page, perhaps anticipating this), there seems no doubt that the entire run of both impressions was produced before February 1900.

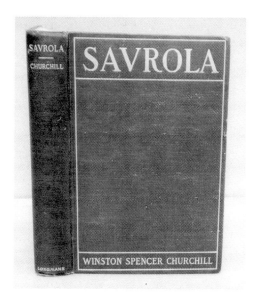

The true first edition of *Savrola* was published by Longmans in New York in late 1899, bound in navy blue cloth blocked gilt. This edition is also known in red cloth blocked white.

DUST JACKETS
None are known to exist, though it is very likely that they were supplied originally.

VARIANTS
A striking variant (thus far encountered only on second impressions) exists in red cloth blocked white instead of the usual navy cloth blocked gilt. This variant has no rules and no rear catalogue.

COMMENTS
Savrola is the first of several Churchill works in which the American edition preceded the English, in this case possibly for commercial reasons: the novel was being serialised in *Macmillan's Magazine* in England as late as December 1899, so Longmans's London office may have held up publication in deference to the periodical; this consideration did not apply in the United States. In fact, the English Edition was made up from the American plates. The 'November 1899' first publication date stated in the second impression has given rise to speculation that *Savrola* preceded *The River War* and deserves to be designated 'A2'. This is unlikely, because *The River War* was published 6 November and, according to Ronald Cohen, the United States Library of Congress did not receive its first copyright copy of *Savrola* until the 18th.

APPRAISAL
A well-made volume using good quality page stock, this edition rarely suffers from the advanced foxing of its English counterpart (partly because America is a drier place!). The most common flaw is wear and chipping to the cloth at the head and

foot of the spine. Because of its precedence, the first impression is an expensive book, especially in fine condition (up to $1,500/£900). Despite the tendency of some booksellers to treat the second impression as a rare discovery, 'not in Woods', it remains a second impression, worth about a third or quarter of the price of a first, conditions being equal.

First English Edition, Home Issue: ICS A3ba
Publisher: Longmans, Green and Co., London, 1900

Medium to dark green cloth blocked gilt on cover and spine, title and author signature on cover, title, byline and publisher name on spine. Black endpapers. Crown 8vo, 360 pages, numbered (2), (i)-(x), 1-345, (3), including two pages of advertisements (for the *Malakand* and *River War*). Dated 1900 on title page but copyright date (on verso) is 1899. Boxed adverts for the *Malakand* and *River War* on the half-title verso of both impressions. Published at 6s. ($1.50).

QUANTITIES AND IMPRESSIONS
Only two impressions are distinguishable: the first and the second. The latter is labelled 'NEW IMPRESSION' on the title page. The first impression consisted of 1,500 copies, printed 30 January 1900. Ronald Cohen (*Finest Hour #74*) states that subsequent printings occurred on 10 February (1,000 copies), 20 February (1,000) and 17 March (2,000). Together with a net 550 sheets transferred to the Home Issue from the Colonial, production totalled 6,050, of which 4,550 copies were labelled 'NEW IMPRESSION' on the title page.

DUST JACKETS
A dust jacket for this edition is reported but not described in the famous Mortlake catalogue, and has not been traced.

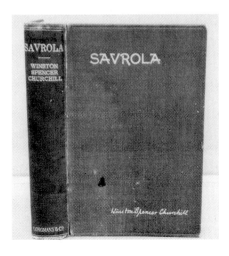

The first English *Savrola* in green cloth was published in January 1900. Three subsequent impressions occurred and 550 more were bound using sheets transferred from the Colonial Issue; all these bear the line 'New Impression' on their title pages but are otherwise indistinguishable.

VARIANTS

A variant cloth exists, distinctly blue rather than the usual green. Some copies have a blank verso title, and one copy was seen with a cancel title (its verso blank) transposed with the half-title (possibly to fill in a shortage from Colonial Library sheets).

COMMENTS

While the 'New Impression' was made up of three different printings, they are indistinguishable from each other. Of the total edition of 6,050, Cohen states, 98 were 'presentation copies'. This does not mean they were Churchill's, for they could also have gone to the publishers and reviewers. In fact, *Savrola* is one of the least inscribed titles in the entire canon. Checking the auction and sales records for the past 30 years, bookseller Glenn Horowitz was able to find only two instances of a signed copy changing hands. Churchill's negative opinion of the novel is perhaps the reason he inscribed so few.

APPRAISAL

The First English Edition does not carry the cachet of the First Edition, for the obvious reason that it appeared second–by as much as three months. Aesthetically, too, it is not as pleasing. Since it was printed on rather pulpy stock, the English climate has rendered unspotted copies a rarity today. Conditions being equal, which they rarely are, the first English is worth about two-thirds the value of the First (American) while the 'New Impression' is about on a par with the second impression of the American edition.

First English Edition, Colonial Issue: ICS A3bb

Publisher: Longmans, Green, and Co., London & Bombay, 1900

Grey cloth blocked pictorially in the 'Longman's Colonial Library' design in navy blue on cover; spine stamped gilt. 8vo, 350 pages. Also published softbound in grey wrappers in Longmans uniform design. Blue printed endpapers; boxed adverts for the *Malakand* and *River War* on the half-title verso. Published simultaneously with the Home Issue. Title page states at bottom in bold face: 'This Edition is intended for circulation only in India and the British Colonies.' Also has two pages of adverts similar to Home Issue. Mentioned by Woods, page 26.

QUANTITIES AND IMPRESSIONS

The first impression of 1,500 was printed 30 January 1900 simultaneously with the Home Issue. Subsequent impressions, labelled 'NEW IMPRESSION' on title pages, were run on 10 February (2,000 copies) and 20 February (1,000) copies, from which 550 copies were transferred to the Home Issue, leaving a total of 3,950. Of these, 1,670 were clothbound (including 21 presentation copies) and 2,280 were published in wrappers (115 presentation copies).

DUST JACKETS AND VARIANTS
Jackets for the hardback presumably were produced but none are reported. No variations reported.

COMMENTS
Like the Colonial *Malakand*, which it matches, this is a physically beautiful book, but even harder to find. Wrapper copies, although they outnumbered the clothbound, have almost completely disappeared. By the time of *Savrola's* publication, Churchill had firmly removed the middle initial 'L.' from his byline. Covers of cloth copies, like 1901 issues of the Colonial cloth *Malakand*, therefore carry the byline 'W. Spencer Churchill', while the spines spell out 'Winston'.

APPRAISAL
A rare gem, but alas hardly ever seen. A very desirable issue, at least equal in value to First Editions.

The first Colonial Issue *Savrola* was bound uniformly with the Colonial *Malakand.* Later impressions bear the line 'NEW IMPRESSION' on their title pages.

First Canadian Issue: ICS A3bc
Publisher: Copp Clark, Toronto, 1900

Olive grey pictorial cloth stamped gilt on spine, navy blue on top board. Crown 8vo, 358 pages, with cancel title for Longmans' export agent in Canada. The title-page cancel reads, 'TORONTO | THE COPP CLARK, CO., LIMITED' above the Longmans, Green line. Copp Clark's name also appears on the spine. Not in Woods. Quantity unknown but probably made up from sheets of the Colonial Issue. Extremely rare and desirable, worth as much or more than a comparable Colonial.

First Illustrated Edition: Woods A3(c)
Publisher: George Newnes, Ltd., London, 1908

A softbound volume, demy 8vo, 128 pages including advertisements, published in May 1908 at 6d (13¢), also offered at 3d. post-free from the publisher. The light, thin wrappers carry blue printed artwork of Savrola and Lucille with the title printed red; the spine carries the title and byline (Rt. Hon. Winston S. Churchill, M.P.)

Paperback *Savrolas*: Left to right: the first illustrated edition (Woods A3c), first French, Spanish and 1957 Beacon Books Edition. The latter's lurid cover did nothing to improve sales!

printed navy. Variations: copies have been encountered with the first two pages blank and printed with adverts.

Contents are printed on pulpy stock which is almost always yellowed, though not usually brittle. This is 'first illustrated edition', carrying frontispiece artwork and an illustration opposite page 30, sought after mainly for this distinction. A companion piece is the Hodder & Stoughton softbound edition of *My African Journey*, but the *Savrola* is more often seen. A fine copy, if it exists, could command $500/£300, but most of them are worn and sell for half this price, or less.

Third Edition: Woods A3(d)
Publisher: Hodder & Stoughton, London, 1915

Red scored cloth-like boards blocked blind with publisher device and vertical columns on top board, spine lettering black 'Savrola by the Rt. Hon. Winston S. Churchill, M.P.') Part of the publisher's 'Sevenpenny Net Novels' series. 16mo, 260 pages, pages (i) to (iv) printed on coated paper; frontispiece portrait.

QUANTITIES AND IMPRESSIONS
25,000 copies were published June 1915 at 7d. (15¢).

DUST JACKETS
The jacket is red with a four-colour reproduction of the frontispiece photo, showing Savrola standing over the dead Molara. The spine panel carries a large '7d. net' in addition to title, byline and publisher; the back face advertises other Sevenpenny novels; flaps are blank.

VARIANTS

Copies exist in distinctly darker red, really burgundy bindings. A handful of copies display the date '1915' on the title page, which probably constitutes a separate state, though whether it preceded or followed the undated title page is unknown. One copy has been found with the '1915' inverted. The contents display no other differences.

COMMENTS

Until the arrival of the Leo Cooper Edition in 1990 this was the most available and least expensive hardbound *Savrola*. It is a nice enough little book, though the pages are subject to yellowing and brittleness, and the red covers and spine will fade easily if subjected to much light.

APPRAISAL

Readily available for a book this old, A3(d) is desirable to round out a collection or as a reading copy. Presence of the evocative jacket turns this rather ordinary book into a collector treasure; unfortunately, I have encountered only a handful of jacketed copies in ten years, usually offered for prices approaching First Editions. Unjacketed, they start around $20/£12 and run up to about $80/£48 for very fine copies.

Two rare dust jackets for *Savrola*, (left) the Hodder & Stoughton 7d Library published in 1915, and (right) the elusive modern reprint published by Cedric Chivers in 1973.

Second American (Fourth) Edition: ICS A3ea
Publisher: Random House, New York, 1956

Navy blue ¾ buckram with red cloth strips 1½in wide at foredges of top and bottom boards, the top board carrying the title gilt, the spine carrying title, byline and publisher's logo gilt, publisher's name and decorative devices in light blue. 8vo, 244 pages, the last three blank. Frontispiece portrait of the author in 1900. Published at $3.50. Woods A3(e).

QUANTITIES AND IMPRESSIONS
A single impression was published 16 April 1956; quantity is not known to the writer.

DUST JACKETS AND VARIATIONS
The jacket, bearing a new subtitle ('SAVROLA | A NOVEL') carries the Philippe Halsman photo of Churchill at 80, overlooking the Chartwell swimming pool. The face is lettered red, black, yellow and white with a white-on-red spine; the rear face carries a photo of WSC c. 1901; the flaps carry a description of the book. No variations are reported.

COMMENTS
Churchill wrote an amusing new foreword to this book, dated 20 January 1956 (not 1965 as per Woods), quoting his original foreword about submitting the book 'with considerable trepidation', and adding that the 55 years since the first edition 'have

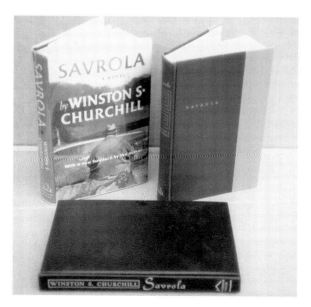

American *Savrolas*. Upright are Random House 1956 editions, with and without jackets; lying flat is the Amereon House limited edition, which had no jacket.

somewhat dulled though certainly not changed my sentiments on this point'. Since this was the last *Savrola* text to be established, Woods leaves off numbering the various editions at this point.

APPRAISAL

A sound reading copy, this one is available in good supply at low prices (up to $75/£45) except for very exceptional jacketed examples (up to $150/£90). Really essential for the amusing new foreword and the various photographs of the author throughout. I do wish Random House would republish this.

Limited Issue: ICS A3eb
Publisher: Amereon House, Mattituck, New York, c. 1988

Black, blue or red cloth blocked gilt on spine. Also known in tan cloth blocked silver on spine and cover. 8vo, 232 pages. Not issued with a dust jacket. A photographic reproduction of the Random House edition, with the same pagination (slightly enlarged) from page 3 onward. A note 'to the reader' on page (iv) states, 'It is our pleasure to keep available uncommon titles and to this end, at the time of publication, we have used the best available sources. To catalogers and collectors, this title is printed in an edition limited to 300 copies–Enjoy!' Whether these copies were produced with the knowledge of the copyright holder is a good question. The book is not distinctive and holds no premium value over the Random House edition, which indeed is more attractive. Amereon's product was most likely not jacketed.

First Paperback Edition: ICS A3f
Publisher: Beacon Books, Odhams Press Ltd., London, 1957

A paperback, 224 pages including two pages of rear adverts, with a four-colour action-style cover showing Savrola confronting Molara and Lucille, all in modern dress. Published 1 April 1957 at 2s. 6d. (35¢). The half-title page contains an excerpt from A.L. Rowse's review of the Random House edition. Mentioned by Woods, page 27.

Sixth Edition: ICS A3g
Publisher: Cedric Chivers, Portway and Bath, 1973

Plain wine cloth blocked with title, author and 'New Portway' on spine. 8vo, 260 pages plus 18-page rear catalogue. Published 'at the request of the London & Home Counties Branch of the Library Association' at £2.20 ($6) or £1.65 to Library Association members. This is one of the hardest editions to find. Though often represented as a 'large type' edition, its type is quite small, about 9-point. The dust jacket has a colour drawing of revolutionaries charging a house, promotion blurb on inside flap, plain pink rear face with Library Association logo, plain rear flap. Extremely rare; $200/£120 would not be too much to pay for a clean copy.

New (Seventh) Edition: ICS A3h
Publisher: Leo Cooper, London, 1990

Black cloth blocked gilt on spine. 8vo, 214 pages, including a two-page rear note on the International Churchill Society, and a new foreword by Tom Hartman. Bright red-orange dust jacket with a cartoon of Savrola on the top face. Text photographically reproduced from the 1974–1975 Collected Works edition. Published at £14.95. There was no paperback version, nor an American issue.

FOREIGN TRANSLATIONS
Note: Contrary to Woods, Dutch and Norwegian editions of *Savrola* do not exist, and there are only two, not three French translations.

Danish: SAVROLA
Published by Steen Hasselbalch, Copenhagen, 1948, 8vo, 207 pages at 10 kr unbound in card covers. Also issued in half dark brown leather and brown marbled paper boards, with illustrated dust jacket. Variants: some hardbound copies have additional type on verso of half-title, viz.: 'UDLAAN OG UDLEJE af denne Udgave er ikke tilladt, Steen Hasselbalch Forlag'.

Finnish: KANSA NOUSEE
Published by Karisto, Helsinki, 1916. This First Finnish Edition is, more significantly the first translation of any Churchill work into a foreign language. 8vo, 224 pages.
     Another edition was published by Karisto in 1956, 40 years after its First Edition; completely reset in paper covered boards of two varieties: red with grey/green stripes and light grey with dark grey strips. Also issued unbound.

French: SAVROLA
Published by Les Éditions du Rocher, Monaco, 1948. The first French Edition was a paperback of 250 pages, wrappers printed black and yellow on white with an illustration of the author. The production included 60 special copies printed on Lafuma pure linen paper of which 50 were numbered (1)–50 and ten ('hors commerce' = not for sale) were numbered in Roman I to X. An off-print or two impressions of the standard edition exist, since copies have been found with and without a cover note that 8,000 are in print. All copies state '8–1948' on spine.

French: SAVROLA (Limited Edition)
Published by À la Voile Latine, Monaco, 1950. The finest presentation of *Savrola* and perhaps the most elegant Churchill work, this unique book was published 15

The most beautiful *Savrola*, À La Voile Latin's Monaco 1950 illustrated edition with André Collot's colour woodcuts, shown here with its two known boxes, the pages unbound as usual.

February 1950 in a limited edition of 1,000 copies. 4to, 282 pages. Intended to be bound by the purchaser, its pages were issued in a slipcase. The most striking feature is the beautiful woodcut artwork by André Collot, engraved by Bracons-Duplessis, much of it in four-colour. (See *Finest Hour* #74 for examples of the artwork including the colour cover.)

The first 50 copies were printed on rag vellum and included a set of black and white illustrations by Collot. Copy #1 also included the sketches and studies of the artist as well as 12 original designs, while #2–13 included two original designs. Copies #51–950 were printed on Lafuma pure linen paper. The remaining 50 copies, numbered 'HC1 to HC50' ('hors de commerce') each including a set of black and white illustrations, were reserved for the author, illustrator, publishers and collaborators. Slipcases: two types are known: grey with spine printed black; and ivory leatherette printed red.

This magnificent edition is overlooked by many collectors because it is not in English. They are missing a great deal. No serious Churchill library is complete without it. Availability is not bad, but prices vary from $750/£450 to $2,000/£1,200 depending on what the dealer had to pay. Virtually all copies I have seen are in their loose, slipcased form.

German: SAVROLA
Published by Verlag Hallwag [Verlag Publishers], Berne, 1948. Black cloth blocked gilt on top board and gilt and red on spine in dust jacket; 8vo, 300 pages.

Spanish: LAS COMPENSACIONES DE LA VIDA
Published by Luis de Caralt, Barcelona, 1950: the first Spanish Edition. 8vo.

Spanish: SAVROLA
Published by Ediciones G.P., Barcelona, 1956. A paperback of 160 pages, published at 12 pesetas. The cover, printed four-colour on white, portrays a contemporary Churchill and medieval buildings.

Swedish: SAVROLA
Published by Skoglunds, Stockholm, 1944, the first Swedish Edition. 8vo, 348 pages, published in cloth and wrappers at 17 kr and 11 kr respectively. Wrapper bears an illustration of Churchill c. 1900 and a scene of the 'rebellion in Laurania', printed black, white yellow and red. Bound versions are known in full blue cloth and half blue cloth with paper covered boards. Jackets for bound versions probably exist.

The Second Swedish Edition was published by B. Wahlströms Bokförlag, Stockholm 1958: completely reset, 8vo, 256 pages, top page edges marbled. No. 13 in a series of 15 from Wahlströms's Ramanbibliotek (fiction library). Bound in half medium blue leather on patterned blue paper covered boards with dust jacket, 6.65 kr.

LONDON TO LADYSMITH
VIA PRETORIA

WOODS A4, COHEN A4

I often wish modern writers who say Churchill was a racist would read his conversation with his Boer captors in *London to Ladysmith*. This was, remember, 1899, when every Englishman alive supposedly believed in the utter supremacy of the white race, English branch.

'Is it right', the guard asked Churchill, 'that a dirty Kaffir [native] should walk on the pavement [sidewalk]–without a pass? That's what they do in your British Colonies. Brother! Equal! Ugh! Free! Not a bit. We know how to treat Kaffirs ... They were put here by the God Almighty to work for us. We'll stand no damned nonsense from them. We'll keep them in their proper places.'

After recording his guard's opinions Churchill states his own: 'What is the true and original root of Dutch aversion to British rule? It is the abiding fear and hatred of the movement that seeks to place the native on a level with the white man. British government is associated in the Boer farmer's mind with violent social revolution ... the Kaffir is to be declared the brother of the European, to be constituted his legal equal, to be armed with political rights ... nor is a tigress robbed of her cubs more furious than is the Boer at this prospect.' After the statements of his captor, Churchill concludes, '[he and I had] no more agreement ... Probing at random I had touched a very sensitive nerve.'

Now it is accurately said that Churchill's view of native Africans was not that of, say, Martin Luther King, Jr half a century later. Churchill was paternalistic, and held, if not in these pages then in the *African Journey*, that immediate equality was impractical and unworkable. But his views in the *Ladysmith* are in striking contrast to those of most contemporary Britons. Of course, whatever improvements might have evolved in a South Africa under pure British government, the Union of South Africa in 1910 led to something different. By combining the Boer-dominated Transvaal and Orange Free State with the British Cape Colony and Natal, in a Union where only whites could vote and Boers outnumbered Britons, Great Britain established the Boer patrimony which the Boers had failed to achieve by arms; and from that Union grew the policy of Apartheid. It is interesting to find Churchill in 1899 representing the same essential approach to native emancipation as the South African reformers of the early 1990s–and agreeable to know that Nelson Mandela is an admirer of Winston Churchill.

Ever in search of adventure, Churchill in 1899 attached himself to the 21st

Lancers and followed the flag to South Africa. There, a rebellion against British authority had broken out among the Boer settlers of the Transvaal and Orange Free State, and a Boer Republic had been proclaimed.

Churchill secured an assignment as press correspondent to the *Morning Post*, but he had scarcely arrived before he was involved in a skirmish which found him 'in durance vile': a prisoner of war in Pretoria, unable to talk himself out of prison by claiming to be a reporter, and nearly mad over the lack of action. Typically, he made a daring escape, travelling overland toward Lourenço Marques, Portuguese East Africa (now Maputo, Mozambique), hiding by day and moving by night. The true-life adventure story of his successful escapade dominates this book, one of the most gripping in the canon, making this one of his most popular books.

The escape story in the *Ladysmith* should be read in tandem with Churchill's later remarks on the subject in *My Early Life*. The latter work, published nearly thirty years later, allowed the author to reveal more about the methods and people involved in his escape. Until 1982, when a South African facsimile edition appeared, this volume was hard to obtain at low prices. More recently, it was combined with *Ian Hamilton's March* as a new title, *The Boer War*.

FROM THE REVIEWS

'The work is not intended to be a history of the war (as was *The River War*) and thus does not cover the causes or opening of the conflict, or events at which Churchill was not present. It begins in October 1899, just after the Boer government of the Transvaal and the Orange Free State declared war on Britain and sent hardy and mobile riflemen pouring into the British South African colony of Natal. The main British force was trapped and besieged at Ladysmith, and Sir Redvers Buller, with a relieving force and the intrepid Winston, set out from England to restore Imperial fortunes.

The narrative is replete with personal incidents: Here Winston indignantly describes a raucous parson who freezes the soldiers into apathy on the eve of battle; there he relates the wounding of his brother Jack, expressing very human relief that Jack will be honourably out of harm's way for a month. Churchill tells with pride of the triumphal entry into Ladysmith, its gaunt but happy defenders, the speeches and the cheering; in conclusion he discusses the terrible situation and enormous difficulties that resulted in the siege of the town, concluding that the relief was worth the terribly high price paid.

One of the fascinations of the *Ladysmith* is that the letters it comprises were not written with benefit of hindsight. Reading them with that advantage today allows a fuller appreciation of the sagacity of the author. As an exciting autobiographical slice from the life of a great man, and as a clear, fast-paced military chronicle and adventure story of the last of Britain's "little wars", *London to Ladysmith* is still well worth reading.'

Stanley Smith in *Finest Hour* #40, Summer 1983.

First Edition: ICS A4a

Publisher: Longmans, Green and Co., London, 1900

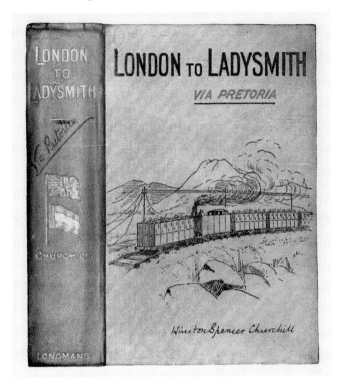

The first edition of *London to Ladysmith via Pretoria*, a superior copy showing little dirt to the fawn-coloured cloth and strong gilt blocking on the spine.

Fawn pictorial cloth. The top board bears a black line-drawing of an armoured train, the title and the author's signature. The spine bears the title, author's name and publisher's name along with two flags, a Union Flag flying straight out over a drooping Transvaal flag. The words 'Via Pretoria' are blocked red on spine and top board; the spine is otherwise stamped gilt, the top board otherwise blocked black. 8vo, 516 pages numbered (2), (i)–(xiv) and (1)–498 (2). The two unnumbered pages advertise *The River War* and the *Malakand*. Boxed adverts for these titles plus *Savrola* are on the half-title verso. In addition, there is a 32-page rear catalogue, printed on thinner paper, of other Longmans' titles. Endpapers faced black. Full colour folding map facing title page, other maps and plans. Published at 6s. ($1.50). Woods A4.

QUANTITIES AND IMPRESSIONS

Woods states that 10,000 copies were published on 15 May 1900, and a second impression of 500 'a few days after', but publishers' catalogues identify the second impression as having been produced in July 1900, nine months after. The second impression is identified by the words 'NEW IMPRESSION' on title page; it also advertises the third impression *River War* on page 1 of the rear catalogue.

Since I have personally handled about 100 New Impressions and know of scores more, I strongly doubt Woods's figure of only 500 copies published. The immense contemporary popularity of Churchill's escape story, coupled with the many New Impressions encountered, suggest that the second printing was more like 5,000 copies, and probably occurred some time later, as suggested by the publisher's catalogues. This theory is supported by adverts for the *Ladysmith* in *Ian Hamilton's March*, published in October 1900, which are headed by the words, FIFTEENTH THOUSAND. If we accept that, the New Impression had 5,000 copies.

DUST JACKETS AND VARIANTS

A jacket bearing the same art as the cover and spine, printed black, has been reported but not verified. The second impression has been found in a distinctly different, coarser brown cloth than the usual fawn cloth common to both impressions.

COMMENTS

A splendid book both aesthetically and from a literary standpoint, the *Ladysmith* is one of the most sought-after titles in the canon, and readily available if not always cheap. Its bibliographical history is straightforward, though the existence of only one subsequent impression suggests that Churchill's period as Boer War hero was brief indeed; many people thought of him in less heroic terms after he began his parliamentary career. Boer War fever abated quickly in Britain; the author went on to other spheres.

Woods is inaccurate in his description of the flags on the spine, describing them as 'Union Jack and Union [of South Africa?] flag'. Actually they are the Union Flag (it is a 'jack' only when flown at the bow of a ship) and the Transvaal flag, although the Union of South Africa flag incorporated both these flags in its design.

APPRAISAL

The as-usual very good first edition, with no serious flaws, no gutter breaks and reasonably clean boards, commands around $600/£360, but can easily vary up and down. The rare fine copy in sparkling condition could break $1,000/£600. The New Impression is also in good supply and costs, of course, much less, usually less than $150/£90 for 'very good' copies. The incidence of truly fine copies of either impression is small: the fawn cloth soils easily, and the thickness of the book and pages induces hinge and gutter breaks. The colour folding map is often encountered torn or misfolded. Collectors should cheerfully pay premiums for clean copies with maps that are not misfolded.

First American Edition, Home Issue: ICS A4ba

Publisher: Longmans Green and Co., New York, 1900

Red buckram, top board title/ author's name blocked gilt and framed by gilt rules in the style of the first edition *Savrola*; spine lettered gilt with title, author's name and publisher name, top page edges gilt. 8vo, 510 pages numbered (i)– (xiv) and (1)-496. Unboxed adverts for the *Malakand, River War* and *Savrola* on half-title verso. Plain endpapers, two-colour (black and red) folding map facing title page, other maps and plans. Published 16 June 1900 at $1.50. Mentioned by Woods, page 30.

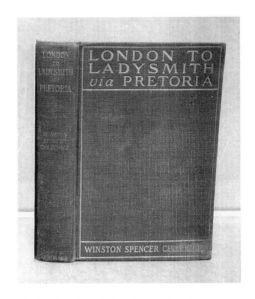

The American first edition of the *Ladysmith* was bound in scored red cloth without the armoured train illustration; its folding map is black and white.

QUANTITIES AND IMPRESSIONS
A single impression of 3,000 copies was produced.

DUST JACKETS AND VARIANTS
No jackets have been reported. I have seen a copy with a debossement on the title page, reading circularly, 'PRESENTED BY THE PUBLISHERS'. I have seen this device on several contemporary titles, including *Lord Randolph Churchill*, published by Macmillan; therefore it is not unique to Longmans, and I have some doubts about its provenance.

COMMENTS
With the same text but not the aesthetic quality of the English Edition, the American Edition lacks the evocative cover illustration and elaborate folding colour map, though it forms a handsome matched pair with the American *Hamilton's March* and provides the minor luxury of gilt top page edges. It is often found in fine condition, although on some copies the gilt spine lettering is dull; but it is almost always in better condition than the English Edition, thanks to the drier American climate and a superior cloth binding. It is also printed on better quality paper which is less inclined toward spotting. This is a very nice contrasting mate to the English Edition.

Inscribed copies are occasionally available. The most spectacular I have encountered was a handsome pair including the American *Hamilton's*, both inscribed by Churchill to the captain of the ship which brought him back to England from his American lecture tour in 1901.

APPRAISAL

Despite its relatively small numbers, the American *Ladysmith* remains in reasonably good supply. Prices do not match those of the English First, though a much larger proportion of extant copies are in fine condition, and are offered frequently at around $300/£180 to $500/£300–surprisingly modest prices given the press run.

Canadian Issue: ICS A4bb

Publisher: Copp Clark, Toronto, 1900

Published both clothbound and in wrappers. The hardback is bound similarly to the First Edition, but the cloth is more ochre than tan in colour. The spine contains an abbreviated title ('LONDON TO LADYSMITH'), a fleur-de-lis design instead of flags, and the Copp Clark imprint. The wrapper copy (said to bear the name of the Montreal News Co.) has not been seen by this writer. 8vo, 510 pages numbered (i)–(xiv) and (1)-496. No adverts on half-title verso. Plain endpapers. Two-colour (black and red) folding map facing title page, other maps and plans. Not in Woods.

Despite its outward resemblance to the English Edition, this volume was made up from sheets, or printed using plates, of the American Edition. Nothing is known to me about quantities or dust jackets. Although the scarcest by far of the three first editions, it is considered peripheral by many collectors and prices have not been higher than comparable American Editions. I believe it is undervalued, and should be acquired before things change.

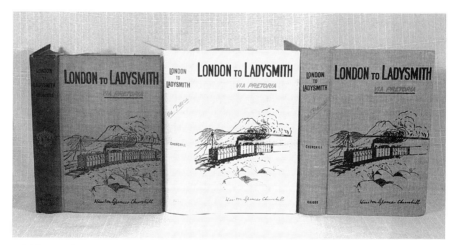

Left: The Canadian issue *Ladysmith* is blocked like its English counterpart; right: in 1982 the work was reprinted in facsimile in South Africa with facsimile binding; and (centre): a handsome dust jacket.

South African Edition: ICS A4c

Publisher: T. W. Griggs & Co. (PTY) Ltd., Durban, 1982

Rough mustard pictorial cloth with title, author's name signature and armoured train illustration on top board and title, author's name and publisher name on spine, all blocked black; 'VIA PRETORIA' blocked red on top board and spine. 8vo, 512 pages numbered (i)–(xiv) and (1)-498, plain endpapers. Black printed folding maps facing front and rear pastedowns, other maps and plans. New foreword, unsigned, on verso of title page. Published at 18.95 rands. Not in Woods.

QUANTITIES AND IMPRESSIONS

The publisher advised me that 1,000 copies were published in one impression.

DUST JACKETS AND VARIANTS

The jacket is printed black, red and yellow-buff on heavy white paper and duplicates the style of the top board and spine. The foreword is reprinted on the front flap; the rear flap and back face are blank. No binding variants exist.

COMMENTS

Since this offprint of the First Edition was the first *Ladysmith* in over 80 years, it was welcomed by both Churchill and Africana collectors, although it was a crude facsimile: the maps are poorly reproduced and the typesetting rather fuzzy. The best feature is the cover, which replicates the famous armoured train, though the original's gilt spine stamping and two-flag spine logo are absent and the cover illustration is heavily inked. 'Some passages reflect the prejudices of the time, and we trust that modern readers will not find references made to race groups offensive, but will rather read them in their historical context', states the publisher's foreword. They might have added that Churchill defended the black Africans in his conversations with the Boers, who made the offensive references cited.

APPRAISAL

This edition has been out of print for many years now, and prices have begun to rise slightly to the realm of $120/£72 for fine examples.

IAN HAMILTON'S MARCH

COHEN A8, WOODS A5

A sequel to *London to Ladysmith*, this volume completes Churchill's coverage of the Boer War, including the liberation of the Boer prison camp in Pretoria where he had been held prisoner. It describes the fighting march of Ian Hamilton's mounted division from Bloemfontein to Johannesburg (Churchill rode a bicycle into 'Jo'burg' a day before the Army arrived) and on to Pretoria, where the author was able to help liberate his former fellow prisoners at the Staats Model School. It is, of course, indispensable to any Churchill library, and it has long been canonised among the more collectible Churchill books.

General Sir Ian Hamilton is of particular interest because of his long friendship with Churchill, which began with this adventure. Hamilton was one of the generals in charge of the fatal 1915 Gallipoli landings (though he never blamed Churchill for the débâcle that followed). When Churchill sold his first country home, 'Lullenden', Ian Hamilton bought it, and they were still in touch when Churchill became Prime Minister during the Second World War. Churchill wrote one of the entries in the Hamiltons' privately published tribute to Lady Hamilton (Jean, London 1942, see Woods Db55/3). Although the *Ian Hamilton* was out of print nearly ninety years, it was recently combined with the *Ladysmith* to form *The Boer War*, and is now readily available in that form.

An example of Churchill's photographic memory (and willingness to store someone else's good phrase for recycling later) is the title of Chapter I, 'A Roving Commission'. Thirty years later, Churchill suggested this to Charles Scribners as an alternative title to *My Early Life*, but the words actually originated as the title of a pre-1900 Henty novel! (Young Winston was a devoted fan of the Victorian novelist.)

FROM THE REVIEWS

'In considerable degree, Mr. Churchill is qualified to do serious military writing. He is a man of talent, courage and boundless energy. He has seen real war as a soldier. He is practised in observing, arranging and presenting military facts. His *River War* is one of the very best books on the reconquest of the Egyptian Sudan ... Of course, Mr. Churchill had adventures in this 400-mile march: he has a talent for adventures. In one fight his horse bolted, and he was left on foot within close range of the Boers, the nearest cover a mile away. He was saved by a gallant trooper, who took him up behind, and who seemed to repent the deed when his own horse was killed by the explosive bullet. But we must not be tempted into relating the experiences of this enterprising young gentleman, and can only stop to say, further, that a very entertaining chapter, quite unrelated to the rest of the book, is a diary of a young officer as a prisoner in Pretoria.'

New York Times Saturday Review of Books & Art, 12 January 1901.

First Edition: Woods A5

Publisher: Longmans, Green and Co., London, 1900

Dark red cloth with title gilt in blind panel with blind rule, ranged upper right; on spine, title, author's name and publisher name gilt. 8vo, 432 pages numbered (2), (i)–(xiv) and (1)–409 (+7). Four of the unnumbered pages advertise other Churchill titles; they are sometimes followed by a 32-page catalogue of Longmans' titles printed on thin paper. Folding map printed sepia, black and red facing page (411); other maps and plans. Frontispiece portrait of Ian Hamilton. Boxed advert for four other works by Churchill on verso of half-title. Black-faced endpapers. Published 12 October 1900 at 6s. ($1.50).

QUANTITIES AND IMPRESSIONS
A single impression of 5,000 copies was produced.

DUST JACKETS AND VARIANTS
No jackets are reported but they are presumed to have been produced. A second state exists with different adverts. Rear catalogues are sometimes absent.

COMMENTS
In appearance this title looks more like a mate to the *Malakand* than the *Ladysmith*, being bound to match the former, but in red rather than green cloth. The rear adverts for Churchill's other works are interesting, in that they show how the totals were adding up: the *Malakand* was up to 7,000 copies, *The River War* to 3,000,

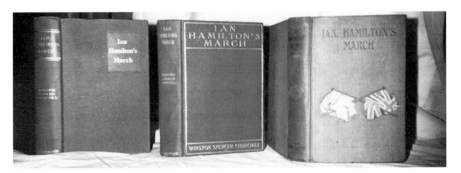

Fine copies of *Ian Hamilton's March* first editions. Left to right: the English, American and Canadian issue. Crossed flags pattern on the latter was a repeat of the wrapper design on the Canadian softbound *Ladysmith*. *(Photo: Patrick Powers)*

Savrola to 10,000, the *Ladysmith* to 15,000. Not many authors could claim to have sold so many copies of so many titles before they were thirty.

APPRAISAL

In value and availability, *Ian Hamilton's March* closely follows *London to Ladysmith*. Although it wouldn't appear to be as easily soiled as the latter, this is indeed the case, and most of the hundreds of copies I have examined over the years are scruffy. A very good copy is a scarcity and a fine one is truly rare, selling for a huge premium. Workaday copies start at $150/£90, get up to $400/£240 for very good copies, and double that at least for the rare fine copy.

Second Edition: ICS A5b
Publisher: Longmans, Green and Co., London, 1900

Identical to the First Edition except for the following points:
Title page: for 'LIEUTENANT H. FRANKLAND' read 'LIEUTENANT T. H. C. FRANKLAND'. Page 108: for 'Maria Corunia Verecker' (mid-page) read 'Maria Corinna Vereker'. Page 109: five lines up from bottom, for 'Hapton' read 'Hafton'. Page 128: seven lines up from bottom, for 'Commander of the Bath' read 'Companion of the Bath'. Page 129: four lines up from bottom, for 'lost my reputation' read 'ruined my reputation'. Page 299: in the italicised paragraph, for 'Lieutenant H. Frankland' read 'Lieutenant T. H. C. Frankland'. I gleaned these points by examining Churchill's own marked copy of the First Edition, prepared for the Second Edition, in the Forsch Collection at the Baker Library, Dartmouth College, and comparing it to my own Second Edition, which itself divulges further alterations:

Title page: 'SECOND EDITION' appears above the name of the publisher. Half-title verso: unboxed adverts for the *Malakand, River War, Savrola* and *Ladysmith*. Of the seven unnumbered rear pages, six now advertise other Churchill titles instead of four. The additional title advertised is *Ian Hamilton's March* itself, which receives identical blurbs on pages 411–412. Each of these adverts is headed by the title, EIGHTH THOUSAND. This is in line with Woods' statement that 3,000 copies of the Second Edition were pressed on 12 October 1900.

We cannot always accept publisher's claims at face value. The self-proclaimed 'Second Edition' of *Liberalism and the Social Problem* is, for example, merely a second impression. But this work has had enough changes to constitute a true Second Edition, and the changes demonstrate Churchill's concern not only with accuracy but with English.

It would be nice to think this edition, so much about which is now known, has great value, but it does not. To the book collector it is merely second to the first. Its value is between a third and a half that of the First Edition, conditions being equal.

First American Edition: ICS A5ca

Publisher: Longmans Green and Co., New York, 1900

Red buckram, top board title/author's name blocked gilt and framed by gilt rules in the style of the American *Savrola*; spine lettered gilt with title, author and publisher name, top edges gilt. 8vo. Either, 426 pages numbered (i-xiv), 1-48 (2) 49-409 (3) or 424 pages eliminating the last blank leaf (411-412). Plain endpapers, frontispiece portrait of Ian Hamilton, three-colour (sepia, black and red) folding map facing page 410, other maps and plans. Published 1 December 1900 at $1.50.

QUANTITIES AND IMPRESSIONS
A single impression of 1,533 copies was produced.

DUST JACKETS AND VARIANTS
Jackets are presumed to exist but have not been reported. Variations include copies with a 32-page rear catalogue, and with advertisements for *London to Ladysmith* and *Savrola* rather than *Ladysmith* and *Hamilton*.

COMMENTS
This edition makes a nice matched pair with the American *Ladysmith*, but is much scarcer. Because of good quality binding and paper stock, it is often found in near-fine condition. A full-fine copy looks spectacular: a very desirable volume.

APPRAISAL
Despite one of the shortest press runs of any Churchill trade title, the American Edition remained in good supply until the early 1990s, but it has now definitely dried up and prices are already galloping. Always priced higher than the American *Ladysmith*, the American *Ian Hamilton* is on a par with the First Edition. About $800/£480 would not be too much to pay for a fine copy.

Canadian Issue: ICS A5cb

Publisher: Copp Clark, Toronto, 1900

Pressed from the American plates and published both clothbound and in wrappers. The hardback is bound in tan cloth, with a unique design of crossed Union Flag and White Ensign in red, white and blue. The wrapper copy front cover is similarly decorated, but uses different title type (on both cover and spine) and adds a facsimile author's signature ranged lower right; also, four vertical 'batons' on centre of spine instead of the Copp Clark logo and fewer endpapers than the hardback. The Copp Clark logos on the back covers/boards are identical in both issues. No adverts appear on half-title versos of either work. 8vo, 424 pages numbered (i)–(xiv) and (1)–410. Plain endpapers, frontispiece portrait of Ian Hamilton. Three-colour (sepia, black and red) folding map facing page 408, other maps and plans. Unlike the Canadian *Ladysmith*, this Copp Clark issue has a unique cover design, which makes it the most beautiful of the *Ian Hamilton* Firsts. Nothing is known about quantities or dust jackets. Easily the scarcest among the three early editions, in either hardbound or wrapper form, a very good buy when obtainable for under $600/£360. Not mentioned by Woods.

COMBINED WORK:
THE BOER WAR

By 1989 (with the exception of the shortlived South African *Ladysmith*) Churchill's twin tracts on the Anglo-Boer war had been out of print almost 90 years. Both were high on the priority list of the International Churchill Society, which launched a campaign in 1985 to encourage the return to print of a dozen long-vanished titles. While ICS did not get new facsimile first editions of each, the texts of the *Ladysmith* and *Hamilton* were combined into the single-volume *Boer War*. Features common to all issues of this edition are as follows: text photographically reproduced from the *Collected Works*, Volume IV (see appendix); new foreword by Tom Hartmann; maps and plans from the Collected Works (redrawn). Not in Woods.

This work was formerly assigned 'A149' in the ICS Amplified Woods list but, on consideration, it is not a separate work and is better considered at this point. This was not, by the way, the first time *London to Ladysmith* and *Ian Hamilton's March* appeared in one volume: Harcourt, Brace and World in New York published a paperback with that title. However, its contents were taken from *Frontiers and Wars*, which is so structurally different that I have covered it under a separate heading under ICS 'A142/1'; Harcourt's book will be found under there.

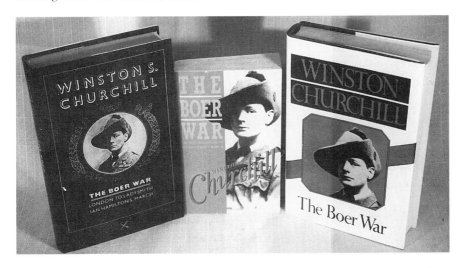

The English, English paperback and American issues of *The Boer War*, a combined work containing the texts from the *Ladysmith* and *Hamilton*, rescued Churchill's text which, save for the South African *Ladysmith*, had not been in print since the early 1900s.

COMBINED WORK: THE BOER WAR

First Edition: ICS A4/5a

Publisher: Leo Cooper, London, 1989

Black cloth stamped gilt on spine, plain boards. Demy 8vo, 408 pages, including a two-page appendix on the International Churchill Society at the rear. Sold at £14.95. Bulks 1½in. Black dust jacket printed white, gold and red, photo of author in uniform of the South African Light Horse on front face. One impression, no variants.

American Issue: ICS A4/5b

Publisher: W. W. Norton & Co., New York, 1990

Maroon cloth stamped silver on spine, plain boards. Demy 8vo, 408 pages, including a two-page ICS appendix. Sold at $19.95. Bulks 1¾in. White dust jacket printed brown, gold and black, cropped version of photo on A4/5(a). One impression.

Paperback Issue: ICS A4/5c

Publisher: Mandarin Paperbacks, London, 1991

Pictorial colour boards. 8vo, sold at £4.99. Photographically reproduced (reduced) from the Cooper Issue. Two impressions.

Second American Issue: ICS A4/5d

Publisher: Dorset Press, New York, 1993

A remainder reprint of the Norton issue. Half brown cloth and red textured paper boards stamped gilt on spine. Demy 8vo, 408 pages lacking the ICS appendix. Sold at discount prices by Barnes & Noble Bookstores. Bulks 1½in. One impression, September 1993.

MR. BRODRICK'S ARMY

COHEN A10, WOODS A6

If anyone thought Churchill's hasty abridgement of *The River War* meant the author would pull in his horns rather than anger the establishment, they changed their minds when they saw *Mr. Brodrick's Army*. Published as a kind of celebration, it consists of what Manfred Weidhorn describes as 'six oratorical onslaughts in two years': the speeches assaulted Secretary of State for War St. John Brodrick and his plan for expanding the permanent peacetime Army from two to three divisions. Churchill, though of Brodrick's Party (but not for much longer), led the Parliamentary opposition to 'Brodrick's Army', invoking the theme of economy expounded by his late father and lambasting Brodrick with some of his best early oratory: '[In] war with any great Power ... three army corps would scarcely serve as a vanguard. If we are hated, they will not make us loved. If we are in danger, they will not make us safe. They are enough to irritate; they are not enough to overawe. Yet, while they cannot make us invulnerable, they may very likely make us venturesome.' (12 May 1901).

Until 1977, when modern facsimiles were published by Dalton Newfield, the *Brodrick's Army* was one of two Churchill books virtually impossible to acquire. Mr Newfield did a great service by making it available in facsimile form as the First American Edition in 1977.

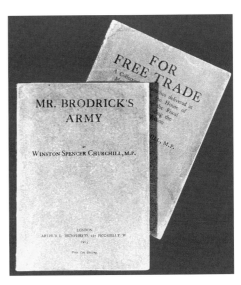

A beautiful original copy of *Mr Brodrick's Army* which, together with its counterpart *For Free Trade*, recently sold for $50,000. *(Photo: Glenn Horowitz)*

FROM THE REVIEWS

'The parallels between Churchill's 1901 opposition to Secretary of State for War St. John Brodrick's Army Reforms and Lord Randolph Churchill's 1886 battle with Secretary of State W. H. Smith over Army Estimates are many and striking–down to the coincidence of Smith's righthand at the War Office being none other than Mr Brodrick. "Alone in opposing his own conservative government, on 13 May 1901 Churchill made his first great oration ... the ex-officer appealed to the very principles on behalf of which his father had resigned and ruined himself ... Thus the son began his long political journey ... " (Weidhorn, *Sword and Pen*, 1974). Even in his initial assault on Brodrick, Winston's identification with Randolph was unmistakable; he made the House listen to him read aloud from speeches his father had delivered in the same room 20 years earlier.

'There is, however, one titanic difference between the generational struggles: Winston won and launched one of the most productive Parliamentary careers in English history, while Randolph lost, resulting first in his resignation as Chancellor of the Exchequer in December 1886, and, soon afterward, the end of his political life.

'Did a sense of injustice, even a need to expiate adolescent shame, motivate Churchill in the Brodrick affair? Many MPs thought yes, including Arthur Lee (later Lord Lee of Fareham, who presented "Chequers" to the nation as a country residence for Prime Ministers). The day after the first anti-Brodrick blast, Lee commented that Winston was wrong "to confuse filial piety with public duty".

'Blatantly oedipal as the roots of his motives might now appear, Churchill was also earnest about his position–"a definitive divergence of thought and sympathy from nearly all those [Conservatives] thronging the benches around me", he later wrote–and the Brodrick controversy marks the onset of his alienation from the Tories, the party of his father and of his class. Sensing the constructive turmoil in Winston, John Burns, the veteran radical Fabian, wrote admiringly to Lady Randolph: " ... to share with his mother the hope that he [Winston] will go further in the career he has chosen and on the excellent lines of his courageous speech ... "'

Glenn Horowitz, *Finest Hour* #70, First Quarter 1991

First [Supposed] Edition: Woods A6(a)
Publisher: Arthur L. Humphreys, London, 1903

Stated by Woods to be a 44-page pamphlet measuring 8⅜ x 5½in, with a completely separate setting from the larger version. Woods assigns this pamphlet appearance priority, but adds that 'there is no clear evidence that this version was ever released and I would therefore regard it as most likely that Churchill, displeased with its appearance, demanded a better production and got it'. Only one copy is reported to exist.

Second [First?] Edition: Woods A6(b)
Publisher: Arthur L. Humphreys, London, 1903

Bound in red card wrappers with title, author's name, publisher, date and price printed black and centred on front face; verso of front face and rear wrapper blank. 8vo, 104 pages numbered (1)–104. Published at 1s. (25c). No variations reported. (Contrary to Woods, the typeface is 14-point, not 12-point Bodoni.)

APPRAISAL
The single rarest Churchill book: in his Note to the First American Edition, Dalton Newfield suggests that 'less than a dozen' copies exist. The distinguished late Churchill collector Harry Cahn mentioned that he had acquired his copy in the 1920s for 2s. 6d., which proved to be a canny investment. Lately, copies have changed hands for five-figure prices, including a fine example paired with a like edition of *For Free Trade*, which commanded $50,000/£30,000 for the pair.

WAS *MR. BRODRICK'S ARMY* A VANITY PRESS PUBLICATION
Bookseller Glenn Horowitz speculates with some authority that the scarcity of the 1903 edition, and Churchill's subsequent *For Free Trade*, is owed to both books having been produced in small quantities, paid for by Churchill himself! See note on page 78.

First American Edition: ICS A6c
Publisher: The Churchilliana Company, Sacramento, 1977

Hardbound, stamped gilt with title, author's name and publisher's logo on both cover and spine. Preceding the actual facsimile are front matter, cartoon (*Westminster Gazette*, 14 May 1901), a preface by Manfred Weidhorn and a publisher's note by Dalton Newfield. The text is completely reset and sandwiched between replica red wrappers, black printed on front face. Endpapers take the form of Churchill's entry in *Who Was Who* 1961–1970. Published in half-brown cloth and half-cream buckram 'collector's binding' at $22.50 and a full brown cloth 'library binding' at $18.50. An outstanding service to the student, scholar, bibliophile and collector which continues to honour the memory of its late publisher, Dalton Newfield. Not in Woods.

LORD RANDOLPH CHURCHILL

COHEN A17, WOODS A8

Winston Churchill's first biographic work, this is an almost strictly political book, concentrating heavily on his father's career after the latter's entering Parliament as the Member for Woodstock in 1880. The author documents Lord Randolph's quarrel–on behalf of his brother, over a lady–with the Prince of Wales ('a great personage') and his subsequent, temporary ostracism from London society; his later meteoric rise from a rambunctious and independent Tory to Leader of the House of Commons and Chancellor of the Exchequer; his precipitous fall from power on the morrow of achieving it; and his declining though occasionally influential final years in the House of Commons.

Lord Randolph has been the subject of six biographies, of which his son's was the second. (T.H.S. Escott wrote in 1895; John Beattie Crozier in 1897; Winston and Lord Rosebery published in 1906, Sir Robert Rhodes James in 1959, R. F. Foster in 1981.) Churchill's is the most elegant stylistically, but critics maintain that filial propriety prevented Winston from an objective viewpoint. This is debatable.

Sir Robert Rhodes James, speaking at a Churchill Center symposium in 1994, said, 'it is beautifully written but not a biography–Lord Randolph never puts a foot wrong'. I'm afraid this statement is not only sweeping, but what Winston Churchill would call a 'terminological inexactitude'. While the author is undeniably his father's champion, charging the Prime Minister, Lord Salisbury, with cynical hypocrisy in accepting Lord Randolph's 1886 resignation as Chancellor, he also lists the tactical miscalculations by Lord Randolph which were the principal causes of that career-shattering episode–and other episodes. 'Mr. Winston Churchill has not unduly obtruded his [views]', said one contemporary reviewer. 'While the book is undeniably positive, there are many such episodes in the life which receive critical appraisal.'

Casual researchers have been all too ready to accept the myth, first voiced in the 1920s by political enemies of Winston, that Lord Randolph died of syphilis, allegedly contracted sometime after the birth of Winston. This has recently been authoritatively rebuffed by the research of Dr John Mather, a member of the Churchill Center's Board of Governors. Later biographers mainly avoided taking a definitive position on the cause of death, and Winston only states that his father's illness was 'a very rare and ghastly disease'. Ghastly perhaps, but syphilis is not rare, and was more common still in Lord Randolph's time. This is not the place to get into Mather's analysis, except to say that whatever Lord Randolph died of, it was highly unlikely to have been syphilis.

Winston's biography was both admired and denounced in its time, John Plumpton wrote in *Finest Hour* #51, 'because it showed Lord Randolph participating in the game of politics for the sheer pleasure of it. Admiration was extended for the clear and frank portrayal of its subject's extravagant behaviour, but the biography's claim that Lord Randolph made the Conservative Party more democratic and popular was challenged. To many readers Lord Randolph was a cynical politician who believed that the gyrations of political parties had value for their own sake.'

'Had he been in America, he would have proved himself a "boss" among ward-politicians', wrote the traditionally-hostile *Blackwood's* magazine in February 1906. The author, Winston, would roundly dispute such notions. 'There is an England', he wrote, 'of brave and earnest men ... of "poor men" who increasingly doubt the sincerity of party philanthropy. It was to that England that Lord Randolph Churchill appealed; it was that England he so nearly won; it is by that England he will be justly judged.'

FROM THE REVIEWS

'Whatever judgment men may pass on the career of Lord Randolph Churchill, no one can dispute the great literary talent shown by his son in the brilliant biography he has given to the public. However important historically the events which he describes, he has known how to make the personality of his father always the predominating interest of the book. It is biography, not history, at which the author has aimed.

'The story is told, if not without partiality, yet with very commendable frankness and with little attempt to keep back from the public extravagances of behaviour and language which in his own day, if they delighted a large section of the democracy, certainly estranged from him no small portion of the steadier elements in the community. Mr. Churchill has succeeded in painting a striking and we believe on the whole a true portrait of a very remarkable man.'

The Edinburgh Review, No. 417, July 1906.

First Edition: Woods A8(a)
Publisher: Macmillan and Co. Ltd., London, 1906

Two volumes
Deep red cloth stamped gilt on spine, blind and gilt on front board. 8vo; the volumes usually bulk 1⅞in and 1¾in with 584 pages numbered (2), (i)–(xviii), (1)–564 and 544 pages numbered (2), (i)–(x), (1)–531, (1) pages. Frontispieces (tissue protected) and other illustrations in each volume. Published 2 January 1906 at 36s. ($9).

QUANTITIES AND IMPRESSIONS
Woods records a single impression of 8,000 copies. However, some sheets may have been used in the Times Book Club issue.

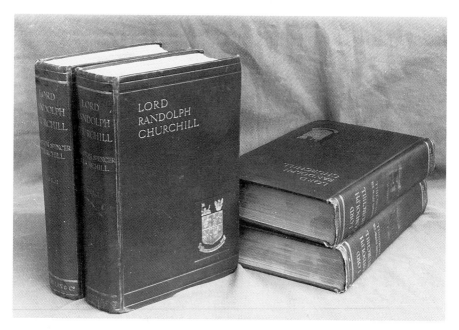

English (left) and American First Editions of *Lord Randolph Churchill*. The English has plain top page edges, smooth red cloth binding and 'Macmillan & Co' on the spine; the American has gilt top page edges, lightly scored red cloth binding and 'The Macmillan Company' on the spine.

DUST JACKETS AND VARIANTS

Jackets printed dark blue on light blue stock bear the title, author's name and publisher's name and logo on spines and the title and author's name on the front face. No binding variants are known although the outside dimensions of these books vary from volume to volume.

COMMENTS

This is a handsome pair of volumes that rivals the beauty of the two-volume *River War*, containing Lord Randolph's coat of arms on the front boards, blocked gilt inside a blind box. Like *The River War*, it was not originally sold in a slipcase, but deserves the modern slipcases which have often been fitted by booksellers. It is aesthetically inferior, however, to the American Edition. It is not uncommon, but is rarely found in pristine condition: page stock was acidic and susceptible to foxing, especially when stored in the damp English climate. Boards and spines tend to bump and chafe. The heavy pages pull at the binding and often cause gutter breaks; examine copies thoroughly for these.

APPRAISAL

Prices for the First Edition range from the low hundreds up to around $1,200/£720, but condition is everything and copies should be examined carefully before purchase.

DUST JACKETS

Although a handful of dust jackets are known to the writer, I have encountered only one complete jacketed set, which would be an extreme rarity for which the owner could name any price.

Identification Note

The English Edition is often confused with the American. It can be quickly identified by the spine legend, 'MACMILLAN & CO'. The volumes are bound in smooth cloth and the page edges are trimmed unevenly on all three sides. The lower title page states 'London' [in Old English] centred over 'MACMILLAN AND CO. LIMITED' and, in small type 'NEW YORK: THE MACMILLAN COMPANY' along with the date '1906'. The American issue is quite different in these respects. Finally, page 531 of Volume II, both the Home and Times Book Club issue (below) contain the names of the English printer, which is absent on American issues.

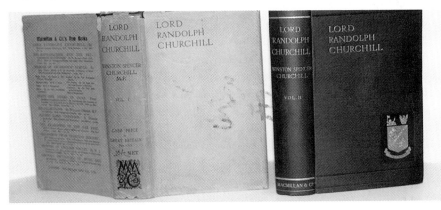

The English first edition *Lord Randolph,* with Volume I in the very rare dust jacket.

First American Edition: ICS A8aa
Publisher: The Macmillan Company, New York, 1906

Two volumes

Cherry red vertically ribbed cloth stamped gilt on spine, blind and gilt on front board. Top edges gilt. Two volumes, 8vo, with 586 and 546 pages respectively. (The four extra pages, identical in each volume, comprise one leaf of adverts for Morley's *Life of Gladstone* and a Tennyson memoir, and one blank leaf. Frontispiece and other illustrations. Published 10 February 1906. Mentioned by Woods, page 36.

QUANTITIES AND IMPRESSIONS

I have no information on the quantity printed, but the use of a different, unlaid paper stock, and the presence of the Norwood Press name on the title-page verso suggests this is a separate issue.

DUST JACKETS AND VARIANTS

Jackets have not been encountered but presumably follow the style of the Home Issue. No variants have been reported.

COMMENTS

The American Edition is often confused with the English. American Editions can be quickly identified by the spine legend, 'THE MACMILLAN COMPANY' (not 'Macmillan & Co.'). They are also bound in vertically scored rather than smooth cloth, the top page edges are gilt and the side and bottom pages are trimmed unevenly. On the lower title page the American issue states 'New York' [Old English] centred over 'THE MACMILLAN COMPANY' and, in small type 'LONDON: MACMILLAN & CO. LTD'. and the date '1906'. The name of the printer, the Norwood Press in Massachusetts, appears at the bottom of the title-page verso. The English Edition is quite different in these respects.

If you plan to own only one First Edition of each Churchill work, I recommend this one. It is better bound than the English, with finer cloth and gilt top page edges; it is rarely subject to the heavy foxing of its UK counterpart; and it costs less, conditions being equal, because it appeared a few weeks after the English. It is nonetheless equally subject to gutter breaks created from careless usage and the pulling apart of aged bindings.

APPRAISAL

Condition being the same, the American Edition costs perhaps 10–20 per cent less than comparable English Editions. It is much scarcer, however, and should be expected to equal the price of the Home Issue over the next decade.

Times Book Club Issue: ICS A8ab

Publisher: Macmillan and Co. Ltd., London, 1906

Two volumes

Reddish brown ribbed cloth stamped gilt and blind on spine (which includes the unique Times Book Club logo), blind on front board. Two volumes, 8vo, shorter and narrower than the Home Issue: a typical copy measures 8¾ x 5½in, usually bulks 1⅞in and 1¾in with 584 and 544 pages respectively. Frontispieces (acetate protected) and other illustrations in each volume. Published May 1906 at 7s. ($1.75).

QUANTITIES AND IMPRESSIONS

These volumes apparently used sheets purchased by The Times Book Club from Macmillan and sold as a huge loss-leader. Randolph S. Churchill's *Winston S. Churchill, Companion* Volume II, Part 1, pages 493–494 records a letter from Churchill to Frederick Macmillan in which WSC calls this a 'shabby trick ... I do hope you will find it will not cause any serious injury to the sale of the [first edition of the] book ... I do not see how you can stop people selling things they have bought below the cost price, but I can quite understand the annoyance and derangement which it causes.' Randolph notes that this move was part of a 'book war' between *The Times* and the publishing trade, although how they were able to obtain sheets so soon after publication is a mystery to me. This book uses the same sheets as the First Edition, slightly trimmed, including even such tipped-in items as Queen Victoria's letter to Lord Randolph (opposite page 154, Vol. II). It is not a typical book club edition.

DUST JACKETS AND VARIANTS
It is not known whether the Times Book Club Issue came in dust jackets; no variants are reported.

COMMENTS
This issue can be quickly identified through the circular logo at the foot of the spines: a belt-like device reading 'The Times 1785'. The spine titles are also smaller than the trade edition's. The page edges are trimmed to smaller dimensions than the original pages, and the books themselves are about ⅛in shorter and ¼in narrower than the originals.

Since it was published at the same time as the First Edition, it is a genuine first edition, made up with identical sheets. Nicely if not elaborately bound (it lacks the gilt coat of arms), it is an adequate if not dramatic looking set of books. The Times Book Club binding is very susceptible to fading, so copies with unfaded or lightly faded spines are rare.

Lord Randolph Churchill reprints. Left to right: the Times Book Club two-volume first edition, 1907 one-volume edition, the 1952 Odhams dust jacket and the book underneath.

APPRAISAL

In 1906 these sets sold for a fifth the price of the First Edition; today they sell for about a third or half the price, condition being equal. The booktrade retail price has hovered around $100/£60 for years, but this is usually for faded sets; a pristine example would be worth at least three times as much. This is a bargain priced version of the original two-volume text.

First Cheap Edition: Woods A8(b)
Publisher: Macmillan & Co., Ltd., London, 1907

Deep red cloth stamped gilt on spine, blind (four horizontal rules) on front board. 8vo., usually bulks 1¾in with 908 pages. Frontispiece (acetate protected) and four other illustrations. Published May 1907 at 7s. 6d. ($1.83). Remainders sold c. 1925 at 10s. ($2.50) with revised dust jackets.

QUANTITIES AND IMPRESSIONS

Woods records a single impression of 3,000 copies; this presumably included enough sheets to warrant a reissue in 1925, because copies of that date, on identical page stock, contain no new printing information. I do not know whether the 1925s were in original or remainder bindings.

DUST JACKETS

The jacket is printed black on light brown stock with title, author's name and Macmillan initial logo on spine and front face. Jackets of the 1925 issue contain the legend '10/- | NET' on the lower spine and the back face advertises, among other titles, Sir Sidney Lee's biography of Edward VII, the second volume of which was to be published in the autumn of 1925. I have not encountered an original 1907 jacket.

VARIANTS

Copies exist with and without gilt top page edges. It might be thought that, if two printings did occur, gilt edges mark the original 1907 issue and plain edges the remainder issue; but if there was only one printing, perhaps it's the other way round–the original uneven page tops might have been shaved and gilded. Unfortunately, the only way genuinely to confirm the date is by the dust jackets, and these are so rare as to make firm conclusions impossible. Vagaries of binding in those years could easily mean that some original page edges were gilt while others were not.

A small number of copies bear a small round 'presentation copy' embossment similar to that mentioned under *London to Ladysmith*, but it is not established that these stamps are the publisher's.

COMMENTS

The one-volume edition can be quickly identified by the lack of a Volume number on the spine. A handsomely bound book despite its plebeian origins, this volume presents the unabridged original text and costs much less than First Editions. It tends to hold up better, and many copies still have the nicely rounded spines they were born with. The pages are not as prone to foxing as the First Editions, but because the paper stock is much thinner, the book has to be read carefully.

APPRAISAL

Not scarce, this edition has maintained a fairly level value over the years. Typical price for a fine copy is from $150/£90 up; a really crisp example might go for a hundred more, but that's the present limit. Well-worn examples can be purchased for much less.

Note: American Cheap Edition (existence questionable)

Copies of the Cheap Edition have been reported bearing the spine inscription 'THE MACMILLAN COMPANY', which was the style and identification of Macmillan's American office on the First American Edition. I have not personally encountered such copies and would be interested to hear of their existence. Presumably they would contain the 'New York' title-page inscription in Old English as on the First American.

Extended One-Volume Edition: Woods A8(c)
Publisher: Odhams Press Limited, London, 1952

Bright red cloth stamped gilt on spine, boards blank. 16mo, usually bulks 1½in, 840 pages. Frontispiece and eight pages of illustrations. Published 5 February 1952 at 21s. ($2.94).

QUANTITIES AND IMPRESSIONS

A single impression of unknown quantity was issued.

DUST JACKETS AND VARIANTS

The jacket is navy blue printed yellow and white, unillustrated; the face has the title (yellow), author's name (white) and a small blurb (yellow). No variants of the book are reported.

COMMENTS

Odhams Press acquired the post-war rights to numerous Churchill titles. Their edition of *Lord Randolph Churchill* was particularly welcome, since the book had been out of print for two decades. Churchill was able to add previously unpublished material, namely Sir Henry Wolff's account of Lord Randolph's resignation in 1886.

This, says our author in his *'Introduction to the New Edition'*, throws 'an intimate light upon his quarrel with Lord Salisbury. Everyone can see now what a mistake he made in breaking with Lord Salisbury at a time when, being Chancellor of the Exchequer and Leader of the House of Commons at only thirty-six, he had every reason to believe that time would be on his side.'

For its new material, the Odhams Edition should be acquired. A handsome book when published, it proved even more susceptible to gutter breaks than the 1906 originals, and unbroken examples are rare. Aside from the two collected editions (see appendix) and a recent special binding of leftover sheets from the *Collected Works*, this represents the last appearance of *Lord Randolph Churchill* to date. It is time for a reprint.

APPRAISAL
Very easy to acquire: as little as a couple of pounds in scruffy condition and not more than $150/£90 in absolute fine, jacketed condition.

Issue from the *Collected Works*

The Churchill Center's concern with making rare Churchill works readily available has resulted in the recent binding of leftover sheets from the Library of Imperial History's 1974–1975 *Collected Works*, accomplished by Mark Weber and offered by the Center's New Book Service. The rebound *Lord Randolph Churchill* contains the 1952 expanded text (reset) and appears in burgundy or red cloth blocked gilt with the Churchill coat of arms on the cover. Sold at $60/£38 and still available at this writing.

FOREIGN TRANSLATIONS

Swedish: LORD RANDOLPH CHURCHILL
Published in one volume by Norstedt: Stockholm 1941, offered in buff cloth or in cardboard wrappers, both with dust jackets.

FOR FREE TRADE

COHEN A18, WOODS A9

The 1906 General Election was the first which Churchill fought as a Liberal. He campaigned for Manchester North-West on a single issue, Free Trade, an institution dear to the hearts of the Manchester cotton manufacturers. Although the constituency had long been Tory, Free Trade had opened an opportunity for the Liberals who, unlike the Conservatives, were firmly committed to it. The Tories had split on the issue after their scion, Joseph Chamberlain, introduced his scheme of 'Fair Trade', which applied protective tariffs on goods from nations outside the British Empire. This was, of course, anathema to the manufacturing community of Manchester– and to Churchill, who had been brought up in Lord Randolph's house as a firm ally of Cobden and Bright, the Anti-Corn Law movement, and the knocking-down of tariffs in general. In that last great Liberal landslide, Churchill and his party were swept into office with 377 seats. Churchill had to fight the seat again in 1908 when he was appointed to the Cabinet (as was then the custom). This time he narrowly lost. Opponents passed out 'Churchill Memory Cards' but they were premature; he was quickly offered and won Dundee, a seat he would hold for the next 15 years through the worst upheavals and disasters of his career.

FROM THE REVIEWS

'Churchill objected to Protection as a policy which favoured industry and monopoly at the expense of the small manufacturer, the consumer, and the shipping industry. It would cripple British exports, reduce the consumer market at home, raise prices, cause hardship to the poor, restrict enterprise, nurture vested interests, corrupt politicians, make the Empire odious to workers, worsen foreign relations and thereby raise defence spending. Its opposite, Free Trade, is the best foreign policy: it encourages international relations, interdependence and peace. He carried on the fight, as he saw it, against "corruption at home, aggression to cover it up abroad", against party tyranny, hollow patriotism, financial exploitation of the public interest by the private sector and the financial combines.

'All this sounds like radical rhetoric, and though it is used on behalf of the free play of forces in the capitalist economy, Churchill is not oblivious to the "sad conditions" of the poor. He sets Free Trade as only a "negative process", a catalyst of progress but not progress itself. To defend Free Trade, an as-yet imperfect Britain must get at deep-seated ills by producing "a positive and practical policy of social reform". She had to think more "about the native toiler at the bottom of the mine and less about the fluctuations of the share market", to "consider the condition of a slum in an English city" to be as important as a "jungle in Somaliland".

'How right Churchill is in these speeches is a question best left to economists and is in any case dependent on the political philosophy of the reader. What should be noted is once again the masterliness of the rhetoric, the excitement that these speeches on a dead issue can still generate. "Dead issue?" The particular context is of interest only to historians, but the principles at stake are still around, albeit in reverse political order ... In another land and a later time, *For Free Trade* is not without its relevance.'

Manfred Weidhorn in the Preface to the American Edition, 1977.

First Edition: ICS A9a
Publisher: Arthur L. Humphreys, London, 1906

Bound in red card wrappers with title, author's name, publisher, date and price printed black and centred on front face; verso of front face and rear wrapper blank. 8vo, 136 pages numbered (i)–(xvi) and (1)–(119), (1). Published at 1s. (25c). No variations reported. Notably, the back wrapper advertises *Mr. Brodrick's Army* (1903), which could not have sold too well even considering the small press run. Contrary to Woods, the typeface is 14-point, not 12-point Bodoni.

Next to *Mr. Brodrick's Army* this is the rarest Churchill title. In his Publisher's Note to the First American Edition, Dalton Newfield suggests that hardly more than a dozen copies of this volume exist. Lately, copies have changed hands for five-figure prices, including a fine example paired with a like edition of *Mr. Brodrick's Army* which commanded $50,000/£30,000 for the pair. Woods A9.

Note: why are *For Free Trade* and *Mr. Broderick's Army* so rare?

'In 1901 Churchill was only a 27 year-old, first term MP. Who would have wanted to publish his early, decidedly ephemeral, political speeches? I believe this was none but Churchill himself, who wanted to distribute them in permanent form to influential MPs and politicians.

'For decades, Arthur L. Humphreys (1865–1946) managed Hatchard's Piccadilly bookshop, running out of it what amounted to a vanity press–the address on both the *Brodrick* and *Free Trade* is '187 Piccadilly, W.', Hatchard's address then and now ...

'How Churchill and Humphreys hooked up remains unknown. A logical candidate for intermediary would be Frank Harris, Oscar Wilde's great friend and Churchill's de facto "literary agent" for *Lord Randolph Churchill*. In 1895, Humphreys published Wilde's first book, *Oscariana*, and, in 1906, Lord Rosebery's defensive monograph on Lord Randolph, though this is a common book.

'Whoever did the introducing, it seems evident that once Churchill determined to see his early reform speeches between covers (two full years had elapsed since the anti-Brodrick speeches) he enlisted Humphreys as his "publisher"–not once but twice.

'It may be coincidental, but by any quantifiable measure the two rarest book-length works in Churchill's canon are *Mr. Broderick's Army* and *For Free Trade*, also the only instances of Churchill's and Humphreys's names being juxtaposed on title pages.'

Glenn Horowitz in *Finest Hour #70*, First Quarter 1991.

American Edition: Cohen A17.2, ICS A9b
Publisher: The Churchilliana Company, Sacramento, 1977

Hardbound, stamped gilt with title, author's name and publisher's logo on both cover and spine. Preceding the actual facsimile are front matter, illustration (WSC addressing the Commons in 1906), a preface by Manfred Weidhorn and a publisher's note by Dalton Newfield. This edition is reproduced photographically from a First Edition. The original text is sandwiched between replica red wrappers, black printed on front face. Endpapers take the form of Churchill's entry in *Who Was Who 1961–1970*. Published in a half-brown cloth and half-cream buckram 'collector's binding' at $22.50 and a full brown cloth 'library binding' at $18.50. An outstanding service to the student, scholar, bibliophile and collector which continues to honour the memory of its late publisher. Not in Woods.

FOR
FREE TRADE

A Collection of Speeches delivered at
Manchester or in the House of
Commons during the Fiscal
controversy preceding the
late General Election

BY

WINSTON S. CHURCHILL, M.P.

LONDON
ARTHUR L. HUMPHREYS, 187 PICCADILLY, W
1906

One Shilling net

The cover of *For Free Trade*, represented by the replica wrapper from the 1977 Churchilliana Company reprint.

MY AFRICAN JOURNEY

COHEN A27, WOODS A12

As Undersecretary of State for the Colonies in 1907, Churchill was theoretically answerable to the Colonial Secretary, Lord Elgin (pronounced 'El-gan') but since Elgin was in the House of Lords it fell to Churchill to speak on Government Colonial policy in the Commons–a pleasant assignment which the ambitious Winston used to the fullest. When Churchill asked his senior for permission to travel to Africa on an extended tour of inspection, his request was granted by what today would be called express mail. Elgin was only too happy to be relieved of his opinionated and talkative junior, at least for a little while.

With eight books and ten volumes already behind him, Churchill saw the advantages of producing a travelogue on Britain's valuable possessions in East Africa. Among these, Churchill waxes most eloquent on Uganda, which he calls 'a pearl', though in one inscribed copy I have seen he writes, 'Uganda is defended by its insects.'

The work was first published in shorter form in *The Strand Magazine* (Woods C35), though the last two chapters in the book do not appear in the periodical. Illustrations in the book were selected from the magazine. The magazine serials contain about 35,000 words, the book 45,000. Even this was not enough for the size book the publishers wanted, so its 12-point type was generously leaded. Both the First and American Editions are important because they appear to include photographs allegedly taken by Churchill, the only such appearance in the canon; the text is important because it shows Churchill raising prescient questions involving the betterment of the East African population. These were issues far ahead of their time, some of which were only being addressed half a century later and, judging by the recent history of Somalia, Rwanda and Zaire, not being addressed very well.

FROM THE REVIEWS

'In Mr. Churchill's book the picture of his travels is vividly and attractively drawn. Here and there he employs a somewhat extravagant language to describe matters of insignificant detail ... but on the whole there is little to criticise and much to praise in the story which he unfolds. East Africa, Mr. Churchill thinks, can never be a white man's country in the true sense of the word, for proof is wanting that "the pure-bred European can rear his children under the equatorial sun and at an elevation of 6,000 feet." The desire of the white man to make East Africa a white man's country does not bring him into collision with the black aboriginal [because] "the white man absolutely refuses to do black man's work." ... Mr. Churchill recommends reserving the highland areas for exploitation at the hands of the white man, while at the same time encouraging the Asiatic to trade and settle in "the enormous regions of tropical fertility to which he is naturally adapted."

'Of the entrancing scenery of Uganda, Mr. Churchill writes with undisguised admiration: "The Kingdom of Uganda is a fairy tale." In the rich domain between the Victoria and Albert Lakes "an amiable, clothed, polite and intelligent race dwell together in an organised monarchy ... " Mr. Churchill trekked north, passing from the regions of equatorial luxuriance to the two great deserts, emerging finally in the tourist-ridden land of Egypt. Speeding down the White Nile to the Sudan and Egypt, he opines that 'the best lies behind. Uganda is a pearl.'

'When he sums up his conclusions as a result of the journey, they comprise the words: "Concentrate upon Uganda", and the steps which should be taken to develop the immense latent wealth of the country are summed up in the three words: "Build a Railway".

The Bookman, London, January 1909

First Edition: ICS A12aa

Publisher: Hodder & Stoughton, London, 1908

Red pictorial cloth, spine blocked gilt; the top board carries a woodcut illustration of Churchill with his bagged white rhinoceros, blocked blue, brown and black and signed 'HR' over the title and author's name, all inside a heavy black rule. Frontispiece illustration (photo of cover scene), protected by tissue. 8vo, 242 pages numbered (2), (i)–(xiv) and (1)–226; 18-page rear catalogue of other Hodder & Stoughton titles printed on the same stock; 46 unnumbered photo pages (61 photos) on coated stock inserted throughout (see illustrations list, pages (ix)–(xiii)); three maps on coated stock facing pages 2, 16 and 92. Endpapers blank. Published December 1908 at 5s. ($1.25).

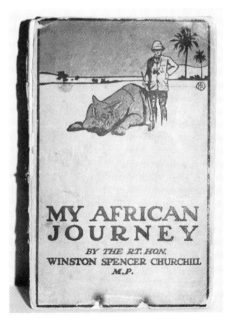

The extremely rare wrapper copy, likely produced for export, is identical internally to the English first edition.

QUANTITIES AND IMPRESSIONS

A single impression of 12,500 was produced.

DUST JACKETS

No jackets have surfaced and it is impossible to speculate on their design; they certainly existed, since Hodder & Stoughton were jacketing copies for several years by 1908.

VARIANTS

Hardbound variant: Copies exist with a small gold 'asterisk' centred above or below the publisher's imprint on the bottom of the spine. Since every such copy that I and others have examined contains evidence of having been first sold in India or the British Colonies, and since the *African Journey* has no separate Colonial issue, the 'asterisk' almost certainly designates an export edition.

Softbound variant: The very rare card-wrapped edition is identical internally to the hardbound First Edition. The following description is provided by Mark Weber, owner of the only copy I know of: 'The paper stock, title page, frontispiece (with glassine) are identical to the First Edition. Wrappers are light card, white on the inside, the outside a light tan. The endpaper is tightly glued onto the outer cover. The front cover illustration is identical to that of the First Edition except that the background is tan instead of red. The blue, black and grey are clearly printed from the same tools. The rear face is blank, although this copy has a bookseller's label from Kobe, Japan, indicating this may be an export edition. The spine is printed black on tan background 'MY AFRICAN JOURNEY' in three lines of serif type similar but smaller than the spine type of the First Edition. The author's name is in three lines, same as the First Edition, but in a sans serif bold font except 'L's have turn ups. Hodder & Stoughton at the spine base is in italic upper/lower case. Supporting my theory that this is another export variation, an asterisk appears below the publisher name.' Woods (page 42) describes this variant in 'cream' wrappers but misdates it 'March 1919' and confuses its price and quantity with the First Cheap Edition (Cohen A25.6, see below).

COMMENTS

This is a physically beautiful book and for that reason one of the most popular Churchill works. Aside from its striking cover, collectors are drawn to its profuse illustrations, most of which disappeared after the First Editions. It is also popular with Africana collectors.

Woods (page 42) confusingly mentions a 'later issue without the illustration or lettering in the top board' (this is the American issue, see next entry); and two paperback editions whose characteristics he confuses: a 'cheap paperback ... published March 1919' came long after what Woods calls 'another, probably subsequent' paperback, whose description is that of the Hodder & Stoughton 1909 edition.

APPRAISAL

My African Journey has held its value well over the years; finding a fine copy is not impossible, but it is increasingly difficult; as always, such examples command a healthy premium: a run-of-the-mill copy might sell for as little as $250/£180, a really fine copy may go for $1,200/£720. Buyers should be extremely careful personally to collate a prospective purchase; be sure to check all illustration pages and maps, which were tipped in and can easily loosen and fall out. The wrapper variant is a hundred times rarer and $2,000/£1,200 would not be too much to pay for one.

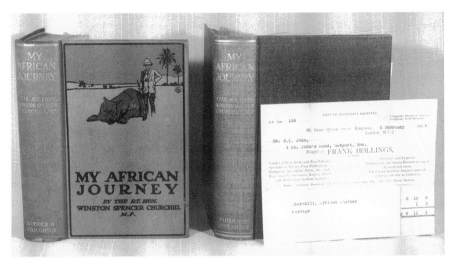

The English and American first editions of *My African Journey*. The plain bound American edition is much scarcer. At right is an invoice from bookseller Frank Hollings, who sold the English first edition shown in 1957 at £8 11s. 3d.

American Issue: ICS A12ab

Publisher: Hodder & Stoughton and George Doran, New York, 1908

Dark red buckram, spine blocked gilt with title, author's name, publisher imprint and a double band (one narrow, one wide) top and bottom. The boards are blank. Frontispiece illustration sometimes protected by tissue shows Churchill with his white rhinoceros. 8vo, about ¼in taller than the First Edition; 242 pages numbered (2), (i)–(xiv) and (1)–226; 46 unnumbered photo pages (61 photos) on coated stock inserted throughout (see illustrations list, pages (ix) to (xiii)); three maps on coated stock facing pages 2, 16 and 92. No rear catalogue. Endpapers blank. Published 17 April 1909 at $1.50. Mentioned by Woods, page 41 (confused as a 'later issue' of the First Edition by Woods, page 42).

QUANTITIES AND IMPRESSIONS

There appear to have been two impressions, the first using English sheets, the second pressed outside England. See variants, below.

DUST JACKETS

A dust jacket is presumed to have existed but none has been found.

VARIANTS

There are three distinct issues, conforming to changes in Hodder & Stoughton's operations in the United States. Each can be clearly recognised from the publisher's imprint at the bottom of the title page. Note that all issues read 'HODDER & STOUGHTON' on the spines.

First Issue: Title page reads 'HODDER AND STOUGHTON | LONDON MCMVIII'. These copies contain the imprint, 'Clay & Sons' on page (iv). Cohen A25.2.

Second Issue: Title page reads 'HODDER & STOUGHTON | NEW YORK AND LONDON' [no date]; page (iv) carries the 'Clay & Sons' printer's imprint. Cohen A25.3.

Third Issue: Cancel title reads 'GEORGE H. DORAN COMPANY | NEW YORK'; page (iv) lacks the 'Clay & Sons' imprint. Since this title page is a cancel, the balance of the contents are most probably made up from existing sheets. Cohen A25.4.

Contrary to Woods, the American issues were not published by Doubleday, Doran, a firm which did not exist until a 1929 merger. In fact, Hodder & Stoughton set up George Doran in business in New York, and *My*

Title pages identify the three issues of the American *African Journey*. Top to bottom: first issue (imprinted 'HODDER & STOUGHTON | LONDON MCMVIII'); second issue ('HODDER & STOUGHTON | NEW YORK AND LONDON'); third issue ('GEORGE H DORAN COMPANY | NEW YORK').

My African Journey

BY

THE RIGHT HON.
WINSTON SPENCER CHURCHILL, M.P.

AUTHOR OF "THE STORY OF THE MALAKAND FIELD FORCE,"
"THE RIVER WAR," "LONDON TO LADYSMITH," "IAN HAMILTON'S MARCH,"
"SAVROLA," "LIFE OF LORD RANDOLPH CHURCHILL"

WITH SIXTY-ONE ILLUSTRATIONS FROM PHOTOGRAPHS BY
THE AUTHOR AND LIEUTENANT-COLONEL GORDON
WILSON, AND THREE MAPS

HODDER AND STOUGHTON
LONDON MCMVIII

My African Journey

BY

THE RIGHT HON.
WINSTON SPENCER CHURCHILL, M.P.

AUTHOR OF "THE STORY OF THE MALAKAND FIELD FORCE,"
"THE RIVER WAR," "LONDON TO LADYSMITH," "IAN HAMILTON'S MARCH,"
"SAVROLA," "LIFE OF LORD RANDOLPH CHURCHILL"

WITH SIXTY-ONE ILLUSTRATIONS FROM PHOTOGRAPHS BY
THE AUTHOR AND LIEUTENANT-COLONEL GORDON
WILSON, AND THREE MAPS

HODDER & STOUGHTON
NEW YORK AND LONDON

MY AFRICAN JOURNEY

BY

THE RIGHT HON.
WINSTON SPENCER CHURCHILL, M.P.

AUTHOR OF "THE STORY OF THE MALAKAND FIELD FORCE,"
"THE RIVER WAR," "LONDON TO LADYSMITH," "IAN HAMILTON'S MARCH,"
"SAVROLA," "LIFE OF LORD RANDOLPH CHURCHILL"

WITH SIXTY-ONE ILLUSTRATIONS FROM PHOTOGRAPHS BY
THE AUTHOR AND LIEUTENANT-COLONEL GORDON
WILSON, AND THREE MAPS

GEORGE H. DORAN COMPANY
NEW YORK

African Journey may have been his first title. The first issue represents export sheets identical to (perhaps part of) the English impression of 12,500; the second issue reflects the publisher's establishing a New York office; the third issue reflects the emergence of George Doran as Hodder & Stoughton's United States distributor.

COMMENTS

Although it offers the serious collector three separate ways to spend money and is much scarcer than the First Edition, the American issue lacks appeal because its plain cover is much less attractive than the First Edition's. It is, however, a more durable binding; having spent their lives in the USA, copies tend to be free of foxing. Be sure all inserted photo and map pages are present before buying.

APPRAISAL

Important in tracing the publishing history, the American issue is less significant as a collector's item; generally, copies sell for not more than 75 per cent of the prices of First Editions in comparable condition, and I do not think it likely that even a fine one would be offered at a four-figure price. I have seen too few to judge which issue is rarest.

Canadian Issue: ICS A12ac
Publisher: Wm. Briggs, Toronto, 1909

Red pictorial cloth, spine blocked gilt; the top board identical to the First Edition. 8vo, endpapers blank. Cancel title page reads 'WILLIAM BRIGGS | 1909'; no publisher's rear catalogue; contents otherwise identical to the First Edition but printed on thinner paper. Apparently printed in England: Clay & Sons imprint on page (iv).

VARIANTS

A softbound wrapper version has been reported, but is not verified.

This is an extremely rare variant. Having never heard of a sale, appraising this one is mere guesswork, but I believe it would command the price of a near-fine (but not a full-fine) First Edition. The Canadian *Ian Hamilton's* has intrinsic value because of its unique binding. The Briggs *African Journey* looks outwardly like a conventional First Edition. Since collectors are attracted by oddity, they would be less tempted by this one than by the Canadian *Hamilton's*.

First Cheap Edition: ICS A12b
Publisher: Hodder & Stoughton, London, c. 1909

Cream-greyish pictorial wrappers. On top wrap, the title (blue) and author's name (black) over a colour illustration of Churchill and his white rhinoceros (similar but

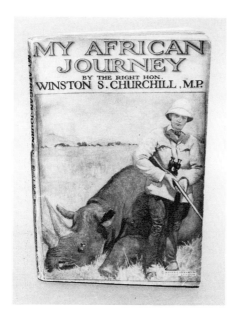

The 1909 cheap edition in colour wrappers sold 20,000 copies but is rare today and very desirable when in the condition shown here. Its front wrapper illustration is unique to this edition.

not identical to the First Edition's cover artwork). 8vo, 96 pages, adverts on pages 1, 2, 6, 93–96 plus inside of wrappers and back wrapper. Type arranged in two-column format, no internal illustrations. Woods (page 42) confuses this with the wrapper variant of the First Edition, which he states was published in March 1919 at 6s. in a quantity of 20,000 copies. The price and quantity undoubtedly refer to this work, but Woods's date is probably a typo for March 1909.

APPRAISAL

This is a production similar to the pulp *Savrola*, A3(c), but much scarcer and more expensive. Very large sums, up to $1000/£600, have been asked and paid for nice copies, which are rarely fine because of the pulpy, usually yellowed page stock. The handsome cover is the chief attribute of this edition.

Holland Press Edition: ICS A12c

Publisher: Holland Press–Neville Spearman, London, 1962

Brown cloth blocked gilt on spine, boards blank. 8vo, 150 pages, frontispiece and four internal photos, map at page (viii). Dust jacket printed orange, brown and black with 'Churchill' the dominant word on the top face, emblazoned across an outline map of Africa with the Nile traced by a white line. The text for this edition was completely reset. One impression was published, quantity unknown. A serviceable reading copy, unfortunately lacking most of the original illustrations. Mentioned by Woods, page 42.

First Paperback Edition: ICS A12d
Publisher: Icon Books, London, 1962

This first modern paperback carries cover illustrated with art and photos that would better be applied to *London to Ladysmith*. 128 pages, no frontispiece or other illustrations; the text was again reset for this edition. Two impressions exist, quantities unknown. Offered at 3s. 6d. Not in Woods.

Heron Edition: ICS A12e
Publisher: Heron Books, London, c. 1965

A pretty little red leatherette volume blocked in decorative gilt with 'Churchill' on top board and four 'attempts' at bands on the spine. Decorative gilt-on-brown endpapers and yellow cloth pagemarker. 16mo, 152 pages including a colophon naming the book's designer, 'William B. Taylor for Edito-Service SA, Geneva'. Printed in Switzerland by photographically reducing the text and photos from the Holland Press edition of 1962. Among the inexpensive editions this is moderately desirable, if a bit hard on the eyes. Not in Woods.

VARIANT
Copies have been observed with and without top edges gilt.

APPRAISAL
Never pay more than $35/£20, unless these get a lot scarcer or I get a lot poorer.

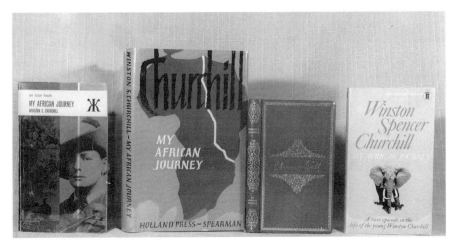

African Journey reprints. Left to right: the Icon paperback, Neville Spearman edition, Heron edition and New English Library paperback.

Second Paperback Edition: ICS A12f
Publisher, New English Library, London, 1972

A paperback subtitled 'A rare episode in the life of the young Winston Churchill.' Tan wrappers with charging elephant on front and photo of the author c. 1900 on the back wrapper, along with prices in eight currencies. Published March 1972 at 25p in the UK. One impression known. Not in Woods.

The New Edition, 1989 : ICS A12g

My African Journey was among the several older Churchill titles reprinted by Leo Cooper and W. W. Norton in 1989–1990. Features common to all issues of this edition are as follows: text photographically reproduced from the *Collected Works*, Volume I (see appendix), including 12 pages of photos from the original work on coated stock; new foreword by Tom Hartman (in addition to the author's original preface); and a map reprinted from the original edition. All issues are essentially the same. They are ideal as reading copies, especially for those wishing to experience Churchill's 'incredible journey' without wear and tear on valuable early editions. Used copies in fine condition are readily available at insignificant prices.

First New Edition: ICS A12ga
Publisher: Leo Cooper, London, 1989

Black cloth stamped gilt on spine, plain boards. 8vo, 136 pages including appendix on the International Churchill Societies; published at £14.95. Black dust jacket printed white, blue and red, photo of author circa 1908. One impression, no known variants.

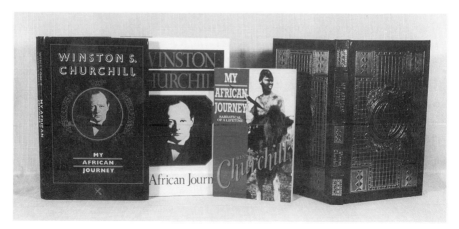

New editions of *My African Journey*. Left to right: the Cooper, Norton, Mandarin and Easton Press limited.

New American Issue: ICS A12gb
Publisher: W. W. Norton & Co., New York, 1990

Dark green cloth stamped silver on spine, plain boards. 8vo, 136 pages including ICS appendix; published at $18.95. White dust jacket printed green, gold and black, cropped and enlarged version of Home Issue jacket photo. One impression, no known variants.

New Paperback Issue: ICS A12gc
Publisher: Mandarin Books, London, 1991

Pictorial heavy colour boards showing an African warrior multicolour. 8vo, 138 pages including an extra leaf with more Mandarin titles on reverse; no illustrations. Published at £4.99. One impression, no variants. ICS A12gc.

Limited Edition: ICS A12h
Publisher: Easton Press, Norwalk, CT, 1992

Part of an extensive, pigskin-bound limited edition of travel books, not sold separately, thus hard for Churchill collectors to find. Reddish brown pigskin elaborately blocked gilt on both cover (a decorative globe device) and spine (three decorative devices separating the title and 'Winston Churchill', along with three raised spine bands). Beige moiré cloth endpapers, tan silk pagemarker, all edges gilt. 8vo, 136 pages numbered (i)–(ii) and (1)–134. (ICS appendix excised). Title page states: 'COLLECTOR'S EDITION | Bound in Genuine Leather'. Illustrations identical to the Cooper-Norton editions, and most likely photographically reproduced from their sheets. However, a special black and white drawing of a charging rhinoceros (artist unstated) was commissioned for the frontispiece of this work. About 2,000 copies were published.

LIBERALISM AND THE
SOCIAL PROBLEM

COHEN A29, WOODS A15

That a young, radical Churchill was once held the scourge of the British Establishment and a traitor to his class is largely forgotten by those who think of him only in the modern or at least the Second World War context. Yet by 1909, when his third book of speeches was published, Churchill was an ardent reformer, the bane of Torydom, Lloyd George's chief lieutenant and ally among the Young Turks of the Liberal Party in their assault on the privileges of the House of Lords, their championing of the earliest forms of welfare legislation, and their campaign for Home Rule in Ireland.

'My father was a Manchester Liberal', said Alistair Cooke, recalling this period for the International Churchill Society in 1988. 'He had been a young man during what he always said were Winston's great years, from 1904 to 1910, during the memorable Liberal Parliament, when the two great radicals, Lloyd George and Churchill, embarked on the reform of British society. This strange alliance–the poor country boy and the aristocrat–abolished sweatshops and gave the miners an 8-hour day. They set up the labour exchanges that led to unemployment insurance. In fact, what Roosevelt later called the "New Deal" was really started by Bismarck in Germany, where Lloyd George sent a colleague to study Bismarck's system. To Americans it is Franklin Roosevelt, inventor of memorable phrases, who has gone down as the man who invented the New Deal.' But FDR was years behind Bismarck, Lloyd George and Churchill.

In *Liberalism and the Social Problem* we part company with the light-hearted, contemplative mood of *My African Journey* and turn to more serious business. There was one other important watershed in the period between these two books: on 12 September 1908, Churchill married Clementine Hozier, and *Liberalism and the Social Problem* is dedicated 'To My Wife'. The dedication was politically as well as romantically apt, since Clementine was a lifelong Liberal, who never quite trusted the Conservatives, even after Churchill had returned to them as Chancellor of the Exchequer in 1924. It was she who urged her husband not to accept the Tory Leadership after Neville Chamberlain's fatal illness in late 1940, and she again who urged Winston to give up politics in 1945 and remain the national figure he had become. Though his wife's advice was often very important and heeded, in these instances Churchill ignored her.

The foreword is by Henry William Massingham (1860–1924), who espoused

Only one fully jacketed copy of *Liberalism and the Social Problem* is known in the world.

many of Churchill's positions on handling the Boers in South Africa and was editor of *The Nation* from 1907 through 1923.

FROM THE REVIEWS

'This grandson of a duke having fulfilled a longstanding wish by crossing the floor to become a "radical" or modern Liberal, questions of tariffs and economics then blossomed into the larger social issue which preoccupied Churchill for four crowded years. *Liberalism and the Social Problem* addresses itself to three important topics of the time: the speeches of 1906–1908 deal mainly with the settlement in South Africa and the vindication of free trade; those of 1908–1909 project various social reforms and attack the Conservatives, the rich vested interests, and the land speculators; the last group of speeches defends Lloyd George's radical "People's Budget" of 1909 and assails the House of Lords in the constitutional crisis between the two houses which the budget caused ...

'If [*Mr. Brodrick's Army* and *For Free Trade*] contain interesting, lucid, clearly structured, sometimes brilliant orations on somewhat dated topics, *Liberalism* is a broad-ranging survey of modern social problems; the issues it discusses are still being fought out today. Its imagery, fervour, rhetoric, variety, compassion and wit, and its careful delineation of the course between the Scylla of Tory reaction and Charybdis of socialism makes it a classic exposition of the pragmatic political basis for the Liberal or progressive Conservative outlook ... '

Manfred Weidhorn in *Sword and Pen: A Survey of the Writings of Sir Winston Churchill,* Albuquerque: University of New Mexico Press, 1974

First Edition: ICS A15a
Publisher: Hodder & Stoughton, London, 1909

Burgundy cloth. The top board bears the gilt signature 'Winston S. Churchill'. The spine bears the title, byline 'THE RT. HON. WINSTON S. CHURCHILL M.P.' and publisher's name. 8vo, 438 pages numbered (i)–(xxiv) and (1)–414. Introduction by Hugh Massingham. The verso of the half-title contains a boxed advert for *My African Journey*. Endpapers are white. Published at 3s. 6d.

QUANTITIES AND IMPRESSIONS
Woods states that a single impression of 5,000 copies was published on 26 December 1909. However, he fails to mention a second impression which followed in 1910 (see below).

DUST JACKETS AND VARIANTS
The only jacket I have ever seen is printed grey on thin white paper, bears a Russell & Sons boxed photo of the author (same as on *The People's Rights*, less snugly cropped), title and byline on the cover and the title, author's name, publisher and '3/6 net' on the spine. All type is dropped out white. The flaps and back face are blank.

There are no variations although Ronald Cohen reports a publisher's 'Advance Copy' so designated in blind on the top board.

COMMENTS
Of interest is the title page author's name 'WINSTON SPENCER CHURCHILL', the last use of the full 'SPENCER' in first editions of Churchill's works. Woods is inaccurate in describing a misdated speech on page 277 as 'May 3, 1903 [Stet 1903. Misprint for 1909]'–on every copy I have seen, this speech is dated (also incorrectly) 'May 4, 1909'. The actual date of this speech was May 3, 1909, and the 'correction' made in the second impression was, as noted below, also incorrect!

APPRAISAL
Liberalism and the Social Problem ranks among the most important Churchill speech volumes. Manfred Weidhorn writes: 'Of the volumes of speeches, *Liberalism, While England Slept,* and [*Into Battle* or] *Blood, Sweat and Tears* (and so to a degree *The Unrelenting Struggle*) stand out as eloquent expressions of Churchill's three greatest periods as orator.'

Unfortunately, the first edition is exceedingly rare and, while most Churchill firsts have come down in price over the last five years, scarcity is maintaining *Liberalism* prices at a high level. The lowest price I have seen for a copy lately was $600/£360. More often, prices run up to and over $1,000/£600. Still, there's hope: a friend and colleague recently found a nice example in an English bookshop marked only £10, and quickly squirrelled it onto his personal library shelves—as well he should. As to jacketed copies, the one mentioned above is the only complete one known to exist. It was bought in London in 1985 for $100/£60, resold in 1990 for $3,500/£2,200, and was offered recently in excess of $10,000/£6,000! This may seem excessive, but it's the only one there is ... so far.

Second Impression: ICS A15b,
Publisher: Hodder & Stoughton, London, 1909

Unmentioned by Woods, this is identical in appearance to the First Edition, with the following exceptions: 1) The title page contains the words 'SECOND EDITION' about 1¼in below the author's name but retains the MCMIX date, even though it seems unlikely that this impression could have been off the press in 1909. 2) The date of the speech on page 277 has been corrected to read 'May 4, 1903'. Unfortunately, they had it wrong again—the correct date was 3 May 1909. Nevertheless, this and the title page make identification of the second impression easy. Despite its title page proclamation, this volume is recognised by Ronald Cohen as a second printing, not a second edition, since it involves no resetting of plates.

The Second Impression is quite a bit less common than the First, although when it is offered, prices are more modest, averaging about half or less than First Editions in comparable condition.

First American Issue: ICS A15c
Publisher: Hodder & Stoughton, New York, 1910

Burgundy cloth without the gilt cover signature; the spine author's name is a plain 'WINSTON S. CHURCHILL'. Woods (page 44) states that this issue was published at $1.50 on 5 February 1910 by 'Doubleday, Doran'. The publisher's name is an error,

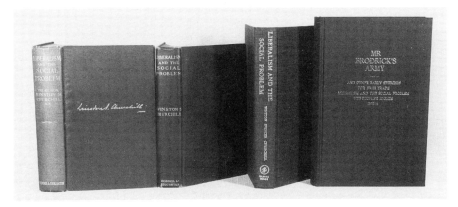

Left to right: the first English and American editions of *Liberalism and the Social Problem*, the only modern reprint (by Haskell House, 1973), and the combined volume from the *Collected Works* (1994).

since Doubleday and Doran were not partners until almost two decades later and the book is plainly published by Hodder & Stoughton's American office. Though Hodder & Stoughton were minor shareholders in the George Doran company (his imprint appeared on the third state of the American *My African Journey*), Doran had no involvement with *Liberalism and the Social Problem*, nor did he publish any other Churchill titles, although his connection with Hodder & Stoughton lasted 16 years. The American Issue apparently uses sheets from, or was pressed from, plates of the English First Edition, since page 277 contains the original date error (see above) and American issues carry that same advert for *My African Journey* (priced at 5s.) as the English.

APPRAISAL

Thanks to America's drier climate this volume tends to hold up better than its English counterparts; one rarely encounters spotted pages or boards. The most common fault is rub marks at the corners of spine extremities. Though much scarcer than the English First, the American Issue commands a lower price because it is not a true First Edition; presentable ('very good') copies can be found for under $600/£360. Fine copies are, however, a rarity, and command much more; no dust jacket data are available. This volume is prized by collectors who like to have the First Editions from each of Churchill's Motherlands.

Second American Issue: ICS A15d
Publisher: Haskell House Publishers Ltd., New York, 1973

Unnoted by Woods, this modern offprint from the Second English impression bears the same distinguishing characteristics of the latter but is about 1in taller and ½in wider, and differently bound: rust brown cloth blocked black on the spine, or grey cloth blocked gilt for a second impression or remainder binding published in 1985. In each case the title (on two lines) and author's name ('WINSTON SPENCER CHURCHILL') read horizontally down the spine; the house logo and publisher's imprint appear vertically at the spine bottom. There were no dust jackets.

While in print, Haskell House issues were budget alternatives to the early editions, but scarcity has forced their prices up to and over $100/£60 for fine copies. Of course this is still much less than any but the scruffiest 1909–1910 copies.

Combined Issue from the *Collected Works*

Collectors should be aware of this product of leftover sheets from Volume VII of the *Library of Imperial History's 1974–1975 Collected Works*, bound in burgundy cloth blocked gilt on cover and spine by Mark Weber and also offered by the Churchill Center New Book Service ($60/£38). This work is entitled (cover and title page): 'MR | BRODRICK'S | ARMY | AND OTHER EARLY SPEECHES | FOR FREE

TRADE | LIBERALISM AND THE SOCIAL PROBLEM | THE PEOPLE'S RIGHTS | INDIA'. The spine reads, somewhat misleadingly, 'FIVE EARLY SPEECHES' with the author's name 'WINSTON S. CHURCHILL'. Later bindings may read simply 'EARLY SPEECHES'. The text of all five works is entirely reset and the pages (516 plus introductory matter) are numbered consecutively.

THE PEOPLE'S RIGHTS

COHEN A31, WOODS A16

'If you were an English Liberal', Alistair Cooke continued in his 1988 peroration, '1904 through 1910 were very stirring years. Here on the one hand you had the crackling, sarcastic, brilliant Lloyd George; and on the other the witty, devastating Churchill, following each other like a great vaudeville team up and down the country. Churchill at one point even spent a week on the road begging–pleading– for the abolition of the House of Lords: "This second chamber as it is, one-sided, hereditary, unpurged, unrepresentative, irresponsible, absentee." It is still there, though shorn of all power.' The Labour victory of 1997 was said by some to assure that the Lords itself might be eliminated altogether.

The People's Rights is part of a trilogy representing that great political vaudeville act as it campaigned for the Liberal Party agenda in the general election of 1910, the other two volumes being Lloyd George's *The People's Insurance* and *The People's Budget*. I have often wondered if the gentlemen who then ran Hodder & Stoughton, their publishers, were, like Churchill, considered 'traitors to their class' and ostracised from all the proper clubs and watering holes. Hodder & Stoughton, which had earlier published a cheap edition of *Savrola*, dished out vast quantities of *The People's Rights/Budget/Insurance*, peddling paperback versions for a mere shilling (25c). In the event, the books did not do Liberalism's 'Terrible Twins' much good. Though Churchill and Lloyd George were each handily re-elected, their party lost its thumping majority, and was never able to dominate affairs as it had between 1904 and 1910.

FROM THE REVIEWS

'Less than a week after publication of *Liberalism and the Social Problem*, Prime Minister Asquith dissolved Parliament following rejection of the Liberal Government's budget by the Conservative-dominated House of Lords. Churchill, President of the Board of Trade, immediately hit the campaign trail with a series of stirring speeches, given during the period 3–11 December 1909. *The People's Rights* is a distillation of these nine days of speeches. Quite unlike his other writings, it follows a textbook or outline form: six chapters, broken down into short paragraphs, headlined in bold face by a statement or rhetorical question. Although this format is effective, it was probably used for speed: a letter to Churchill by the chairman of Hodder & Stoughton, written 16 December, indicates that the printers had already received the text and had suggested deletions of repetitious matter!

'The book opens with Churchill's famous criticism of the House of Lords and continues with a plea for a balanced budget. (His arguments are not unfamiliar.) The cases for Free Trade, a graduated income tax, luxury tax and surtaxes on unearned income, also familiar topics today, are also deftly argued. Churchill shows a paternalistic but genuine concern for improving the lot of the working classes, but remains clear that this must be accomplished under Parliamentary systems (excluding the House of Lords). Socialism is mentioned only once, and abruptly dismissed; trade unions and labour are not mentioned at all. Clearly he felt that a government-operated system of "labour exchanges", along with the Liberal programmes being advocated, would adequately improve the lot of the masses without more radical reforms.

'The result of the political campaign was a two-seat majority for the Liberals, whose budget was passed by the House (with the help of Labour and the Irish Nationalists) in April 1910. The Lords, who had been threatened with the promotion of enough Liberal peers to carry the budget, assented. The Parliament Act, reducing the power of the Lords, and the National Insurance Act, were passed a year later. Despite these victories the seeds of discontent had been sown. The long descent of the Liberal Party coupled with the rise of the Labour Party had begun. *The People's Rights* remains as evidence of Churchill's contribution in this great turning point in British history.'

John P. Nixon, Jr in Finest Hour #56, Summer 1987

First Edition, First State: ICS A16aa
Publisher: Hodder & Stoughton, London, 1910

Hardbound: Burgundy cloth blocked gilt with title and author's name on front cover and spine, and publisher's imprint on spine bottom. Softbound: Yellow-orange paper printed black and green with halftone photo of the author on the cover and the same imprints on the spine plus the price ('1/- NET'). Inside front wrapper bears a boxed advert for other political works by Dr T. J. Macnamara and Churchill. Both versions 16mo, 160 pages numbered (i)–(viii) and 1–152. Pages 149–152 contain an index.

QUANTITIES AND IMPRESSIONS
Woods states that 5,000 copies were published 'on the week ending 14 January 1910, price 1s' (presumably the price refers to the wrapper copy). There were no subsequent impressions although there was a second state (see below) which may increase the actual quantity produced.

DUST JACKETS AND VARIANTS
No dust jackets to the hardbound version have been observed. Ronald Cohen conjectures that its jacket was simply unprinted glassine.

Several variants of the wrapper copy are known in which Hodder & Stoughton's imprint at the bottom of the front wrap is reduced to small type and the space gained occupied by the imprints of various newspapers, including but not necessarily limited to *The Daily News* (London and Manchester), *The Yorkshire Observer* and *The Liverpool Post and Mercury*.

The Daily News and *The Yorkshire Observer*, at least, carry their names in their distinct title script. The latter is called *The Yorkshire Observer* EDITION, but this word is absent on *The Daily News* version.

COMMENTS

Woods's description of the hardbound copy ('cherry-red cloth, flecked with pink') is erroneous; he must have inspected a worn or faded copy, which can appear this way. Woods is also incorrect in his description of page [viii], which actually acknowledges *The Liverpool Post and Mercury* and *The Bolton Journal and Guardian*, as well as *The Manchester Guardian*, for granting permission to print extracts. The Bolton paper may also be one of those to place its imprint on certain wrapper copies (see variants above).

The two Lloyd George companion works, *The People's Budget* and *The People's Insurance*, were bound of the same material; softbound versions of *The People's*

Left: *The People's Rights* was published in hardback, but copies are extremely rare; the softbound is far more often encountered, which is to say hardly at all anymore. A pair in the condition of these two is a rare prize indeed.

Budget were printed red and black on the same orange-yellow paper. I have not examined a softbound *People's Insurance.*

APPRAISAL

The People's Rights is the third rarest Churchill book after *Mr. Brodrick's Army* and *For Free Trade.* As a result, prices are formidable. Brilliant hardbound copies (which are not unknown) have sold recently for $7,500/£4700, while near-fine wrapper copies have topped $5,000/£3,000. A defective copy lacking the back wrap with a well-worn spine is presently on offer at $2,200/£1,400: the cheapest I've seen in years. I don't know of a copy inscribed by Churchill; I would like to know if one exists.

The extreme scarcity is owed to the fact that this was in essence a political pamphlet, dealing with issues that were mostly soon passé, and most copies were discarded. Indeed most lists of Churchill's works in his later books omit any mention of *The People's Rights.*

Of all Churchill first editions, this is the one most in need of deacidification. Both hardbound and wrapper copies were printed on cheap, pulpy, acidic paper which is fast deteriorating, and the pages are somewhat browned even on the best of copies. The worst are becoming brittle, and starting to crack and dissolve, especially around the edges. Each copy of this rare work deserves top priority preservation efforts.

First Edition, Second State: ICS A16ab
Publisher: Hodder & Stoughton, London, 1910

In this second state (mentioned by Woods, page 45), the index on pages 149–152 is replaced with a second Appendix ('Labour Exchanges and Unemployment Insurance'). This state has never been observed hardbound. Among wrapper copies there is little to choose between the two, and no difference in value, for all 1910 copies are so rare that collectors lacking *The People's Rights* rarely hesitate when they find, and can afford, a copy. Those who can afford two own one of each: a better investment than mutual funds.

Second Edition: ICS A16ba
Publisher: Jonathan Cape, London, 1970

The answer to the needs of most collectors who are shocked by the prices of First Editions, this handsomely produced hardbound edition includes both appendices and the original index, plus a new and good introduction by Cameron Hazlehurst, a research fellow at Nuffield College, Oxford. Entirely reset, it contains 192 pages bound in brown cloth blocked gilt on spine, and a colourful dust jacket printed sepia, red and orange, based on the original wrappers. It is now fairly uncommon, and fine jacketed copies have been known to top $100/£60.

Second Edition, American Issue: ICS A16bb

Publisher: Taplinger Publishing Co. Inc., New York, 1971

The only edition ever to appear outside England, this is identical to the Cape Edition save for the Taplinger imprints on jacket, spine and title page. It was published on 3 March 1971 at $6.50, according to a reviewer copy slip in my own copy. It sells for the same price as the Cape Edition.

Combined Issue from the *Collected Works*

Collectors should be aware of this product of leftover sheets from Volume VII of the *Library of Imperial History's 1974–1975 Collected Works*, bound in burgundy cloth blocked gilt on cover and spine by Mark Weber and also offered by the Churchill Center New Book Service ($60/£38). This work is entitled (cover and title page): 'MR | BRODRICK'S | ARMY | AND OTHER EARLY SPEECHES | FOR FREE TRADE | LIBERALISM AND THE SOCIAL PROBLEM | THE PEOPLE'S RIGHTS | INDIA'. The spine reads, somewhat misleadingly, FIVE EARLY SPEECHES with the author's name 'WINSTON S. CHURCHILL'. Later bindings may read simply 'EARLY SPEECHES'. The text of all five works is entirely reset and the pages (516 plus introductory matter) are numbered consecutively.

Handsome reprints of *The People's Rights* were offered by Taplinger (New York, 1971, left) and Jonathan Cape (London, 1970, right). In the centre is Taplinger's reviewer's slip for their copy.

THE WORLD CRISIS

COHEN A69, WOODS A31

Many connoisseurs of Churchill and the Churchill style, who were introduced to him through *The Second World War* or *A History of the English-Speaking Peoples,* soon found that an even more readable multi-volume work existed. For a long, dry spell in the 1970s and 1980s, a complete edition of *The World Crisis* was unobtainable, except as an expensive first edition (the post-war Scribners edition had a small press run and has always been harder to find than the first). Efforts by the International Churchill Society produced a modern reprint by the Easton Press (still available at this writing). More recently, The Churchill Center has offered an inexpensive alternate by combining two-volume 1939 Odhams Editions with bindings from *Collected Works* sheets of the two volumes Odhams did not publish: *The Aftermath* and *The Eastern Front.* Thus the complete original text, and Churchill's 1931 additions incorporated by Odhams, are again available at relatively modest prices.

Whenever I am asked to recommend a 'big work' by Churchill, I always name *The World Crisis.* Like all of his war books where he is involved, it is highly biased and personal, tending to magnify and defend his own role in affairs. But one of his endearing characteristics was his unabashed honesty. Of *The World Crisis* he declared that it was 'not history, but a contribution to history'; later, of *The Second World War,* he would say similarly, 'This is not history; this is my case.'

I cannot think of another twentieth-century statesman who not only spent most of the two World Wars in high office but was able to write of them in such superb English, with such eloquence and verve. Even those who do not usually read war books will be entranced by Churchill's account of the awful, unfolding scene, written as if the reader were a colleague, observing over his burly shoulder the march of events.

It is well briefly to explain the arrangement of the original volumes. Though commonly described as a six-volume work, *The World Crisis* is more accurately five volumes in six books: the middle two volumes, subtitled 1916–1918, were issued in two parts; they were sold as a pair, slipcased together in the USA and Canada. I usually refer to them as 'Volumes 3a and 3b'. Thus the last two volumes, *The Aftermath* and *The Eastern Front,* are correctly Volumes IV and V respectively, and the whole set is '5-in-6', as usually described by knowledgeable booksellers.

This causes some confusion, since English Editions from Volume II on carried sequential stars on their spines. The two 1916–1918 books have three and four stars, *The Aftermath* five and *The Eastern Front* six. Scribners added to the muddle by labelling the 1916–1918 volumes 'Volume I' and 'Volume II'. In later impressions and editions, such as the 1963–1964 Scribners, the books were simply redesignated Volumes I through VI. Nevertheless, the most accurate description is '5-in-6'.

Volume I goes back to 1911 and the great power rivalries to trace the background and dramatic opening of the war, more or less as *The Gathering Storm* traces events leading up to the Second World War. Volume II, 1915, is the most personal, largely devoted to Churchill's failed efforts to break the deadlock in Europe by forcing the Dardanelles, knocking Turkey out of the war and succouring the Russians. Volume III, 1916–1918 (both parts) covers the carnage on the Western Front, the German victory over Russia and almost-victory over the Allies in 1918, and the final, exhausted end of the war. *The Aftermath* chronicles events in which Churchill was involved during the ten years after victory, including the Irish Treaty; *The Eastern Front's* subject is self-explanatory, dealing with the titanic battles between Russia and the German-Austrian armies.

FROM THE REVIEWS

'Carnage on an unprecedented scale was the salient feature of the *First World War*, and the writing on that carnage is largely responsible for the modern disgust not only with war but also with politics in general ... Churchill knew everything about the war's horror that the other writers knew, but he rejected their conclusions: for him, the war did not mean the death of political life as men had previously known it. In examining the political and military failures that were responsible for the slaughter and in suggesting how prudence might have averted disaster, Churchill reasserted the dignity of the political life, which the war had made men regard as ignominious, unnatural, and mad ...

'Churchill is an exemplar of the political life that the Great War is alleged to have repudiated forever. He renders the war as nightmare but also makes clear that the nightmare did not take place in a void. While he recognises the truth of the soldier's story–as a battalion commander in France, he was beloved by his men and renowned for his fearlessness–he knows it is a fragmentary truth. The soldier's story is the heart of his history, but his own greater understanding informs it. *The World Crisis* celebrates the Allied triumph–especially the British part in it–but mourns the European tragedy. The history is decidedly partisan, leaving no doubt that the right side won, yet it is withering in its appraisal of both sides' folly. The spectacle takes place under a pitiless emotional overcast that is relieved by only the rarest glimmers of magnificence. The virtues that Churchill honours as pre-eminent are, awfully, those of the men who were smashed in the general wreckage. It is above all to demonstrate how the chronic infirmity of political and military command made them suffer as they did that Churchill writes this history ... '

Algis Valiunas in *The American Spectator,* April 1991

First Edition: ICS A31aa

Publisher: Charles Scribners Sons, New York, 1923–31

Five volumes in six parts

Dark brown cloth blocked gilt, 8vo. Vol. I published April 1923 at $6.50, 604 pages numbered (i)–(xiv) and (1)–(590). Vol. II published October 1923 at $6.50, 592 pages numbered (i)–(xiv) and (1)–578. Vol. III (in two parts) published 1927 in a slipcase at $10; Part 1 ('Vol. I') 320 pages numbered (i)–(xviii) and 1-302; Part 2 ('Vol. II') 338 pages numbered (i)–(x) and 1–326 (two pages misnumbered ix–x). Vol. IV *The Aftermath* published 1929 at $5, 520 pages numbered (i)–(xvi) and 1–502 (+2). Vol. V *The Unknown War* published 1931 at $5, 414 pages numbered (i)–(xviii) and (1)-396. All volumes illustrated with maps and charts (and a photo in Vol. I).

Later impressions have binding variations which I shall leave to the bibliographers; first editions are bound as follows:

Vol. I: 'THE WORLD CRISIS' and 'WINSTON S. CHURCHILL' on top board (inside blind box rule) and spine; 'SCRIBNERS' on lower spine. (A single star appeared on the spine starting on some but not all impressions.)

Vol. II: 'THE WORLD CRISIS' and 'WINSTON S. CHURCHILL' on top board (inside blind box rule) and spine; spine usually contains two stars, the subtitle '1915' and the 'SCRIBNERS' imprint.

Vol. III: Plain top boards; spines are lettered with the main title, author's name and Scribners imprint and subtitles '1916–1918 and VOL. I or VOL II'.

Vol. IV: 'THE AFTERMATH' and 'WINSTON S. CHURCHILL' on top board (inside blind box rule) and spine; spine is subtitled '1918–1928.'

Vol. V: 'THE UNKNOWN WAR' and 'WINSTON S. CHURCHILL' on top board (inside blind box rule); spine adds 'THE EASTERN FRONT' and the 'SCRIBNERS' imprint.

A remarkable set of American first editions, all in their dust jackets; we encounter a set like this once every ten years.

IMPRESSIONS

At least this many impressions are known: Vol. I, four (1923, 1924, 1928, 1930). Vol. II, two (1923, 1929). Vol. III, one for each part (1927). *The Aftermath*, three (March, April, September 1929). *The Unknown War*, three (1931 twice, 1932).

Identifying first impressions: Volumes I and II carry the date 1923 on title-page and no reprint information on the title-page verso. Volume III, both parts, carry the date 1927 on title-page. *The Aftermath* carries the date 1929 on title-page and no reprint information on title-page verso. *The Unknown War* carries the date 1931 on title-page and the block letter 'A' on title-page verso.

DUST JACKETS

Volumes I and II: Off-white or cream paper printed black, flaps blank except for $6.50 price, book descriptions on front faces. Volume I back face details 'Important New Scribners Publications', Volume II back face contains an advert for Volume I.

Volume III: These two books were originally slipcased, and their jackets are thus plain, except for the legend '$10.00 | Two Volumes' on the upper front flaps and jacket spine lettering identical to the books themselves, printed black on off-white or cream paper. The very rare slipcase carries two tipped-on labels: a title/author's name/publisher label on the back and a boxed description of the books, printed dark brown on cream laid paper, on one side.

The Aftermath: Grey paper printed navy blue, flaps blank except for $5 price, book description on front face with title/author's name/publisher in an odd, bold

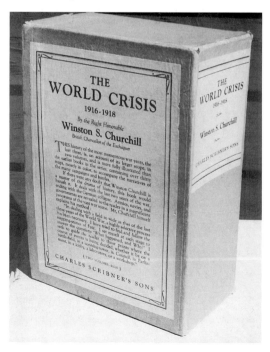

Rarity among rarities. Scribners, like Thornton Butterworth, issued the 1916-1918 volumes in two parts, but Scribners also boxed theirs; this is the only box I have ever seen. The books inside are in as-new condition, the jackets perfect.

face not used elsewhere; spine is lettered to match the book's spine.

The Unknown War. Grey-threaded paper printed deep red with titles, author's name and publisher spine imprint in a unique, bold typeface. Description of the book on front face, advert with review blurbs for the Abridged Edition (Woods A31b) on back face. Front flap contains '*The Unknown War* ... $5.00' above a blurb for *A Roving Commission*; backflap contains a blurb promoting *The Aftermath*.

Although all *World Crisis* jackets are extremely rare, collectors should pay close attention to the descriptions of them, since later impression jackets may be different; first impressions with later impression jackets are 'married pieces', and worth no premium.

COMMENTS
All volumes are illustrated with maps and charts which can be checked by consulting the list of illustrations in the front of each. Some maps are fold-outs. Points to look for: Vol. II 1915: six-entry errata slip tipped between pages (x) and (xi). *The Unknown War.* a large colour fold-out map, usually tipped ahead of the index starting at page 389. This is also the only volume with a frontispiece (Emperor Franz Joseph), and contains seven other photographs.

APPRAISAL
It is not widely known that Volume I at least appeared in America before its British counterpart, making this the true first edition. But Scribners volumes do not wear as well as the British, particularly Volume I, which was bound in an inferior cloth that in most cases quickly discoloured and faded, while the gilt turned black. Later volumes, and later impressions of Volume I, used a much better cloth and brighter gilt, and these are often found in fine condition. Jacketed sets are extremely rare and command prices up to and over $5,000/£3,000. If they include the even rarer Volume III slipcase, add another 10 per cent. Typical unjacketed sets with Volume I 'faded and discoloured as usual' were selling for plus or minus $600/£360 in 1997; a perfect Volume I would double their value, but such examples are hardly ever seen. This is a highly desirable, true first edition and a prime investment.

The American Edition had fewer reprints than the English, so non-first editions are less often encountered. They sell for half or less the price of firsts. However, reprints of Vol. I are prized because of the deplorable state of most first editions of that volume.

First English Edition: ICS A31ab
Publisher: Thornton Butterworth Ltd., London, 1923–31

Five volumes in six parts
Navy cloth blocked blind on cover, blind and gilt on spine, 8vo. Vol. I published 10 April 1923 at 30s., 544 pages numbered (2), (i)–(vi) and (1)–536. Vol. II published

Rare and beautiful, the first English (left) and American editions of *The World Crisis* in their original dust jackets.

30 October 1923 at 30s., 560 pages numbered (1)–557 (+3). Vol. III (in two parts) published 3 March 1927 at 42s.; Part 1, 292 pages numbered (1)–(292); Part 2, 308 pages numbered (i)–(x) and 293–589 (+1). Vol. IV *The Aftermath* published 7 March 1929 at 30s., 476 pages numbered (1)–474 (+2). Vol. V *The Eastern Front* published 2 November 1931 at 30s., 368 pages numbered (1)–368. All volumes variously illustrated with maps and charts.

Later impressions have binding variations, including different thicknesses; first editions are bound as follows (all with blind publisher's logo on top board and two thick blind rules on top and bottom of top board and spine):

Vol. I: 'THE WORLD CRISIS 1911–1914' and 'WINSTON S. CHURCHILL' on top board (inside blind box rule). The same titling plus 'THORNTON BUTTERWORTH' imprint gilt on spine. No star on spine.

Vol. II: 'THE WORLD CRISIS 1915' and 'WINSTON S. CHURCHILL' on top board (inside blind box rule). The same titling plus 'THORNTON BUTTERWORTH' and two stars gilt on spine.

Vol. III: 'THE WORLD CRISIS 1916–1918 Part. I. (or Part. II.)' and 'WINSTON S. CHURCHILL' on top board (inside blind box rule). The same titling plus 'THORNTON BUTTERWORTH' and three stars (Part I) or four stars (Part II) gilt on spine.

Vol. IV: 'THE WORLD CRISIS', 'THE AFTERMATH' and 'WINSTON S. CHURCHILL' on top board (inside blind box rule). The same titling plus 'THORNTON BUTTERWORTH' and five stars gilt on spine.

Vol. V: 'THE WORLD CRISIS', 'THE EASTERN FRONT' and 'WINSTON S. CHURCHILL' on top board (inside blind box rule). The same titling plus 'THORNTON BUTTERWORTH' and six stars gilt on spine.

EDITIONS, IMPRESSIONS AND QUANTITIES

At least this many impressions are known: Vol. I, eight (first edition April 1923; second edition April 1923, reprinted same month; third edition November 1923, reprinted July 1924, May 1927, December 1927, February 1930). Vol. II, six (October 1923 thrice, December 1923, May 1927, February 1929). Vol III, five (January 1927, March 1927 twice, April 1927, September 1930). *The Aftermath*, three (two in March 1929; the third in June 1929). *The Eastern Front,* two, both November 1931.

Identifying first impressions: All first impressions carry the legend 'First Published' followed by a single date on the verso of the title-page. All later impressions carry notes of subsequent printings in this place.

Quantities (according to Woods). Vol. I: 7,380 first editions, 16,462 total. Vol. II: 7,500 first editions, 14,260 total. Vol. III: 7,523 first editions, 14,598 total. *The Aftermath:* 7500 first editions, 11,000 total. *The Eastern Front:* 5,150 first editions, 7,994 total.

DUST JACKETS

These volumes are sometimes found with non-first edition dust jackets, so carefully check jackets to be sure they are not 'married'. The descriptions of first edition jackets follow:

Vol. I: Printed navy on grey paper. Title, author's name, publisher, price and 'MAPS AND CHARTS' on front face and spine; quote from page 188 also on front face. Contents blurb on front flap. No adverts for subsequent volumes or review blurbs for Vol. I on flaps or back face.

Vol. II: Printed dark brown on tan paper. Front face and spine similar to above. Contents blurb on front flap, Vol. I press notices on back flap, advert for Vol. I on back face.

Vol. III: Printed black on grey paper. Front face and spine similar to above, but face blurb is not by Churchill. Contents blurb on front flap, six titles of 'General Literature' on back flap, adverts for Vols. I and II on back face. Aside from the distinguishing legends 'Part I.' and 'Part II.' (no period after 'Part') on spines, jackets for the two parts are identical.

The Aftermath: Printed black on greenish-grey paper. Front face, front flap and spine arranged similarly to Vol. III. Back flap contains blurb for Beaverbrook's two volumes, *Politicians and the War.* Adverts for Vols. I, II and III on back face.

The Eastern Front: Printed black and red on green paper (which has often faded to a brown colour). Front face, front flap and spine similar to above. Back flap contains press notices for *My Early Life.* Advert for the abridged and revised *World Crisis* on back face. The jacket was unaltered for the second impression.

VARIANTS

Later impressions of Volume I sometimes occur with a single star on the spine, uniform with numeration stars on other volumes. Commencing with the third impression, Volume III (both parts) is distinctly thinner from the use of thinner paper. The single spine star designating Volume I is always present after the first three printings, that is, commencing with the 'Third Edition, first impression'.

COMMENTS

Woods's listing of two impressions of *The Eastern Front* has been challenged, but Woods is right: several copies of the second impression have been spotted; their title-page verso notes publication in November 1931, the same month as the first.

All volumes are illustrated with maps and charts which can be checked by consulting the list of illustrations in the front of each. Some maps are fold-outs. Points to look for: Vol. I, 1911–1914: a 13-item errata slip can occur in several places, including p. (vi), p.1 and elsewhere. Vol. III, 1916–1918 Part 2: A three-item errata slip is tipped onto the half title. *The Aftermath:* A two-item errata slip is tipped onto page 9 (Woods says between 10 and 11, which may be a variation). *The Eastern Front:* a large colour fold-out map is tipped onto the last free endpaper, following page 368. This is also the only volume with a frontispiece (Emperor Franz Joseph), and contains seven other photographs.

APPRAISAL

Although not the true first edition, the English is more aesthetically desirable, being bound in a more durable and uniform material and equipped with shoulder notes on each page which summarise the subject of that page. Probably for that reason, it is more popular among collectors who wish to own only one edition. Jacketed sets are extremely rare and command prices in excess of $5,000/£3,000. The main problem with these volumes is spotting of pages and page edges from their damp life in England, and 'bubbling' of the cloth, especially on *The Aftermath.* Fine unjacketed sets can bring up to $1,500/£900, although they are often available at lower prices; very good sets with routine wear sell for half or a third as much, while later impressions rarely cost more than $500/£300 for a set. For this kind of money you might prefer one of the later sets, such as the full-leather Easton Press edition.

Times Book Club Issue: ICS A31abb
Publisher: Thornton Butterworth Ltd., London, 1923–27

All volumes were sold cheaply by the Times Book Club, which usually used first printings, except for *The Eastern Front,* which is a second. The TBC binding has larger stars and cruder lettering; copies usually contain sticker labels on rear pastedowns. This is the second instance of a Times Book Club issue of one of Churchill's works (see *Lord Randolph Churchill*). Collectors instinctively avoid anything non-standard looking, even if they don't know what it is; in this case they are certainly right, for this is a book club issue despite first printing sheets. A full set is rare but not worth a great deal.

Canadian Issue: ICS A31ac

Publisher: Macmillan Company of Canada, Ltd., Toronto, 1923–31

Five volumes in six parts

Published in Canada from the American plates, this issue is identical in all respects to the latter, save for Macmillan imprints on title-pages (cancels), spines and dust jackets. The Canadian Macmillan logo also appears on dust jacket spines. Curiously, the jacket flaps I have examined contain no prices. These issues are quite rare; I have never found a complete set for sale and most collectors who are building sets are doing so one volume at a time. Ostensibly equal in value to the American Edition, the Canadian Issue is probably somewhat less important, and should not quite reach price levels of the Scribners set.

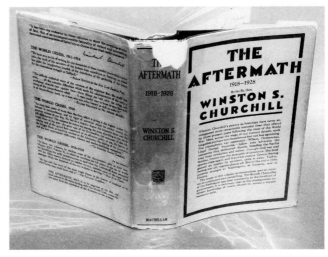

Canadian jacketed *World Crisis* volumes are even scarcer than the British or American; offprinted from the Scribners jackets, they contain the Macmillan logo and name on their spines.

Australian Issue: ICS A31ad

Publisher: Australasian Publishing Co. Ltd., Sydney and Melbourne, 1923

Two volumes: 1911–1914 and 1915

Published from the English plates, this issue is identical to the latter, save for Australasian Publishing Co. imprints on title-pages and dust jacket spines. There is no publisher's imprint, however, on the spines of the books. After Volume II, a separate Australian issue was not produced, and the Australian market received the standard English issues of the other volumes. Although these two volumes are interesting anomalies, there is very little interest in them among collectors, and fine copies can usually be had for up to $150/£90. Jacketed copies sell for about 50 per cent more.

The Australian edition differs only in the first two volumes, which are blank on the lower spine and imprinted 'Australasian Publishing Co.' on jacket spines. From Volume III on, Australians were offered standard English editions.

Second American Edition: ICS A31ae
Publisher: Charles Scribners Sons, New York, 1963–64

Six Volumes

Published one volume at a time over two years, this was an offprint of the original Scribners volumes with smaller page margins resulting in smaller books: 5½ x 8½in compared to the original 6¼ x 9in. The volumes are numbered consecutively, so 1916–1918 is no longer labelled 'Volume I' and 'Volume II' but Volume III and IV. Thus *The Aftermath* becomes Volume V and *The Unknown War* Volume VI. All are bound in medium blue cloth blocked gilt on top board and spines. Dust jackets, printed red, black and light blue on white paper, display some of the internal illustrations, and each contains the subtitle: 'THE FIRST WORLD WAR AS CHURCHILL SAW IT'. Interestingly, the title-page verso indicates that Churchill renewed his copyright in 1951.

Identifying first impressions: The codes mentioned in the following notes are Scribners, taken from versos of the title-page versos; they help to identify first impressions, although I strongly suspect that Volumes III–VI were never reprinted. The complete work went out of print in the early 1970s; I believe that only Volume I, and possibly Volume II, saw reprints to maintain full sets in stock.

Volume I: Published at $7.50 in January 1963, coded A1.63 [MH]; second impression August 1965 coded B8.65 [MH]; third impression February 1970, coded C.2709 [MH].

Volume II: Published at $7.50 in August 1963 coded A8.63 [MH].

Volume III: Published January 1964 at $7.50 simultaneously with Volume IV, coded A-1.675 [MH].

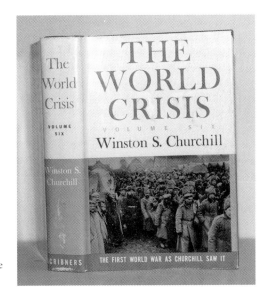

The Second American Edition was the first fully illustrated six-volume *World Crisis*; volumes were issued during a 24-month period in 1963–1964, and complete sets are scarce today.

Volume IV: Published January 1964 at $7.50 simultaneously with Volume III. Coded 'A–1.64[MH]'.

Volume V: Published July 1964 at $7.50 simultaneously with Volume VI. Coded 'A–7.64[MH]'.

Volume VI: Published July 1964 at $7.50 simultaneously with Volume V. Coded 'A–7.64[MH]'.

APPRAISAL

Except for *The Great War*, which was a textual abridgement, this was the first illustrated edition of *The World Crisis*. That is the chief factor it has to recommend it. The books themselves, offprinted from the Scribners originals, are shorter, squatter, and bound in a cheap blue material which doesn't seem to hold up well. Even jacketed copies often have a soiled, rumpled appearance, and the dust jackets are usually faded or grotty. I have built up my fine jacketed set volume by volume over ten years of constant upgrading. Until the Easton Press Edition (below), this set was hotly sought after, but its value has declined somewhat. The typical worn set should sell for less than $150/£90; in rare fine condition with decent dust jackets, expect to pay up to three times as much.

Easton Press Limited Edition: ICS A31af
Publisher: The Easton Press, Norwalk, CT, 1991

My finest hour, bibliographically speaking, was when the Easton Press requested my help in designing a new limited edition of the original *World Crisis* for their the ultimate set, the *World Crisis* I would take with me if confined to a desert island. Like a kid turned loose in a sweet shop I specified the best text (Thornton Butterworth's First English Edition, with its novel shoulder notes and beautiful folding maps), coupled with the best illustrations (Scribners, from their post-war edition above). Easton Press added an elaborate binding in leather and gilt with raised spine bands, gilt page edges and silk page markers, and priced the new set so low that the value of *World Crisis* first editions was cut by half–the fine first edition sets I was selling for $1,500 were soon down to $750, although they have since recovered. From the bookseller standpoint I had committed a kind of hara-kiri ... but many more people now own *The World Crisis*.

With the exception of the tacky bookplates, which are thankfully laid-in (and please throw them away), the Easton Press produced a good aesthetic achievement for the money. While not as perfect as classic morocco leather bindings, the pigskin boards are strong and durable and the quality of the offprinting is high. Easton's full colour reprints of the original folding maps–including the fine folding map at the end of *The Eastern Front*–are, if anything, better than the originals.

There's always a nit, however, and it is my fault. When recommending the use of Scribners post-war illustrations, I forgot that the original *Eastern Front* itself contained eight illustrations, including the frontispiece. Easton, with wads of new Scribners photos to insert, naturally left them out. But I failed to remind them also to omit the original illustration list from page 13–so there it sits, directing the reader to plates that don't exist!

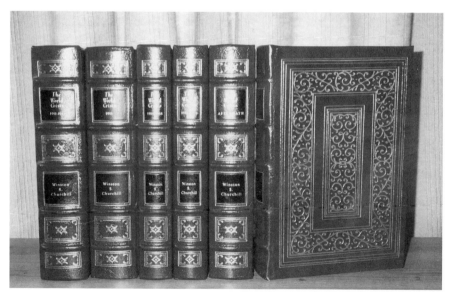

The Easton Press edition, first published 1991, was still in print as this book went to press. The pigskin binding is a bit stiff, but the quality of the contents (offprinted using the first English edition text and photos from the second American edition) cannot be faulted. *(Photo: Douglas Hall)*

Easton's price was only $260/£165–hundreds less than any complete set then available. The first printing quickly sold out, but in 1996 they were reissued at the same price, using an improved, more supple pigskin binding. The set is still available at this writing.

First Abridged and Revised Edition: ICS A31ba
Publisher: Thornton Butterworth Ltd., London, 1931

Medium green cloth (bright green on third impression). The top board bears the title ('THE WORLD CRISIS 1911–1918 Abridged & Revised Edition') author's name and publisher logo debossed blind. Two thick blind rules at top and bottom of top board and spine. The spine bears the title, author's name, publisher's name imprint, all gilt. 8vo, 832 pages numbered (1)–831 (+1). The half-title verso contains a boxed advert for 12 of Churchill's other works. Illustrated with maps and plans. Published 26 February 1931 at 21s.

QUANTITIES AND IMPRESSIONS
Woods lists 5,000 first impressions and 3,000 second impressions (January 1932) but fails to mention a third impression in bright green cloth (October 1937).

DUST JACKETS AND VARIANTS
A striking jacket is printed black and red-orange on thin, bright green paper (which

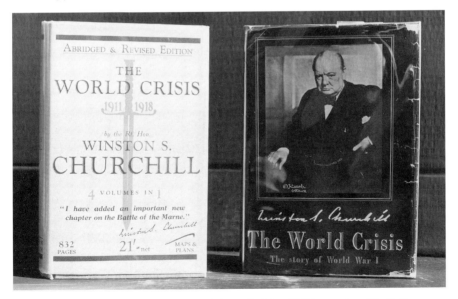

Abridged and revised editions. Left: the first English (1931); right: a 1949 impression of the Scribners American edition with Karsh's famous portrait on its dust jacket.

is often faded); a variant jacket is printed on thicker, lined cream stock. Both these jackets carry a contents blurb on the front flap, an advert for *The Aftermath* on the back flap, and an advert for *My Early Life* on the back face. A second state jacket adds *The Eastern Front* to the back flap.

COMMENTS

Often passed up by collectors as a mere abridgement, this volume is essential to the complete library because Churchill added new material and considerable revisions. Aside from his new foreword there is a completely new chapter on the Battle of the Marne. Also, writes Churchill, 'I have had to record a somewhat different account of Lord Fisher's resignation from that which appeared in the original edition. Mr. Asquith's disclosures in his "Memoirs" and Lord Fisher's own biographers have cast a less charitable light upon the conduct of the old Admiral than that in which I had viewed it.' (Asquith's memoirs disclosed that Fisher had written an incredible letter offering to remain at the Admiralty if vested virtually with dictatorial powers, refusing to serve either under Churchill or his successor, Arthur Balfour). As such, a copy of this work belongs on the shelf of every serious Churchill library.

APPRAISAL

Dust jackets are extremely rare; when found, $500/£300 would not be too much to pay for a jacketed copy. Routine lightly worn unjacketed copies sell for much less, $75/£45 being typical. The later impressions seem much less common than the first edition.

American Abridged and Revised Edition: ICS A31bb

Publisher: Charles Scribners Sons, New York, 1931

Navy cloth, boards blank. Spine blocked gilt with abbreviated title (THE WORLD CRISIS) author's name and SCRIBNERS imprint. 8vo, 880 pages numbered (i)–(xii) and (1)–866 (+2). The half-title verso lists six of Churchill's previous works. Illustrated with maps and plans. Published February 1931 at $5.

IMPRESSIONS

There are at least three impressions: 1931, 1942 and 1949. The first impression is easily distinguished by its 1931 date on the title-page and block letter 'A' on title-page verso. Colours also aid identification: the 1931 is navy, the 1942 medium blue, the 1949 vertically scored red cloth.

DUST JACKETS

The original dust jacket is printed black on yellow paper with the title, author's name, description and '$5' appearing next to a photo of Churchill walking. The front flap contains a contents blurb, the back flap reviewer comments on *The Aftermath,* and the back face reviewer comments on *My Early Life.* Post-war jackets bear a Karsh photo of Churchill and facsimile signature on the front faces.

COMMENTS

I had understood that according to *The New York Times,* this work was published on 7 February 1931, 19 days before the English Edition, making this the true first edition. The new Cohen Bibliography, however, indicates that the London edition takes priority.

APPRAISAL

Unjacketed copies are worth about the same as the English Editions, say $75/£45 for the typical somewhat worn example and double that for exceptionally fine examples. A jacketed copy is another proposition. I know of only two or three of these in existence, and the last one on the market carried a price of $500/£300. I know because I bought it, and I do not feel that I paid too much.

Canadian Abridged and Revised Issue: ICS A31bc

Publisher: Macmillan Company of Canada Ltd., Toronto, 1931

Produced with American plates and identical to the American Edition with the exception of Macmillan imprints on spine, jacket and title-page. I have never seen the jacket but presume it is similar to the American. The same notes as to rarity and value apply here as to the American Edition.

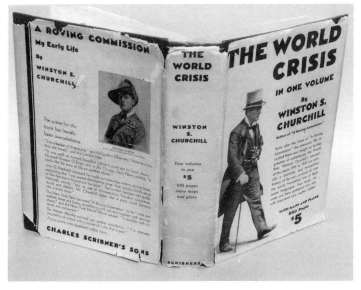

Jacketed copies of first Abridged editions are all rare; Scribners', and the similar Canadian Macmillan, are the rarest. This fine jacketed copy recently changed hands for the price of a complete American first edition.

Second Abridged and Revised Edition: ICS A31bd
Publisher: Macmillan & Co. Ltd., London, 1941

When Thornton Butterworth went out of business in 1940, most of their Churchill works were subsequently published by Macmillan, including the Abridged and Revised *World Crisis*. (Cohen's Bibliography contains considerable detail on this period.) There are three impressions, all on thin wartime paper: 1941 (dark blue cloth), 1942 (very dark blue-black cloth) and 1943 (rougher, lighter blue cloth). All these are easily identified by dates on their title-page versos. All impressions sold for 18s. Today the reprints are common: a fine Macmillan First in like dust jacket might approach $100/£60, but certainly no more; lesser copies and later impressions sell for as little as $10/£5.

Identifying first impressions: The title-page verso of the Macmillan First lists all three 1930s impressions followed by the line, 'Transferred to Macmillan & Co. Ltd.– 1941'. Later impressions give the first publication date, the transfer dates and the reprint date ('1942' or '1942, 1943'). Although all dust jackets are printed red and black on cream paper, first impression jackets are different: their paper is heavier, scored material and the back face advertises (in order) *My Early Life, Great Contemporaries, Step by Step* and *The World Crisis*. Later impression jackets are printed on lighter, cheaper paper and their back faces advertise (in order) *My Early Life, Thoughts and Adventures, Great Contemporaries* and *Step by Step*. Later jackets add *The World Crisis, The Aftermath* and *The Unknown War* to back face adverts.

This is a budget alternative to 1930s editions and is just as readable, since all the original fold-out maps are preserved.

First Paperback Abridged Edition: ICS A31be
Publisher: Landsborough Publications Ltd., London, 1960

This thick 'Four Square Book' reprints the Abridged Edition for the first time as a paperback. The cover portrays Churchill and a war memorial, the back cover the Cenotaph in London. 958 pages, illustrated with maps, published at 7s. 6d. A second and third impression were issued, both in 1964.

Mentor Paperback Abridged Edition: ICS A31bf
Publisher: New English Library, London, 1968

Two volumes
Reprinted from plates of the Four Square paperback (pagination identical throughout) but divided into two volumes of 496 and 460 pages. The covers portray a white sculpted head of Churchill against a blue (Vol. 1) or green (Vol. 2) background. Published at 10s. 6d. in a blue and green slipcase.

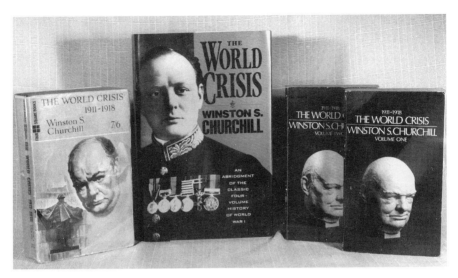

Abridged *World Crisis* later issues. Left to right: the first paperback (1960); Scribners new edition (1992); and the Mentor two-volume paperback (1968).

Second American Abridged and Revised Edition: Cohen A69.16, ICS A31bg

Publisher: Charles Scribners Sons, New York, 1992

Subtitled *An Abridgement of the Classic Four–Volume History of World War I*. Greatly anticipated (because the Abridged Edition had been out of print in hardback for over 40 years), this recent production proved to be a disappointment. Cheaply bound in quarter cloth and cardboard, it was offprinted from an earlier Scribners Edition, but the elaborate and beautiful fold-out maps were either eliminated or reduced to crudely drawn replicas. Also, the jacket photo of Churchill as First Lord of the Admiralty has been poorly coloured and all the medal colours are wrong. This book provides the lyrics, but not the music. Only those demanding completeness need acquire it; others will be happier with Macmillan editions. Published at $35; simultaneously published by Maxwell Macmillan of Canada at C$45. 880 pages.

Sandhurst Edition: Woods A31c

Publisher: Thornton Butterworth Ltd., London, 1933

A limited edition of 1,354 copies compiled by Churchill from the Abridged and Revised Edition, illustrated with maps. This is a textbook which, as it states, was 'Privately printed for the Royal Military College, Sandhurst'. 16mo, 512 pages numbered (1)–511 (+1). Bound in red cloth, publisher's logo blocked blind on top board. Spine printed black with 'THE WORLD CRISIS', author's name, 'Sandhurst Edition' and publisher's name. Woods records its price as 13s. 6d.

Because of Churchill's association with Sandhurst, and because his chapter selections shed light on his military thinking, this is a desirable though scarce edition of *The World Crisis*. It contains a completely reset text in which Churchill selected various chapters from his 1931 Abridged and Revised volume. It was once deemed very valuable, but many copies have turned up recently. The rare fine example is likely to cost $750/£450. However, most were used as cadet textbooks so the typical example is well-worn, often underlined and/or marked with marginal notes. These sell for rather less, down to $200/£120 or so.

THE GREAT WAR: ICS A31d (26, 3 and 4 vols.)
Publisher: George Newnes Ltd., London, 1933–34

The brief mention in Woods (page 51) quite fails to do justice to this beautiful work, which, though its text is abridged, constitutes the first illustrated edition of *The World Crisis*. It began as a serialisation, issued in 26 magazine-format parts every fortnight between September 1933 and October 1934. Part 1 contains a brand new foreword by Churchill; Part 26 contains appendices and index. After these were published, Newnes offered the parts cased in three volumes, and later in a four-volume set jointly produced with The Home Library Book Company.

First Appearance (26 Parts): Measuring 7 x 10in, these are square-bound magazines, each with cover photo, title and author's name dropped out against a medium blue background. Part 1's spine is blank; the other spines are numbered with the title and author's name repeated. Inside and back wrapper faces contain adverts for the series, other Newnes publications, even life assurance! Wrappers were omitted from the bound volumes noted below.

Second Appearance (3 Vols.): Bound volumes (520, 520, 672 pages numbered consecutively with eight pages of preliminaries per volume, comprising 98 chapters. Two styles of publisher-authorised bindings were offered, both by A. W. Bain & Co. Ltd. of Cambridge Heath, London.

The 'Library Binding': half crimson morocco leather, cloth sides, blocked 22 ct. gilt on spine with title, volume number, author's name and a decorative design (globe exploding four ways). Offered at 8s. ($2) per bound volume (not including internals), or 4s. 6d. ($1.12) for each case alone.

The 'Standard Binding': royal blue cloth blocked blind and gilt on top board and blind on spine with title, author's name, volume number, publisher's name, and decorative design (globe exploding from the top). Offered at 5s. ($1.25) per bound volume (not including internals) or 2s. 6d. (66p) for each case alone. Note: spine volume numbers appear in both Roman and Arabic, sometimes interchangeably within sets.

Later Bindings: Though not mentioned by Newnes, I have examined other binding variations, most commonly a plain red cloth with the title blocked gilt and a blind wreath design on the top board. The title, author's name and volume number are blocked gilt between faint blind boxes on the spine. I have seen enough of these to conclude that they were a later, possibly cheaper, publisher's binding, not a 'freelance' variation.

Yet another binding, in plain red cloth blocked gilt on spine only, may be a private binding.

Third Appearance (4 Vols.): Bound volumes (392, 456, 492, 452 pages numbered consecutively with eight pages of preliminaries per volume, comprising 98 chapters) in 'Red Cape Levant Moroquette' (leatherette) with gilt top page edges. A wreathed sword device is blocked blind on the top board and silver and gilt on the spine. The title appears in gilt on top board and spine; spines also contain gilt author's name, volume number and Newnes name. The outside board edges of each volume are bevelled: a nice touch.

This most elaborate and final variation of *The Great War* was an instalment mail offer by the Home Library Book Company, 23–24 Tavistock Street, London in conjunction with Newnes, announced late 1934 and running into 1935. A 1934 advert states, '5/- [$1.25] brings the four superb volumes carriage paid to your door!' A 2 February 1935 advert reduces this to only '3/-' (75¢). Whether these were the prices of each volume (which seems cheap), or simply a 'hook' to bait the customer I have not determined.

APPRAISAL

All variants of *The Great War* contain the same pages, profusely illustrated and captioned, though it's doubtful, judging by their English, that the captions are Churchill's. They certainly offer wonderful graphics to support the author's towering

Four forms of *The Great War.* Left to right: the first of 26 individual parts (the form originally published); sample volumes of the half-leather and royal blue cloth three-volume binding; and one of the four-volume Home Library bindings. *The Great War* is also known in at least two rather plain red three-volume bindings.

prose, and, since they constitute the first illustrated *World Crisis*, the serious collector really ought to own one. I know bibliophiles who own six.

Originally 1s. each, the individual parts cost little as odd volumes, but a full set of 26 can bring up to $300/£180 in fine condition, much more in custom-made boxes, or half as much in as-usual condition with wear and chips.

The most luxurious set is the three-volume half-leather Library Binding, but both the Standard and Home Library bindings are splashier and more colourful. Half-leather bindings are rarely found in top condition because the leather tends to dry out and crack over the years; well-preserved with the leather still supple, they can be worth $600/£360. Fine examples of the cloth and Home Library bindings can cost almost as much.

THE UNKNOWN WAR, Keystone Issue: ICS A31e
Publisher: Thornton Butterworth Ltd., London, 1937

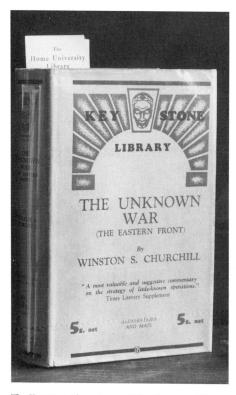

The Keystone Library issue of *The Unknown War* was a reprint sold by Thornton Butterworth at 5s. starting in 1937. The dust jacket is uniform with other Keystone Library Churchill titles.

Bound in medium blue cloth (rougher material than the first edition) with publisher's logo blocked blind on the top board and the title, author's name and publisher's name blocked gilt on the spine. The dust jacket is printed black and red on scored pale green paper and is quickly identified with its red Keystone Library logos.

The Keystone Library was a low-priced series of Thornton Butterworth titles which had run their course as trade editions and were now offered as low priced reprints. Aside from a title-page cancel (bearing a red Keystone Library logo) and a new dust jacket, this is a direct reprint from the English first edition plates, and still includes the excellent colour folding map tipped in following page 368. There was one impression only, offered at 5s. ($1.25).

Churchill tended to second-guess his English publishers when recommending titles. *The Unknown War* was the one he sold to Charles

Scribner, and evidently he finally prevailed with his English publisher on this one. 'The Eastern Front' appears as a subtitle on the spine, title-page and (in parentheses) on the dust jacket.

Apparently sales of this issue were few because it is quite rare today. This has caused it to sell for inflated prices, up to $300/£180 for fine jacketed examples. A somewhat worn copy in a chipped and dirty dust jacket was on offer in 1997 at $125/£80. This is a lot to pay, but since first editions are rarely offered by themselves–dealers hoard them to make up full sets–it is a good buy at that price.

Odhams Edition: ICS A31f (2 vols.)
Publisher: Odhams Press, London, 1939

I have Dr Gordon Cohen to thank for pointing out to me that these thick volumes are not abridgements, but the entire text of the first four volumes, including Churchill's revisions from the 1931 Abridged and Revised edition. Entirely reset, they constitute a new and separate edition of over 1,400 pages with comprehensive, if not elaborate, maps and illustrations. It is therefore quite desirable, both bibliographically and for collectors who want the complete text but not the financial burden of a first edition. Of course it lacks the final two volumes of the complete work, but these can be acquired separately (see some of the following entries).

The Odhams Edition was published at 7s. 6d. ($1.83) the set and promoted by the *Daily Herald*. William Manchester's *The Last Lion* (Vol. II, page 306, US edition) quotes a late 1930s letter from Churchill to his wife: 'Tomorrow the *Daily Herald*

Odhams editions: left, one of the 1939 two-volume issues, which originally came without dust jackets; right, one of the 1949 issues, which divided the text into four volumes. The latter is much scarcer.

quotes a late 1930s letter from Churchill to his wife: 'Tomorrow the *Daily Herald* began distributing the new cheap edition of the *World Crisis* which Odhams have printed. It can be sold for 3s. 9d. for each of the two volumes–a miracle of mass production. They expect to sell 150,000! I like to feel that for the first time the working people will hear my side of the tale.'

The work is bound in both greyish blue and deep red leatherette with a raised bust of Churchill surrounded by a circular title/author's name and blind rules on the top boards. Spines contain the title 'THE WORLD CRISIS 1911–1918', author's name and one or two gilt stars designating the volume number, blocked gilt. There are several binding variations:

Navy blue cloth, plain top page edges, author signature blocked blind on top board. (In this form the work is uniform with a two-volume edition of Lloyd George's war memoirs.)

Deep red cloth, red stained top page edges, author signature blocked gilt on top board, printed marbleised yellow-brown endpapers.

As above with a more elaborate spine: title/author's name gilt on a blind panel; three groups of debossed spine ribs; 18 pairs of gilt decorative rules.

DUST JACKETS

Originally the volumes were not jacketed and were shipped in grey cardboard boxes (one volume per box). In 1942 or later, the famous Karsh 'angry lion' portrait, taken in Ottawa in late 1941, was the basis of an attractive dust jacket, printed orange and black on white paper and marked 'VOL. I.' or 'VOL. II.' on the lower spine. These jackets have been found on all three binding variants, always bearing the same price: 8s. 6d. ($2.12) for the two volumes. Clearly, the jacket was unavailable for pre-1942 copies. Since the boards are quite elaborate for a cheap work, and since no other jacket has been observed on thousands of copies, it is clear that the Odhams Edition was originally issued without jackets.

APPRAISAL

This edition is very easy to come by, selling for only a few dollars or pounds in very good condition, although better examples bring a premium. Combined with reprints of *The Aftermath* and *The Eastern Front* it forms the least expensive full text of *The World Crisis* available, recently at $150/£90. It is an obvious choice for readers on a budget. Alternatives are the post-war four-volume Odhams issue or the new Barnes & Noble issue (see below).

THE AFTERMATH, Macmillan Issue: ICS A31g
Publisher: Macmillan & Co. Ltd., London, 1941

Officially retitled 'THE AFTERMATH | being a sequel to | THE WORLD CRISIS', this work was transferred to Macmillan after Thornton Butterworth went into

Butterworth plates and bound in dark navy cloth blocked gilt 'THE AFTERMATH | A Sequel to | THE WORLD | CRISIS' with author's and publisher's names on the spine. A second impression was issued in 1944. Dust jackets are printed red and black on off-white paper.

Identifying first impressions: this is distinctly taller than the 1944 impression: 9½in high against 9in. Dust jackets look the same, but the 1941 jacket is on slightly yellower paper and the type and photo of the author are reduced to fit the smaller dimensions of the 1944 impression. The half-title verso of the 1941 bears the first publication date and Macmillan transfer date 1941; the reprint adds, 'Reprinted ... 1944'. This is a modestly priced *Aftermath* compared to first editions, but expect to pay a premium for a fine jacketed 1941 impression, which looks and feels like a first edition.

THE UNKNOWN WAR, Macmillan Issue: ICS A31h
Publisher: Macmillan & Co. Ltd., London, 1941

This reprint from Thornton Butterworth sheets was published simultaneously and uniform with the Macmillan *Aftermath,* but had only one impression of just 600 copies. Its size, binding and jacket are uniform with the Macmillan *Aftermath*, but it is considerably rarer, and commands a higher price–not nearly as high, of course, as Eastern Front first editions. Because the binding and spine lettering are quite close to the latter, it does not look out of place among Thornton Butterworth editions, and is a budget substitute for the latter. But it is highly collectable in its own right, since it is so rare; the jackets are especially uncommon.

Note: THE UNKNOWN WAR, 'Hodder & Stoughton Edition' (Formerly ICS A31i) This work is mentioned by Woods (page 55), who describes it as a cheap edition published in 1941 at 6s. ($1.50). Since it has never been encountered among the publisher's records or hundreds of copies examined by dealers and collectors, I doubt very much that it ever existed.

Second Odhams Issue: ICS A31j (4 Vols.)
Publisher: Odhams Press Ltd., London, 1949

An offprint or reprint of the pre-war Odhams two-volume edition broken down into four volumes, this post-war issue is more manageable to read, but unfortunately rare. Only one impression occurred, in September 1949. As usual with post-war Odhams works, the sets were offered in two binding variants:

STANDARD
Bright red cloth; title and one to four stars (indicating volume) blocked gilt and black, and author signature blocked gilt, on top board; title/star(s), author's name

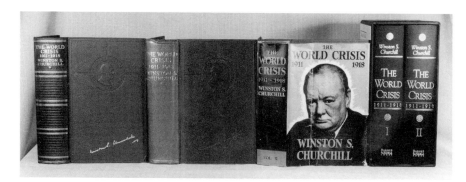

Left to right: two styles of Odhams 1939 bindings; the Odhams dust jacket which wrapped remaining Odhams; the recent reprint by Barnes & Noble booksellers.

and publisher's name blocked gilt and black on spine, separated by repeat publisher's devices and gilt rules.

DELUXE
Red leatherette; author signature blocked gilt with blind rules on top board; title, star(s), author's name between heavy rules blocked gilt on leather spine label; spine decorated with multiple devices, rules and the Odhams name, also gilt.

DUST JACKETS
The familiar Odhams style, printed pink and black on white paper, bearing title, author's name and stars to indicate volume on front face and spine and Odhams name printed black on lower spine.

APPRAISAL
My favourite Odhams edition, recommended if you can find it. Fine jacketed copies usually cost up to $150/£90; routine unjacketed copies with some wear cost a pittance. There seems no difference in value between the two binding styles, although Odhams sold the deluxe for a premium back in 1949.

Barnes & Noble Edition: ICS A31k
Publisher: Barnes & Noble Inc., New York, 1993

The mail order and chain booksellers Barnes & Noble have done Winston Churchill many services, producing cheap copies of numerous books by and about him over recent years. One of their latest was this fine offprint of the two-volume Odhams Edition, bound in half black cloth and stamped gilt on the spines, sold in a black, heavy cardboard slipcase. Available only from Barnes & Noble, at the bargain price of $29.95/£19. Now out of print.

In 1995, The Churchill Center presented a certificate of appreciation to the

In 1995, The Churchill Center presented a certificate of appreciation to the President of Barnes & Noble for his efforts in keeping Churchill in print, along with copies of *The Aftermath* and *The Eastern Front,* which we hoped he would consider for reprinting alongside this work, thus creating a complete *World Crisis* that would certainly sell for under $100/£60. After months of silence he sent them back; he did not even want them as gifts? The Churchill Center duly produced its own reprints: see below.

Bound Volumes from the *Collected Works*

Navy boards blocked blind on top boards and gilt on spines with main title, subtitle, author's name, five or six stars indicating volume, and the name of Thornton Butterworth, the original publisher. Both are reset, based on the original Thornton Butterworth text, leftover from the 1974–1975 collected edition (and, as a result, printed on 500-year archival paper, but thinner than the originals). Note that *The Eastern Front* contains all the original photos and illustrations, save for the elaborate folding map following the index.

To Mark Weber of London goes the credit for salvaging leftover sheets of *Collected Works* and binding them as replicas of the original Thornton Butterworth cases–down even to the publisher's name in gilt on the spines: the first appearance of Thornton Butterworth since 1940. Although one colleague laughingly called this 'an act of bibliographic obfuscation', the books cannot be mistaken for first editions. The internals bear *Collected Works* markings, being entitled Volume XI (*The Aftermath*) and Volume XII (*The Eastern Front)* from that 34-volume collection. They remain available at this writing at $60/£38 each.

FOREIGN TRANSLATIONS

Woods (page 51) mentions some but not all of the following; by 'Yugoslavian' he apparently means the Serbo-Croat edition.

Danish: DEN STORE KRIG (2 vols.)
Translation of *The Great War*, published by Hasselbalch: Copenhagen 1935. Only 89 of the original 98 chapters were published, originally in 33 separate parts. The parts were later bound in two thick quarto (8½ x 11½in) volumes in half brown leather, half blue leather and, say some Danes, in wrappers. Elaborately illustrated with 38 colour plates of world leaders, each tipped onto a heavy backing page. Though pagination differs, black and white illustrations are the same as in the Norwegian Edition. 1,576 pages. Books came in specially designed cardboard boxes.

Dutch: DRIE JAAR WERELDBRAND 1916–1918
A thin abridgement of Volume III, published in rose wrappers printed black with a

photo of the author by *De Telegraaf:* Amsterdam 1927. 102 pages, illustrated, plus wrappers.

Finnish: MAAILMANSODAN JALKISATO
Translation of *The Aftermath,* published by W. S. Oberstrom: Porvossa, Finland 1929.

French: LA CRISE MONDIALE (4 vols.)
Published by Payot: Paris in grey wrappers, consisting of the following volumes: Tome I *1911–1914* (1925), Tome II *1915* (1926), Tome III *1916–1918* (1930) and Tome IV *1919* (1931). 1,946 pages. This work had several impressions but is usually found in well-worn condition at low prices. Glassine wrappers often found with this work are not original; French booksellers put these on everything.

German: WELTKRISIS (4 vols. in 5)
Published by Koehler (1924–1926) and Amalthea (1928–1931) in four volumes and five parts: *1911–1914* (1924), Zweiter Band *1915* (1926), *1916–1918* (2 vols., 1928) and *Nach Dem Kriege* (*The Aftermath*) (1931). An interesting set: the font is old style German; Volumes I and II came bound and unbound; the *1916–1918* pair is bound in deep green and dark blue cloth. *Nach Dem Kriege* is found only in large card wrappers.

German: DIE WELT KRISE 1911–1918 (2 vols.)
Abridged edition, published by Verlag am Stutz Herdeg: Zurich 1947, bound in dark blue cloth; grey dust jacket with white titles.

Italian: LA CRISI MONDIALE (4 vols. in 5)
Volumes I and II published by Società Anonima Poligrafica Italiana in Rome; Volumes III and IV published by Tipo-Litografia della R. Accademia Navale in Livorno. The four volumes in five parts were as follows: Vol I *1911–1914* (1929), Vol II *1915* (1930), Vol III *1916–1918* (2 vols., 1930) and Vol IV Il *Dopoguerra* (*The Aftermath*) (1931).

Japanese:
Contrary to prior reports there was no Japanese Edition.

Norwegian: VERDENSKRIGENS HISTORIE (2 vols.)
The Great War, published by J. W. Cappelen: Oslo 1935–1936; first published in separate parts bound in cream illustrated card wrappers printed red; later beautifully bound. This is the most richly produced of the foreign translations: two thick quarto (11½ x 8½in) volumes bound in half crimson leather blocked gilt with spine bands and contrasting cloth boards. Profusely illustrated in black and white

The World Crisis, this should be it. (An alternate is the Danish Edition.) Expect to pay about $200/£120 in Norway, perhaps less in USA or UK owing to a deplorable lack of interest in foreign translations.

Portuguese: AS MINHAS MEMORIAS
Published by Pereira: Lisbon 1941. Quite likely a multi-volume set using the Odhams 1911–1918 text; three volumes have been discovered covering 1911–1914 and 1915.

Serbo-Croat: SVETSKA KRIZA 1911–1918
Abridged edition published in Zagreb, Yugoslavia, 1936.

Spanish: LA CRISIS MUNDIAL 1911–1918
Abridged edition published by Los Libros de Nuestro Tiempo: Barcelona, 1944

Swedish: VÁRLDSKRIGEN 1911–1918 (1 & 2 vols.)
Abridged edition published by Skoglund: Stockholm 1931. Offered in orange card wrappers or as a single volume bound in blue cloth.

Swedish: DET STORA KRIGET (3 vols.)
The Great War, published by Skoglund: Stockholm 1935 (Vols. 1 & 2) and 1936 (Vol. 3); first published in nine slim softbound volumes priced at 4.5 kr., or four thicker volumes. These were later bound in half mottled red-brown or tan and dark green leather and plain or marbled cloth. At 7¾ x 10½in, smaller in size than the Danish/Norwegian versions but stretched out to three volumes, the Swedish Edition

Sample volumes of Scandinavian editions of *The Great War,* beautifully bound in half or quarter leather.
Left to right: Swedish, Danish and Norwegian.

contains its own set of black and white photos, no colour plates and 95 of the original 98 *Great War* chapters. The volumes originally sold for 26 kr. each; in Sweden today, a bound set costs over $200/£120, but sets on the American second-hand market cost much less because there is little demand. Recommended for its unique photos.

Combined Work: SEKYE INMOOL TAE HOI KOROK (Korean)
Literally 'The Great Memoirs of Our World'. Taken from the abridged texts of *The World Crisis* and *The Second World War.* Published by Korean Publishing Corp., Seoul: 1989, 325 pages.

MY EARLY LIFE /
A ROVING COMMISSION

COHEN A91, WOODS A37

Modern historians have soundly established that Winston Churchill took certain liberties with episodes in his autobiography, which covers the years from his birth in 1874 to his first few years in Parliament. Jim Golland (*Not Winston, Just William?*, Harrow: 1988) showed that young Winston was scarcely the school dunce he suggests he was; some researchers believe he was not nearly so ignored and abandoned by his parents as he implies. His nephew, Peregrine Churchill, aided by Lady Randolph Churchill's archives, concluded that Winston's mother spent a surprising amount of time with him and his brother Jack before they left for school– and that Winston 'was a very naughty boy; his parents were very concerned about him'. On the other hand, biographers have shown that Churchill's entry into Sandhurst, and in due course into the cavalry, were rather less than personal achievements, and a letter has recently surfaced stating that his famous escape from the Boer Prison camp in Pretoria was the act of a 'bounder'–although Churchill himself, through libel suits, and his official biographer, have long since proved that he acted honourably.

None of this affects the wonderful treat provided by this most approachable and readable of Churchill's books. Harold Nicolson had it right in his 1930 review when he likened *My Early Life* to 'a beaker of Champagne'. If the reader was drawn to Churchill by *The Second World War*, his autobiography will come as a revelation; the war memoirs chronicle a very public struggle against national extinction; the autobiography charts a young man's private struggle to be heard. But the same style and pace are there, the same sense of adventure, the piquant humour, the ability to let the reader peer over the author's shoulder as events unfold.

Of course Winston was born with 'certain advantages', as William Manchester points out in his introduction to a recent edition of *My Early Life*: '... One must realise that his youth was virtually incomprehensible to most people then alive. He had been born into the English aristocracy at a time when British noblemen were considered (and certainly considered themselves) little less than godlike. His grandfather was Viceroy of Ireland ... These dominant forces–the class into which he had been born–were masters of the greatest empire the globe has ever known, comprising one-fourth of the earth's surface and a quarter of the world's population, thrice the size of the Roman Empire at full flush. They also controlled Great Britain herself, to an extent that would be inconceivable in any civilised nation today. One per cent of the country's population–some 33,000 people–owned two-thirds of its wealth, and that wealth, before two world wars devoured it, was breathtaking.'

Nevertheless, Churchill had little handed to him, once family influence had placed him where he wanted to be. He could not have embarked on those thrilling war junkets to Cuba, India, the Sudan and South Africa without the influence of his mother and other great personages; but once there he was on his own, and he acquitted himself well. In his autobiography he records these experiences in words which will live as long as any twentieth-century author is read.

My Early Life begins with Churchill's first memories, of the 'Little Lodge' in Dublin where his father lived as secretary to his grandfather, the Duke of Marlborough. The family had gone to Ireland in a kind of imposed exile after a serious quarrel broke out between Lord Randolph and the Prince of Wales, whose disapproval had ostracised Randolph and Jennie from London Society. Winston's description of his nurse, Mrs. Everest, is heartwarming and undoubtedly accurate; impressions of his schools may be familiar to many who were sent away to school. The story of his years at the Royal Military Academy; his adventures as a war reporter in Cuba, India and South Africa; and above all the famous charge of the 21st Lancers at Omdurman are elegantly written and will hold the reader's attention to the end. Here and in his later account of entering politics and Parliament, we can see Churchill's emerging political philosophy, studded with remarkably advanced views on British society and the Empire.

The text was not entirely fresh when the book appeared in 1930: Churchill had been writing autobiographic books since 1898. But the book melded his experiences together, added a lot, and had a huge printing over the years. It has been reprinted in 14 major English editions, 15 foreign languages and countless impressions—more than any of his other books except *The Second World War*. There is a copy for every reader, be it a cheap paperback or a rare first edition.

It is notable that *My Early Life* was one of the two Churchill works excerpted by the Nobel Library—for Sir Winston's 1953 Nobel Prize in Literature was won not for his war memoirs but the totality of his work. This book presents Churchill at his dazzling best as chronicler and memoirist, written at a time when he had freshly entered into the political wilderness, when most people, including himself on occasion, considered that his political career was over.

FROM THE REVIEWS

'[*My Early Life*] is his finest literary achievement ... better than anything which has gone before. Its variation and development in the matter of style are the greatest of its charms. One fancies one hears the small boy, the youth at Sandhurst, the young soldier, the slightly older politician each telling his story in his own way. Of course no gentleman cadet, still less a small boy, could write like that; that Mr. Churchill should contrive to bewitch his readers into the momentary impression that they can is proof that he has at his command the art of the autobiographer.'

The Times Literary Supplement, 1930.

'However fascinated we may be with what Churchill did, the impression cannot be avoided that he was a singularly pushing and cock-sure young man. But his story is told with such frankness and charm that its appeal, especially to those with any spirit of adventure, cannot be resisted.'

F. D. Dulles in *The Bookman,* 1930.

First Edition: Woods A37(a)
Publisher: Thornton Butterworth Ltd., London, 1930

Plum cloth. The top board bears the gilt title, subtitle and author's name with the publisher's device and two thick rules at top and bottom debossed blind. The spine bears the same material as on the cover (but no logo) and 'THORNTON BUTTERWORTH' gilt at the bottom. 8vo, 392 pages numbered (1)–392, with frontispiece, maps, plans, one folding map and 16 tipped-in illustrations. The verso of the half-title contains a boxed list of the author's other works. Endpapers are white. Published 20 October 1930 at 21s. ($5.25).

QUANTITIES AND IMPRESSIONS
Six impressions occurred, not all of them recorded by Woods. Their dates, with Woods's quantities where stated are: October 1930 (two impressions of 5,750 and 2,500 respectively), November 1930 (1,500), December 1930 (1,500) and September 1931 (1,000; Woods misdated this impression as 'August 1932'.) This fifth impression adds four more titles to the book list on the half-title verso.

The two lettering formats of the first edition *Early Life*, with five-line and three-line titles. First states come in either of these styles, second states only with the five-line title.

After a run of 'Keystone Editions' in the later 1930s (see below), Thornton Butterworth produced what they called a 'New Impression' in December 1940. This was in fact the sixth impression of the trade edition. It was bound in violet cloth, with no lettering on the cover, and priced at 7s. 6d. ($1.87).

Identifying first impressions: these carry only the original publishing date on the title-page verso, thus: 'First published ... 1930'.

VARIANTS

States: There are two distinct states, which are easily identified. The first state (ICS A37aa) lists 11 Churchill titles on the half-title verso, which is integral with the rest of the pages. The second state (ICS A37ab) adds 'THE WORLD CRISIS 1911–1914', which had been inadvertently omitted, by means of a cancel (pasted-in substitute page) of the half-title.

Bindings: Volumes are also bound in two distinctly different cloths: smooth and roughly textured. The top board is also found either with five lines of type 'MY | EARLY LIFE | A ROVING COMMISSION | WINSTON S. | CHURCHILL) or with three lines (MY EARLY LIFE | A ROVING COMMISSION | WINSTON S. CHURCHILL'. First states are reported in smooth cloth with five lines and rough cloth with three or five lines. Second states are reported in smooth or rough cloth but only with five lines.

Times Book Club variant: A book club edition of the first impression was offered by the Times Book Club, bound in a smooth, dark red cloth virtually identical to that of the first edition *Lord Randolph Churchill*, blocked on spine only: 'MY EARLY | LIFE, WINSTON S. CHURCHILL' and, at the base, 'BUTTERWORTH'. Reported copies are second states. Most carry the black and gold Times Book Club label on the rear pastedown.

DUST JACKETS

The first impression dust jacket, which is very

MY EARLY LIFE

A ROVING COMMISSION

The Rt. Hon.
WINSTON S. CHURCHILL
C.H., M.P.

Illustrations and Maps

$4.50

THOMAS NELSON AND SONS, LTD.

THORNTON

Most of the spine of the Canadian dust jacket to *My Early Life*. The books sold in Canada are uniform with the English edition.

rare, is printed black on solid plum paper, carries a contents blurb on the front flap, a list of 13 'autobiographies & biographies' on the back flap, and adverts for four *World Crisis* volumes (*1911–1914, 1915, 1916–1918* and *The Aftermath*) on the back face. A reproduction dust jacket was produced (by me) which looks the same but can easily be distinguished, since it is printed black and plum on heavy white paper: the underside is thus white, not plum. These jackets are usually, but not always, marked 'reproduction' on the underside of the spine area. Unscrupulous booksellers have passed this off as a 'variant dust jacket'–it's a variant, all right, but it was produced half a century later!

I have not seen any original jackets to the second through fourth impressions and cannot say whether or not they match the first. The fifth impression jacket is printed navy blue on white paper and its back face lists just three *World Crisis* volumes. The sixth impression jacket (1940) is entirely new, carrying a light red photo of Churchill on the face with the short title 'MY EARLY LIFE', byline 'WINSTON CHURCHILL' and price '7s. 6d. Net' the titles in white. It is printed black on white on the spine and back face. The back face advertises *Step by Step, Great Contemporaries*, all volumes of *The World Crisis* including the one-volume edition, and *India*.

Canadian jacket variant: First Editions exist (in first and later impressions) with special dust jackets for the Canadian market, the jacket spine imprinted 'THOMAS NELSON | AND SONS, LTD' over the Thornton Butterworth name. The price $4.50 appears on the spine and front face. The back face is mostly blank except for a statement that the work is published in the USA by Scribners as *A Roving Commission*.

COMMENTS

It is interesting that the author's preface was signed 'Winston Spencer Churchill', the first time in many years that the author had spelled out 'Spencer', perhaps recalling his schoolboy years when he chafed that 'Spencer-Churchill' (as he was known at Harrow) placed him too far down in the alphabetic order ...

When the many variations of the First Edition were revealed in *Finest Hour* in the 1980s there was a great rush among collectors to acquire the ones they didn't have. Partly for that reason the supply of nice copies has narrowed to a trickle. However, no value premium should attach to any particular variant. Woods's description of the First Edition fails to mention the second state, the binding variations, the Times Book Club variant or the Canadian dust jacket, and is wrong in dating the fifth impression.

APPRAISAL

The dust jacket is so rare that reproductions have been printed (see above), and the seller of a fine copy in a complete jacket can virtually name its price. Most jackets that do exist have pieces torn or missing. Even fine unjacketed copies are rare, because the plum cloth didn't wear well and is very susceptible to fading. The

Vastly different in appearance as well as title: the English and American first editions of *My Early Life / A Roving Commission* in their rare dust jackets.

typical 'very good' copy with a faded spine sells today from $300/£180 to $500/£300, but the price soars as condition improves. The second through fifth impressions are 'first edition look-alikes' and can be acquired at modest prices, around $50/£30 for very good copies and perhaps double that in fine condition. Jackets for later impressions are equally rare; I know of only two, for example, for the 1940.

First American Edition: Woods A37(b)
Publisher: Charles Scribners Sons, New York, 1930

Bright red cloth (changed to brick red for third impression, grey for fourth). The top board bears the gilt title 'A ROVING | COMMISSION and WINSTON S. | CHURCHILL' gilt in a grid of blind vertical and horizontal rules. The spine bears the title, author's name and SCRIBNERS blocked gilt, with a grid of blind rules on its top half. 16mo, 392 pages numbered (i)–(xiv) and (1)–(377), (1); with frontispiece, maps, plans, one folding map and 16 tipped-in illustrations. Published 23 October 1930 at $3.50.

IMPRESSIONS
At least four impressions were published, two in 1930, one in 1931, one in 1932. The First Edition of 1930 can be identified by the block letter 'A' below the publisher's name on the title-page verso. All impressions carry the publication date on the title-page (the second impression, title-page dated 1930, lacks the letter 'A').

DUST JACKETS
The first impression dust jacket (also used on the second impression) is printed red and navy on white paper and can be identified by its back face, which carries quotes from the book (preface and page 60). The jacket was altered for the third impression, where its back face contains excerpts from reviews of the work. A reproduction first impression jacket, produced by this writer, is marked on

Where Churchill got the American title for his autobiography. Henty's *Roving Commission* was published in 1900.

A ROVING COMMISSION

OR THROUGH THE
BLACK INSURRECTION OF HAYTI

BY

G. A. HENTY

Author of " With Frederick the Great " "The Dash for Khartoum"
" Both Sides the Border " &c.

WITH TWELVE ILLUSTRATIONS BY WILLIAM RAINEY, R.I.

LONDON
BLACKIE & SON, Limited, 50 OLD BAILEY, E.C.
GLASGOW AND DUBLIN
1900

the back face: 'REPRODUCTION DUST JACKET | CHURCHILLBOOKS, BURRAGE ROAD, CONTOOCOOK, NH 03229, USA'.

COMMENTS

A Roving Commission was remembered by Churchill as the title to Chapter 1 in his *Ian Hamilton's March* 30 years before; even this was not original, having been the title of a Victorian military novel by G. A. Henty, which Winston undoubtedly read as a boy.

The American Edition stole a march on the English by correcting a bad error, which has persisted in every English issue of *My Early Life* to date. The Duke of Cambridge (commander in chief of the army, 1856–1895), was approached by Lord Randolph to get Winston into the 60th Rifles (which Winston dodged, preferring the more dashing 4th Hussars). Though mentioned twice in the First Editions (British pages 50–75, American pages 36–61), he is incorrectly referenced in their indices as the 'Duke of Connaught'. Scribners editors quickly caught this, replacing Connaught by Cambridge in their 1930 second impression. (A page-by-page comparison finds that this is the only change in the second impression, and Cambridge remains properly referenced in all American editions published since.)

But the index error was never corrected in English editions, and in 1944 the Reprint Society compounded it, altering the text to read 'Connaught' to comply with the index! That double-error persisted in English Editions until Leo Cooper made it

"*More exciting than any novel.*"
—London Times.

A Roving Commission

My Early Life

by

Winston S. Churchill

author of "The World Crisis," etc.

"Like a beaker of champagne," says a reviewer in the *London Observer* of Mr. Churchill's zestful volume of recollections, and continues: "I am sure that as long as there are young men and women they will thumb with delight the tale of adventure told by Mr. Churchill with the skill of a Dumas."

It is packed with excitement, tense with action, glowing with life, this narrative of hairbreadth 'scapes in South Africa, wartime adventures in Egypt, India, and Cuba, red-hot political campaigns and amusing youthful scrapes at home. Moreover, it is an incomparable picture of the shaping of a man.

Profusely illustrated
$3.50

CHARLES SCRIBNER'S SONS, NEW YORK

Desirable jacketed editions of the *Commission*. Left to right: the American first, second and third editions and, at far right, the Scribners and Scribner-Macmillan 'Hudson River Editions', part of a series of important books reprinted by the publisher.

worse in his 1989 edition of *My Early Life,* altering 'Cambridge' to read 'Connaught' on page 75 (but missing the other Cambridge on page 50), and Cooper's American counterpart, W. W. Norton, picked up the same gaffes.

Happily the muddle doesn't exist in the latest American Touchstone Edition (off-printed sans index from a Scribners Edition). The Americans thus had the Duke of Cambridge right throughout all but two of all their issues, while the British have messed up Cambridge in every impression ever published. The only English Edition that is faultless is in the *Collected Works* (see appendix), which was offprinted from the First Edition but left out the index with its erroneous entry.

APPRAISAL

Fine copies of the First Edition are almost never seen, and are even scarcer in the original dust jacket. Like the English Edition they are prone to fade, and when exposed to light, quickly bleach to almost white. They also seem to attract dirt. A genuinely fine copy in a whole, untorn dust jacket is certainly worth $1,500/£900 today, perhaps more. Near-fine copies in good dust jackets sell for $500/£300 and up. Without dust jackets, fine copies are almost unheard of, but would be worth up to $300/£180, while the typical worn and faded copies cost as little as $40/£24. Later impressions are not often seen, but $50/£30 should buy quite a decent one. Occasionally one shows up with a dust jacket; if it happens to be the second impression, its jacket should be saved to transfer to a first impression, which is entirely ethical since the jackets were identical.

Keystone Library Issue: ICS A37ac
Publisher: Thornton Butterworth Ltd., London, 1934

Bound in smooth plum cloth exactly like the First Edition. The dust jacket is printed black and medium blue on scored pale green paper and is quickly identified with its blue Keystone Library logos. The logo also appears printed blue on the title-page. Page (3) lists other Keystone titles, page (4) lists 16 Churchill titles. 2,000 copies published 20 February 1934 at 7s. 6d. ($1.87) but quickly reduced to 5s. ($1.25).

There were two later impressions, each in different bindings: January 1937 (like the above with gilt titles on top board but less glossy plum cloth; and January 1940 (purple cloth, on top board blank).

DUST JACKETS

Variations occur on the back faces. First impression, first state lists 'additions for Spring 1934', listing seven titles including this one. Second state lists 'Recent Additions, Spring 1935': six new and some older titles. Second impression advertises *Thoughts and Adventures* and *The Unknown War*. Third impression advertises the revised and extended edition *Great Contemporaries*. All jackets except the first state carry the 5s. price.

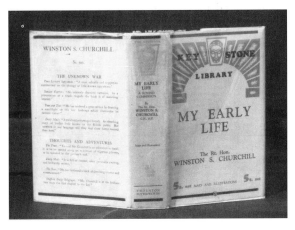

Butterworth's Keystone Library issue of *My Early Life* appeared in 1934 at 7s. 6d., but was quickly knocked down to 5s., less than quarter the price of the first edition.

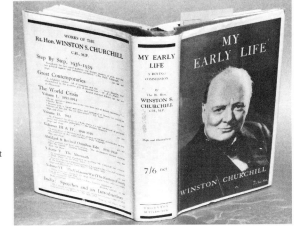

Thornton Butterworth's final effort on behalf of Churchill was the 1940 impression of *My Early Life*, carrying a new dust jacket with a photo of our author.

APPRAISAL

The Keystone Library was a low-priced series of previous Thornton Butterworth titles. Aside from a title-page cancel (bearing the Keystone Library logo) and a new style of dust jacket, this is a direct reprint from the English first edition plates, including the frontispiece and tipped-in map and illustrations. A good buy now as then, it can usually be obtained for trifling amounts, but the rare fine jacketed copy is worth up to $150/£90.

Second American Edition: Woods A37(c)

Introduction by Dorothy Thompson
Publisher: Charles Scribners Sons, New York, 1939

Navy blue cloth. The top board bears the gilt title 'A ROVING | COMMISSION and WINSTON S. CHURCHILL' blocked silver. The spine carries the same words plus SCRIBNERS. 16mo, 396 pages numbered (i)–(xviii) and (1)–377, (1); with frontispiece, maps, plans, one folding map and 16 tipped-in illustrations. Published 1939 at $2.50; later impressions raised to $3.50.

IMPRESSIONS

There are three impressions, each distinctly different. The first (1939 on title-page, code 'AA' on title-page verso) is the only one bound in rough navy cloth and with the title and author's name on the cover. The second (1940 on title-page, code 'BB' on verso) is bound in smooth navy cloth with the top board blank. The third (1941 on title-page, no code on verso) is bound identically to the second. Both later impressions bulk slightly thicker than the first.

DUST JACKETS

The dust jacket, which didn't vary, is printed navy blue and orange on white, lists six other 'famous books by Winston S. Churchill' on the back flap and advertises Helen P. Kirkpatrick's *Under the British Umbrella* on the back face. The same jacket is occasionally found wrapped around the Third American edition, apparently by the publishers who were getting rid of extra copies; it doesn't fit well, since the Third is a thinner book. Such jackets should be removed and carefully preserved for use on Second Editions, which are much scarcer and more desirable.

COMMENTS

This edition contains significant new material. In an expanded preface, Churchill offers 'some further account of my American forebears', not all of it quite accurate, as later genealogists have shown; these lines were continued in later American editions. The preface is now signed 'Winston S. Churchill' and the 'Chartwell Manor, 1930' is omitted. Also added (to this edition only) is an introduction by newspaperwoman Dorothy Thompson, who calls Churchill 'one of the finest living writers of English prose' and 'a stormy petrel of politics. For the past decade he has been the most pugnacious, eloquent, and scathing critic of British policy. He happens to have been right, and that is the reason he is again in the Cabinet at last ... It would be impossible to imagine England without him.' Winston must have loved it.

An amusing note about the 'AA' and 'BB' letters on the title-page verso of the first two impressions is recorded by the noted bibliophile David A. Randall, in his *Dukedom Large Enough* (New York: Random House 1960). Asked about the 'AA', Randall checked with Scribners and was informed it was 'normal procedure. After all, it was a new edition with a new Introduction, and the new material had to be copyrighted, hence the double "A". This was nice, reassuring, logical and right out of headquarters, and I so reported. Some months later I met a girl at a party somewhere who was working for Scribners, at the press. She was a Bryn Mawr graduate, I recall, and I simply happened to mention this anomaly. "Oh, I remember", she replied. "I was asked about that. I put in those double 'A's. The page looked prettier that way." '

APPRAISAL

Prized for its unique introduction, the Second American is a very scarce book, especially in decent condition. Because this is not a First Edition, the impression has little to do with value: condition is everything. A near-fine second impression in a like dust jacket is worth up to $150/£90. Jacketed copies of any kind sell for at least half that, though run-of-the mill unjacketed examples command little more than a few dollars or pounds. This book is worthy of any Churchill library for its unique material, which was expunged from the succeeding edition, and appears nowhere else.

Macmillan Issue: ICS A37d

Publisher: Macmillan & Co. Ltd., London, 1941

Bound in navy cloth, spine only blocked gilt with title, author's name and 'MACMILLAN'. Maps, plans, one folding map and 16 tipped-in illustrations. Published 1941 at 10s. 6d ($2.62). Four impressions: 1941, 1942, 1943, 1944.

When Thornton Butterworth went into liquidation, this title and others were obtained by Macmillan. The first impression spine title reads 'MY EARLY | LIFE' and its title-page verso states 'Transferred to Macmillan & Co. Ltd., 1941' with no subsequent reprint information (although it does list all the previous Thornton Butterworth printings). First impressions are printed on thicker paper than later impressions, which also carry the spine title in three lines. Later impressions are thinner and bound in smooth dark navy cloth. All impressions were printed in pulpy wartime paper, but seem to be holding up well regardless.

Dust jackets are printed red and black on heavy white scored paper and first impression jackets advertise *My Early Life, Great Contemporaries, Step By Step* and

The World Crisis (one vol. edn) on the back face. This is a garden variety *Early Life*, nicely bound, an inexpensive hardbound alternative to the valuable first editions.

Third American Edition: ICS A37e
Publisher: Charles Scribners Sons, New York, 1941

Grey cloth, spine only blocked gilt with 'A ROVING | COMMISSION | WINSTON S. | CHURCHILL' and 'SCRIBNERS', 382 pages numbered (i)–(xii) and (1)–370. Illustrated with maps, plans, one folding map and 12 photos on six tipped-in sheets. Price in 1951: $3.50.

This cheapened edition had numerous impressions, including, but not necessarily limited to, 1941, 1942, 1944, 1945, 1949 and 1951. The frontispiece was relegated to one of a reduced number of illustrations. The index and Dorothy Thompson introduction disappeared, although Churchill's notes on his American forebears were retained in the preface.

Dust jackets vary but all are designed around the photo of Churchill in the uniform of the South African Light Horse. The 1941–1945 jackets are printed red and black on white paper; the 1951 is printed dark blue and brown on light blue. A handful of first impressions carry the orange and blue Second Edition jacket advertising Dorothy Thompson's introduction, which of course is not there; these appear to have been wrapped around the books when new, possibly to ease a shortage.

This edition is available regularly for pocket change; fine jacketed copies are worth perhaps $35/£22.

Reprint Society Edition: ICS A37f
Publisher: The Reprint Society, London, 1944

Cream, loose woven cloth with black leather spine label containing title, author's name and decorative border gilt. 5 x 7½in, 392 pages numbered (1)–392, frontispiece and nine illustrations tipped in on slightly heavier, uncoated paper. Top page edges stained dark blue. Dust jacket printed orange and navy blue on white paper. (This edition compounds the Cambridge–Connaught error mentioned under Cohen A87.2: the fictitious Duke of Connaught appears here in both the index and the text.)

A book club edition in the 'World Books' series, whose Broadsheet for May 1944 indicates that this is 'The June Book'.

APPRAISAL

A nicely produced book despite wartime limitations, retaining most of the original photos and the tipped-in folding map. Fairly common, it has no value except in fine jacketed condition, when it is worth around $50/£30.

Note: In the Broadsheet mentioned above, this is referred to as a 'World Books Edition'. Although distinct Reprint Society and World Books editions of *Great Contemporaries* exist, I have not encountered a specific World Books edition of *My Early Life*.

First School Edition: Not in ICS
Publisher: Albert Bonnier, Stockholm, 1946

8vo, 188 pages in card wrappers printed brown on cream. The front photograph is of Churchill's welcome at Durban after his escape from the Boer prison camp in 1900. This is an abridged version in English intended for use in schools teaching English Language courses. Introductions are in Swedish and English, the latter thanking Churchill for permission to reprint. Twenty pages of rear notes explain difficult words or phrases, and a folding map at the end shows South Africa and Churchill's journey. This volume was only recently discovered by Mark Weber, who had never seen one before. It is extremely rare and interesting.

Odhams Edition: ICS A37g
Publisher: Odhams & Co. Ltd., London, 1947

8vo, 384 pages numbered (i)–(x) and (1)–374. At least eight impressions: 1947, 1948 (April, August), 1949, 1957, 1958, 1965, 1966. A 1954 impression is also possible. Completely reset, the volume now included a frontispiece and eight illustrations between pages (viii) and (ix), and the former folding map was now printed over a double page spread. There are distinct forms of this Edition.

Odhams was a mail order bookseller, which helps explain the lack of prices on dust jackets. Deluxe bindings of first four impressions were shipped in grey cardboard boxes with *Step by Step, Great Contemporaries* and *Thoughts and Adventures* at 32s. ($6.40) post-paid to mail order clients.

Bindings: Through 1958, copies appeared in the two bindings: standard (bright red cloth blocked gilt and black on top board and spine, page edges unstained) and deluxe (red leatherette with author signature blocked gilt on top board and black leather title/author label on spine combined with multiple devices, rules and the Odhams name, also gilt, page edges stained red.) Boxes containing the 'deluxe' binding are marked 'CHURCHILL SET D/L'. The first impression is identified on the verso of its title-page by no date beyond 1947 and the code 'S.947Q'. Dust jackets were printed black and yellow on white paper (price on flap in 1958).

In March 1965 Odhams reissued *My Early Life* in the same format but printed on thicker paper with new bright red leatherette boards: a circular drawing of Churchill printed maroon on the cover, the spine blocked gilt with two black sections to resemble leather labels. This edition was sold individually at 18s. ($2.52) in a dust jacket printed red and black on mottled cream paper. It was also sometimes combined with *Painting as a Pastime* and Thomson's *Churchill: His Life and Times* without jackets in a red slipcase–though more often, Heath's *Churchill Anthology* was slipcased with the other titles.

VARIANTS

The 1958 impression exists in plain medium red cloth with no black panels, top board blank, the spine imprinted with the title, author's name and 'ODHAMS' at the base. It is not a library rebind as the titling is in Odhams' standard font, with the usual spacer artwork and leading.

All the Odhams editions are of incidental value, although the First Impression of 1947 is quite rare. The 1965 is the most handsomely presented version, and may often be found in fine jacketed condition for around $30/£18.

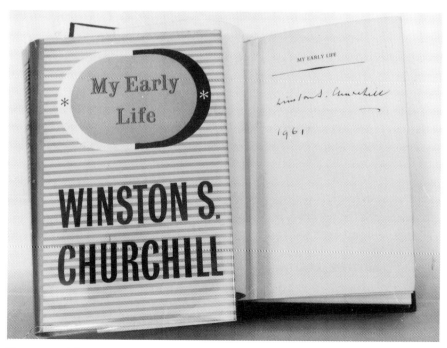

The post-war Odhams edition in a jacket uniform with other Odhams Churchill titles; this copy was inscribed by the author in 1961.

First Canadian Edition: ICS A37fb

Publisher: The Reprint Society of Canada, Ltd., Montreal, 1948

Cream leatherette with black leather or leatherette spine label similar to the Reprint Society edition and internally offprinted from it. Dust jackets printed bright yellow or tan on white paper. Although a mere book club issue, this is the first individual Canadian Edition and therefore of some interest. I paid $75/£45 for my copy years ago, and haven't seen another since.

Fourth American Edition: ICS A37h

Publisher: Charles Scribners Sons, New York, 1958

Physically identical with the Third American Edition, except for the absence of illustrations, this version is significant in adopting the main title *My Early Life* for the first time in the United States.

Hardbacks: Originally published in blue cloth blocked gilt on spine, they saw at least ten impressions: 1958, 1960, 1964, 1965, 1966, 1968, 1977, 1980, [?] and 1988. The last four impressions were in the 'Hudson River' series of low-volume reprints of important past Scribners titles (Cohen A87.14). The 1988 impression is marked for the merged company of Scribners Macmillan. Hudson River volumes, blue cloth blocked silver on spines, carry dust jacketed printed black and blue on cream laid paper.

Paperbacks: Originally 5¼ x 8in, 384 pages numbered (i)–(xii) and (1)–372, first published September 1960 at $1.45. (This first impression is coded 'A–9.60 [C.]' on the verso of the title-page.) After at least three impressions in the 1960s and 1970s; the September 1972 issue carries a full-cover photo of Churchill in the uniform of the South Africa Light Horse. This paperback was reissued in 1987 at $10.95. The first impression is identified by a row of numbers from 10 down to 1 on the verso of the title-page; it carries a maroon, blue and black cover with a photo of Churchill as MP for Oldham.

Second School Edition: ICS A37i

Introduction by Andrew Scotland
Publisher: Odhams Press Ltd., London, 1958

Blue cloth blocked gilt on top board (title, author name and 'SCHOOL EDITION') and on spine (author and title reading vertically upwards, 'ODHAMS' reading horizontally. 280 pages numbered (i)–(x) and 11–280. Maps and plans within the text. A small (5 x 7½in) hardback issued as a school textbook, this edition contains a reset text including a one-page introduction by Andrew Scotland who interprets the work for young people. Very popular at a time when British schools were still proud of Britain's history, it saw at least 13 impressions. The first impression, dated

October 1958 and coded 'T.1058.Q' on the title-page verso, is very rare, but the edition has little value. Impressions noted: 10/58, 2/59, 11/59, 3/60, 10/60, 3/61, 10/61, 4/62, 10/62, 2/63, 7/63, 12/63 and 7/64.

First Paperback Edition: ICS A37j

Publisher: Collins Fontana Books, London & Glasgow, 1959

Paperback, 384 pages numbered (1)–382 (+2) plus two unnumbered pages containing four photos on coated stock. First published at a shilling (14p), this edition saw 18 impressions through 1980; the impression can be determined from information on the title-page verso, and the first impression is rare. Although Fontana announces on page 6 that the text 'is that of the first edition', it has been reset for paperback format. The first several impressions had unillustrated covers, printed black, pale green, pale blue and red on white paper; over the years covers became more elaborate.

Manor Books Edition: ICS A37k

Publisher: Manor Books Inc., New York, 1972

Paperback, 384 pages numbered (i)–(xii) and (1)–372, plus 16 pages of photos and cover photo from the Columbia Pictures film, 'Young Winston', starring Simon Ward. Photograph-ically reproduced from a Scribners edition, sold at $1.50. One impression known.

New Edition: ICS A37L

Publisher: Leo Cooper, London, 1989

Black cloth, blocked gilt on spine, offprinted from the *Collected Works* 1974 edition. 390 pages numbered (1)–390 plus 16 pages of photos on coated stock. Published at £14.95.

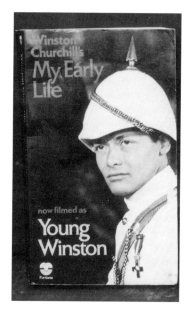

Two of the many varieties of Fontana's paperback: a 1974 issue picturing Simon Ward in the role of the concurrent film, 'Young Winston'; and an early 1990s reprint with a photo of the author as he appeared at the end of *My Early Life*.

This edition is significant in having an excellent five-page foreword by Tom Hartman and a note on the International Churchill Society, which collaborated in the reprint, following Churchill's text. The dust jacket is printed black and red on white paper with the titles dropped out white.

New Paperback Issue: ICS A37m
Publisher: Mandarin Paperbacks, London, 1989

Photographically reproduced (reduced) from the Cooper Edition with the illustrations omitted, this oversize (5 x 7¾in) paperback was published at £5.99. The cover design, by Alison Wright, is based on a portrait of Churchill aged 5.

Touchstone Edition: ICS A37n
Introduction by William Manchester
Publisher: Simon & Schuster, New York, 1996

Paperback, 396 pages numbered (i)–(xiv) and (1)–372, 5½ x 8½in. The cover design takes three photos of Churchill in his youth against a large format of the MP for Oldham as background, with a facsimile of WSC's signature printed light blue on dark blue at left. Notable for its evocative new introduction by Manchester (pages (vii)–(xx)), it is unindexed and unillustrated. Published at $14, still in print at this writing.

FOREIGN TRANSLATIONS

Danish: DE UNGE AAR
Published by Steen Hasselbalchs Forlag: Copenhagen 1931; over 40,000 copies in at least seven impressions: 1931, 1945, 1948, 1949 (smaller, thinner), each unbound or half brown leather; 1956 (yellow card wraps or full brown leather in slipcase); and 1963 (paperback). Also published by Schönbergske: Copenhagen 1973 (paperback).

Dutch: MIJN JONGE JAREN / EEN WARE ZWERFTOCHT
Published by Allert De Lange: Amsterdam 1947, hardbound. Later published by Uitgeverij Het Spectrum: Utrecht 1948, 1950; both paperbacks.

Finnish: NUORUUTENI
Published by Otava: Helsinki 1954 (bound in red cloth or unbound).

French: MES AVENTURES DE JEUNESSE
First published in pale green illustrated wrappers by Payot: Paris, 1931. Later French translations include MES JEUNES ANNÉES, Paris: Club français du livre 1960, 1965;

MÉMOIRES D'UN JEUNE HOMME, Paris: édition Spéciale 1972 and MES JEUNES ANNÉES (in French Braille).

German: WELTABENTEUER IM DIENST
Published by P. List: Leipzig, 1931 (brown cloth), Munich, 1946 (smaller, cheap half cloth binding), Rowohlt: Munich, 1951 (no. 36 in a paperback series; at least two impressions, 100,000 copies). A later paperback (stated fourth edition) entitled MEINE FRUHEN JAHRE was published by P. List: Munich 1965.

Hebrew: SHACHARIT CHAYAI
Published by the Omanuith Co. Ltd.: Tel-Aviv, 1944.

Icelandic: BERNSKUBREK OG ÆSKUPREK
Published by Snœlandsintgáfan: Reykjavik 1944. Bound in dark red or brown cloth; also in white card wrappers; all had dark blue dust jackets.

Italian: MEMOIRIE (1874–1903)
Published by Garzanti: Milan, 1946, stated second edition, 1947. Retitled GLI ANNI DELLA MIA GIOVINEZZA and published by Garzanti: Milan 1961 (a new translation with altered text).

Japanese: information needed

Korean: NAE JOLMUN NAL EUI CHUUK
Published by Pum jo Sa: Seoul, 1987; published in the Jong sun Sekye Munhak (World Literature Series) by Chong rim: Seoul, 1991.

Foreign translations of *My Early Life* abound. These in Portuguese (left and middle) and Danish.

Norwegian: UNGDOM
Published by Gyldendal Norsk: Oslo, 1935 (in cloth or wrappers); 1945 (same appearance, retitled MINE UNGAER); 1956 (retitled UNGDOM, reset, smaller format, cream cloth boards). A paperback was published in 1973.

Portuguese: MINHA MOCIDADE
Published by Editora Nord-Sul: Rio de Janeiro, 1941; three impressions, one in the late 1980s or early 1990s. Later published as MEMORIAS DA MINHA JUVENTUDE by Editorial Seculo: Lisbon, 1947 and Carlos y Reis: Lisbon, 1974.

Slovene: MOJA MLADA LETA
Published by Cankarjeva Zaloz: 1976

Spanish: MÍ PRIMERA JUVENTUDE / UNA MISION ERRANTE
Published by Editorial Clarid: Buenos Aires 1941.

Swedish: MIN UNGDOM
Published by Norstedt: Stockholm, 1931. Reprinted 1934, 1948 (Albatross Series: smaller, cheaper), 1953 (three printings), 1954, 1955 (published by Vingforlaget, part of Norstedt), 1963 (Vingforlaget), 1972 (Pam Books, reset paperback). A Swedish School Edition was published by A. Bonniers: Stockholm 1936, reprinted 1946. The volumes record at least 31,000 Swedish copies.

INDIA

COHEN A92, WOODS A38

This book was proposed by Churchill to Thornton Butterworth, his current English publisher, on 21 March 1931, when the author offered a package of seven 'very good speeches ... I have taken much more trouble with them than any book.' His object, of course, was to gain support for his campaign against the India Bill, over which he had broken with his party leadership, believing these relatively modest reforms would lead to the loss of India to the Empire. Thornton Butterworth responded enthusiastically, saying that he agreed with Churchill's cause. But he was possibly more interested in recementing a relationship that had only just survived Churchill's threat to drop him in a dispute about *World Crisis* royalties. To the initial seven speeches Churchill added three earlier addresses and a pithy introduction, and *India* was published in cloth and paperback two months later.

Eminently a product of its time, *India* was fast overtaken by what Churchill called the 'Gathering Storm' of the Second World War. Although our author usually favoured republication of his earlier books, he saw no reason to revive *India*. After all, that cause had been lost when the India Bill had passed Parliament in 1935. Churchill even sent Gandhi his best wishes for success, and lent tacit approval to Attlee's plan to grant India Dominion status (thus *de facto* independence) in 1948. What he did not approve was the sudden rush to leave India under Attlee's Viceroy, Lord Mountbatten, who arbitrarily moved Britain's departure date up to August 1947. British authority thus ended before boundaries could be worked out between Moslems, Hindus and Sikhs; a vast shift of population occurred, amid bloody attacks by the various sides against each other. Later Churchill would exclaim to Mountbatten, 'What you did in India was like striking me across the face with a riding crop.'

India remained a forgotten book, inaccessible to many, an unfortunate loss for students of rhetoric and political science. In 1990, this writer was able to publish a new American Edition with a new introduction by Manfred Weidhorn, excerpts of which form our reviewer's notes for this title.

FROM THE REVIEWS

'Setting aside the merits of the substance of these speeches, one must admit that as rhetorical exercises they are impressive. They were made when Churchill was at the height of his oratorical powers and one of the best speakers in the House of Commons. While not always on a level with some of the masterpieces of other phases of his career, they have their moments. There are numerous deft touches of irony and sarcasm, as when he refers to himself and his followers with a climactic, appropriate word: "A few die-hards and reactionaries, and other untouchables". And, on Gandhi: " ... a seditious Middle Temple lawyer of the type well-known in the East, now posing as a fakir, striding half naked up the steps of the Viceregal palace to parley on equal terms with the representative of the King-Emperor".

'Stanley Baldwin has much to answer for at the bar of history, but in this matter he was right. While Churchill carried on about how the facts were against Indian independence, Baldwin likewise urged people to face up to the truth. The principal fact "today", he concluded, was that "the unchanging East has changed". With that one nugget, the usually pedestrian Baldwin shoots the usually eloquent Churchill, with his romantic, Victorian, imperial rhetoric, right out of the water.

'Of course some of Churchill's prophecies were not so erratic. What would happen to the rest of the British Empire, he asked rhetorically, if it lost its centrepiece? That loss, he went on, "would mark and consummate the downfall of the British Empire ... [It would be] final and fatal [and] reduce us to the scale of a minor Power." He was also right in warning about sectarian strife and Hindu domination in the wake of the British departure; in fact, several million lives were lost in the fighting between Hindus and Moslems during the weeks and months following independence. The Sikhs even today resort to violence against what they consider Hindu oppression. He warned also about balkanisation of the subcontinent masquerading as a nation; in fact, Moslem Pakistan broke away from a mainly Hindu India only to have Bangladesh in turn break away from it, and tensions and clashes have long reigned in places like Kashmir.

'Most Pakistanis and Indians, would, of course, say that all this was the price necessary for independence and dignity and that it was well worth paying. A Tory in 1776 might have reasonably argued that Britain's holding onto the American colonies would spare them the fate of undergoing either balkanisation or a brutal civil war, and he would have been correct. Yet how many Americans wish to undo the Revolution for that reason?

'We would like genius to be discerning and moderate, to be a little bit more like the rest of us. Few geniuses have been so. Churchill had the vices of his virtues. In judging him we err by unconsciously depending on the wisdom of hindsight. No one could tell at the time how the campaigns of 1931 and 1940 would turn out. If responsible voices across the political spectrum in 1931 told Churchill that the imperial age in India was over, just as many responsible voices in 1940 said that Hitler could not be beaten and should be negotiated with. If Churchill had been amenable to prudence in 1931, he would have spared everyone embarrassment, but that same prudence would have dictated in 1940 negotiations with Hitler. Only the pugnacious mule of 1931 could see his way through the impossibilities of 1940. A more civilised, common-sensical soul like Halifax did negotiate with Gandhi. And, had Halifax rather than Churchill been made Prime Minister on 10 May 1940, he would have certainly negotiated with Hitler.

'Genius exacts its high price. If we like the way 1940 turned out, we have to comprehend 1931.'

Manfred Weidhorn, Yeshiva University
In the foreword to the First American Edition

First Edition: Woods A38
Publisher: Thornton Butterworth Ltd., London, 1931

Hardbound: Orange cloth blocked black with 'INDIA' and 'CHURCHILL' on front cover and spine, publisher's logo debossed on lower right corner of cover, and publisher's imprint on spine bottom. Softbound: Orange paper printed black with 'SPEECHES BY, THE RT. HON. WINSTON S.' and '1/- NET' added to front face, INDIA – CHURCHILL and the price (two times) on spine. Inside wrappers are blank; back wrapper contains adverts for *My Early Life,* the Abridged *World Crisis* and *The Aftermath.* Both versions 8vo, 144 pages numbered (1)–141(3). Pages 142–144 contain membership information on the Indian Empire Society. Published 27 May 1931 at 1s. (25¢) for the softbound version and 2s. (50¢) for the hardback.

IMPRESSIONS
Two impressions occurred, the second almost immediately after the first–both are dated May 1931. The second impression (softbound version) was identical to the first except for dark green instead of orange wrappers, although there are variants (see below).

The very rare orange cloth *India* in its two binding variations, with black type reading across and down the spine. Both are among the rarest of Churchill's hardbound volumes, much less often seen, for example, than the *Malakand* or *The River War.* The left-hand variant came first.

VARIANTS

Hardbound: Bindings are known with two spine variations, one with 'INDIA, CHURCHILL and THORNTON BUTTERWORTH' blocked horizontally, another with 'INDIA - CHURCHILL' (only) blocked vertically down the spine in much larger typeface. There are no other differences.

Softbound: There are first impressions in green wraps; second impressions in orange wraps; *and* second impressions in orange cloth (spine type reading down); all are rare. Woods also reports a first impression with the price of 2s. 6d. on its cover, which seems odd, since the hardback itself only cost 2s.; the 2s. 6d. variant may have been a prototype copy.

DUST JACKETS

The dust jacket for hardbound copies is printed black on orange paper and looks like the softbound wrapper, except that it carries the price '2/- net'. The front flap promotes the book, the back flap the 1911-1914, 1915 and 1916-1918 volumes of *The World Crisis*.

COMMENTS

Softbound copies on the market today outnumber hardbound copies by at least twenty to one, which offers a clue as to their original press runs. The books were printed on pulpy paper, and it is rare to encounter a copy entirely free of spots.

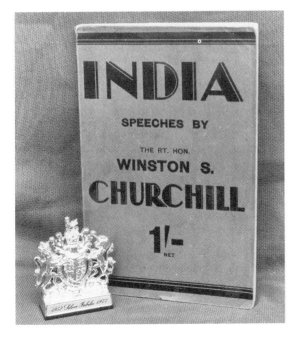

India is more commonly seen in wrappers; this one, printed black on dark green, is the second impression. Second impressions in orange wraps and cloth are known to exist.

APPRAISAL

Jacketed hardbacks are extremely rare: I have encountered only four or five in 15 years. Such a copy, with the book underneath in pristine condition, could command a price in excess of $2,500/£1,500. Unjacketed hardbound copies can exceed $1,500/£900 in fine condition, but are worth much less in worn condition. Softbound first impressions in excellent condition were worth up to $1,000/£600 in 1997, but generally sold for less and half that much would buy a nice example. Green wrapper second impressions were selling simultaneously for $150–250/£90–150. Any of the variants mentioned above are extremely rare and would command a towering premium.

First American Edition: ICS A38b

Publisher: Dragonwyck Publishing Inc., Hopkinton, NH, 1990

Orange cloth blocked black with 'INDIA' and 'CHURCHILL' on front cover and spine, publisher's logo debossed on lower right corner of cover, back cover and bottom of spine, two large blind rules across covers and spine. 8vo, 188 pages numbered as follows: front matter (i)–(xl); replica wrapper (xli)–(xlii); text (1)–144; replica wrapper 146–147.

QUANTITIES AND IMPRESSIONS

2,000 copies were published at $35 in May 1990, including 100 copies of the limited edition at $100 (see below).

VARIANTS

A leatherbound limited edition of 100 was published in orange leather blocked gilt in all places blocked black or blind on the standard edition, all edges gilt, with black endpapers and a gold satin page marker.

DUST JACKETS

The dust jacket, printed orange and black on white coated stock and unique to this edition, was designed by Charlotte Thibault. The front face groups portraits of Churchill, Gandhi, Nehru, Britannia, and an Indian Rajah and George V around the author's name, title, new subtitle *(Defending The Jewel In The Crown)* and cover blurb *(His Rare Book–Out Of Print For 60 Years)*. The front flap describes the book, the back flap Churchill and Weidhorn; the back face contains quotes from the text and comments by Robert Pilpel 'On Reading Churchill'.

COMMENTS

Our intent was to publish enough copies to keep this volume in print a long time, and it is still available at this writing, helping to fill many a hole in a library. In 1997 it was chosen as the book discussion topic for the International Churchill Conference in Toronto.

APPRAISAL

The standard edition continues to sell at a special price of $25 to members of The Churchill Center or Churchill Societies. No limited editions have been sold to my knowledge, but in the event they would likely command their original price.

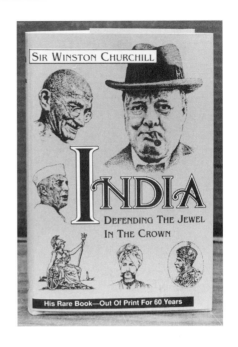

This writer was proud to publish the first American edition of *India* in 1990; it remains in print. The dust jacket was unique to the volume, but beneath it is a replica of the cloth original.

Dragonwyck's *India* was issued in a gilt-blocked leatherbound limited edition with satin page marker (right), as well as the standard cloth.

THOUGHTS AND ADVENTURES /
AMID THESE STORMS

COHEN A95, WOODS A39

The broadest range of Churchill's thought between hard covers, *Thoughts and Adventures* comprises essays on a vast array of subjects, attesting not only to the breadth of the author's comprehension but of his personal experience. Not yet sixty when it was published, Churchill had already seen enough of the world from high office to fill several political careers; he had read widely, his photographic memory recording it all for reference; he had lived through what was then thought to be the greatest convulsion in history, the 'War to End Wars'. Here he provides a charming and attractive sampler. 'Quite a few essays in it are as carefully constructed as short stories', writes Manfred Weidhorn. 'In other pieces, Churchill, little concerned with apologetics, criticism or sources, wanders nimbly around and through his subject, like a Montaigne or a Lamb. The flexibility of the style is striking. Whether sounding the dark ubi sunt motif or descanting lightly upon hobbies, Churchill, as the *Times Literary Supplement* reviewer noted, seems always a happy young warrior enjoying himself and sure of his convictions.'

Of minor interest is that Churchill's longtime private secretary, Eddie Marsh, wrote the foreword while Churchill was indisposed, according to Marsh's biographer Christopher Hassall. 'Stylistically, it is doubtful whether anyone would ever have known', commented Fred Woods, quoting as proof the following lines from the foreword: ' ... now confusion, uncertainty and peril, the powers of light and darkness perhaps in counterpoise, with Satan and Michael doubtfully reviewing their battalions ... ' Adds Woods: 'One can only admire the quality of the pastiche.'

The *Thoughts* may be divided into several clear subcategories. First are Churchill's musings on his own career–'A Second Choice', 'Personal Contacts', 'The Battle of Sidney Street', 'Election Memories', 'The Irish Treaty'–and the tools by which he made himself relax amid those political storms: 'Hobbies' and 'Painting as a Pastime'. This is a remarkably frank collection in which he has few axes to grind– no defence of his actions over such as the Dardanelles, as in *The World Crisis*, a franker account of how he helped stitch together the Irish Treaty than appears in *The Aftermath*. 'Painting as a Pastime' appeared as an article in 1921, and would later appear as a freestanding book, but here Churchill uses it as an example of 'Hobbies' which, he insists, are absolutely indispensable as an escape device for people otherwise enmeshed in their careers.

The Great War, memories of which still dominated thought in the 1930s, is covered in 'The German Splendour', 'My Spy Story', 'With the Grenadiers', 'Plugstreet', 'The U-Boat War', 'The Dover Barrage', 'Ludendorff's "All or Nothing"', 'A Day with Clemenceau' and 'In the Air'. One might consider that these are among the aspects of the war that most struck the author. Again we see his ability to evaluate fairly, and even to praise the enemy.

Then there is Churchill on Politics ('Cartoons and Cartoonists', 'Consistency in Politics', 'Parliamentary Government and the Economic Problem'), the latter a thoughtful consideration of the future of democracy in the midst of world depression. The 'Cartoons' essay is illustrated with some of Churchill's favourite parodies of himself, and he singles out the great David Low for praise tempered by political criticism: a 'green-eyed Antipodean radical' who jeers at 'the fatted soul' of the British Empire. (Low disagreed with Churchill over almost everything–until the Second World War came and Low drafted a famous cartoon entitled *All Behind You, Winston.*)

Most intriguing today are Churchill's musings on the future in a remarkable set of essays: 'Shall We All Commit Suicide?', 'Mass Effects in Modern Life' and 'Fifty Years Hence'. Here we see Churchill imagining the future with H. G. Wells, or inviting readers to imagine alternative history. Editing a fine article on these essays by Professor Paul Alkon in the Spring 1997 *Finest Hour*, I was astonished to find Churchill speculating on 'a race of artificially bred beings' just as Scottish scientists were announcing that they had cloned a sheep, with the media issuing solemn assurances that human clones were not far behind.

Falling into none of the above categories is 'Moses', a subject Churchill and David Ben-Gurion would later argue about in friendly meetings in their old age, Ben-Gurion setting out to prove that Jesus was a greater man, while Churchill would champion Moses! One recent reviewer suggested that the Moses essay was misplaced: Churchill's thought is so evergreen that it obviously should have appeared in *Great Contemporaries* ...

While the book seems to have sold slowly in the USA, it certainly did well in the UK. On 14 December 1932 Mr Butterworth bubbled to Churchill that 6,903 copies had been sold: 'We are truly delighted at this success which confounds the Jonahs of the bookselling trade.'

FROM THE REVIEWS

'There is much here that we could do without: some poor stuff which is best forgotten or, at least, ignored; but there are many things of splendour, too, many delights and sparkling episodes. What great advantages he had! Immersed in making the country's history, he met and knew intimately all sorts and conditions of folk;

holding office at most critical times, he was still unbowed by the heavy weight of politics which had smothered so many of his contemporaries. He could provide full-scale portraits of very famous and important persons who had strutted the boards in his youth; and he knew enough of the inherent weaknesses of Man to predict a future for the human race.

'What is more, he could write. It was a pity that he took the easy path to writing, but I cannot blame him. There was clamour for his work: his name alone sold copies of magazines and papers; he lived and wrote, as he said, "from mouth to hand" and he deserved what he earned.

'Oddly, perhaps, I think Churchill was rather ashamed of *Thoughts and Adventures*. For a writer of genius it was all too easy hack work, and rather a comedown for a former Chancellor of the Exchequer. Had his break with Baldwin and his party not happened, few, if any, of these articles would have been written.'

Henry Fearon, *Churchill's Works: A Commentary and Catalogue*

First Edition: Woods A39(a)
Publisher: Thornton Butterworth Ltd., London, 1930

Khaki cloth. The top board bears the gilt title and author's name with two blind rules top and bottom and publisher's device debossed blind. The spine bears the same material as on the cover (but no logo) and 'THORNTON BUTTERWORTH' gilt at the bottom. 8vo, 320 pages numbered (1)–(320), with frontispiece; Chapter 2 illustrated with cartoons. The half-title verso contains a list of 13 of the author's other works. Endpapers are white. Published 10 November 1932 at 18s. ($4.50). Note: Woods also gives '4 November' as the date for the second impression, possibly a typo for 14 November.

QUANTITIES AND IMPRESSIONS
Title-page versos state that four impressions of this edition (as distinct from the subsequent Keystone Edition) were produced–November 1932 (three) and December 1932. But Woods lists five impressions with four in November, one in December, and may be right (see 'Comments'). Woods notes 4,000 copies of the first edition and 6,000 in the later impressions, for a total run of 10,000. Seventy per cent were sold by the end of the year. Identifying first impressions: these carry only the original publishing date on the title-page verso, thus: 'First published . . 1932'.

VARIANTS
Bindings: First editions exist bound in dark green instead of khaki cloth; all later impressions were bound in dark green cloth.

DUST JACKETS
The first impression dust jacket, which is rare, is printed black on tan paper, carries

a contents blurb on the front flap, 'Points about THE HOME UNIVERSITY LIBRARY' on the back flap, and adverts for *My Early Life, The World Crisis* (all original volumes, numbered I–VI, plus the Abridged Edition) and *India* on the back face. The second impression jacket is identical.

Third and fourth impression jackets are the same format but overprinted in red on front face (in space gained by moving the author closer to the title): 'The Opinion of the Press is summarised in the words of the Morning Post 'A TONIC FOR THE TIMES'. The front flap now carries press comments. Another jacket has been reported printed navy blue on white paper, which I have not seen personally.

COMMENTS

A letter to Churchill from George Thornton Butterworth, dated 16 December 1932, provides some clues as to the difference between impressions proclaimed by Woods and the books themselves: ' ... Our first printing, as you know, was 4,000 copies, but before publication we felt it necessary to put on a new printing of 1,000. These copies came in just within half an hour of our being out of print; the same happened with the third edition; and with the 4th edition we had to "wangle" deliveries from 11 o'clock in the morning until 5 o'clock in the evening when supplies were ready for distribution. The sheets were delivered by passenger train and the cases were made by the binders in advance.'

I construe from this that the 'new printing of 1,000' which Butterworth said was undertaken 'before publication' used first edition sheets which indicated no second impression. If Butterworth then hastily ordered an extra 1,000 cases for them, this might account for the variant green bindings sometimes found. If Butterworth produced yet another impression after he wrote this letter, it would account for the five impressions noted by Woods.

The first edition, at least in khaki cloth, is elusive in fine condition because the khaki soiled and scratched easily; those which do exist usually are under their original dust jackets. The variant dark green binding holds up better and is highly sought after, because it is much scarcer and aesthetically more pleasing.

APPRAISAL

The dust jacket for this work is almost as scarce as the jacket for *My Early Life,* though in contrast to the latter, it has not been replicated. A truly fine jacketed copy is today worth up to $1,500/£900, but a well-worn jacket depreciates the value even if the book beneath remains bright. The typical 'very good' copy, with rubmarks and scratches and sans dust jacket, sells for around $100/£60 to $150/£90. Later impressions cost about one quarter of the prices mentioned above.

Green cloth first editions tend to command slight premiums. If, however, it emerges that the green ones were part of Butterworth's hasty second impression (see Comments), you and I may have paid too much for our copies.

First American Edition: Woods A39(b)

Publisher: Charles Scribners Sons, New York, 1932

Carmine cloth. The top board bears the gilt title 'AMID | THESE STORMS and WINSTON S. | CHURCHILL' gilt in a grid of blind vertical and horizontal rules. The spine bears the title, author's name and 'SCRIBNERS' blocked gilt, with a grid of blind rules on its top half. 8vo, 320 pages numbered (1–4), 5–319, (1), with frontispiece; Chapter 2 illustrated with cartoons. Published 25 November 1932 at $3.50.

IMPRESSIONS

Only one impression was published. Do not be misled by the absence of a letter 'A' on the title-page verso. Scribners omitted this usual sign of a first edition, which they had begun using in 1930, from *Amid These Storms* and no copy has ever surfaced with the 'A'. (Perhaps this was another case of someone at Scribners deciding that 'the page looked prettier that way'–see comment under the Second American Edition of *My Early Life*.)

DUST JACKETS

The dust jacket is printed red and black on white paper and bears a silhouetted photo of Churchill in Flanders, 1916 wearing his French *poilu's* helmet. A promotion blurb appears on the front flap, a blurb for *A Roving Commission* appears on the back flap; adverts for the Abridged *World Crisis, The Aftermath* and *The Unknown War* on the back face.

COMMENTS

When Charles Scribner told Churchill he thought the title *Thoughts and Adventures*

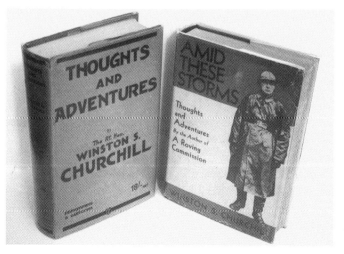

Jacketed copies of both the English (left) and American first editions of *Thoughts* are almost equally scarce and highly prized. The American jacket illustrates Churchill in Flanders in the First World War, wearing his French *poilu's* helmet.

dull and unsuitable for the American market, Churchill replied, 'What about *Amid These Storms?*' Thus for the second time a Churchill book appeared in America with a different title, and again the alternative was suggested by the author. Scribners did retain *Thoughts and Adventures* as a subtitle, and in the book's most recent appearance in America it reasserted itself–unfortunately, for *Amid These Storms* is more evocative, and more fun. The pressing seems to have been made from the British plates, since there is no difference in pagination, type size or arrangement from page 5 onwards.

APPRAISAL

Like its identically bound cousin, *A Roving Commission,* fine copies of *Amid These Storms* are almost never seen; the dust jacket is almost as scarce, though no mass reproductions have been created. Like the *Commission,* copies are highly susceptible to fade, and soil easily. A genuinely fine copy in a whole, untorn dust jacket is worth up to $1,500/£900 today. Near-fine copies in good dust jackets sell for less, down to $500/£300. Without a dust jacket few copies have remained fine, but they are sometimes encountered with faded spines and otherwise bright boards; such copies are worth perhaps $250/£150. Routine worn copies command as little as $40/£24.

Keystone Library Issue: ICS A37ab
Publisher: Thornton Butterworth Ltd., London, 1934

Bound in textured dark green cloth with two blind rules at top and bottom of top board and spine. Title, author's name and publisher's logo blocked blind or gilt on the top board; the title, author's name and publisher's name blocked gilt on spine. The Keystone logo is printed blue on the title page. Page (1) lists other Keystone titles, page 2 lists 16 Churchill titles. Published 26 September 1933 at 5s. ($1.25).

QUANTITIES AND IMPRESSIONS

The first impression was of 3,000 copies, but judging by the many variant bindings, these may not all have been bound at once. Second impression, February 1934.

VARIANTS

First impressions exist with both gilt and blind titles on the top board. There are at least three variant green cloths, differing in shade and texture. Just to make things really confusing, a Keystone first impression has been found in the exact khaki cloth of the First Edition. Clearly this bargain line of books took advantage of whatever binding materials were lying around.

DUST JACKETS

There are two states to the first impression jacket: (1) large blue Keystone logo at top of front flap and seven press comments; (2) no logo and nine press comments, plus a much smaller 5s. price on the back face. The second impression carries a different jacket with the back face starting with 'Additions for Spring 1934', but also has the front flap with Keystone logo at top.

APPRAISAL

The Keystone Library was a low-priced series of previous Thornton Butterworth titles. Aside from a title-page cancel (bearing a red Keystone Library logo) and a new dust jacket, this is a direct reprint from the English first edition plates, including the frontispiece and illustrations. A good buy now as then, it can usually be obtained for trifling amounts, but the rare fine jacketed copy is worth up to $150/£90.

Keystone Editions were sold in Canada (and possibly Australia), with the sterling prices on the dust jackets obliterated by ⅝-inch circular punched holes. The books themselves are otherwise identical to the home versions. These have some additional value, but not a lot.

Macmillan Edition: ICS A39c
Publisher: Macmillan & Co. Ltd., London, 1942

Bound in navy cloth, spine only blocked gilt with title, author's name and 'MACMILLAN'. Reset in smaller type, 272 pages numbered (1)–272. No frontispiece, but the cartoons remain in Chapter 2. Published 1942 at 10s. 6d ($2.62). Three impressions: 1942, 1942, 1943.

This title and others were obtained by Macmillan and the first impression reads 'Transferred to Macmillan & Co. Ltd., 1942' with no subsequent reprint informa-

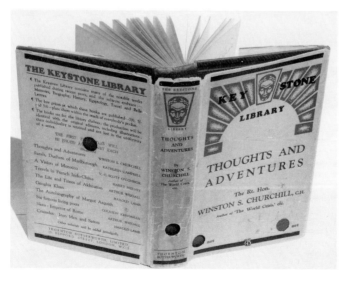

A Keystone issue of the *Thoughts* sold in Canada carries neat holes to obscure the sterling prices, but no Canadian prices are substituted and the book underneath is a standard Keystone issue.

tion. There is no size difference between the impressions. Dust jackets are printed red and black on heavy white scored paper and do not vary between impressions. The back face advertises *My Early Life, Great Contemporaries, Step By Step* and *The World Crisis* (one vol. edn). Commonly found, often in its jacket and nicely bound, this is an inexpensive hardbound alternative to the valuable first editions.

Odhams Edition: ICS A39d
Publisher: Odhams & Co. Ltd., London, 1947

Completely reset, this volume carries no frontispiece but retains the Chapter 2 cartoons. Notably, it contains a publisher's note on page (vii), quoted among the reviews above. Bound in two styles: standard red cloth blocked gilt and black on top board and spine, page edges unstained; deluxe red leatherette with author signature blocked gilt on top board and black leather title/author label on spine combined with multiple devices, rules and the Odhams name, also gilt, page edges stained red. Dust jackets printed black, mauve and light blue on white paper. Identifying first editions: verso of title page contains no date beyond 1947 and the code 'S.947Q'. 8vo, 384 pages numbered (i)–(x) and (1)–246. Four impressions: September 1947, April and August 1948, January 1949.

Odhams was a mail order bookseller, which helps explain the lack of prices on dust jackets. Deluxe bindings of the first four impressions were shipped in grey cardboard boxes with *Step by Step, My Early Life* and *Great Contemporaries* at 32s. ($6.40) post-paid to mail order clients. This title was offered c. 1954 (with *My Early Life* and *Step by Step*) to buyers of Malcolm Thompson's *Churchill: His Life and Times*, by Odhams under the general series title, *The People's Home Library*. All the Odhams editions are common except the first Impression of 1947, although no special premium attaches to it. Copies may often be found in fine jacketed condition for around $30/£18.

Books For Libraries Issue: Cohen A91.6, ICS A39e
Publisher: Books for Libraries, New York, 1972

A reprint photographically reproduced, probably from the 1932 Scribners Edition, and still entitled 'AMID THESE STORMS'.

Ayer Issue: ICS A39f
Publisher: The Ayer Company (Publishers) Inc., Salem, NH, 1984

A library reprint photographically reproduced, probably from the 1932 Scribners Edition, since it is identical down even to the frontispiece (crudely rephotographed, but still there). Possibly another pressing of the Books for Libraries issue, which Ayer stocked in other Churchill titles. Bound in wedgwood blue shiny cloth blocked white on spine only: 'Churchill' (reads across), 'AMID THESE STORMS' (reads down),

'AYER' (reads across). This issue carried a price of $28 and finally went out of print in 1995.

The New Edition, 1990

The first new trade edition in many years had two hardback and one paperback issues. Features common to all issues are as follows: text photographically reproduced from the *Collected Works* (see appendix); new foreword by Tom Hartman (in addition to the author's original Preface); appendix on the International Churchill Societies; maps and plans from the *Collected Works* (redrawn) pages.

First New Edition: ICS A39ga
Publisher: Leo Cooper, London, 1990

Black cloth, blocked gilt on spine, offprinted from the *Collected Works* 1974 edition. 248 pages numbered (I)–(x) and (1)–238, no frontispiece, cartoons in Chapter 2. Pages (vii)–(ix) contain a new foreword by Tom Hartman, pages 237–238 contain a note on the International Churchill Society, which collaborated in the reprint. The dust jacket is printed black and red on white paper with the titles dropped out white or grey. Published at £16.95.

New American Issue: ICS A39gb
Publisher: W. W. Norton & Co., New York, 1991

Brown cloth stamped silver on spine, plain boards with 'WSC' debossed blind. Pagination as above. 8vo, sold at $22.95. White dust jacket printed brown, gold and black, photo of author as a young Member of Parliament on front face. One impression, no known variations.

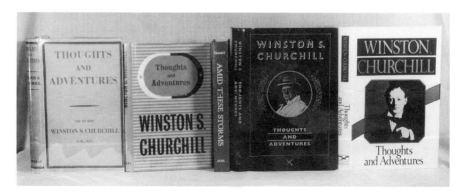

Thoughts and Adventures reprints. Left to right: Macmillan, Odhams, Ayer (not issued with dust jacket), Cooper and Norton.

New Paperback Issue: ICS A39gc
Publisher: Mandarin Paperbacks, London, 1991

Photographically reproduced (reduced) from the Cooper Edition, this (5 x 7¾in) paperback was published at £5.99. The front wrapper bears the subtitle *Through Stormy Years*.

FOREIGN TRANSLATIONS

Danish: TANKER OG OPLEVELSER
Published by Steen Hasselbalch Forlag: Copenhagen, 1948 in card wrappers and leatherbound.

French: REFLEXIONS ET AVENTURES
Published by Delachaux et Niestle: Neuchâtel, Switzerland, 1944. A new edition entitled REVIVRE MA VIE was published by Olivier: Paris 1981.

At least two impressions. Published in wrappers with allegorical artwork summarising the contents, and in tan cloth.

German: GEDANKEN UND ABENTEUER
Published by Amstutz Herdeg: Zurich, 1943. Three impressions.

Korean: THOUGHTS AND ADVENTURES
Published by Sang Rok Mun: Seoul, 1956.

Spanish: PENSAMIENTOS Y AVENTURAS
Published by Los Libros de Nuestro Tiempo: Barcelona, 1943, in both red and medium blue cloth.

Swedish: TANKER OCH MINNEN
Published by Norstedt: Stockholm, 1933; four impressions, card wrappers or cloth, except for the third impression, which was a unique softbound book. A new edition entitled TANKER OCH AVENTYR was published by Albatross/Norstedt in 1949, second impression (paperback) 1953.

Combined Work: CHURCHILL ON MEN AND EVENTS, Cohen A269
Subtitled: *A Selection from 'Thoughts and Adventures' and 'Great Contemporaries' made by Andrew Scotland, M.A., Ph.D.*, this work was published by Ginn & Co. Ltd., London, 1965. So far as I am aware, it is the only work to combine chapters from both of Churchill's mid-Thirties collections of essays. Frontispiece has a drawing of T. E. Lawrence by Augustus John.

MARLBOROUGH:
HIS LIFE AND TIMES

COHEN A97, WOODS A40

One million words long and ten years in the making, *Marlborough* is Churchill's greatest biography. It may be his greatest book. To understand the Churchill of the Second World War, the majestic blending of his commanding English with historical precedent, one has to read *Marlborough*. Only in its pages can one glean an understanding of the root of the speeches which inspired Britain to stand when she had little to stand with. The great teacher Leo Strauss, commenting spontaneously to his University of Chicago class after hearing of Churchill's death, called *Marlborough* 'the greatest historical work written in our century, an inexhaustible mine of political wisdom and understanding, which should be required reading for every student of political science'.

Churchill came to the Premiership in May 1940 fresh from having published the final volume of *Marlborough*, and having written the first drafts of his *History of the English-Speaking Peoples*. No finer grounding in Britain's destiny, or her sense and purpose in the battle against Hitler, could have been available. Churchill commandeered the English language and sent it into battle, as Edward R. Murrow and John F. Kennedy said; he could not have done so without a thorough grounding in the life and times of John Churchill, First Duke of Marlborough. Desmond MacCarthy in his *Sunday Times* review cannily pointed to the intrinsic appeal of *Marlborough* and its author when he commented that 'the half-successful are more interesting'. Both Marlborough and his biographer were in the end half-successful; both stood against tyranny, both ended as spent political forces, one at least lived to see a greater tyranny arise upon the ashes of its predecessor. 'I have accomplished much', mused Churchill in old age, 'only to accomplish in the end nothing'.

The late Henry Fearon, who sniffed at *Thoughts and Adventures* as 'hack work', judged that *Marlborough* proved that the 'wilderness years' were not wasted. Indeed even its critics agree with Fearon that this majestic biography is a major contribution to English literature. Winston Churchill emerges here as 'a superb historian, a scrupulous (though not unbiased) authority on eighteenth-century war and politics, an accurate assessor of human nature in all its diversity and conflicting strains of good and evil. Few historians rival his marshalling of facts, planning of the work, his sense of purpose, the sheer rambunctious vigour of his tale.

This is not to say that the work is flawless; quite the contrary. Churchill took up this biography with the primary intention of vindicating John Churchill from the charges, notably by Thomas Babington Macaulay, that he was an unprincipled charlatan, an avaricious warmonger. This task largely occupies the first volume which, wrote Lord Blake, 'is the least satisfactory–too polemical about Macaulay who was wrong but not as wrong as Churchill alleged. He had come to hate Macauley for traducing the great Duke, his ancestor, though in his youth Macaulay's *History and Essays* were paramount influences on his style. The ensuing three volumes are masterly.'

Actually Churchill held some private reservations about Marlborough. 'What a downy bird he is', Winston wrote his wife: 'He will always stoop to conquer'. In the book, however, Churchill paints the portrait of a saint whose greatest problem was the confused, stubborn, small-minded politicians with whom he had to deal. 'Yet [Churchill] too is undone', notes Manfred Weidhorn, for the book 'leaves one with a jaundiced view of all politics ... Churchill is so rapt by the complexities, the sporting aspect, the glamour of politics, that this point eludes him, even as he is too engrossed in military strategy to notice the human suffering it produces. *Marlborough* leaves us with a compelling portrait of a supreme hero, though we remain uncertain whether this Marlborough with his "harmony of interests" ever existed.'

FROM THE REVIEWS

'There are no flat tracts in this long book; the current of events through it never grows languid. Packed with details as it is, few of its pages give one a sense of being overcrowded ... The naturally energetic movement of Mr. Churchill's mind, his intense interest in the historical significance of events and their relation to the characters and motives of those concerned in them, his profound admiration (most infectious) for the chief actor of all, and his training in political life are considerations which help to decide one question: Will its length prevent it winning in the future as many readers as its merits and interest undoubtedly deserve?

'[It is not easy] to recall any full length English biography to put above it. Morley's "Gladstone"? Moneypenny's and Buckle's "Disraeli"? Trevelyan's "Garibaldi"? No: I don't feel inclined to do that ... The merits of Mr. Churchill's book lie in its narrative power; its limpid impetuosity which may well carry a reader on to the end, though he may be daunted by the length of the river; a gift for clear popular exposition; an intense interest in military history, and a rare instinct for strategy; and finally a sense, educated in the school of experience, of the nature of the problem (perpetually recurring) of how to get people actuated by different motives and ideas to work towards some common aim in politics and war ...

'When a man's achievement is obvious, emphasis upon it seems commonplace to posterity. The half-successful are more interesting. As with a very high mountain, the reputation of Marlborough was recognisable at a glance as belonging to the higher ranges; but it is only when one starts to walk up such a mountain and looks down from its top upon the imposing protuberances that one realises its real mass and altitude. And this is what Mr. Churchill has enabled us to do.'

Desmond McCarthy in *The Sunday Times*, 11 September 1938

First English Edition: Woods A40a, ICS A40aa
Publisher: George G. Harrap & Co. Ltd., London, 1933–38

Four volumes

Plum cloth, bevelled outer edges, blocked gilt on top board (Marlborough Arms) and on spine (titles), gilt top page edges, 8vo. Vol. I published 6 October 1933 at 25 s. ($6); 616 pages numbered (i)–(iv) and (1)–612. Vol. II published October 1934 at 25s., 666 pages numbered (1)–651 (+5). Vol. III published 23 October 1936 at 25s., 612 pages numbered (i)–(ii) and (1)–608 (+2). Vol. IV published 2 September 1938 at 25s., 672 pages numbered (1)–(671), (1). All volumes variously illustrated with portraits, maps, plans and facsimiles. Spines are lettered 'MARLBOROUGH | HIS | LIFE AND TIMES (space) WINSTON S. | CHURCHILL (space) VOL. [I–IV]' and, at the bottom, 'HARRAP'.

EDITIONS, IMPRESSIONS AND QUANTITIES

The following impressions are known: Vol. I, two (both October 1933); 'New Revised Edition' November 1934. Vol. II, two (both October 1934). Vol. III, one (October 1936). Vol. IV, one (September 1938). Volume I only had a second edition.

Identifying first editions: All first editions carry the legend 'First Published' followed by a single date on the verso of the title page. All later impressions or editions here carry notes of subsequent printings.

Quantities (according to Woods). Vol. I: 17,000 (but this total includes the 'Presentation Edition' of 1939, see A93.4). Vol. II: 15,000. Vols. III and IV: 10,000 each.

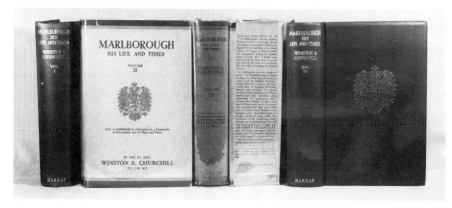

A lovely jacketed first edition *Marlborough*, one volume opened to show the front flap, which should never carry mention of a later impression at bottom left corner. This is a really fine trade binding: note Harrap's bevelled boards.

DUST JACKETS

Volumes I and II are commonly found with non–first edition dust jackets, some of which have been clipped to eliminate inscriptions indicating later impressions, which appear at the lower left corner of the front flap. To be certain, front flaps should be unclipped. All jackets are printed deep plum with the Marlborough Arms gilt on heavy, mottled grey (Vol. I), cream (Vols. II and III) and light green (Vol. IV) paper.

A jacket on a proof copy of Volume I carries a price of 30s., which was reduced to 25s. when the book went on sale.

VARIANTS (ICS A40ab)

All four volumes exist in purple cloth with unbevelled edges, gilt top page edges and an abbreviated title (deleting 'HIS LIFE AND TIMES') At least the first two were offered by The Times Book Club; most of them have small TBC labels affixed to the rear pastedowns. Since these purple sets often crop up in Australia, Mark Weber theorises that they are an export variant. ICS has designated this 'A40ab' to distinguish it from the first trade edition.

COMMENTS

Among Churchill's publishers, Harrap probably produced the most beautiful trade editions. Printed by the Ballantyne Press, each volume is replete with finely reproduced facsimiles of documents, portraits and magnificent maps and plans; each carries a thorough bibliography and index. Churchill's dedication to the Grenadier Guards appears in Volume I only, but each volume has its own preface, written at Chartwell, Westerham (the first appearance of Churchill's home village in the prefaces of his books). Collectors of fine bindings tell me that they have made room for this trade binding on their shelves because of its physical magnificence.

APPRAISAL

Although *Marlborough* is the one pre-war Churchill work that is fairly common in dust jackets, truly fine copies are scarce. Volumes I–III were and are susceptible to severe fade; the slightest chip in a dust jacket can almost instantly produce a bleached spot on the binding, especially the spines. A near-fine jacketed set can be had today for $1,000/£600 to $1,200/£800. Buyers should be careful to avoid jackets that state 'second impression' on the lower left corner of the front flap, or flaps where this has been cut away. Without jackets, the first three volumes are almost always 'faded as usual'; such sets, otherwise fine, command only in the realm of $300/£180. Sets including later impressions cost somewhat less. There is not much demand for the plainer, variant purple binding, although this is less susceptible to fading.

Churchill was immensely proud of *Marlborough* and inscribed many copies for his friends and colleagues (including some of his most strident political opponents). Enormous prices have been demanded and sometimes realised for inscriptions with good associations, such as Baldwin or Chamberlain; the value of such copies depends heavily on that association, and collectors should be reticent about spending sums like $20,000 /£12,000 (a recent asking price) for a set inscribed to an individual of no importance.

Signed Limited Edition: Woods A40a

Publisher: George G. Harrap & Co. Ltd., London, 1933–38

Four volumes

The only signed trade edition in the Churchill canon and one of only two publisher's leatherbound first editions (the other is presentation binding of *The Second World War*) this consists of 155 four-volume sets sold by advance subscription. The binding (by Leighton Straker Ltd., not Sangorski and Sutcliffe, as Woods states) is orange morocco, elaborately trimmed with five raised spine bands decorated with gilt, marbled endpapers and a tipped-in page signed by the author. Each book had an acetate dust jacket and came in a grey cardboard slipcase with paper labels, the

Copy no. 65 of the limited edition *Marlborough* bound in full orange leather by Leighton Sraker Ltd.
Churchill's signature and the number appear on a cancel in Volume I. Only 155 were produced: the only
signed edition in the canon. *(Photo: David Mayou)*

first of which bears the number of the set. A total of 150 sets were numbered (1)-150, but 155 sets were produced. In one of the latter which has surfaced, the word 'special' (possibly in Churchill's hand) appears in the number space; another carries the word 'presentation', but not in Churchill's hand. (Blenheim Palace's copy is number 15.) Thicker pages mean volumes bulk thicker than trade editions.

Clearly this is the most desirable of the first editions, and I believe most of the 155 copies have survived. For years a fine set (most have been well cared for) commanded $7,500/£4,500 almost every time, but lately prices have begun to gallop up to over $10,000/£6,000, especially when the original slipcases are still intact. Yet 20 years ago the sets could be had for a quarter that much or less. Such a rise in value suggests that this set remains a solid investment.

First Edition, Canadian Issue: ICS A40ac

Publisher: Ryerson Press, Toronto, 1933–38

Four volumes

The Canadian issue is internally identical to the British but bound in cheaper, plain unbevelled purple cloth boards without the Marlborough Arms, blocked gilt on spine only. Top page ends are purple (Vols I-III) or gilt (Vol. IV). Jackets are similar to the British but do not contain a price on the front flap.

Volumes I–III and jackets bear the imprint 'RYERSON PRESS'. Volume IV bears 'HARRAP' imprints but is bound uniformly with the previous Canadian volumes. Except among advanced collectors there is less demand for this variation and prices run about 20 per cent lower than the First American edition, conditions being equal. Conversely, the Canadian issue is more attainable; you could own a jacketed set of this first edition for as little as $500/£300.

First American Edition: Woods A40b

Publisher: Charles Scribners Sons, New York, 1933–38

Six volumes

Emerald green cloth, blocked gilt on spine, 8vo. Vols. I and II published 1933 at $6 the pair; Vol. I, 320 pages numbered (i)–(vi) and (1)–311 (+3); Vol. II, 312 pages numbered (1)–311 (+1). Vols. III and IV published 1935 at $6 the pair; Vol. III, 368 pages numbered (1)–364 (+4); Vol. IV, 296 pages numbered (1)–296. Vol. V published 1937 at $3, 612 pages numbered (i)–(ii) and (1)–608 (+2). Vol. VI published 1938 at $3, 672 pages numbered (1)–670 (+2). All volumes variously illustrated with portraits, maps, plans and facsimiles. Spines are lettered 'MARLBOROUGH | HIS LIFE | AND TIMES' | [dates of the volume] | (line) | 'WINSTON S. | CHURCHILL' (space) 'VOL. [I–VI]' and, at the bottom, 'SCRIBNERS'. A double gilt line is blocked at top and bottom of each spine. Dates of the volumes are I, 1650–1688; II 1688–1702; III, 1702–1704; IV 1704–1705; V 1705–1708; VI 1708–1722.

The first American *Marlborough* as originally issued, with Volumes 1/II and III/IV (equivalent to the British Volumes I and II) slipcased and with plain dust jackets, Volume V (= British Volume III) in a red, black and white jacket, and Volume VI (= British Volume IV) in a blue and gold jacket. *(Photo: Patrick Powers)*

EDITIONS, IMPRESSIONS AND QUANTITIES

Scribners opted to divide the British Volumes I and II into four volumes, labelled I–IV; Volumes V–VI contain the same contents as the British Volumes III and IV. There was only one impression of each volume before the Second World War. Volumes I and II, at least, were reprinted in 1946 and 1950.

Identifying first editions: All first editions carry the letter 'A' beneath the 'all rights reserved' paragraph on the verso of the title page. The 1946 and 1950 reprints carry these dates on their title pages, and no 'A' on their versos. The reprints are printed on thinner paper and thus bulk thinner.

DUST JACKETS AND SLIPCASES

Volumes I and II were originally wrapped in plain white dust jackets with the spine titles printed green, and sold as a pair in a white illustrated slipcase printed green and black. Volumes III and IV were treated similarly, their slipcase printed blue and black. Volume V was sold singly, in an illustrated white dust jacket printed red and black. Volume VI was sold singly in a blue and gold dust jacket. After all six volumes were published, Scribners applied the blue and gold dust jackets to each and sold them for $16.50 as a set, boxed in a dark green slipcase. Jackets for the 1946 and 1950 reprints were blue and gold on the front

After the final volume, Scribners jacketed all *Marlboroughs* in blue and gold and sold them as a slipcased set. *(Photo: Wallace Johnson)*

face but blank on the flaps and back face, lending credence to the thought that only Volumes I and II were reprinted, to make up some sets, originals of Volumes III–VI being in good supply.

VARIANTS

None noted. In a boxed six-volume set I have found a 3 x 5in white card printed 'With the Compliments of the Author', but no volumes are inscribed; sets with the card were probably sent to a number of American recipients on behalf of Churchill.

COMMENTS

The Scribners set is nicely presented and the earlier volumes are easier to read than their bulky British cousins, but the binding is workaday with none of the special touches of George Harrap. As a result, collectors desiring only one first edition usually prefer the British. Like all multi-volume works, the first volumes sold best, and Scribners Volumes I and II are quite common. Volumes III and IV are less common, and Volumes V and VI are scarce. Collectors who quickly find the first two volumes may wait a long time before completing their Scribners sets.

APPRAISAL

Despite the greater popularity of the British edition, the First American sells for a high price, especially in its 'first state' (slipcases and original dust jackets) or when boxed in its 'second state' (one slipcase, uniform blue and gold jackets). Such sets command up to $1,200/£800 on today's market. Unjacketed sets bring half that in fine condition, but the spine gilt tarnishes easily, and 'as-usual' sets with dulled spine lettering sell for up to $300/£180. Odd Volumes I and II cost only a few dollars or pounds; the rest sell for much more because the later volumes are much scarcer, and hoarded by dealers trying to make up sets. I would assume that the post-war reprints would sell for less, but in 15 years as a Churchill bookseller I have never encountered these in a complete six-volume set.

BLENHEIM (First Derivative Edition), Woods A40c
Publisher: Publisher's Guild/Harrap, London, 1941

Paperback, 128 pages, illustrated with maps and plans, number 2 in the Guild Books Series, bound in paper wrappers printed orange (not red as per Woods) and black, 16mo. Published February 1941 at sixpence; 64,750 copies were sold in four impressions. Woods misclassified this paperback extract, which really belonged in his reprints section, but it is mentioned here for followers of Woods. Its subject, of course, is the Battle of Blenheim, which Churchill recounts in majestic style. Copies still sell for only a few dollars or pounds; the exceptional pristine copy, with insignificant wear, may however cost up to $75/£45.

'Limited Presentation Edition', ICS A40ad
Publisher: George G. Harrap & Co. Ltd., London, 1939

Four volumes

In 1938 Harrap were confronted with the same overstock of volumes as Scribners. Scribners boxed and rejacketed their original volumes, Harrap produced what its jackets proclaim was a 'Limited Presentation Edition', reprinting the 1934 second edition of Volume I to replenish that volume, and rebinding all the volumes in medium purple cloth blocked silver on spines only. Jackets are distinctively printed in black and orange on cream stock. Unjacketed copies can quickly be identified by their spine designations: one to four stars instead of volume numbers. The first two volumes being reprints, this is not a first edition, and the only thing that limited it was the size of Harrap's stock. Fine jacketed sets nevertheless bring several hundred dollars and up to £250; ordinary, unjacketed sets should not cost more than $100/£60. Bindings fade easily, bleaching almost white. Collectors fortunate enough to own an unfaded set should take care to keep the volumes away from sun or artificial light.

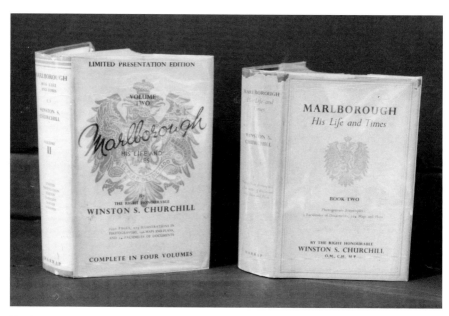

Two later and more affordable *Marlboroughs*. Left, one of the four-volume 'Limited Presentation Edition', which should not be confused with the signed limited edition (page 168): this was merely a rebinding in purple cloth of leftover sheets, and some sheets were reprinted to make up the sets. Right: one of the post-war two-volume editions, combining the complete text (and many corrections by the author) into two volumes using thinner paper and smaller type.

Two-Volume Edition, Woods A40d
Publisher: George G. Harrap & Co. Ltd., London, 1947

Two volumes

After the war, paper restrictions forced Harrap to reconfigure *Marlborough* into a two volume edition, labelled 'Book One' [1650–1705] and 'Book Two' [1705–1722] on the spine and jackets. They comprise 1052 and 1080 pages respectively and were always sold as a pair. There were seven impressions: 1947/49/55/58/63/66/69, the last two reprinted by photo-lithography. Identifying first editions: The original states on its title-page verso: 'This edition in two Books first published 1947'; later impressions are so indicated in this space. The 1947 dust jacket is distinct, printed on very thin paper with a blurb for BBC's *The Listener* on the back flap and the Harrap prancing horse logo worked into a multi-ruled design on the back face.

Only the 1947 first edition has value, selling for up to $300/£180 in fine condition with near-fine dust jackets. Unjacketed copies plummet in value and even fine jacketed reprints rarely cost more than $200/£120–usually much less.

Note: The publisher issued a handful of 1947 first impressions in leather presentation bindings, worth about double the value of a normal binding.

First Paperback Edition, ICS A40e
Publisher: Sphere Books, London, 1967

Four volumes

The cheapest version of the complete text was published in four white-wrapped volumes, boxed in a cream slipcase printed sepia. A second impression was boxed in a multicolour slipcase, and in a third impression the wrappers were changed to a different colour for each. This unabridged set should not be mistaken with the Scribners four-volume paperbacks, which are abridged. Not often seen, the sets have become valuable with the rise in price of hardbound volumes. Typical prices in fine condition with the slipcase: $50/£30.

Abridged Edition, ICS A40f/g
Publisher: Charles Scribners Sons, New York, 1968

One volume hardbound, four volumes paperback

Scribners applied an introduction by Henry Steele Commager, who controversially edited this extensively abbreviated edition, leaving in most of the soldiering while trimming much of the politics. The 1,020-page hardback, published March 1968, was bound in black cloth, blocked gilt on the spine, with an illustrated dust jacket printed black, pink and gold on white stock.

Identifying first editions: The verso of the title page contains the Scribners code 'A–3.68[V]'; this edition has seen at least five impressions. Trade Edition jackets have a price on the front flap and a description of the volume on the back face. A book club edition exists, and can be identified by its dust jacket, which repeats the front face illustrations on the back face and carries no price on the front flap.

Later, the text was divided into four volumes (still abridged). My own set is boxed, the slipcase illustrated with scenes from the PBS television series, 'The First Churchills', and each volume contains the verso code 'A–1.71 (C)' that indicated January 1971 publication. The paperbacks may, however, have appeared before 1971. On the secondhand market these volumes are of trifling value: $25/£15 for a fine first issue hardback, less for the paperbacks.

Folio Society Edition, ICS A40h

Publisher: The Folio Society, London, 1991

The most recent appearance of the original four volumes in hardback, this set was completely reset and carried an introduction by Maurice Ashley, Churchill's chief literary assistant during the writing in the 1930s. The most luxurious rendering since the 1930s signed limited edition, it carries colour frontispieces and is bound in maroon buckram elaborately blocked gilt on the cover and spine. Top page edges are stained dark red. The volumes are contained in a maroon buckram slipcase blocked gilt with the Marlborough Arms on two sides. The Folio Society offered this limited edition at $300/£180, with the usual claims that its exclusivity rendered it a prime investment. Although it is a most handsome edition, it remains a reprint, and in my experience readymade collectors' items rarely hold their value. If offered a set today, I should think that half the original price would be about right.

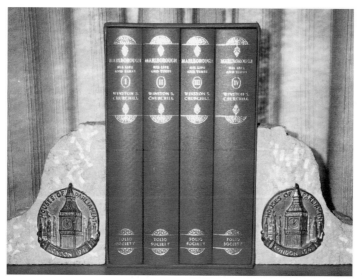

The most recent four-volume hardbound *Marlborough* was produced by the Folio Society in London in 1991, bound in red buckram and slipcased. *(Photo: Douglas Hall)*

FOREIGN TRANSLATIONS

Danish: MARLBOROUGH / OG HANS TID (4 vols)
Published by Hasselbalch: Copenhagen, one volume at a time in 1949, 1950, 1951, 1952. Sold in card wraps with pictorial dust jackets, blue leatherette or maroon leather.

Dutch: MARLBOROUGH / ZIJN LEVEN EN SUN TIJD (4 vols.)
Published by Kroonder: Amsterdam 1947–1948. A particularly desirable foreign edition, this set duplicates in smaller scale the style of the original Harrap Edition, with the Marlborough Arms blocked gilt on top boards, a luxurious red buckram binding, and handsome dust jackets: definitely worth a place in the advanced library.

French: MARLBOROUGH / SA VIE ET SON TEMPS (4 vols.)
Published by Robert Laffont: Paris 1949–1951 in multicolour paperback wrappers.

German: MARLBOROUGH (2 vols.)
First published in purple cloth with white dust jackets by George D. W. Callwey: Munich 1968; the volumes subtitled *Der Weg zum Feldherrn 1650–1705* and *Der Feldherr und Staatsmann 1705–1722*. Second edition published in smaller format by Manesse: Zurich in cloth and dark red leather bindings.

Italian: MARLBOROUGH (2 vols.)
Published by Mondadori: Rome 1968, based on the American Abridged Edition; bound in green leatherette. Republished by Mondadori in 1973 in one volume entitled MARLBOROUGH – LA VITA E I TEMPI DEL DUCA DI FERRO.

Swedish: MARLBOROUGH/ OCH HANS TID (4 vols)
Published by Skoglund: Stockholm 1934–1937 in cloth, half leather and unbound.

Miscellaneous *Marlboroughs*: the four-volume English paperback (left), unlike the American, is *not* abridged but a complete text; the Dutch edition (centre, with and without dust jacket) is a particularly fine presentation; the French edition (right) was issued in paper wrappers.

GREAT CONTEMPORARIES

COHEN A105, WOODS A43

In *Bargaining for Supremacy* (University of California Press, 1977), James R. Leutze accused Churchill of being 'oddly unaware of other people's reactions ... not much interest in others'. That charge has stuck, and rare is the Churchill critic who fails to repeat it. The reader of *Great Contemporaries* will come away with entirely the opposite impression. No one could have written such vivid essays on the great personages of his time without comprehension, understanding and regard for them.

Take for example the Labour Chancellor of the Exchequer, Philip Snowden, with whom Churchill (the preceding Chancellor) hotly debated all the great issues of socialism versus capitalism in the 1930s. After a lengthy account of their antagonisms Churchill adds: ' ... never have I had any feelings towards him which destroyed the impression that he was a generous, true-hearted man ... the British Democracy should be proud of Philip Snowden'. A generous tribute–and typical.

Of the 25 personalities eventually described (the 1938 Revised Edition added four to the original 21), 16 are British. With the exception of four military figures and an eclectic threesome (Shaw, George V, Baden-Powell) all of these represent the cultured, urbane British political leadership of the late nineteenth and early twentieth centuries. Three of them–Balfour, Rosebery, Asquith–had been Prime Ministers. Several of the others had wished to be, including Lord Curzon, for whom Churchill reserves some of his most penetrating and witty prose:

'Here was a being gifted far beyond the average level: equipped and caparisoned with glittering treasures of mind and fortune; driven forward by will, courage and tireless industry; not specially crossed by ill luck; not denied a considerable span: and yet who failed to achieve the central purpose of his life. Why did he fail, and how did he fail? ... Surely in this limited sphere no inquiry could be more rich in instruction.'

In 1923, Arthur Balfour had prevented Curzon from being named Prime Minister by leaving a sick-bed for the Palace, where he convinced the King that a Premier needed to come from the House of Commons. Churchill writes: 'When late that night Balfour returned to his sick-bed ... he was asked by some of his most cherished friends who were staying with him, "And will dear George be chosen?" "No", he replied placidly, "dear George will not"'.

Churchill concludes this sketch of 'a long and strenuous career with ultimate disappointment' with a magnanimous epitaph few would object to: 'The morning had been golden; the noontide was bronze; and the evening lead. But all were solid, and each was polished till it shone after its fashion.'

The same penetrating evaluation, humour and understanding permeates the sketches of those outside politics: King George V, Baden-Powell, George Bernard Shaw (a classic essay) and the four military figures, Generals Haig and French, Admiral Fisher and Lawrence of Arabia. Lawrence was always a romantic hero to Churchill, who failed to enlist his further efforts after Lawrence had helped him create modern Iraq and Jordan at the 1921 Cairo Conference: 'All you will see of me', Lawrence told Churchill, 'is a small cloud of dust on the horizon'.

There are nine foreigners: three German/Austrian (the ex-Kaiser, Hindenburg and Hitler); two Russians (Savinkov and Trotsky, one executed, one about to be); Spain's King Alfonso XIII, America's Roosevelt, and the two greatest Frenchmen of the age, Foch and Clemenceau. (The latter inspired a famous peroration when he told Churchill in the midst of the First World War, 'I will fight in Paris, I will fight behind Paris ... ') The Hitler essay, recently quoted out of context by revisionists anxious to suggest that Churchill once approved of Hitler, was actually thought too belligerent by a Foreign Office colleague, who recommended it be dropped–Churchill ignored him. Of Roosevelt, whom he did not then know, Churchill is respectful, but dubious about the New Deal: 'Is it better to have equality at the price of poverty or well-being at the price of inequality?' (This is hardly an out-of-date question). Our author was also judicious, quickly trimming his Russian essays from an edition published after Stalin became Britain's ally, and his Roosevelt piece shortly after meeting FDR. (But all three were right back in the mix again after the war!)

FROM THE REVIEWS

'This book is about mankind and about a few prominent men–great, evil, stupid, silly, wise. Occasionally the dark stream of melancholy which is part of Churchill's being is revealed, as when by the bedside of the dying Balfour he reflects on "the tragedy which robs the world of all the wisdom and treasure gathered in a great man's life and experience, and hands the lamp to some impetuous and untutored stripling, or lets it fall shivered into fragments on the ground". Of course this also applies to ordinary mortals–people unknown who will inherit no known grave– though Churchill does not say so.

'There runs through all the pieces an overriding cordiality and liking for the subject, for Churchill was not a hater. Only once, over Hitler, would he be totally unforgiving. While recognising its failures and foolishness he retained compassion, and hope for mankind. He was never cynical. His judgements are of justice, tempered with magnanimity.

'The book is also about Churchill as he sees himself, with the personalities which shaped his judgements and character. He outlines the debt he owes, the knowledge gained, from observing their qualities and defects. At this distance we see him absorbing those lessons of leadership for the moment when he was to become Prime Minister of a nation alone, at its most solemn hour.'

H. Ashley Redburn in *Finest Hour #36*, Summer 1982

First Edition: Woods A43(a)
Publisher: Thornton Butterworth Ltd., London, 1937

Dark blue cloth. The top board bears the title and author's name blocked gilt and the publisher's device and two thick rules at top and bottom debossed blind. Top page edges stained dark blue. The spine bears the same material as on the cover (but no logo) and 'THORNTON | BUTTERWORTH' gilt at the bottom. 8vo, 336 pages numbered (1)–335 (+1), with 21 tipped-in illustrations and a 5-page index. The verso of the half-title contains a list of 16 of the author's other works. Endpapers are white. Published 4 October 1937 at 21s. ($5.25).

IMPRESSIONS AND QUANTITIES
Six impressions occurred, which the volumes themselves date as September (2), October (2), November and December 1937. Woods's dates, which he told me were taken from publisher records, were October (3), November and December (2). The first impression had 5,000 copies; the next five impressions had 2,000 each for a total of 15,000. Identifying first editions: title page verso contains the line, 'first published ... 1937' with no further reprints indicated.

VARIANTS
I have encountered a copy in which the footnote in the Bernard Shaw essay, page

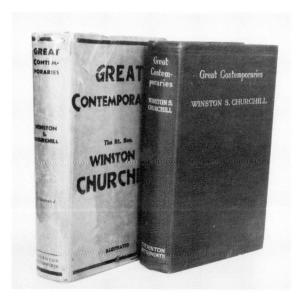

First editions of *Great Contemporaries*. The dust jacket is printed black on orange paper, the binding is dark blue cloth. Second impression jackets are the same as firsts, but starting with the third impression, jacket-flap copy differs.

57 ('Alas we laughed too soon') is preceded by the sentence: 'Written in 1929'. This book was otherwise conventional, the leaf appeared integral with the other pages. I have never seen another example.

First Edition sheets were bound cheaply by the Times Book Club in smooth navy cloth, crudely blocked on spine only: 'GREAT | CONTEM- | PORARIES' then 'WINSTON S. | CHURCHILL' and, at the foot, 'BUTTERWORTH'. They carry the typical TBC small gold on black paper label on rear pastedowns.

A short, narrow variant exists in dark blue, rough cloth, with block spine lettering omitting "THORNTON" and a jacket trimmed to fit: perhaps a salesman's ("traveller's") copy. Canadian jackets may also exist with sterling prices obliterated.

DUST JACKETS

Jackets are printed black on light orange paper. The first and second impression dust jackets are identical: book blurb and list of chapters on front flap. Commencing with the third impression, front jacket flaps began to quote book reviews. Later jackets occasionally crop up on first editions, a combination devoutly to be avoided.

COMMENTS

Great Contemporaries is a straightforward production with no variants or states (except for the oddly printed page 57 in one example). It is, of course, an important part of the canon and belongs in every library, where it will be read and referred to regularly. Many of the situations confronted by its cast of characters are not unknown more than sixty years on. The characters themselves are intrinsically interesting; the book is avidly sought after, for example, by students of T. E. Lawrence (and well it should be, for the Lawrence essay is a gem).

APPRAISAL

Fine jacketed copies sell today for $500/£300 or up to double that; although by shopping around you stand a good chance to finding one at the lower figure. Lesser examples in dirty jackets cost as little as $300/£180, fine unjacketed copies up to $250/£150. The price of the typical very good, somewhat worn but sound first edition was $100/£60 15 years ago and is the same today. Reprints (all first edition look-alikes) should not cost more than $50/£30 unless in jackets, in which case double that price.

First American Edition: ICS A43ab

Publisher: G. P. Putnam's Sons, New York, 1937

Dark blue cloth blocked silver and red. The top board bears the title in silver on a ⅜-inch high red band near the top; five similar red bands appear on the spine reading 'GREAT | CONTEMPORARIES | [decorative device] | CHURCHILL' toward the top and 'PUTNAM' toward the bottom. Top page edges stained red. 8vo, 312

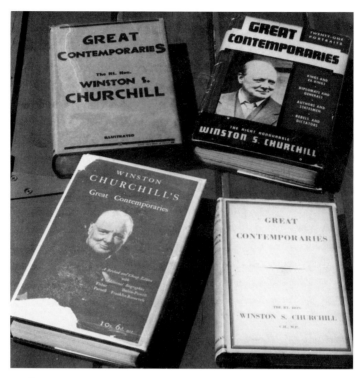

A collection of *Great Contemporaries*. Top: the first English and American editions.
Bottom, the 1938 revised and extended edition (very rare in dust jacket) and the
Macmillan edition from 1942.

pages numbered (+2) (i)–(x) and (1)–300, with 21 tipped-in illustrations and a 7-
page index. Endpapers are white. Published October 1937 at $4.

IMPRESSIONS
Three impressions are known. Identifying first editions: title-page verso contains
no indication of a later impression.

VARIANTS
Some books exist with unstained top page edges. Some later impression sheets are
rumoured to have been bound in red-orange cases blocked blue and silver on spines
only, instead of the style described above, I have never seen one.

DUST JACKETS
Printed black and dark blue on white paper, with an illustration of the author
(outside Chartwell, wearing his 'at home' style four-in-hand tie) on the front face.
First edition jackets may differ from those on later impressions. They contain excerpts
from the book on Shaw, Trotsky and Lawrence (front flap); Lawrence (continuation)

and Savinkov (back flap), and a three-paragraph promotional blurb on the back face.

Later impression dust jackets contain alterations to the back face: a new subtitle ('THE NEW NON-FICTION BEST SELLER'), with the third paragraph of the original promotion blurb replaced by two paragraphs of review excerpts from *The New York Times* and the *Boston Herald*. (Although I have seen this jacket wrapped around a first edition, with no evidence that it had been 'married', I strongly doubt that it belongs there, though the publisher or dealer might have replaced a defective original jacket when it was new.)

COMMENTS

Woods failed to mention the American edition of *Great Contemporaries,* an elegant production which was entirely reset and edited with American spelling ('fiber' for 'fibre', 'color' for 'colour', etc.) The type style and leading make for a more readable book; its wider, taller size and more interesting dust jacket make it aesthetically superior to the English edition. The two reprints must have been small; I have never seen either, and rely for descriptions on notes from their owners. Interestingly, the American edition was never updated with the four additional articles added in 1938.

APPRAISAL

Prices for the American edition have never rivalled those of the English, possibly because (thanks to Woods) many collectors don't know it exists. The binding was of high quality so fine, unjacketed copies are readily available, but the dust jacket was likely to chip, and a really clean jacket is a rarity. Such a jacket wrapped around an equally fine book could command $600/£360, but more worn jacketed copies run only two-thirds as high, and near-fine unjacketed copies cost only about

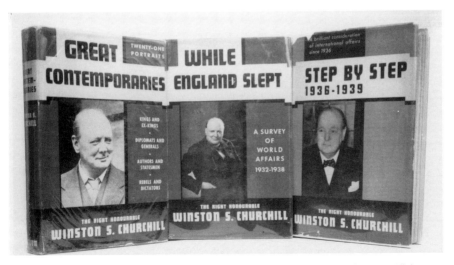

Putnam followed their *Great Contemporaries* with two other titles (see next two chapters). All three were uniformly bound and jacketed, but the jackets were printed respectively, blue, red and green.

$50/£30. Of the four Churchill works published by Putnam between 1937 and 1941, this is the hardest to find in a dust jacket.

Revised, Extended Edition: Woods A43(b)
Publisher: Thornton Butterworth Ltd., London, 1938

Navy blue cloth. The top board bears the title and author's name blocked gilt and the publisher's device and two thick rules at top and bottom debossed blind. Top page edges unstained. The spine bears the same material as on the cover (but no logo) and 'THORNTON | BUTTERWORTH' gilt at the bottom. 8vo, 388 pages numbered (1)–(387), (1), with 25 tipped-in illustrations and a 5-page index. The verso of the half-title contains a list of 17 of the author's other works. Endpapers are white. Published 7 November 1938 at 10s. 6d. ($2.63).

IMPRESSIONS AND QUANTITIES
There were two impressions, the second in May 1940 according to the volume. Woods says August 1939, the only explanation for which is that the issue was held up with the outbreak of war, and hastened into publication when Churchill became Prime Minister. This theory is supported by Woods's figures for press runs: 5,000 for the first, 28,000 for the second. The second impression bears the publisher's Keystone Library logo on its title page.

VARIANTS
A distinct variation of the first impression exists printed on much thicker paper and bulking a full 2 inches instead of the usual 1¾.

DUST JACKETS
Jackets of the standard first edition are printed blue and black on white paper. The face bears a photo of the author printed blue and the title, 'WINSTON CHURCHILL'S Great Contemporaries', proclaiming itself 'A Revised and Cheap Edition with 4 Additional Biographies', which it names. Type is dropped out white. The spine contains similar information but the correct title above '(Revised Edition)'. The front flap promotes this edition, the back flap the Keystone Library; four additional books and '10/6' are on spine, reviews blurbs are on back face.

The variant binding carries a white dust jacket without a photograph. The 1940 second impression is reported with a Keystone Library style dust jacket; whether this is original to the book I am unable to confirm.

COMMENTS
Churchill added four essays to this edition, on Parnell, Baden-Powell, Roosevelt and Fisher. The latter *(Lord Fisher and his Biographer)* is really a review of Admiral Bacon's anti-Churchill Fisher biography. Our author is also circumspect with regard

to Roosevelt, entitling that chapter 'Roosevelt from Afar', perhaps to suggest that Churchill was not close enough to pronounce definitively on Roosevelt's domestic policies (which he generally abhorred at the time). This edition, or some later version of it, belongs in every Churchill library for the extra material.

APPRAISAL

Highly prized for its four additional essays, the Revised is a rather uncommon edition, and the extra-thick variant is a real rarity. Jackets border on the unknown; I have seen five in 15 years. As a result, the Revised commands more than the first edition: up to $1,000/£600 for a fine copy in a whole dust jacket. Any jacket, however incomplete, is prized, but poorer condition lowers the price. The book itself doesn't wear well, and unjacketed copies invariably show dulled gilt; these sell for much less, $50-100/£30-60. Second impressions, despite Woods's high press run figure, show up less often, are worth a little less.

Reader's Union Edition: ICS A43c
Publisher: Reader's Union Ltd. & Thornton Butterworth Ltd., London, 1939

Light blue cloth blocked maroon (triple wavy line, title and facsimile signature on top board, 'Churchill's GREAT CONTEMPORARIES' on spine, reading up). 8vo, 388

Left: the Reader's Union edition in blue cloth blocked maroon; right: the French edition published by Gallimard in Paris just before the start of the Second World War.

pages numbered (1)–387 (+1), with 25 illustrations in two gatherings between pages 126–127 and 254–255 and a 5-page index. Half-title verso contains a list of 17 of the author's other works; title page verso explains this edition. No endpapers. Published at 2s. 6d. (63¢). Variants: Various shades of blue cloth are reported.

This book club production from the Revised, Extended Edition sheets (trimmed slightly, but type not reduced) was an excellent value, giving all that the latter gave at one-fifth the price. Entirely unmentioned by Woods, it was the last pre-war edition with all 25 of Churchill's essays intact. There was probably no dust jacket. Market value incidental, though $50/£30 for an exceptionally fine copy would be worth paying.

Reprint Society Edition: ICS A43d
Publisher: Reprint Society Ltd., London, 1941

Cream buckram with brown leatherette spine label containing the title and author's name inside a decorative double border. 16mo, 352 pages numbered (i)–(viii) and (1)–344, with eight pages of photographs on coated paper grouped between pages (viii) and (1). Dust jacket printed dark brown on thin white stock; spine and front face have a repeat pattern of light green wreaths on a faint lilac background. Published at 3s. 6d. (88¢).

Another book club edition, containing only 23 essays: the Soviet Union was now in the war, and Churchill thought it judicious to excise his essays on Savinkov and Trotsky, both by then murdered by Stalin. The Hitler chapter, considering all that had happened, was retitled 'Hitler and His Choice, 1935'. With wartime paper restrictions in place, this volume measures only 5 x 7½in. Its chief importance to the collector lies in its use of different photos (15 of the protagonists, plus one of the author). Value incidental, except for fine jacketed copies which are worth up to $100/£60.

World Books Issue: ICS A43e
Publisher: Reprint Society Ltd., London, 1941

Tan cloth blocked maroon on top board (title) and spine (title), decorative mark, author name and World Books logo. Contents identical to the Reprint Society Edition. Dust jacket printed green on thin white stock with wreath pattern identical to the above. Published at 2s. 6d. (63¢).

World Books, in Reigate, Surrey, was another outlet for the Reprint Society with an even more generous discount pricing policy.

Note: Although both Reprint Society variations contain a note that they were published 'by arrangement with Macmillan & Co. Ltd.', both carry 1941 dates while the first Macmillan Edition carries 1942; therefore their place in the order.

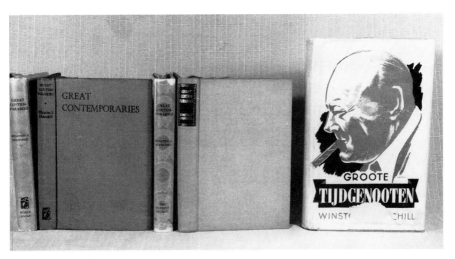

Left: The World Books and centre: Reprint Society *Great Contemporaries*, shown with and without their dust jackets; right: the handsomely jacketed Dutch edition.

Macmillan Issue: ICS A43f

Publisher: Macmillan & Co. Ltd., London, 1942

Black cloth blocked gilt on spine (title, author name, publisher name). 16mo, 294 pages numbered (i)–(vi) and (1)–287 (+1). No illustrations. Dust jacket printed black and red on heavy off-white paper. Published 1942 (not '1943' per Woods) at 8s. 6d. ($2.13). Second impression, 1943.

The product of wartime inflation? Macmillan first published *Great Contemporaries* in 1942, using the same plates that had produced the two book club editions immediately preceding, but taking further economy measures: dropping the individual title pages for each entry, dropping the photo section and (since America was now an ally, dropping that diffident chapter on Franklin Roosevelt). The result saved almost 60 pages. Although slightly taller and wider than the Reprint Society's production, the Macmillan Edition has no aesthetic significance, and is important only to illustrate the political exigencies of the time.

VARIANT DUST JACKET
The decision to excise Roosevelt must have come at the last moment, because the first state Macmillan dust jacket fails to omit him from the front flap copy. (The back face of this jacket promotes *Great Contemporaries* among three other Churchill works published by Macmillan.) The second state jacket omits Roosevelt from the front flap. (The back face replaces the blurb for *Great Contemporaries* with one for *Thoughts and Adventures*.) There is no difference in the books themselves. Curiously, the first state jacket does appear on some second impressions as well as firsts.

Odhams Edition: ICS A43g

Publisher: Odhams & Co. Ltd., London, 1947

8vo, 320 pages numbered (i)–(x) and (1)–309 (+1) with 16 pages of photographs between pages viii and ix. Four impressions: 1947, 1948 (2), 1949. Completely reset, the Odhams Edition includes a frontispiece and eight illustrations between pages viii and ix, and the former folding map was now printed over a double page spread. Later impressions have been reported, but I have not seen any. (Odhams offered this title in 1954 to buyers of Malcolm Thompson's *Churchill: His Life and Times*, under the general series title, 'The People's Home Library'.)

There were two Odhams bindings: standard bright red cloth blocked gilt and black on top board and spine, page edges unstained; deluxe red leatherette with author signature blocked gilt on top board and black leather title/author label on spine combined with multiple devices, rules and the Odhams name, also gilt, page edges stained red. Dust jackets printed black, yellow and dark yellow on white paper. The first impression is identified on the verso of its title page by no date beyond 1947 and the code 'S.947Q'.

Odhams was a mail order bookseller, which helps explain the lack of prices on dust jackets. Deluxe bindings of first four impressions were shipped in grey cardboard boxes with *Step by Step, My Early Life* and *Thoughts and Adventures* at 32s. ($6.40) post-paid to mail order clients.

Odhams published all 25 of Churchill's sketches from the 1938 Revised, Extended Edition; the books are plentiful and of incidental value, although the first impression is quite rare. The only distinctive feature of this edition is a number of new photographs.

Fontana Paperback Edition: ICS A43h

Publisher: Collins Fontana, London, 1959

The first paperback was published in 1959 at 5s. (70¢), and at least four impressions followed through 1972, when it sold for 45p. The text was reset for this edition though curiously, Fontana used the Odhams foreword with its 1947 dating. Sixteen pages of photographs, some new to the work, were incorporated on coated paper; in later editions these were divided into two gatherings of eight pages each. Trifling value: the cheapest way to read the full text.

Books for Libraries Issue: ICS A43i

Publisher: Books for Libraries, New York, 1972

A reprint edition published in hardback, listed in contemporary editions of Books in Print. Issued without dust jacket.

University of Chicago Edition: ICS A43j

Publisher: University of Chicago Press, Illinois, 1974

Published in both cloth and paperback on 12 February 1974 at $7.95 in hardback, $4.95 in paperback; at least two impressions. The hardback's dust jacket and the paperback's cover carry the famous Karsh 'growling lion' photograph from 1941. Offprinted from the 1938 Revised, Extended Edition, including muddy reproductions of the original tipped-in photographs. By eliminating the blank pages (versos of essay titles, versos of photographs), the publishers were able to retain the original pagination.

The New Edition, 1990

The last of seven new trade editions produced by Leo Cooper (five issued by Norton in the USA) had two hardback and one paperback issue(s). Features common to all issues are as follows: text photographically reproduced from the *Collected Works*, (see Appendix); new foreword by Tom Hartman (in addition to the author's original Preface); see Appendix on The Churchill Center.

First New Edition: ICS A43ka

Publisher: Leo Cooper, London, 1990

Black cloth, blocked gilt on spine, offprinted from the *Collected Works* 1974 edition. 270 pages numbered (i)–(xii) and (1)–252 (+6). Eight pages of photographs (some new to the title) on glossy stock between pages 84–85, 116–117, 148–149 and 180–181. Pages (ix)–(xi) contain a new foreword by Tom Hartman, pages 251–252 contain a note on the International Churchill Society, which collaborated in the reprint. The dust jacket is printed black, green and red on white paper with the titles dropped out. Published at £16.95.

New American Issue: ICS A43kb

Publisher: W. W. Norton & Co., New York, 1991

Grey cloth stamped gilt on spine, plain boards with 'WSC' debossed blind. 264 pages numbered (I)–(xii) and (1)–252. 8vo, sold at $22.50. White dust jacket printed purple, gold and black, photo of author c. 1910 on front face. One impression, no known variations.

New Paperback Issue: ICS A43kc

Publisher: Mandarin Paperbacks, London, 1991

Photographically reproduced (reduced) from the Cooper Edition, this (5 x 7¾in) paperback was published at £5.99.

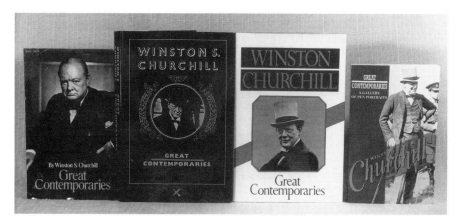

More modern issues of *Great Contemporaries*. Left to right: the University of Chicago, Cooper, Norton and Mandarin issues.

FOREIGN TRANSLATIONS

Dutch: GROOTE TIJDGENOOTEN
Published by Universum-Editie: 1937; blue cloth, white dust jacket printed orange and black. A second edition was published by Jedes: Amsterdam (no date).

French: LES GRANDS CONTEMPORAINS
Published by Gallimard: Paris, 1939. Card wrappers printed brown and navy.

German: GROSSE ZEITGENOSSEN
Published by Allert De Lange: Amsterdam, 1938 (German text, not Dutch, black cloth). A much abbreviated paperback second edition (containing only Rosebery, Chamberlain, Balfour, Asquith, Parnell, Curzon, Shaw, Lawrence, Fisher, Clemenceau, the Kaiser, Alfonso XIII and George V) was published by Fischer Bücherei: Frankfurt & Hamburg 1959.

Hebrew: GADAULE HADOR
Printed and published in Palestine.

Norwegian: STORE SAMTIDIGE
Published by Cappelens: Oslo, 1938 in card wrappers and in yellow cloth. Contains only Shaw, Chamberlain, French, Savinkov, Asquith, Lawrence, Birkenhead, Foch, Haig, Balfour, Curzon, Snowden, Clemenceau and George V.

Portuguese: GRANDES HOMENS CONTEMPORANEOS
Published by Companhia Editora Nacional: Rio de Janeiro, Brazil, 1941. Black cloth.

Spanish: GRANDES CONTEMPORANEOS
Published by Los Libros de Nuestro Tiempo: Barcelona, 1943. A paperback edition was published by Plaza & Janes, 1960.

Swedish: STORA SAMTIDA
Published by Skoglund: Stockholm 1937–1954 in several impressions. The first edition is much thicker than its successor and was offered unbound or bound in blue cloth, both in jackets. The first edition jacket is white printed orange and black. An expanded edition was published in 1954. A Swedish edition was also published in Helsinki, Finland, Swedish being Finland's second language.

Combined Work: CHURCHILL ON MEN AND EVENTS, Cohen A269
Subtitled: *A Selection from 'Thoughts and Adventures' and 'Great Contemporaries' made by Andrew Scotland, M.A., Ph.D.,* this work was published by Ginn & Company Ltd., London, 1965. So far as I am aware, it is the only work to combine chapters from both of Churchill's mid-Thirties collections of essays. Frontispiece has a drawing of T. E. Lawrence by Augustus John.

ARMS AND THE COVENANT / WHILE ENGLAND SLEPT

COHEN A107, WOODS A44

'For five years I have talked to the House on these matters–not with very great success. I have watched this famous island descending incontinently, fecklessly, the stairway which leads to a dark gulf. It is a fine broad stairway at the beginning, but after a bit the carpet ends. A little farther on there are only flagstones, and a little farther on still these break beneath your feet ... if mortal catastrophe should overtake the British Nation and the British Empire, historians a thousand years hence will still be baffled by the mystery of our affairs. They will never understand how it was that a victorious nation, with everything in hand, suffered themselves to be brought low, and to cast away all that they had gained by measureless sacrifice and absolute victory–gone with the wind! Now the victors are the vanquished, and those who threw down their arms in the field and sued for an armistice are striding on to world mastery ... We should lay aside every hindrance and endeavour by uniting the whole force and spirit of our people to raise again a great British nation standing up before all the world; for such a nation, rising in its ancient vigour, can even at this hour save civilisation.'

This finest (and most ominous) pre-war warning of Winston Churchill occurs on the penultimate page of *Arms and the Covenant.* It is available in no other Churchill book, for the last four paragraphs of that famous speech on 24 March 1938 are absent from the *Complete Speeches.* Those words summarise the theme of this volume, a precursor to the official theme of *The Gathering Storm:* 'How the English-speaking peoples through their unwisdom, carelessness, and good nature allowed the wicked to rearm.' 'Years later', wrote William Manchester in *The Last Lion,* Volume II (1988), 'the White House revealed that a copy of *While England Slept* ... had lain on President Roosevelt's bedside table, with key passages, including an analysis of the President's peace initiative, underscored'. The 41 speeches, all but two delivered in the Commons, were collected by Churchill's son Randolph, then carefully reviewed and revised by Churchill himself. 'It is common knowledge that Mr Churchill devotes more time than any other modern orator to the preparation of his speeches', said the publisher. Imagine then the keenness and polish of these, having been subjected to Churchill's editing a second time round.

Together they remind me of a concert with three movements: a light, sometimes even humorous beginning ('Germany Disarmed'); a gathering solemnity ('Germany Rearming'); a terrible crescendo ('Germany Armed'), ending in the awful finale of March 1938. Part One begins with Churchill's 1928 'Disarmament Fable': once all the animals agreed to disarm, but the buffalo and stag wished to keep horns as defensive weapons, while the lion and tiger said teeth and claws were ancient and honourable weapons that should also be allowed. The discussion broke up and the animals 'began to look at one another in a very nasty way'. Part Two traces the sad, dreary progress of German rearmament and Britain's refusal, first to see it and later to match it. Part Three recounts the accumulating result of Britain's lethargy: the lagging defence programme, the arrogance of the dictator nations, Eden's resignation as foreign secretary, the Austrian *Anschluss*.

The book appeared well before Munich, a time when prevailing opinion held that Hitler had made his last demands, and few save Churchill insisted otherwise. 'The idea that dictators can be appeased by kind words and minor concessions is doomed to disappointment', he told the League of Nations Union on 2 June. 'Volcanic forces are moving in Europe, and sombre figures are at the head of the most powerful races ... we must stand by the League Covenant, which alone justifies a general rearmament; and on the basis of the Covenant we must unite with other countries desiring freedom and peace.'

Three weeks later, *Arms and the Covenant* was published. The American Edition did not appear until late September, so its publishers had three further months and the Munich pact in which to contemplate a title. They entitled it appropriately: *While England Slept*.

FROM THE REVIEWS

'The vigorous and moving criticism of British international policies which Winston Churchill has been voicing, in Parliament and elsewhere, make up the text of an absorbingly interesting volume ... It could hardly be more timely, for in the immediate past (and unfortunately still in the present) have come about the very threats to Anglo-French peace and freedom which Churchill has been forecasting ... In all this brilliant Englishman's sharp forecasts on China, Spain, Italy, Austria, Czechoslovakia, now become history instead of prophecy, there is absorbing interest. A few years may tell how accurate are his predictions of events which fate has not yet unrolled for our inspection. A really thrilling book. '

The Baltimore Sun, 1938

First Edition: Woods A44(a)
Publisher: George G. Harrap & Co. Ltd., London, 1938

Blue cloth blocked with thin double-line border on top board. Spine blocked gilt with title and author name within a three-line border toward the top and the

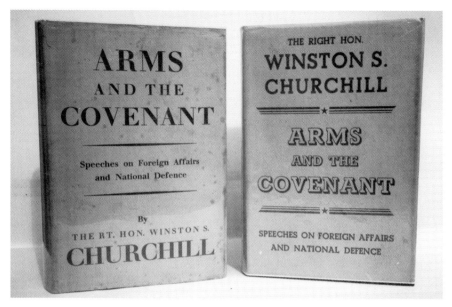

First editions of *Arms and the Covenant* in their two styles of dust jacket. The original (left) is printed dark blue on light blue paper and carries a price of 21s. Remainders were sold at 7s. 6d. with a red-on-yellow jacket so priced (right).

Harrap logo and name toward the bottom. Top page edges stained blue. 8vo, 468 pages numbered (1)–(466), (2), frontispiece (Steichen photo of Churchill) before title page. The verso of the half-title contains a list of 17 of the author's other works. Endpapers are white. Published 24 June 1938 at 18 s. ($4.50).

IMPRESSIONS AND QUANTITIES
A single impression of 5,000 was issued, but not all were sold, and the book was reissued in June 1940 at 7s. 6d. ($1.87). According to Woods, 3,381 were sold at the original price and 1,382 at the lower price, leaving 237 unaccounted for. (Contrary to Woods, there was no Odhams reprint.)

VARIANTS
None encountered.

DUST JACKETS
The original dust jacket is printed dark blue on laid blue paper, carrying the 18s. original price on the front flap. The front face carries the title, author's name and a subtitle 'Speeches on Foreign Affairs and National Defence'. The remainder issue (original binding) is wrapped in a new dust jacket printed red on yellow paper, carrying the 7s. 6d. price.

COMMENTS

Although some collectors insist on acquiring copies in both jackets, the books underneath are uniform throughout. The binding is susceptible to fading and copies should be kept out of direct light. *Arms and the Covenant* holds a special place in the literature as the forerunner to Churchill's classic war speech volumes and really sets the stage for them. Although it is unfortunately not indexed, each speech is preceded by a useful 'Diary of Events' compiled by Randolph Churchill, which helps place the speech in context. It is a shame so few were listening: the *Covenant* had the lowest sale of any Churchill book in the 1930s.

APPRAISAL

Fine blue jacketed copies have been offered for between $750/£450 and $1000/£600 if the jacket is clean and unchipped–being of good stock, it often is. Red and yellow jacketed copies are much rarer and generally cost 10–15 per cent more on the antiquarian market. Fine, unjacketed copies bring up to $250/£150, while 'very good' examples showing some wear can cost up to $150/£90. Readers on a budget would do better to look for the American edition.

First American Edition: Woods A44(b)
Publisher: G. P. Putnam's Sons, New York, 1938

Dark blue cloth blocked silver and red. The top board bears the title in silver on a ⅜-inch high red band near the top; five similar red bands appear on the spine reading 'WHILE | ENGLAND SLEPT | [decorative device] |CHURCHILL' toward the top and 'PUTNAM' toward the bottom. Top page edges stained red. 8vo, 415 pages numbered (i)–(xii) and (1)–404, frontispiece (Steichen photo of Churchill) before title page. The verso of the half-title contains a list of 18 Churchill works (including this one). Endpapers are white. Published 30 September 1938 at $4.

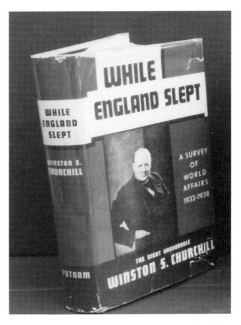

The first American edition with its unique title, *While England Slept*, is printed red and black on white paper.

IMPRESSIONS

Four impressions were issued in the following quantities: 5,000 (September 1938), 2,500 (October 1938), 1,000

(October 1940), 1,000 (September 1941). Identifying first editions: impressions are not individually dated: all title pages contain the 1938 date. However, the title-page verso of first editions contains no indication of a later impression.

VARIANTS

Some books may exist with unstained top page edges. The fourth impression was bound in red-orange cases blocked blue and silver on spines only, instead of the style described above.

DUST JACKETS

Printed black and red on white paper, with the Steichen frontispiece photo on the front face. First edition jackets contain the book description on the front flap, three English review excerpts on the back flap, and a description of *Great Contemporaries* on the back face. The second impression jacket is identical while the third impression advertises *Rufus Isaac First Marquess of Reading* on the back flap and *The Voice of Destruction* on the rear face. The fourth impression jacket contains American review excerpts on the front flap, an advert for *The Reconstruction of Europe* on the back flap, and adverts for three other books including *Churchill's Blood, Sweat, and Tears* on the back face.

COMMENTS

This volume was completely reset with American spelling by the publisher. Although not quite as handsome as Harrap's (who were in a class by themselves for elegant trade bindings), it is nicely produced and uniform with Putnam's *Great Contemporaries; Step by Step;* and *Blood, Sweat, and Tears,* with an interesting dust jacket. The quantity produced, almost double that of the English edition, suggests that the American public was readier to listen to Churchill–but note that the last two impressions came almost two years after the first two. Also, Putnam had the advantage of publishing in the aftermath of Munich, when many outside Britain began to conclude that he had been right all along.

APPRAISAL

Like *Great Contemporaries,* the American edition has never approached the price of the English, although it is encountered infrequently in the dust jacket. The binding was of high quality so fine unjacketed copies are more common; the dust jacket is susceptible to wear and a fine book and jacket might cost $600/£360, but most jacketed copies run less. Near-fine unjacketed copies cost up to $125/£78, but scruffier ones can often be found for half that much. Reprints would cost about half these prices book for book, but their press runs were small and the first edition is most often encountered. *While England Slept* is the most available of only three known editions of this work.

Books for Libraries Issue: ICS A44c
Publisher: Arno Press, Inc., New York, 1971

Purple leatherette blocked gilt on spine only; an offprint of *While England Slept* with identical pagination; the frontispiece is reproduced on regular page stock. This volume was offered at $35 until 1996 by N. W. Ayer, after which it finally, and regrettably, went out of print. It is one of the Churchill titles most in need of a reprint, for it contains many lessons that are not entirely irrelevant to later times.

FOREIGN TRANSLATIONS

Danish: MENS ENGLAND SOV
Published by Gyldendal: Copenhagen, 1939, 4,000 copies unbound in bright orange-red wrappers, priced at 8.75 kr.

Swedish: NÅR ENGLAND SOV
Published by Skoglund: Stockholm, 1938 in cream card wrappers (12.50 kr); or in blue cloth (17.50 kr). Both carried orange, white and black jackets with a quote from Churchill's 7 November 1933 speech.

STEP BY STEP 1936-1939

COHEN A111, WOODS A45

Some think *Step by Step* is another speech book. In fact it comprises 82 newspaper articles, from the German reoccupation of the Rhineland in March 1936 through the Spanish Civil War, the Rome–Berlin–Tokyo Axis, Hitler's absorption of Austria and Czechoslovakia, President Roosevelt's inquiry about what Hitler and Mussolini intended for the States on their borders, to Churchill's May 1939 prediction that Hitler would next attack Poland. Interestingly, Churchill had planned the last article to be 'Will Hitler Make Napoleon's Mistakes?' (first published in *Illustrated,* 4 March 1939, Woods C411/1). At the last moment he substituted 'Turkey's Significance as a Partner in the Peace Bloc' (*Daily Telegraph,* 18 May 1939). Perhaps he didn't wish to give Hitler any helpful hints.

After the events described here, it is a measure of the author that *Step by Step* ends with an upbeat Epilogue: 'Here then, in an hour when all is uncertain, but not uncheered by hope and resolve, this tale stops. Great Britain [is] ready to confront and to endure what may befall. The shock may be sudden, or the strain may be long-drawn: but who can doubt that all will come right if we persevere to the end'. The phrase 'all will come right' had been learnt and remembered by Churchill in its Boer original from the Dutch farmers fighting Britain in South Africa nearly forty years before; it was part of his capacious store of maxims carefully filed in his photographic memory.

Another of his qualities, magnanimity, was more extemporaneous. Of Neville Chamberlain, whom he had fought and debated with repeatedly for two years, Churchill writes: 'Everyone must sympathise with Mr. Chamberlain in his grievous responsibility. No Prime Minister in modern times has had so much personal power to guide affairs. Everything that he has asked of the nation has been granted; and when he has not asked what many thought necessary, no steps have been taken to compel him. There never has been in England such a one-man Government as that under which we have dwelt for the last year. He has taken the whole burden upon himself, and we can only trust that he will not be found unequal to it.'

FROM THE REVIEWS

'Churchill rushed the articles into print in book form almost on the eve of World War II, as though to provide the nation with a tract for the war about to be fought. The ideas and rhetoric are similar to those in his speeches of the period, but because the articles do not treat domestic issues, they show a greater concentration and continuity. In fact, chance has imposed on this work a structure which gives it some of the qualities of an intentionally literary composition. Quickly changing circumstances and unexpected events generate much suspense and excitement; thus, Churchill's joy over France's initial standing by Czechoslovakia is followed in the very next piece, "The Austrian Eye-Opener", by the electric effect on everyone of Hitler's sudden seizure of Austria. This is, in short, solid drama as well as a neat little history of the period.'

Manfred Weidhorn in *Sword and Pen,* 1974

First Edition: Cohen, ICS A45a
Publisher: Thornton Butterworth Ltd., London, 1937

Dark green cloth. Top board stamped blind, publisher's device ranged lower right and two thick rules top and bottom which extend across the spine. Spine blocked gilt with title and author's name at top and publisher's name at bottom. Top page edges unstained. 8vo, 368 pages numbered (1)–(366), (2), one internal map and a folding map of 'Modern Europe' tipped in after page 368. The verso of the half-title contains a list of 18 of the author's works. Endpapers are white. Published 27 June 1939 at 12s. 6d. ($3.13).

IMPRESSIONS AND QUANTITIES
Woods records three impressions: 7,500 in June 1939, 1,500 in November 1939, 1,800 in February 1940; but there was a second impression in June 1939, making four in all. Identifying first editions: title-page verso contains the line, 'first published ... 1939' with no further reprints indicated. Note: a typographical error on page 7 (citing page 252 instead of page 352 for 'After President Roosevelt's Message') persists in all impressions.

VARIANTS
None noted.

DUST JACKETS
Jackets are printed black with lilac decorative borders and rules on heavy cream-white paper: on front flap, book title/author name (top) and price (lower right corner); on back flap, blurb for *Great Contemporaries*; on back face, description of *Step by Step*.

COMMENTS
By the time this work appeared the public was thoroughly aroused, and *Step by Step* enjoyed good sales. As a result, it is not uncommon on the secondhand market today, despite having had only one reprint in the last half century. An important

work, it belongs on the shelf of every Churchill reader. A discerning critic, Professor Manfred Weidhorn, calls it 'enthralling ... journalism at its best'.

APPRAISAL

My own fine jacketed first edition cost $650/£390 ten years ago and would cost more today. The white jacket soils easily, and although it is not rare I seldom see really clean examples. The books hold up better; clean firsts with bright gilt are relatively common; these cost up to $300/£180, but prices drop off quickly as condition worsens, to under $100/£60 for worn examples. Reprints in jackets cost about $100/£60, half as much without jackets, a quarter as much if well-worn.

First American Edition: ICS A45b

Publisher: G. P. Putnam's Sons, New York, 1939

Dark blue cloth blocked silver and red. The top board bears the title in silver on a ⅜-inch high red band near the top; five similar red bands appear on the spine reading 'STEP | BY STEP | [decorative device] |CHURCHILL' toward the top and 'PUTNAM' toward the bottom. Top page edges stained red. 8vo, 336 pages reset and numbered (i)–(xii) and (1)–324, frontispiece Wide World photo of the author opposite title page. Endpapers are white. Published 25 August 1939 at $4.

First editions of *Step by Step*. Left: the English with its white dust jacket, rarely seen this clean. Right: the American, its jacket printed light green and black on white paper.

IMPRESSIONS
Two impressions are known: August 1939 (5,000 copies) and November 1940 (750). Identifying first editions: title-page verso contains no indication of a later impression.

DUST JACKETS AND VARIANTS
Jackets are uniform with Putnam's *Great Contemporaries* and *While England Slept*. Printed black and medium green on white paper, with an Acme photograph of the author on the front face. First edition jackets contain the price and book description (front flap), a blurb for Chamberlain's *In Search of Peace* (back flap), and a description of *Great Contemporaries* on the back face. Second impression jackets advertise *Rufus Isaac First Marquess of Reading* on back flap and *The Voice of Destruction* on rear face.

COMMENTS
The American First is taller and more elegant than its English counterpart and includes a frontispiece, but it lacks the two maps of the Thornton Butterworth Edition. Many collectors believe the differences are sufficient to warrant owning one of each. Like the other Putnam productions, the text has been completely reset with American spelling.

APPRAISAL
Although jacketed copies are far more common than the preceding Putnam titles, only an immaculate jacket wrapped around a fine book will bring more than the $650/£390 estimated for an English First in similar condition. But condition is crucial: in my catalogue I offered a fine copy in a rather worn jacket (half its spine missing) for $275 for years without a taker. Unjacketed copies are almost common and should not cost more than $60/£36 unless in exceptionally nice condition. Reprints are less often seen but certainly worth less.

Macmillan Edition: ICS A45c
Publisher: Macmillan & Co. Ltd., London, 1942

Navy cloth blocked gilt on spine (title, author name, publisher name). 8vo, 358 pages numbered (1)–358, one internal map and a folding map of 'modern Europe' tipped in after page 358. No illustrations. Dust jacket printed black and red on heavy textured cream paper. Published March 1942 at 10s. 6d. ($2.63). Second impression 1943 bound in smooth cloth with dust jacket printed on distinctly inferior, thin, unscored paper. The second impression dust jacket replaces *Thoughts and Adventures* with *Step by Step* on the rear face.

There were two interesting deletions (no doubt supervised by Churchill) to the Macmillan Edition: 'Enemies to the Left' (4 September 1936) and 'The Communist Schism' (6 October 1936), both critical of the Communist international movement.

Much as he omitted Trotsky and Savinkov from *Great Contemporaries*, considering the sensibilities of his new Soviet ally, Churchill with his usual thoroughness dropped these articles from *Step by Step* lest they be brought to the attention of Stalin. The latter was not blind, however, and several times chided Churchill for his anti-communist views. But the Prime Minister usually managed to josh Stalin along and turn the subject humorous. On one occasion Churchill said the British electorate was getting pinkish; Stalin replied that pink was a healthy colour.

Macmillan Editions are relatively common and inexpensive. The first should not cost more than $50/£30 for an immaculate copy in a jacket. The reprint or unjacketed firsts sell for less. This edition should be acquired for its unique textual alterations.

Odhams Edition: ICS A45d

Publisher: Odhams & Co. Ltd., London, 1947

8vo, 368 pages numbered (i)–(xvi) and (1)–352 with two maps integral with the text. Four impressions: 1947, 1948 (2), 1949. (Odhams offered this title in 1954 to buyers of Malcolm Thompson's *Churchill: His Life and Times*, under the general series title, 'The People's Home Library'.)

Copies appeared in the two Odhams bindings: standard bright red cloth blocked gilt and black on top board and spine, page edges unstained; deluxe red leatherette with author signature blocked gilt on top board and black leather title/author label on spine combined with multiple devices, rules and the Odhams name, also gilt, page edges stained red. Dust jackets printed black, medium blue and light blue on white paper. The first impression is identified on the verso of its title page by no date beyond 1947 and the code 'S.947Q'.

Odhams was a mail order bookseller, which helps explain the lack of prices on dust jackets. Deluxe bindings of first four impressions were shipped in grey cardboard boxes with *Great Contemporaries, My Early Life* and *Thoughts and Adventures* at 32s. ($6.40) post-paid to mail order clients.

Completely reset, the Odhams Edition includes a new publisher's note at page (ix) and a paragraph listing Churchill works at page (viii). The former folding map was now printed over a double page spread. More importantly, time had moved on, the Iron Curtain had descended, and Churchill made sure the two original articles on Communism were reinstated. Both bindings are commonplace and should not cost more than $25/£15 in the finest condition.

Books for Libraries Issue: ICS A45e

Publisher: Books for Libraries Press, Freeport, New York, 1971

Medium blue cloth blocked blind on top board (publisher's logo) and silver and red on spine ('CHURCHILL', title, publisher's logo silver, title on red panel between silver bars); an offprint of the Putnam edition with identical pagination; the frontispiece is reproduced on regular page stock. This volume was offered at $35 until the early 1990s by N. W. Ayer. A companion to *While England Slept*, it needs to be reprinted.

FOREIGN TRANSLATIONS

Danish: SKRIDT FOR SKRIDT
Published by Gyldendal: Copenhagen, 1939 (2,300 copies), issued in dark blue wrappers.

French: JOURNAL POLITIQUE 1936–1939
Published by Amiot-Dumont: Paris, 1938. In addition to the trade edition (bound in wrappers) there was a limited edition of 130 on high quality paper by Rives.

German: SCHRITT FÜR SCHRITT 1936–1939
Published by Allert De Lange, Amsterdam, 1940. Issued in wrappers or light blue cloth, both with turquoise dust jacket printed dark blue and red. Another edition was published by Jedes: Amsterdam (no date).

Italian: PASSO A PASSO
Published by Mondadori: Rome, 1947, bound in half dark blue cloth and medium blue paper covered boards; dust jacket carries full-colour portrait of the author. Reprinted 1982.

Norwegian: MOT STUPET
Published by Nasjonalforlaget: Oslo, 1963, bound in half white cloth and paper covered boards; possibly also issued unbound.

Polish: KROK ZA KROKIEM
Published by Zaloga: Warsaw, 1939

Spanish: PASO A PASO
Published by Editorial Clarid: Buenos Aires, 1943

Swedish: STEG FÖR STEG 1936–1939
Published by Skoglund: Stockholm, 1939; bound in red, orange and white card wrappers, blue cloth or half leather and marbled boards; jackets printed blue and black on white. Priced at kr9.50 unbound, kr13.50 bound.

INTO BATTLE /
BLOOD, SWEAT, AND TEARS

COHEN A142, WOODS A66

In February 1941, after hearing that Lend-Lease had passed the US Congress and broadcasting to America, 'Give us the tools and we will finish the job!', Churchill took a moment to inscribe a copy of *Into Battle* to the supplier of his favourite whiskey, Sir Alexander Walker. That copy is on my desk as I write. Opening it at random, I find an earlier broadcast to America: 28 April 1939, just after Hitler had responded mockingly to Roosevelt's letter asking that he declare if he had any further hostile intent toward Germany's neighbours. I am struck at once by the evenness of Churchill's reply. Here is a man described by Hitler (and more than one latter-day revisionist historian) as a mindless warmonger, intent on dragging Britain into a war she couldn't win out of singleminded hatred and burgeoning ego:

'It is quite natural that Herr Hitler should not like the way in which the Great War ended ... But when Herr Hitler complains of the reparations exacted from Germany, we are surely entitled to point out that far more than was ever extracted in reparations was lent to Germany, part by Britain, but mostly by the United States of America, the bulk of which is not likely to be repaid ... If there be encirclement of Germany, it is not military or economic encirclement. It is a psychological encirclement. The masses of the peoples in all the countries around Germany are forcing their governments to be on their guard against tyranny and invasion ... Nothing can now stop this process except a change of heart in the German leaders, or a change of those leaders. But there is no country ... that would tolerate for one moment the idea of attacking Germany, or of trying to impede her peaceful development and legitimate growth. On the contrary, the return of Germany to the circle and family of Europe, and to the wide, lofty uplands of a progressive, tolerant, prosperous civilisation, remains the sovereign hope of the British, French and American democracies. And this is what is going to happen in the end.' All he was saying, in the words of another time, was 'Give Peace a Chance'.

The idea of publishing a book of his speeches was suggested by Desmond Flower, Literary Director of Cassell, with whom Churchill had contracted to write *A History of the English-Speaking Peoples,* which he had drafted and then set aside when war came. The obvious political and propaganda value of such a book clearly appealed to the author, and six further volumes would follow. *Into Battle* takes up where *Arms and the Covenant* leaves off, containing every major Churchill peroration from May 1938 through November 1940. Like its predecessor, it was edited with a Preface by Randolph Churchill. It is without doubt the most inspiring of all his speech volumes. All the great orations are there: 'I have nothing to offer but blood, toil, tears and sweat ... You ask what is our aim? I can answer in one word–Victory ... Arm yourselves and be ye men of valour ... Fight on the beaches ... Their finest hour ... Never was so much owed by so many to so few'. Here are charted the uneasy months of the 'phoney war', the sudden German conquest of Denmark and Norway, the Blitzkrieg in the west, the Belgian surrender, the French collapse, the change of Prime Minister. What a tale they tell.

It should be remembered that almost half the book consists of speeches delivered before war was declared–in which Churchill's arguments only seem like common sense. At the time, things were different. Britain had lost the cream of a generation in the First World War. 'The British people would do anything to stop Hitler, except fight him', Alistair Cooke told the 1988 International Churchill Conference, adding, as he looked around a room of 300 Churchillians: 'Had all of you been there at the time, not one in ten of you would have been with him.'

Into Battle went through twelve impressions in Great Britain. In its North American guise, *Blood, Sweat, and Tears,* it sold more copies than any previous Churchill work, paid off all of Winston's debts and most of Randolph's, and accounted for nearly 60,000 copies in the American market alone. More than any other book to come out of the war, it bolstered the fainthearted, gave strength to the weak and encouraged the strong. Here between two hard covers, in Ed Murrow's words, was the English language mobilised for battle. It deserved to be a best-seller, and it probably introduced Winston Churchill to more Americans and Canadians than any other of his books. To paraphrase a comment often made about Churchill himself, no one ever left this book without feeling braver.

FROM THE REVIEWS

'When Nature gave Winston Churchill the urge to be an orator of the front rank, she gave him at the same time certain physical handicaps. His stammer, the hard and somewhat metallic quality of his voice, his limited register and restricted power of cadence, have all militated against the achievement of his ambition. At times, too, his temperament has seemed to worsen the situation, for his love of verbal color has made some of his speeches seem garish, and his innate aggressiveness has lent a note of stridency to many of his speeches both in the constituencies and in the House. Yet here also he has triumphed through the integration effected by a supreme purpose. Now at last he has become the superb master of his instrument as well as the master of an individual style that perhaps has no peer today.

'"Majestic" is, to me, the word that comes nearest to indicating Churchill's essential oratorical quality; it is something that wells up from deep within the man himself. From the day when he captivated the Commons by his maiden speech at the age of twenty-seven, he has always revelled in the organ tones of rhetoric. Time has been when, to some of his critics, the rhetoric seemed more apparent than the majesty, and when it seemed that he had needlessly adorned the passing episode with a brocaded panoply of diction that ill became its meagre form. But here again the man and the moment have fused into a higher manifestation. In Britain's crisis, the grandeur of his manner has matched the gravity of the occasion ...

'This book could be analyzed with profit as an anthology of English prose wherefrom one might learn much concerning both the orator's technique and the Prime Minister's personality. It could be considered as the raw material of the historian ... But there is something else to consider about this book: Churchill's speeches have themselves become major events in the war. His great appeals–particularly those of last summer–have steadied the nerves and steeled the will of his people in their supreme ordeal. His own tenacity has both reflected and invigorated that of the whole British commonwealth. More than that, there is in these pages a patriotism which burns at such intensity that it has transcended the boundaries of a state until it has become the beacon of the Western way of life.'

Cecil H. Driver in The Yale Review, June 1941

TRANSLATIONS OF WAR SPEECH VOLUMES

Numerous non-English editions of Churchill war speeches were published. Some closely follow the various English editions but most do not, and even those with the same titles add or delete speeches according to the preference or politics of their publishers. Several have misleading titles. The Norwegian *Blod, Svette og Tarer (Blood, Sweat and Tears)* actually includes speeches from that title and *The Unrelenting Struggle*. Accordingly, I have found it less confusing to group them by language after my entry on *Victory. (Secret Session Speeches,* where the translations exactly coincide, lists them in the usual place.)

First Edition: Woods A66(a)
Publisher: Cassell and Co. Ltd., London, 1941

Light blue cloth blocked gilt with title, author's name (with titles 'P.C.', 'M.P.') and 'CASSELL' on spine. 8vo, 322 pages numbered (i)–(viii) and (1)–313 (+1), with frontispiece (Cecil Beaton photo of the author) opposite title-page. Published February 1941 at 8s. 6d. ($2.13).

IMPRESSIONS AND QUANTITIES
Eleven impressions (incorrectly termed 'Editions' in the volumes): February (5), April, July and November 1941; January 1942; December 1943; May 1945. Woods records 30,000 copies for the first edition and 29,700 more for the reprints, but lists only seven impressions. This is belied by notes in the books themselves. Mr Woods

told me he had obtained this information from the publisher's records; the figures may refer to printings of sheets that were stockpiled until each new impression was required. Identifying first editions: title-page verso contains the line, 'First Published 1941' with no reprints indicated, and the code 'F.141' (printed in January).

Commencing with the sixth impression, six lines of the poem *Into Battle* by Julian Grenfell, a First World War soldier-poet, appear on the title-page.

VARIANTS
Some trade copies of the first edition were bound in a smoother, dark blue cloth. Publisher's presentation copies were bound in full black pebble grain morocco.

In December 1943, some tenth impressions were bound in navy half morocco and blue cloth, top edges gilt for corporate presentation. Many bear a gift bookplate from the General Fire Appliance Company Ltd., London.

Note: Woods states that a single leaf ('War with Germany', 3 September 1939) was tipped into a majority of a 'second issue'. No such examples have been encountered until the second impression. Since the books themselves record five February 1941 impressions and Woods only one, Woods was probably confusing one of the later February impressions with the first. (Incidentally, this extra page '128a/b' was never added to the contents page.)

DUST JACKETS
Jackets are printed red fading into black on white paper, and have often been switched. True first impression jackets advertise Quentin Reynolds's *The Wounded Don't Cry* on the front flap; Rosita Forbes's *The Prodigious Caribbean* and Stefan Zweig's *The Tide of Fortune* on the back flap, and notes about *Into Battle* on the back face. Identical jackets were used on the second impression and half of the

Churchill's first book of Second World War speeches. Left: the English first edition. Centre: the American first and book club editions, spines facing out, each flanked by its respective dust jacket (note the priced jacket for the first edition and the absence of a price and Book-of-the-Month Club logo on the book club edition). Right: taller and more elegant, the Canadian edition by McClelland & Stewart of Toronto.

third impression. Later jacket flaps were altered. Many collectors believe the words 'Book Society Choice' (jacket face and spine) designate a book club dust jacket. Not so: all jackets for *Into Battle* are so inscribed; the Book Society simply sold trade editions.

COMMENTS

A key speech book, easy to come by in ordinary worn condition, but perfect, unspotted copies are now at a premium. Strongly recommended for its majestic oratory, *Into Battle* belongs on every library shelf.

APPRAISAL

This was once a book you could find anywhere for a couple of dollars or a pound or two. It still is, but they're not first editions. Jacketed firsts have risen dramatically. Truly fine, unspotted copies in near-fine, unchipped dust jackets command up to $250/£150. Fine copies sell for about a third that much. No premium attaches to the binding variant and there is little demand for half-morocco presentation bindings because they are invariably later impressions.

Canadian Edition: ICS A66ca
Publisher: McClelland & Stewart Ltd., Toronto, 1941

Dark red cloth blocked gilt (title between two rules on top board) title, author's name ('CHURCHILL') and publisher's names between multiple rules on spine. 8vo, 496 pages numbered (i)–(viii) and (1)–488, with frontispiece (Cecil Beaton photo of the author, with facsimile signature) and eight other photographs printed sepia on coated stock, tipped in before pages 73, 89, 169, 185, 265, 281, 361 and 377. Top page edges stained red. Published March 1941. Second edition (also 1941) bound in different cloth with three speeches added and 536 pages numbered (i)–(viii) and (1)–525 (+3).

IMPRESSIONS

Identifying first editions: aside from the extra pages, the contents of both editions are identical, showing no difference in title-pages or versos. All first editions I have seen were bound in a red cloth with obvious vertical scoremarks; later editions are bound in a more evenly textured red cloth or a vertically scored grey cloth, blocked navy. I refer readers to the Cohen Bibliography, which I trust will sort out these mysteries.

VARIANTS

I have found both first and second editions with and without the photographs, and there is no list of illustrations to confirm or deny their presence. There are also two binding variants of the second edition (see above). Many believe all red copies are first editions; not so.

DUST JACKETS

Jackets are uniform with, but of course larger than. the Putnam American edition, printed dark red and navy on cream stock with the title, author name and book blurb on both front and back faces. Jackets contain no price and do not vary between editions.

COMMENTS

The most elegant rendering of this work, the Canadian Edition is substantially taller and wider than the American, printed on much finer paper than the British, and the only one of the three English language editions to contain (sometimes) internal illustrations. It is completely reset, and omits one speech from *Into Battle* (curiously, Churchill's first speech as Prime Minister, 13 May 1940). The second edition adds three speeches whose inclusion is obvious from lighter type on contents page (vi): *The War Situation* (19 December 1940), *To the Italian People* (23 December 1940) and *Give Us The Tools* (9 February 1941).

APPRAISAL

Aesthetically the most desirable English language war speech volume (later Canadian issues were more mundane), this edition is under-appreciated by collectors, to many of whom it is unfamiliar.

I find it difficult to secure customers for editions other than English and American; I don't know why, because in many cases collectors are missing something worthwhile. McClelland & Stewart deserve top marks for this beautiful work. Market value: up to $150/£90 for a fully equipped (all photos and dust jacket) first edition. Anything less sells for a quarter that much.

Canadian Edition, Dominion Issue: ICS A66cb

Publisher: Dominion Book and Bible House, Toronto, 1941

This issue consists of the enlarged, 536-page text bound in dark blue cloth blocked as follows: on top board, 'The Rt. Hon. Winston S. Churchill, P.C., M.P'. is reversed out on large gold rectangle; on base of spine, 'DOMINION'; spine otherwise blocked like other Canadian Editions. The title-page is altered with the name of this publisher.

American Edition: ICS A66b

Publisher: G. P. Putnam's Sons, New York, 1941

Dark blue cloth blocked silver and red. The top board bears the Churchill Coat of Arms debossed blind at lower right and the title in silver on a ⅜-inch high red band near the top; five similar red bands appear on the spine reading 'BLOOD, SWEAT, | AND TEARS | [decorative device] | CHURCHILL' toward the top and 'PUTNAM' toward the bottom. Top page edges stained red. 8vo, 472 pages, reset and numbered (i)–(x) and (1)–462, frontispiece (Beaton photo with facsimile signature) opposite title-page. Endpapers are white. Published 14 April 1941 at $3.

IMPRESSIONS

Two impressions are known, of 50,000 and 11,700 copies respectively, both in April 1941. Identifying first editions: title-page verso contains no indication of a later impression.

VARIANTS

A rare variant of the first edition is bound in black cloth, blocked red and silver as usual on the spine, but blank on the top board (no title, no debossed coat of arms). While this binding bears all the marks of a reprint or book club edition, it has a standard trade dust jacket and carries no indication of a later printing on its title-page verso.

A second impression inscribed to Bullitt McClure, President of Westminster College when Churchill made his famous *Iron Curtain* speech in March 1946, exists with red-orange bindings like later impressions of other Putnam Churchill titles; but most second impressions I have seen are blue like the first. The top boards of second impressions are sometimes blank.

DUST JACKETS

Printed red and blue on cream coated stock. Uniform with, but smaller than, the Canadian Edition, except on the back face, where a drawing of Churchill by K. S. Woerner is printed blue. The front flap contains the price '$3.00' at upper right and

Left to right: half morocco corporate presentation binding of *Into Battle*; one of the Winnipeg-Regina-Saskatchewan issues of the excerpted work, *Their Finest Hour*; and Capricorn's excerpt, *Churchill in His Own Words*.

(most importantly) no Book of the Month Club logo (see next entry).

COMMENTS
The American First is bound uniformly with earlier Putnam's titles, but is shorter, and the debossed coat of arms is unique. The text looks at first like a reduced offprint of the Canadian, but is in fact completely reset and (like all other Putnam Churchills) is translated into 'American'.

It has no internal illustrations, but more importantly, it contains three speeches not in either the first English or Canadian editions: *War* (3 September 1939) later added as an extra leaf to 'Into Battle'; 'We will Never Cease to Strike' (9 November 1940); 'United States Cooperation' (9 January 1941); and three speeches not in the English or first Canadian editions: 'The War Situation' (19 December 1940), 'To the People of Italy' (23 December 1940) and 'Put Your Confidence in Us' (9 February 1941). Interestingly, these last three are retitled by Putnam.

For its importance in establishing a further text, this is bibliographically a significant edition.

APPRAISAL
The American First had an enormous press run and is very common in the United States. A fine jacketed copy sold for $75/£45 a decade ago, and rarely commands more than that today. Lesser copies can be had for whatever one chooses to pay. Do not confuse this with the Book Club issue (below). The text is desirable, since it contains more speeches than most other editions.

Book of the Month Club Issue: ICS A66b
Publisher: G. P. Putnam's Sons, New York, 1941

Red buckram blocked gilt and blue. The top board bears a large Churchill Coat of Arms debossed blind at upper centre between two gilt rules surmounting the widely spaced initials 'W S C'; the spine bears the title (without commas) and 'CHURCHILL' between two gilt-on-navy decorative bands and the name 'PUTNAM' in gilt at the bottom. Top page edges stained blue. 8vo, pagination as per the First American Edition. Dust jacket similar to American First but printed on uncoated light buff paper; front flap contains no price, and a more tightly leaded book blurb allows room at the bottom for the Book of the Month Club logo. Variant binding: a few of these volumes are bound in a finely woven linen-like cloth instead of buckram.

A rare example of a book club edition bound more nicely than its trade counterpart, this is truly handsome, especially in the linen-like cloth. It's also cheap; $30/£18 should buy the best one in creation, and I sell ordinary copies for as little as a dollar. The only pitfall is that many collectors mistake it for the First American Edition, which it patently is not.

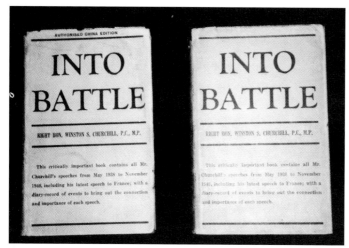

The Kelly & Walsh *Into Battle*, published in Shanghai. Two states of the dust jacket are shown: one with 'Authorised China Edition' at top, the other blank in this space. Any copy of this work is extremely rare and desirable.

China Edition: Not in Woods or ICS

Publisher: Kelly & Walsh: Shanghai (no date but actually 1941)

Bound in red cloth, completely reset with distinct pagination. Dust jackets printed black on brown wrapping paper in three states: one reads 'AUTHORIZED CHINA EDITION' at the top; the other is blank. I have not examined the third. Flaps and rear faces of jackets are blank; the front face carries title, author name between horizontal rules, and a blurb; the spine carries title, author and logo. This is more likely a legitimate than a pirated edition.

Odhams Edition: ICS A66ea

Publisher: Odhams & Co., Ltd., London, 1966

Entitled *Churchill in His Own Words*, this paperback was offprinted from the Putnam *Blood, Sweat, and Tears*. By eliminating separate title leaves and mingling the chronologies with the text, the work was reduced to 352 pages without abridgement: it contains all the speeches in the comprehensive First American Edition.

Capricorn Issue: ICS A66eb

Publisher: Capricorn Books, New York, 1966

Entitled *Churchill in His Own Words*, this 'Capricorn Giant' paperback was the American issue of the above, with identical contents, published at $1.95. It was subtitled *Years of Greatness | The memorable wartime speeches of the Man of the Century*.

This book was a companion to Capricorn's *Churchill in His Own Words: Years of Adventure*, a reprint of *Great Destiny* (A Churchill Anthology in Britain) edited by F. W. Heath, which cleverly excerpted passages from *My Early Life,* the first four war books, the *African Journey, World Crisis* and *Step by Step* to knit a neat little autobiography. *Great Destiny* in its hardbound form was jacketed uniformly with the 1941 Putnam Edition of *Blood, Sweat, and Tears,* published 25 years earlier.

EXCERPTED WORK:

THEIR FINEST HOUR: Woods page 90
Publishers: Winnipeg Free Press, Regina Leader-Post, Saskatoon Star-Phoenix, 1941

Bound in card wrappers printed black, green and in yellow, red-orange. 8vo., 80 pages numbered (1)–80 plus wrappers. Front wrappers carry a photograph of Churchill wearing a naval hard helmet and peering through binoculars. Contains 21 speeches from *Into Battle,* from *Blood, Toil, Tears and Sweat* (13 May 1940) to *The Passing of Neville Chamberlain* (12 November 1940). Published at 25p.

Copyright conflicts caused withdrawal of what was to be a series after this first and only edition (marked 'Vol. I'), was produced, with the imprint of three western Canada newspapers. Contrary to Woods, the booklets were individually published by each newspaper, not by the Winnipeg paper in conjunction with the other two. The booklets have quite an allure and command hefty prices today. $150/£90 is not atypical for the most common variety (Winnipeg Free Press, printed yellow–green–black). Premiums are often paid for the Regina or Saskatoon imprints, or copies printed in red-orange instead of yellow.

THE UNRELENTING STRUGGLE

COHEN A172, WOODS A89

The second volume of Churchill's war speeches sold over 30,000 copies in Britain and over 20,000 in the United States and Canada. For the first time a separate Australian edition was also published. Son Randolph had gone off to war, so the editing and introduction were assigned to Charles Eade, then editor of the *Sunday Dispatch*, who edited *The Unrelenting Struggle*, successive war speech volumes and the 1952–1953 three-volume Definitive Edition. Internal illustrations were adopted for the first time by Cassell, who were nevertheless restricted to pulpy, acidic page stock because of wartime economy standards.

The volume contains 72 of Churchill's speeches, broadcasts and messages to Parliament from November 1940 to the end of 1941, a period marked by many setbacks, and some disillusionment with the Prime Minister. The strength and fortitude he always exhibited in the face of bad news may inspire latter-day readers with much smaller problems. 'I may not agree with all the criticism', Churchill tells the House of Commons in January 1941: 'I may be stirred by it, and I may resent it; I may even retort–but at any rate, Debates on these large issues are of the very greatest value to the life-thrust of the nation, and they are of great assistance to His Majesty's Government.' What a contrast to the modern notion that we must at all costs avoid debate and 'gridlock', mouthed by politicians who really believe otherwise.

Not all the subjects of this book are depressing: there was the attack on the Italian fleet at Taranto, the early battles in North Africa and the victory of Sidi Barrani, the watershed meeting with Franklin Roosevelt in Newfoundland and the resulting Atlantic Charter, and that great speech to the US Congress the day after Christmas 1941, the penultimate entry. 'This long series of portentous events', says the publisher, 'is all recorded here in Mr. Churchill's own forceful words that even now, when the breathless tide of war has borne us onwards, place them in perspective and give them their due significance.'

FROM THE REVIEWS

'Whether he is rendering periodic accounts of the war to the House of Commons, or exhorting civil defence workers or munition makers to greater efforts, or speaking for England to a great ally, or a small people in distress, Mr. Churchill has always the secret of using the natural language for the idea. And when the ideas are great, natural language cannot fail of sublimity. These speeches have not the epigrammatic sparkle of Disraeli's, or the poetic splendour of Bright's, or the grand philosophic sweep of Burke's, or the tormented moral passion of Cromwell's. But they will be read in after ages because they will be recognized as coming nearer to the faithful interpretation of the feelings of those to whom and for whom the orator spoke than the words of any of these illustrious predecessors.'

Times Literary Supplement, 3 October 1942

First Edition: ICS A89a

Publisher: Cassell and Company Ltd., London, 1941

Light blue cloth blocked gilt with title, author's name (with titles 'C.H., M.P.') and 'CASSELL' on spine. 8vo, 360 pages numbered (i)–(x) and (1)–349 (+1), with frontispiece (J. Russell and Sons photo of the author) and four internal photographs on two coated paper leaves inserted between pages 70–71 and 230–231. Published 24 September 1942 at 12s. 6d. ($3.13).

IMPRESSIONS AND QUANTITIES

Four impressions (incorrectly termed 'Editions' in the volumes): June and November 1942, December 1943, August 1946, according to the volumes. Again Woods differs, listing a first impression of 10,900 and four later impressions of 23,500. I have never encountered an impression dated later than August 1946. Identifying first editions: title-page verso contains the line, 'First Edition ... 1942' with no reprints indicated, and the code 'F642' (printed in June).

VARIANTS

A minority of copies, including some first editions, were bound in smooth, medium blue cloth. A very few in the standard binding were blocked navy instead of gilt.

The Unrelenting Struggle first editions. Left to right: English, American, Canadian (spine only is shown; the face is identical to the American) and Australian (with its own unique dust jacket). Later Australian war speech volumes styled their jackets after the English.

Publisher's presentation copies were bound in full black pebble grain morocco.

In December 1943, some second impressions were bound in navy half morocco and blue cloth, top edges gilt for corporate presentation. Many bear a gift bookplate from the General Fire Appliance Co. Ltd., London.

DUST JACKETS

Jackets are printed light brownish orange fading into black on white paper. First impression jackets advertise *Into Battle* ('Eighth Edition') on the front flap (second impression jacket advertises the 'Ninth Edition'); the BBC ('LONDON CALLING OVERSEAS') and notes about this volume on the back flap. Since later jackets often find their way onto first editions, buyers of firsts should be certain the jacket is correct.

COMMENTS

With speeches of even more importance to the ever-widening war, *The Unrelenting Struggle* is essential reading.

APPRAISAL

Although this important speech volume is easy to find in ordinary condition, fine jacketed firsts have become scarce and have lately been priced up to $150/£90; I expect to see them at well over that price inside a decade.

American Edition: ICS A89b
Publisher: Little, Brown and Company, Boston, 1942

Red cloth blocked gilt and black. Title and author's name separated by thick rule blocked gilt on black inside thin gilt frame on top board and spine. Also on spine are wavy lines top and bottom and publisher's name, all gilt. 8vo, 382 pages numbered (i)–(x) and (1)–371 (+1). Published 21 October 1942 at $3.50.

IMPRESSIONS AND QUANTITIES

Two impressions: October 1942 (15,000 copies) and February 1944 (1,000). Identifying first editions: title-page verso contains the line 'FIRST EDITION'. Also, the second impression is ⅜in shorter.

VARIANTS
None noted.

DUST JACKETS

Jackets are printed black and red on white stock with the Karsh 'growling lion' photograph on the front face. First Edition jackets contain a book blurb running on both flaps and quotes from the book on the back flap.

COMMENTS
The nicest binding of a war speech volume by Little, Brown, who replaced Putnam as Churchill's American publisher. War economies would soon affect Little, Brown productions, which became smaller and were printed on cheaper stock. Unfortunately the American Edition contains no illustrations.

APPRAISAL
Extremely common, *The Unrelenting Struggle* is often overpriced by dealers. A fine jacketed copy should not cost more than $50/£30, and lesser copies sell for incidental prices. Every collection I acquire lately seems replete with copies; I sell unjacketed firsts for a couple of dollars.

Canadian Issue: ICS A89c
Publisher: McClelland and Stewart Ltd., Toronto, 1942

An offprint from the Little, Brown American Edition, the Canadian Issue differs only in detail: McClelland and Stewart on the title-page, no publisher name on spine, no price on jacket flap, and 'McCLELLAND | AND STEWART' ("AND" replacing "&") printed black on a red panel on the jacket spine. Pricing as for the American Edition; in my experience, fairly common.

Australian Edition: ICS A89d
Publisher: Cassell and Company Ltd., Melbourne, 1942

Bound in rough white cloth blocked blue-black on spine with the wording identical to the English edition. Although wholly set and printed in Australia by Wilke & Co. of Melbourne, it follows the pagination of the English Edition and contains the same frontispiece and four internal photographs. There may, however, be small textual alterations (see an example of this in the Australian *End of the Beginning*). Published 1942 at A 13s. 6d.

VARIANTS AND DUST JACKETS
Two variant bindings are reported: dark blue cloth and black cloth with a moiré pattern, blocked gilt. The dust jacket is unique, printed black and red on white paper with the spine lettered black; the jacket face contains the line 'BOOK SOCIETY RECOMMENDATION' at bottom. There was only one impression; each copy contains the line 'First Edition - - 1942' on its title-page verso. (Do not be misled by later impressions listed on dust jackets of later Australian titles; these jackets were offprinted or copied from British jackets.)

The Australian Edition is an interesting production, and important in that it expanded Churchill's speech volumes to a fourth major English-Speaking Nation. (The Australians did not publish a separate *Into Battle* but the front flap of this book's dust jacket advertises the English Edition at A 12s. 6d.) Because of its uniqueness and desirability, there should be more interest in this edition, which sells for up to $75/£45 in jacketed condition. Truly fine copies would cost more; most jackets have offset their titles onto the white boards.

European Issue: ICS A89e

Publisher: The Continental Book Company AB, Stockholm, 1942

Bound in half tan cloth and laid paper blocked gilt on spine: 'CHURCHILL | THE | UNRELENTING | STRUGGLE' between two gilt rules; a third rule at spine bottom. (The rules are also reported in brown.) Interestingly, the top board bears the coat of arms from the Harrap Editions of Marlborough. Cream laid endpapers. Pagination per the first edition; frontispiece but no internal photographs. The jacket face looks like the English Edition but the jacket is printed on coated stock with several alterations: spine base blank where 'CASSELL' usually appears; flaps blank; rear face advertises this book.

This interesting offprint of the first edition was published for distribution in what was left of free Europe; the title-page verso carries the message, 'This edition must not be introduced in the British Empire or in the U.S.A.' Churchill's usual Swedish publisher, Skoglund, would produce two volumes of the collected *War Speeches* after the war, and were not inactive during it. This is the only example of a war speech volume published in English in a non-English-speaking country, and is thus of some interest to the collector. Rarely seen, it sells for up to $150/£90, much more in the dust jacket.

Books for Libraries Issue: ICS A89f

Publisher: Books for Libraries, New York, 1978

A hardbound offprint, issued without dust jacket. Stocked until the early 1990s by the N. W. Ayer Company in Nashua, NH.

THE END OF THE BEGINNING

COHEN A178, WOODS A94

The nadir of Churchill's war is captured in this collection of speeches, broadcasts and messages for January to December 1942. The onslaught of Japan; the quick loss of Malaya, Rangoon, Singapore and two capital ships; defeats in Africa, where Rommel sent his motorised cadres deep into Libya and threatened Egypt; the continued U-boat threat to Britain's North Atlantic lifeline; the German siege of major Russian cities: all tried Churchill's courage and Britain's faith. Over 20 pages of *The End of the Beginning* comprise the Prime Minister's response to a no-confidence motion in the House.

'All will come right', Churchill said again and again, and the book ends on a tide of hope, captured in the speech at the Lord Mayor's Day luncheon in London on 9 November 1942, with the Battle of Alamein now history:

'I have never promised anything but blood, tears, toil and sweat. Now, however, we have a new experience. We have victory–a remarkable and definite victory. The bright gleam has caught the helmets of our soldiers, and warmed and cheered all our hearts ... Rommel's army has been defeated. It has been routed. It has been very largely destroyed as a fighting force ... The Germans have received back again that measure of fire and steel which they have so often meted out to others. Now this is not the end. It is not even the beginning of the end. But it is, perhaps, the end of the beginning. Henceforth Hitler's Nazis will meet equally well armed, and perhaps better armed troops. Henceforth they will have to face in many theatres of war that superiority in the air which they have so often used without mercy against others of which they boasted all round the world and which they intended to use as an instrument for convincing all other peoples that all resistance to them was useless.'

Sombre it may be, but like all Churchill's books this one is not without levity. On one of the last pages, an oft-repeated Churchill quip is published. A Member of Parliament had asked whether the titles 'Minister of Defence' and 'Secretary of State for War' were logical, whether they shouldn't be changed to 'Minister for War' and 'Secretary of State for the Army'.

Churchill responded: 'Sir, we must beware of needless innovation, especially when guided by logic.'

FROM THE REVIEWS

'My first impression is of this great man's astonishing vitality. I fancy this quality is less rare among politicians here than in England. It is not always a desirable quality: unless yoked with intelligence, it can be as much a nuisance as a tornado: unless coupled with honesty, it can be a wilful menace. In Mr. Churchill you have it combined with exceptional intelligence, honesty so great that he has suffered political exile and the contemptuous condescension of men infinitely his inferiors, and a gift for direct speech unequalled in our time: and the consequence is a great statesman.

'The great speeches in this book are familiar. To reread them is to be struck again by the exactness of Mr. Churchill's thought, his weighed use of words, the fine eloquence of his more vivid passages, and his uncanny skill in a certain half-savage, half-playful bantering. How good he is in his comments on "that bad man's" oratory in last October. "The most striking and curious part of Hitler's speech was his complaint that no one pays sufficient attention to his victories. Look at all the victories I have won, he exclaims in effect. Look at all the countries I have invaded and struck down. Look at the thousands of kilometers that I have advanced into the lands of other people. Look at the booty I have gathered, and all the men I have killed and captured. Contrast these exploits with the performances of the Allies. Why are they not downhearted and dismayed? How do they dare to keep up their spirits in the face of my great successes and their many misfortunes?" And a little after comes the bold and prophetic sentence, "He sees with chagrin and amazement that our defeats are but stepping-stones to victory, and that his victories are only the stepping-stones to ruin."'

R. Ellis Roberts, *Saturday Review of Literature,* 28 August 1943

First Edition: ICS A94a
Publisher: Cassell and Company Ltd., London, 1943

Light blue cloth blocked gilt with title, author's name (with titles 'C.H., M.P.') and 'CASSELL' on spine. 8vo, 272 pages numbered (i)–(xiv) and (1)–258, with frontispiece (Walter Stoneman photo of the author) and four internal photographs on two coated paper leaves inserted between pages 66–67 and 162–163. Published 29 July 1943 at 11s. 6d. ($2.30)–not 12s. 6d. as per Woods.

IMPRESSIONS AND QUANTITIES
Four impressions (incorrectly termed 'Editions' in the volumes). Woods records three impressions, 16,000 of the first and 16,500 reprints, but his dates are not confirmed by the volumes. Identifying first editions: title-page verso contains the line, 'First Published ... 1943' with no reprints indicated, and the code 'F.543' (printed in May).

VARIANTS
A minority of copies, including some first editions, were bound in smooth, medium

blue cloth. Publisher's presentation copies were bound in full black pebble grain morocco.

In December 1943, some second impressions were bound in navy half morocco and blue cloth, top edges gilt for corporate presentation. Many bear a gift bookplate from the General Fire Appliance Co. Ltd., London.

DUST JACKETS

Jackets are printed black and yellow fading into mauve on white paper. First impression jackets advertise *Into Battle* ('Ninth Edition') and *The Unrelenting Struggle* ('Second Edition') on front flap; by the third impression, jackets advertised the 'Tenth' and 'Third Editions' respectively. The rear flap advertises the BBC ('BRITAIN CALLS THE WORLD'), the back face contains notes about this volume. Since later jackets often find their way onto first editions, buyers of firsts should be certain that the jacket is correct.

COMMENTS

A companion to the previous war speeches with a masterly 21-page defence of his Government by Churchill in the vote of confidence debate (July 1942), which he eventually won by 475 votes to 25, this is an important chronicle of the war and the bleakest period for the Coalition Government.

APPRAISAL

Although this speech volume is easy to find in ordinary condition, fine, unspotted, jacketed first editions have become scarce and have lately been priced up to $100/ £60; I expect to see them at well over that price in a few years.

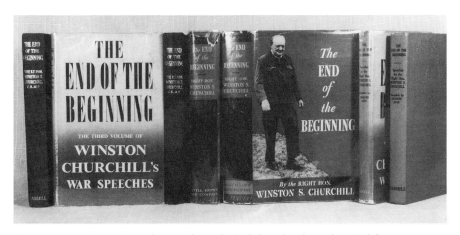

The End of the Beginning first editions. Left to right: English (and its dust jacket), English presentation and American bindings (spines only), Canadian and Australian. The latter is shown in and out of its dust jacket. Author's name on the spine omits Churchill's honours.

American Edition: ICS A94b
Publisher: Little, Brown and Company, Boston, 1943

Red cloth blocked gilt and black. Title and author's name separated by thick rule blocked gilt on black inside thin gilt frame on top board and spine. Also on spine are wavy lines top and bottom and publisher's name, all gilt. 8vo, 336 pages numbered (i)–(xiv) and (1)–322. Published 19 August 1943 at $3.50.

IMPRESSIONS AND QUANTITIES
The first impression (6,000 copies) was the same size (8¾ x 5¾in) as the American *Unrelenting Struggle*, but with wartime restrictions, later impressions were trimmed (8½ x 5⅝in) to save paper. There were six later impressions, all in 1943: August (1,000 and 1,000); September (2,000 and 1,000) October (1,000) and December (1,000). Identifying first editions: title-page verso contains the line FIRST EDITION with no reprints listed.

VARIANTS
None noted.

DUST JACKETS
Jackets are printed black and red on white stock with a silhouetted photograph of Churchill demonstrating his 'Siren Suit' (taken at the White House). All jackets contain a book blurb on the front flap, *Unrelenting Struggle* blurb on back flap, and praise of Churchill by Raymond Gram Swing on the back face. Later impression jackets are of course smaller, and front flaps indicate the impression, for example, 'FIFTH PRINTING'.

COMMENTS
Uniformly and attractively bound with the Little, Brown *Unrelenting Struggle*, this edition was reset but the contents were not altered; there is no frontispiece nor any internal illustrations.

APPRAISAL
I have found that first editions are very scarce, encountering only one or two in the last ten years; even my own copy is not a good one, and $100/£60 would be a fair price for a fine jacketed example. Reprints, on the other hand, are in reasonably good supply and sell for less than one-quarter as much.

Canadian Issue: ICS A94c
Publisher: McClelland and Stewart Ltd., Toronto, 1943

An offprint from the Little, Brown American Edition, the Canadian Issue differs only in detail: the McClelland and Stewart name in place of Little, Brown on the spine and title-page, no price on jacket flap, and McCLELLAND | AND STEWART printed black on a red panel on the jacket spine. The binding is coarser and lighter red than the American, and the gilding is duller. One impression known. Copies are not uncommon; fine examples in jackets sell for around $50/£30.

Australian Edition: ICS A94d
Publisher: Cassell and Company Ltd., Melbourne, 1943

Bound in rough red cloth blocked black on spine with more words than the English Edition: title, 'Speeches | by the | Right Hon. WINSTON S. | CHURCHILL | space | Compiled by CHARLES EADE., and CASSELL' at bottom. Although wholly set and printed in Australia by Wilke & Co. of Melbourne, it follows the pagination of the English Edition and contains the same frontispiece and four internal photographs. However, the frontispiece faces the half title, not the title-page; and the internal illustrations are between pages 114–115 and 146–147. Published 1943 at A 12s. 6d.

In at least one respect the Australian issue establishes a new text: Churchill's quip about logic (see introduction) is followed by his next sentence: 'Statutory sanction would be required'; this appears only in the Australian issue. There may be other examples of textual changes.

Cassell Australia now adopted the dust jacket style of the English Edition, and the Australian jacket contains exactly the same material as the latter, although reset and printed in Australia. There was only one impression: its title-page verso contains the line 'First Australian Edition, 1943'. (Do not be misled by later impressions listed on dust jackets of later Australian titles; these jackets were offprinted or copied from British jackets.)

Its place in the pantheon of Churchill's books is significant, but the Australian Issue seems to appeal only to comprehensive collectors. Current value of near-fine jacketed copies is around $75/£45; full-fine copies are rare and cost more than ordinary copies, which are of low value.

Books for Libraries Issue: ICS A94e
Publisher: Books for Libraries, New York, 1978

An offprint published in hardback, listed in contemporary editions of *Books in Print*. Issued without dust jacket. Stocked until the early 1990s by the N. W. Ayer Company in Nashua, New Hampshire.

ONWARDS TO VICTORY

COHEN A194, WOODS A101

The fourth war speech volume takes a decidedly more upbeat tone as the fortunes of war turn in favour of the Allies and Churchill begins to envision victory. The Casablanca meeting and 'unconditional surrender' policy, which Roosevelt enunciated and Churchill supported despite private misgivings; the end of Mussolini; the Russian victory at Stalingrad and the Red Army's vast new offensive along the thousand-mile front; and the great air offensive against the German homeland all gave much to rejoice over. In the East, the war against Japan was progressing, with New Guinea and the Solomons on the way to liberation; General Wavell, sacked by Churchill from the North Africa command, was leading his forces from India into Burma. There was also the final rout of Rommel in North Africa, and *Onwards to Victory* contains that priceless exchange between Churchill and General Alexander (pages 24–25, first edition):

Churchill (August 1942): '1. Your prime and main duty will be to take or destroy at the earliest opportunity the German-Italian army commanded by Field Marshal Rommel, together with all its supplies and establishments in Egypt and Libya. 2. You will discharge or cause to be discharged, such other duties as pertain to your Command without prejudice to the task described in paragraph 1, which must be considered paramount in His Majesty's interests.'

Alexander (September 1943): 'Sir, The Orders you gave me on August 15, 1942, have been fulfilled. His Majesty's enemies, together with their impedimenta, have been completely eliminated from Egypt, Cyrenaica, Libya and Tripolitania. I now await your further instructions.'

For this writer, the greatest speech in *Onwards to Victory* is that clarion call for Anglo-American brotherhood issued by Churchill at Harvard on 6 September 1943: 'Twice in my lifetime the long arm of destiny has reached across the oceans and involved the entire life and manhood of the United States in a deadly struggle ... To the youth of America, as to the youth of all the Britains, I say "You cannot stop". There is no halting-place at this point. We have now reached a stage in the journey where there can be no pause. We must go on. It must be world anarchy or world order ... All these are great possibilities, and I say: "Let us go into this together. Let us have another Boston Tea Party about it" ... If we are together nothing is impossible. If we are divided all will fail.' How remarkable it is today, with all the dragons slain, that his words remain as sound a guide as ever.

This book follows the layout of previous speech volumes, with a chronology of events inserted periodically to keep the speeches, broadcasts and messages in context.

FROM THE REVIEWS

'Assuming supreme responsibility four years ago when so little seemed left, how could Churchill save so much? What are the driving motives behind his virile, straightforward and never boastful speeches?

'Above all, Churchill is the heir to that great tradition, which began with Burke, of the British Empire, with its far-flung responsibilities. Only by its world bases would the empire stop world-conquering tyrants, and in peace protect that world by exercise of laws of progress and moderation. Churchill holds that the empire's disintegration would open the floodgates to disaster as immeasurable as the dissolution of our Union would have caused in North America. The strategy of peace does not demand a breaking-down, but an even wider and more flexible integration.

'Churchill became the leader in the crisis without indulging in wishful thinking or holding out alluring promises. From the front bench of the House he called England back to her early inspiration, to human liberty and duty. He spoke to Englishmen as to a free and mature people, not enchanting them with brave new worlds, but filling their hearts with a sense of stern responsibility and historical greatness. In the common sense, the humanity, and the fortitude of his words lives the tradition which made the House of Commons the example of civil liberty everywhere.'

Hans Kohn, *The New York Times Book Review*, 23 July 1944

First Edition: ICS A101a
Publisher: Cassell and Company Ltd., London, 1944

Light blue cloth blocked gilt with title, author's name (with titles 'C.H., M.P.') and 'CASSELL' on spine. 8vo, 288 pages numbered (i)–(x) and (1)–278, with frontispiece (Winston, Mary and Clementine, June 1943) and five internal photographs on two coated paper leaves inserted between pages 118–119 and 182–183. Published 29 June 1944 at 12s. 6d. ($2.50).

IMPRESSIONS AND QUANTITIES
Three impressions (incorrectly termed 'Editions' in the volumes): 1944, 1945, 1946, according to the books themselves. Woods records four impressions through 1947, 15,000 of the first and 12,500 reprints; but his dates are not confirmed by the volumes. Identifying first editions: title-page verso contains the line, 'First Published ... 1944' with no reprints indicated, and the code 'F.544' (printed in May).

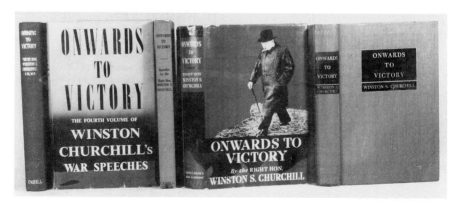

Onwards to Victory first editions. Left to right: English (and its dust jacket), Australian (spine only showing), American (in jacket) and Canadian (out of jacket).

VARIANTS

Publisher's presentation copies were bound in black pebble grain morocco.

DUST JACKETS

Jackets are printed black and orange fading into dark blue on white paper. True first impression jackets advertise *Into Battle* ('Tenth Edition'), *The Unrelenting Struggle* and *The End of the Beginning* on the front flap; the BBC (THE VOICE OF BRITAIN) on the back flap, and notes about this volume on the back face. The second impression jacket advertises the 'Eleventh Edition' of *Into Battle*.

COMMENTS

Uniformly bound with the earlier Cassell war speech volumes, this one marks the turning of what Churchill called the 'Hinge of Fate' and the bright prospects of final victory.

APPRAISAL

Like earlier speech volumes, *Onwards to Victory* is easy to find in scruffy condition, but much scarcer as a fine first in a jacket. Such copies have brought up to $100/£60 lately, and will continue to rise in value. Paper stock in Britain was of even poorer quality by 1944, and most copies spot easily, especially on the page edges.

American Edition: ICS A101b
Publisher: Little, Brown and Company, Boston, 1944

Red cloth blocked gilt and black. Title and author's name separated by thick rule blocked gilt on black inside thin gilt frame on top board and spine. Also on spine are wavy lines top and bottom and publisher's name, all gilt. 8vo, 370 pages numbered (i)–(xii) and (1)–358. Published 13 July 1944 at $3.50.

IMPRESSIONS AND QUANTITIES
One impression of 9,000 copies.

VARIANTS
None noted

DUST JACKETS
Jackets are printed black and red on white stock with a silhouetted photograph of Churchill walking in a topcoat. All jackets contain a book blurb on the front and back flap and praise of the author on the back face.

COMMENTS
Uniformly bound with the earlier Little, Brown war speeches, this edition was reset but the contents were not altered; no frontispiece nor any internal illustrations.

APPRAISAL
Increasingly uncommon, the American Edition commands up to $50/£30 in fine jacketed condition.

Canadian Issue: ICS A101c
Publisher: McClelland and Stewart Ltd., Toronto, 1944

An offprint from the Little, Brown American Edition, the Canadian Issue differs only in detail: the McClelland and Stewart name in place of Little, Brown on the spine and title-page, no price on the jacket flap, and 'McCLELLAND | and STEWART' printed black on a white panel on the jacket spine. One impression was published. It is uncommon, fine examples in jackets selling for around $50/£30.

Australian Edition: ICS A101d
Publisher: Cassell and Company Ltd., Melbourne, 1944

Bound in light blue cloth blocked navy on spine with more words than the English Edition: title, and publisher's name plus 'Speeches | by the | Right Hon. WINSTON S. | CHURCHILL,' [comma but no titles; these were added later–see 'Variants']. Although wholly set and printed in Australia by Wilke & Co. of Melbourne, it follows the pagination of the English Edition and contains the same frontispiece and internal photographs. However, the frontispiece appears facing the half title, the photograph facing the first free endpaper; and the internal illustrations are between pages 118–119 and 134–135. Published at A 12s. 6d.

Again this volume is produced in the image of the English; dust jacket colours are similar but a bit lighter and the flaps advertise four non-Churchill books. There was a single impression; its title-page verso contains the line 'First Australian Edition,

1944'. (Do not be misled by later impressions listed on dust jackets of later Australian titles; these jackets were offprinted or copied from British jackets.)

VARIANTS

The binding described above also comes in medium green and dark blue cloth, both blocked black. A second state binding (or perhaps a binding by other binders) contains the titles 'C.H., M.P.' which were omitted from the first bindings. These have been noted in the standard light blue cloth, as well as medium green, brick red and orange.

The Australian Issue appeals to Australians and advanced collectors elsewhere. Current value of near-fine jacketed copies is $75/£45; full-fine copies are rare and cost more.

THE DAWN OF LIBERATION

COHEN A214, WOODS A107

Printed in March 1945 but not published until after V-E Day, the fifth book of war speeches appeared almost anticlimactic, but its array of speeches, messages, broadcasts and replies to Parliamentary questions involve the last great events of the war: D-Day and the invasion of France, the Soviet steamroller in the East, the futures of Poland (grim) and Greece (hopeful); the V2 rocket bombs halted finally by the Allied armies rolling into Europe. Chronologically the text covers utterances from 22 February to 31 December 1944. Churchill was travelling even more in 1944 than in previous years, so many speeches are from abroad: Italy, Quebec, Moscow, Paris and Athens.

Everywhere that *The Dawn of Liberation* falls open holds something of interest. A random flip lands on page 69, with Churchill addressing the Commons on Empire Unity: 'We had a pretty dreary time between these two wars. But we have great responsibilities for the part we played–so we have, all of us–and so have the Americans in not making the League of Nations a reality and in not backing its principles with effective armed forces, and in letting this deadly and vengeful foe arm at his leisure. But underneath, the whole Empire and ourselves in these islands grew stronger and our resources multiplied. Little was said about our growth. Little was visible of our closer union; while the forces which had sent the Anzac Corps to the Dardanelles, and afterward to the Hindenburg Line, and carried the Canadians to Vimy Ridge, were all growing, unseen, unnoticed, immeasurable, far below the surface of public life and political conflict.'

There is also a looking ahead, a surveying of the future, that is not evident in the earlier war speech volumes, Churchill assuming, of course, that he would lead Britain into the post-war years: 'We must remember that we shall be hard put to it to gain our living, to repair the devastation that has been wrought, and to bring back that wider and more comfortable life which is so deeply desired. We must strive to preserve the reasonable rights and liberties of the individual. We must respect the rights and opinions of others, while holding firmly to our own faith and convictions': good advice for any nation or time.

FROM THE REVIEWS

'[Churchill's] eloquence can be by turns lofty and severe, humorous and playful, with a touch of Bunyan, a touch of Macaulay, a touch that seems American. Some phrases ring like trumpets: "hard and obstinate"; "fell and ferocious"; "the eye of the spirit"; "scarred and armed with experience". "Drive on through the storm", he was saying almost a year ago today, "now that it reaches its fury, with the same singleness of purpose and inflexibility of resolve as we showed to the world when we were all alone".

'He has a sort of cackling homeliness at times that is almost touching, so honest and boyish is it: "When you have to hold a hot coffee pot it is better not to break the handle off until you are sure you can get another equally convenient and serviceable, or at any rate until there is a dish-cloth handy." He says he never thought "that the empire needed tying together with bits of string". He turns scriptural and says he must pick his way "among heated plowshares". He says, with apparent ingenuousness, "There is nothing like talking things over and seeing where we can get to". He has a nice way with his parliamentary opponents: "In an unconceivably short space I shall be seated, and the honorable gentleman, if he should catch the chairman's eye, will then be able to fall upon me with all his pent-up ferocity". He discusses the strategy of "Corporal" Hitler and adds, "Altogether, I think it is much better to let officers rise up in the proper way". He resents having this "squalid caucus boss and dictator" compared with Napoleon.

'This brilliantly successful journalist and lecturer, who at 30 was taking thousands of dollars from American audiences by putting on one of the best one-man shows of the time; this expert parliamentarian, thrusting, parrying, turning the laugh, moving even his opponents to applause; this war correspondent Prime Minister, whose "reviews of the war" are as good as any reporting that has been done during this conflict; this statesman is not really a man of ideas. He is an Elizabethan and an American in being a man of action.'

R. L. Duffus, New York Times Book Review, 5 August 1945

First Edition: ICS A107a
Publisher: Cassell and Company Ltd., London, 1945

Light blue cloth blocked gilt with title, author's name (with titles 'C.H., M.P.') and 'CASSELL' on spine. 8vo, 338 pages numbered (i)–(x) and (1)–327 (+1), with frontispiece (The King and Dominion Prime Ministers) and five internal photographs on two coated paper leaves inserted between pages 100–101 and 228–229. Published 26 July 1945 at 12s. 6d. ($2.50).

IMPRESSIONS AND QUANTITIES
Two impressions (incorrectly termed 'Editions' in the volumes): 1945 and 1947. Identifying first editions: title-page verso contains the line, 'First Published 1945' with no reprints indicated, and the code 'F.345' (printed in March). The first impression numbered 14,250 copies.

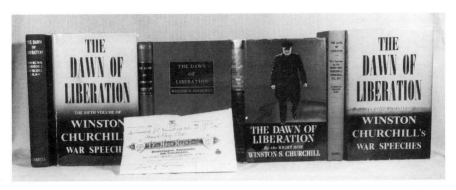

The Dawn of Liberation first editions. Left to right: English (and its dust jacket), American (sans jacket), Canadian (in its jacket) and Australian (spine and jacket face shown). Laid in front is a Hugh Rees (booksellers) receipt for the English edition at 12s. 6d., sold to Air Commodore J C Quinnell, CB, DFC in 1945.

VARIANTS
Publisher's presentation copies were bound in black pebble grain morocco.

DUST JACKETS
Jackets are printed black and yellow fading into purple-blue on white paper. True first impression jackets advertise *Into Battle, The Unrelenting Struggle, The End of the Beginning* and *Onwards to Victory* on the front flap; the BBC (THE VOICE OF BRITAIN) on the back flap, and notes about this volume on the back face.

COMMENTS
An important companion to the other war speech volumes, uniformly bound and jacketed.

APPRAISAL
The reprint, for which I do not have production figures, must have been small because almost every volume I encounter is a first edition. Somewhat more easily found in fine condition, it has been selling for around $60/£36 for such copies and half as much for more worn copies in well chipped jackets. Reading copies can be had for pocket change.

American Edition: ICS A107b
Publisher: Little, Brown and Company, Boston, 1945

Red cloth blocked gilt and black. Title and author's name separated by thick rule blocked gilt on black inside thin gilt frame on top board and spine. Also on spine are wavy lines top and bottom and publisher's name, all gilt. 16mo, 431 pages numbered (i)–(xiv) and (1)–416 (+2). Published 2 August 1945 at $3.50.

IMPRESSIONS AND QUANTITIES
One impression of 3,500 copies.

VARIANTS
None noted.

DUST JACKETS
Jackets are printed black and red on white stock with a silhouetted photograph of Churchill in a uniform striding toward the camera. The jackets contain a book blurb on the front flap, a publisher's note on the back flap, and praise of the author on the back face.

COMMENTS
Although uniform with earlier Little, Brown war speeches, this is substantially thinner because paper rationing had by then come to America. 'In 1941 this volume would have been larger, or thicker, or heavier, and perhaps all three of these, and might have been set in a larger type face with wider margins to the page', states the publisher on the rear jacket flap. This edition was reset but the contents were not altered; there is no frontispiece nor any internal illustrations.

APPRAISAL
Now fairly hard to find, the American Edition was selling recently for upwards of $50/£30 in fine jacketed condition. I believe its price will begin to rise to the level of the equally scarce American post-war speech volumes.

Canadian Issue: ICS A107c
Publisher: McClelland and Stewart Ltd., Toronto, 1945

An offprint from the Little, Brown American Edition, the Canadian Issue was printed on standard paper and is nearly 50 per cent thicker, though of the same height and width. The differences are the McClelland and Stewart name in place of Little, Brown on the spine and title-page, no price on jacket flap, and 'McCLELLAND | AND STEWART' printed white on the jacket spine. The back jacket flap makes no mention of economy standards and instead advertises *While There is Time* by Stephen Leacock. The red cloth is coarser and lighter than the American Edition. The solitary impression is uncommon but not expensive: up to $50/£30 for fine jacketed copies.

Australian Edition: ICS A107d
Publisher: Cassell and Company Ltd., Melbourne, 1945

Bound in light blue cloth blocked navy on spine with more words than the English Edition: title, and publisher's name plus 'Speeches | by the | Right Hon. WINSTON

S. | CHURCHILL, | C.H., M.P.' 8vo, 326 pages numbered (i)–(xii) and (1)–314 (+2). Wholly set and printed in Australia by Wilke & Co. of Melbourne. Illustrations are the same as the English Edition but the frontispiece photo is between pages 20–21 and the other photos are between pages 52–53 and 147–148. Published at A 12s. 6d.

This reset text has different pagination from the English edition but contains the same material; jacket colours are similar but lighter and the flaps advertise the four previous Churchill war speech volumes (front), the BBC (back) and the contents of this volume (back face). The solitary impression carries on its title-page verso the line, 'First Australian Edition 1945'. There may be binding variants though I have not seen any. Current value, up to $90/£56 for a truly fine copy in a near-fine dust jacket.

VICTORY

COHEN A223, WOODS A112

The 'broad, sunlit uplands' Churchill strove for had been reached, he must have thought, as he stood on the balcony of Buckingham Palace with the Royal Family to receive the plaudits of the VE-Day crowd (frontispiece of this volume). But *Victory* is ironically named: while its largest sections deal with the last eight months of the war–Yalta, Greece, the United Nations, the deaths of Lloyd George and Roosevelt, the German surrender, VE-Day, the Atomic bomb and the surrender of Japan–a substantial section covers the General Election–in which his party was trounced and Churchill, to world consternation, was thrown out of office.

Among his election messages, *Victory* offers the famous 'Gestapo' speech of 5 June 1945, the one some say lost Churchill the election:

'My friends, I must tell you that a Socialist policy is abhorrent to the British ideas of freedom. Although it is now put forward in the main by people who have a good grounding in the liberalism and radicalism of the early part of this century, there can be no doubt that Socialism is inseparably interwoven with totalitarianism and the abject worship of the state. It is not alone that property, in all its forms, is struck at, but that liberty, in all its forms, is challenged by the fundamental concept of Socialism ... No Socialist Government conducting the entire life and industry of the country could afford to allow free, sharp, or violently-worded expressions of public discontent. They would have to fall back on some form of Gestapo, no doubt very humanely directed in the first instance ...'. [Italics in the original text.]

His wife and daughter Sarah pleaded with him not to use the word 'Gestapo'. A latter-day member of the Labour Party, Barbara Castle, remarked that the idea of unassuming little Clem Attlee as Himmler just wasn't a picture worth trying to draw. But as one looks at the excesses of many bureaus, regulators, authorities and councils 50 years later–certain 'environmental' or 'safety' initiatives, the pigeonholing of people by ethnicity or race, the creation of government agencies for just about everything, confiscatory taxation ever to increase their budgets, and the arrogance with which many of them treat the citizenry–one wonders how far wrong Churchill was. True, they don't kill or maim people. But if these agencies are not the product of 'abject worship of the state', whatever else are they?

Quoting the 'Gestapo speech' at the 1995 International Churchill Conference, William F. Buckley, Jr remarked: 'It was the fate of Winston Churchill to return to power in 1951 resolved not to fight the socialist encroachments of the post-war years. He, and England, were too tired, and, as with Eastern Europe and Poland, there was nothing to be done. There was no force in Europe that could move back the Soviet legions, no force in Great Britain that would reignite, until twenty-five years later, the vision Mr. Churchill displayed, speaking to the BBC microphones on June 5th, 1945, since nobody else was listening.'

For me *Victory* will always remain a sombre book. It was perhaps the experiences limned here that caused Churchill to muse in old age that he had accomplished a great deal, only to accomplish nothing in the end; and to point sadly to the motto of the Marlboroughs: 'Faithful but Unfortunate'.

FROM THE REVIEWS

'It is not encouraging for the future to have presented to us out of context the portrait of a world statesman turned local politician. That, unfortunately, is the effect created by *Victory*, a collection of speeches, statements, messages to friends and supporters in the hour of triumph for the cause he led so nobly when it was all but lost. It is somewhat disheartening to be reminded by the record that the Prime Minister, who exhorted his people to face their trial so that in a thousand years history would say "this was their finest hour", had to apologize to them in the end for his compromises with principle and had to exhort them to re-elect him and his party lest the freedom they had fought to defend vanish from their island home.

'Here in this volume we have Mr. Churchill in defeat. It was his privilege in the eight months covered by this volume to announce to his people more victories and triumphs than had come to them in the whole five and a half years of their struggle for survival. Yet there is none of that clarion call of certain leadership with which he inspired and led Great Britain through its darkest hour. Indeed, after his return from the conference with the late President Roosevelt and Marshal Stalin at Yalta, where the partition of Poland was agreed upon, we find the Prime Minister frankly confessing his uncertainty in the face of the complex problems of peace.

'Yet Mr. Churchill could not help looking ahead. As the war ended he saw the liberated countries of southeastern Europe saddled with "police governments", their people beset by the fear–not it is true of aggression–but of political persecution. Yet he was sustained by confidence in the good-will of the Soviets, or rather of Stalin, whom he had come to respect as a man who scrupulously keeps his word.

'Here and there, it is true, we find flashes of the old Churchill inspiration and eloquence. But they are few and far between in the mass of prosaic and pedestrian prose which Mr. Eade has assembled. One can only hope that students of future generations will be attracted to those earlier speeches in which Britain's wartime leader seemed imbued with the spirit of St. George and hurled defiance at the foe in the classic Elizabethan English which suits him so well.'

Raymond Daniell, *New York Times Book Review*, 25 August 1946

First Edition: ICS A112a

Publisher: Cassell and Company Ltd., London, 1946

Light blue cloth blocked gilt with title, author's name (now with three titles: 'O.M., C.H., M.P.') and 'CASSELL' on spine. 8vo, 252 pages numbered (i)–(xii) and (1)–239 (+1), with frontispiece (Churchill and Royal Family, VE-Day) and five internal photographs on two coated paper leaves inserted between pages 84–85 and 148–149. Published 27 June 1946 at 12s. 6d. ($2.50).

IMPRESSIONS AND QUANTITIES
One impression of 38,000 copies, but existence of two states (see below) suggests more than one press run.

VARIANTS
States: In the first state, page 177 is incorrectly numbered '77'. In the second state, the page has been properly numbered. Since the correctly numbered page 177 is integral, not inserted by means of a cancel, we may assume the change was noticed and corrected during the press run. This must have occurred early, for the first state is much scarcer than the second.

Publisher's presentation copies were bound in black pebble grain morocco.

DUST JACKETS
Jackets are printed black and blue fading into purple-blue on white paper. No jacket variations are reported.

COMMENTS
Although wartime economy standards were still in effect, *Victory* is more uniformly produced and seems to contain slightly better paper, for it is less often found badly

First editions of *Victory*. Left to right: English (with jacket), American, Canadian and Australian (in and out of jackets).

spotted, and bindings are often bright. The existence of two states lends interest.

APPRAISAL
An easy book to find, but fine copies in bright, unchipped dust jackets are always prized, and worth up to $80/£48 in the first state. However, they can be found for less. The second state, which is much more common, sells for up to $60/£36.

American Edition: ICS A112b
Publisher: Little, Brown and Co., Boston, 1946

Red cloth blocked gilt and black. Title and author's name separated by thick rule blocked gilt on black inside thin gilt frame on top board and spine. Also on spine are wavy lines top and bottom and publisher's name, all gilt. 16mo, 320 pages numbered (i)–(xii) and (1)–307 (+1). Published 7 August 1946 at $3.50.

IMPRESSIONS AND QUANTITIES
One impression of 5,000 copies.

VARIANTS
None noted.

DUST JACKETS
Jackets are printed black and red on white stock with a silhouetted photograph of Churchill giving the V-sign. The back face promotes, among other titles, Arthur M. Schlesinger, Jr's *The Age of Jackson* and Henry Steele Commager's and Allan Nevins's *America*. In 1968, Commager would edit the abridged edition of *Marlborough*. No jacket variations noted.

COMMENTS
This is a thin volume comparable in size to the American *Dawn of Liberation*. This edition was reset but the contents were not altered; there is no frontispiece nor any internal illustrations.

APPRAISAL
The scarcest of the Little, Brown war speech volumes, the American Edition can command $75/£45 in fine jacketed condition.

Canadian Issue: ICS A112c
Publisher: McClelland and Stewart Ltd., Toronto, 1946

An offprint from the Little, Brown American Edition, the Canadian Issue is the same size but slightly thinner. The differences are the McClelland and Stewart name in place of Little, Brown on the spine and title-page, no price on jacket flap, and 'McCLELLAND | and STEWART' printed black on a white panel on the jacket spine. The red cloth is coarser and lighter than the American Edition. Published August 1946, one impression. Unlike earlier Canadian issues, copies of *Victory* are truly scarce, and hotly sought after by collectors wishing to complete their Canadian volumes. Fine examples in jackets are worth up to $80/£48.

Australian Edition: ICS A112d
Publisher: Cassell and Company Ltd., Melbourne, 1947

Bound in light green buckram blocked black on spine with more words than the English Edition: title and publisher's name plus 'War | Speeches | by the | RIGHT HON. | WINSTON | S. | CHURCHILL, | P.C., M.P'. 8vo, 248 pages numbered (i)–(xii) and (1)–235 (+1). Wholly set and printed in Australia by Wilke & Co. of Melbourne. Illustrations are the same as the English Edition and in the same places. Published at A 12s. 6d.

This edition was published very late–later in fact than the Australian *Secret Session Speeches*. Its reset text has slightly different pagination from the English edition but contains the same material. The dust jacket is printed black and light blue fading into dark blue; no variations reported. There was only one impression, whose title-page verso contains the line 'Australian Edition ... 1947'. There may be binding variants though I have not seen any. Value as for the other Australian war speech volumes: $75/£45 for a fine copy in a near-fine dust jacket, but most examples sell for less.

FOREIGN TRANSLATIONS OF WAR
SPEECH VOLUMES

From INTO BATTLE through VICTORY:
Since few non-English editions of the first six war speech volumes precisely follow the contents of the corresponding English titles, I thought it more convenient to group them separately. Readers interested in a particular language should acquire all the volumes listed. See also foreign translations uniform with the first collected edition (*War Speeches 1940–1945,* Cohen A218, Woods A113), and translations of *Secret Session Speeches* (Cohen A221, Woods A114).

Czech
DO BOJE (F. R. Vorovy: Prague, 1946)
NELITOSTNY ZAPAS (F. R. Vorovy: 1947)
KONEC ZACATKU (Stoleti Prerdu: Prague, 1947)
VZHURUK VITEZSTVI (F. R. Vorovy: Prague, 1947)
CZHURU KVITEZSTVI (F. R. Vorovy: Prague, 1948)
COTERVA NKY OSVOZONY (F. R. Vorovy: 1948)

Danish
I KAMP (Gyldendal: Copenhagen, 1948)
DEN HAARDE DYST (Gyldendal: 1948)
MAALET I SIGTE (Gyldendal: 1948)
SEJR (Gyldendal: 1948)
TALER (Gyldendal Ugleboger: Copenhagen, 1965)
The 1948 titles were large softbound books with illustrated wrappers, subsequently bound in two volumes, half navy morocco and patterned paper covered boards labelled Taler I–II and Taler III–IV. The 1965 is small parperback size and comprises 280 pages with speeches selected from the original works.

Finnish: WINSTON CHURCHILL SOTA-KRONNIKA (2 Vols)
Subtitled 1939–1943 and 1944–1945. Published by W. Soderstrom: Helsinki, 1946, 1948 respectively. Collected editions unbound and in paper boards.

French
L'ENTRÉE EN LUTTE, (Heinemann & Zsolnay: London, 1943)
LA LUTTE SANS RELÂCHE (Heinemann & Zsolnay: 1943)

LA FIN DU COMMENCEMENT (Heinemann & Zsolnay: 1943)
EN AVANT VERS LA VICTOIRE (Heinemann & Zsolnay: 1944)
L'AUBE DE LA LIBÉRATION (Heinemann & Zsolnay: 1945)
VICTOIRE (Heinemann & Zsolnay: 1946)
DISCOURS DE GUERRE 1940–1942 (Shenval Press, UK, 1945)
The first six titles are uniformly bound in white wrappers printed blue and red.
Discours de Guerre is a small paperback.

German
REDEN 1938–1940 (Putnam: New York, 1941). This interesting volume bears a dust
jacket uniform in style to the English *Into Battle*, contains the Putnam text from
Blood, Sweat, and Tears, and was apparently distributed by the British Legation in
Berne, Switzerland. Blue cloth blocked blue on top board and spine; orange stained
top page edges.
REDEN 1938–1940 (Europa Verlag: Zurich, 1946)
INS GEFECHT (Europa Verlag: 1946)
DER UNERBITTLICHE KAMPF (Europa Verlag: 1947)
DAS ENDE DES ANFANGS (Europa Verlag: 1948)
VORWARTS ZUM SIEG (Europa Verlag: 1948)
ENDSIEG (Europa Verlag: 1950)
The Europa volumes are uniformly bound in coarse and smooth tan cloth with dust
jackets whose colours change with the volume. Together with the German Edition
of *Secret Session Speeches* (see separately under that title), these comprise seven
volumes sequentially numbered 'Band 1' through 'Band 7'.
REDEN (Ullstein Bücher: 1955; speeches 1938–1945, 212 pages).

Italian: IN GUERRA: DISCORSI PUBBLICI E SEGRETI (2 vols.)
Published by Rizzoli: Milan 1948. Subtitled 1938–1942 and 1943–1945. Bound in

A selection of foreign translations. Left to right: the French and German versions of *Into Battle*, the
Swedish *Victory* and the Spanish *Dawn of Liberation*. The German *Reden* was published by Putnams in
New York but contains a card with the compliments of the British Embassy's press attaché in Berne,
Switzerland.

white card wrappers printed black, later hardbound wrapped in medium green dust jackets with white spines. L700 per volume. Includes *Secret Session Speeches*.

Korean
KOZ (Seoul Newspaper Company: Seoul 1947; Institute of International Affairs: Seoul, 1949).

Norwegian
BLOD, SVETTE OG TÅRER (Cappelens: Oslo, 1946; softbound and quarter leather)
MOT SEIER (Cappelens: 1946; softbound and quarter leather)
VED MÅLET (Cappelens: 1947; softbound and quarter leather)
On all quarter leather editions, two jackets have been noted: illustrated on thin paper, and unillustrated on heavy paper.

Romanian: DISCURSURI DE RAZBOIU
Published by Pilot Press: London 1945. Subtitled O Culegere a Discursurilor Tinute de Primul Ministrue al Maeri Britanni, intre Mai 1940 si Octombrie 1943.

Russian: IZBRANNIE RECHI 1938–1943
Published by H.M. Stationery Office: London, 1945.

Spanish
SANGRE, SUDOR & LÁGRIMAS (Editorial Clarid: Buenos Aires, 1941)
EL FIN DEL PRINCIPIO DEL ASISMO A LA VICTORIA (Editorial Clarid: Buenos Aires, 1944)
ADELANTE HACÍA LA VICTORIA (Los Libros de Nuestro Tiempo: Barcelona, 1944)
ALBA DE LIBERACIÓN (Los Libros de Nuestro Tiempo: 1945)
VICTORIA (Los Libros de Nuestro Tiempo: 1947)
HACÍA LA VICTORIA (Ediciones Minerva: Mexico City, 1945).

Swedish
BLOD, SVETT OCH TÅRAR (Skoglund: Stockholm, 1941; soft and clothbound; a 1941 second edition adds three May 1938 speeches.)
OFÖRTRÖTTAD KAMP (Skoglund: 1942; soft and clothbound)
SLUTET AV BÖRJAN (Skoglund: 1943; soft and clothbound)
FRAM MOT SEGERN (Skoglund: 1944; soft and clothbound)
BEFRIELSENS GRYNING (Skoglund: 1945; soft and clothbound)
SEGER (Skoglund: 1945; soft and clothbound)
KRIGSKRÖNIKA (2 vols, Skoglund: Stockholm and H. Schildt: Helsinki. Volume I (1945) is entitled simply Krigskrönika; Volume II (1947) is entitled Krigskrönika 1944–45. Soft and clothbound.

Soft and clothbound Swedish titles came with a dust jacket. They were later combined with the Swedish post-war speech volumes in a 4-volume leatherbound set.

Turkish: BU HARVIN ICNUZY
Published by Basimeri: Istanbul, 1942.

Combined Work in Korean
A Korean translation of *Blood, Sweat, and Tears* is combined with quote extracts *(The Wisdom of Winston Churchill)* in a volume published by Lim Ik yong: Seoul, 1966.

WAR SPEECHES 1940-1945

COHEN A224, WOODS A113

The first collected edition of the war speeches, this softbound work is derived from the first six war speech volumes (*Into Battle* through *Victory*). In *Artillery of Words*, Frederick Woods wrote: 'With these speeches, together with *Arms and the Covenant,* we have the clearest possible picture of Churchill the gladiator, the fighter, waging war with words as well as with bombs and bullets. No one knew better than he the propaganda value across the world not only of his constant refusal to admit defeat (though he acknowledged passing set-backs in the House of Commons) but also of his never-tiring assertions of eventual victory.'

In 1954, accepting the congratulations of Parliament on his 80th birthday, Churchill uttered his famous assessment of his role as spokesman for Britain:

'I was very glad that Mr. Attlee described my speeches in the war as expressing the will not only of Parliament but of the whole nation. Their will was resolute and remorseless and, as it proved, unconquerable. It fell to me to express it, and if I found the right words you must remember that I have always earned my living by my pen and by my tongue. It was the nation and the race dwelling all round the globe that had the lion heart. I had the luck to be called upon to give the roar. I also hope that I sometimes suggested to the lion the right places to use his claws.'

First Edition: Woods A113
Publisher: Cassell and Company Ltd., London, 1946

Softbound in wrappers printed black and light blue on white stock. 16mo, 284

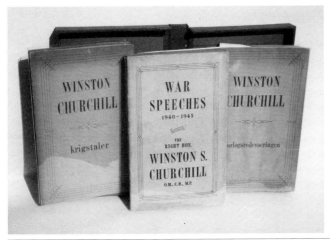

Uniformly bound editions of *War Speeches 1940-1945*, all in light blue wrappers printed black. Left to right: Danish, English and Dutch. The Dutch, published 1945, is the true first edition. All were published in London by Cassell.

pages numbered (i)–(x) and (1)–271 (+3) plus coated paper frontispiece (J. Russell Sons photo of the author) facing the title page and tipped onto a blank free endpaper. Published July 1946 at 5s. ($1.25).

IMPRESSIONS AND QUANTITIES
One impression of 20,000 copies.

VARIANTS
None reported. Several collectors report copies without frontispieces, but examination has always shown that these were removed by a previous owner: the Russell photograph is highly framable.

COMMENTS
Though a cheap production on pulpy paper, this is a significant work: the first collected edition of *War Speeches*, establishing the collected text later expanded in 1952–1953 with a definitive 3-volume edition. Though ignored for years by collectors, it has since become recognised as an important volume. Probably published mainly for export, it is very rare both in Britain and abroad.

APPRAISAL
Not so many years ago copies could be bought for a few pounds or dollars; today prices of near-fine copies (the aging of the paper makes really fine ones very rare) are high and rising, and can reach into hundreds, and some collectors have cheerfully paid $1,000/£600 for exceptional copies. Its cheap materials mean that there are many worn or defective copies, so it is possible to own one without nearly such a high investment, but one has to look around. There are also stories of the proverbial fine copy offered for a fiver by some obscure secondhand bookshop, but these are very old stories...

TRANSLATIONS
(UNIFORM WITH THIS VOLUME)

Danish: KRIGSTALER
Published by Cassell: London, 1946.

Dutch: WINSTON CHURCHILLS OORLOGSREDEVOERINGEN
Published by Cassell: London, 1945. The first world edition of the Cassell paperback collected *War Speeches*, thus highly collectible. Adds one speech not in the English edition (21 September 1943) but lacks the last 16 speeches of the English edition (1944–1945). This edition contains a frontispiece photograph of the author.

WAR SPEECH VOLUMES
PUBLISHED AS BOOKS

Readers are referred to the Cohen or Woods bibliographies for a complete account of the many war speeches published singly or in groups as separate works; some of these constitute the true first appearance of the speech, preceding their appearance in the war speech volumes.

Four speeches or speech groups hardbound in limited editions of special interest to collectors are mentioned here, as some collectors do not consider a collection of Churchill's 'books' complete without them.

ADDRESSES DELIVERED IN THE YEAR NINETEEN HUNDRED AND FORTY TO THE PEOPLE OF GREAT BRITAIN, OF FRANCE, AND TO THE MEMBERS OF THE ENGLISH HOUSE OF COMMONS, BY THE PRIME MINISTER, WINSTON CHURCHILL

Woods D(a)5
Publisher: Grabhorn Press, San Francisco, 1940

A limited edition of 250 copies published for Ransohoff's Department Store in San Francisco by the Grabhorn Press. Bound in quarter beige buckram and orange cloth. Fo., 82 pages numbered (6+) (i)–(ii) and (1)–68 (+6) inclusive of free endpapers. Printed black and orange, the title page (i) contains a stylised Union Flag printed orange. Includes 1940 speeches of 13 May (excerpts); 19 May, 18 June, 20 August, 11 September and 8 October 1940 to the House of Commons; and the broadcast of 21 October to the French Nation. Published at $7.50.

This marvellous, huge (10¾ x 15¾in) large-type edition is not a reprint (per Woods) but the first appearance in volume form of these speeches, later published in *Into Battle*. This was recognised by Ronald Cohen, who includes the work in his Section 'A'. Wrote the late Dalton Newfield: 'Because they used "self-endpapers" these books almost always have one or two gutterbreaks; Grabhorn should have known better. Still very desirable, though.'

The late Robert Hastings, whose famous Churchill collection was recently auctioned by Christie's, had a handwritten letter from Robert Ransohoff (August 1960), stating that his store had requested 500 copies of this and the 1941 title following, but Grabhorn had refused, saying that that would depreciate the value of the books. Ransohoff told Hastings that all 250 copies sold out by noon of the

The first large, finely printed Grabhorn Press commemorative edition (1940 addresses) bound in half buckram and orange cloth, with the first Overbrook Press limited edition (speech to the US Congress, 1941). Only 250 of the former and 1,000 of the latter were published.

first day, and that Henry Morgenthau had wanted 18 copies of this title for a British Embassy reception. Ransohoff filled Morgenthau's order by begging copies back from customers who had bought more than one, including himself and his brother! The price I state above is from this letter. Grabhorn produced many such limited editions for Ransohoff's.

VARIANT

Robert Hastings owned a copy with a large Union Flag blocked gilt on the top board, perhaps one of Morgenthau's 18.

APPRAISAL

Highly desirable, this work has seen prices as high as $800/£480, although the usual range is $350/£218 to $600/£375. They will probably go higher, since Ronald Cohen recognises this work as a full-fledged 'Section A' title.

BROADCAST ADDRESSES TO THE PEOPLE OF GREAT BRITAIN, ITALY, POLAND, RUSSIA AND THE UNITED STATES BY THE PRIME MINISTER OF THE BRITISH EMPIRE, WINSTON CHURCHILL

Woods D(a)8

Publisher: Grabhorn Press, San Francisco, 1941

A limited edition of 250 copies by the Grabhorn Press, bound in quarter beige buckram and light blue cloth. Fo., 78 pages numbered (8+) (i)–(iv) and (1)–60 (+6)

Grabhorn's second limited edition contains a beautiful three-colour printed frontispiece of the Royal Arms. At right is Overbrook's second limited edition (600), of Churchill's 1943 speech to Congress.

inclusive of free endpapers. Printed black, medium blue and gold, page (i) containing the British Royal Arms printed blue and gold. Includes the 23 December 1940 broadcast to the Italians and the following 1941 world broadcasts: 9 February, 27 April, 3 May ('to the Polish People'), 22 June and 24 August. Published at $7.50.

A companion to the previous Grabhorn production, also classified by Ronald Cohen as an 'A' title. A third colour makes it even more elaborate than its predecessor. Equally desirable, though slightly more common than the first Grabhorn book, the BROADCASTS have sold for at least $600/£360. See details of the publishing under the previous title.

AN ADDRESS BY THE RT. HON. WINSTON S. CHURCHILL, PRIME MINISTER OF GREAT BRITAIN, 26 DECEMBER, 1941

Woods A84(c)
Publisher: Overbrook Press, Stamford, CT, 1942

A limited edition of 1,000 copies bound in red cloth (not buckram per Woods). 16mo, 28 pages numbered (i)–(vi) and (1)–17 (+5) printed black and dark red. Paper title label ranged upper left on top board. A pretty little piece, by no means the first appearance of the famous speech to Congress: 'What kind of a People do they think we are?' Its appearance and status as a limited edition caused many to be saved over the years and the supply is quite reasonable at present. Fine copies can run to $250/£150 but can often be found for less. It was preceded by both British

Library of Information and American Government Printing Office editions, but is the only version of the speech in hardbound form.

AN ADDRESS BY WINSTON S. CHURCHILL, PRIME MINISTER OF GREAT BRITAIN

Woods A93(b)
Publisher: Overbrook Press, Stamford, CI, 1943

A more limited and much scarcer edition of 600 copies printed (per a publisher's note on page 21) 'For the members of the Congress, facing vast new responsibilities'. 16mo, 22 pages numbered (1)–21 (+1) printed black and dark red. Bound in black paper-covered boards with red paper title centred in top half of top board containing the title 'AN ADDRESS BY | WINSTON S. CHURCHILL | Washington – 19 May 1943 | The Overbrook Press : Stamford, Connecticut', surrounded by decorative border, all gilt. Churchill's second speech to Congress is here published, not in its first appearance but certainly its most luxurious. Despite the lower run of the Ransohoff works, this is the hardest to find of the four speech volumes mentioned herein. Fine copies now command up to $600/£360 and will go higher.

SECRET SESSION SPEECHES

COHEN A227, WOODS A114

Herbert Morrison is responsible for this book. On 19 December 1945 Morrison, Leader of the House of Commons in the Labour Government which had replaced Churchill's, moved to lift the ban on revealing the proceedings of five wartime Secret Session debates. Six months later Churchill published his seventh and final volume of war speeches, containing all five of his contributions to those sessions. It earned him over $50,000.

'It is impossible to guarantee that the speeches as now printed are a completely accurate, word-for-word report of what Mr. Churchill said in Secret Session', notes the book's editor, Charles Eade. 'It is likely that he occasionally changed words and phrases to suit the mood and temper of the House but such alterations must have been only of a minor character ... [The speeches] form a necessary contribution to the history of the War and explain many events which were puzzling at the time.'

Four speeches are on the life-and-death 'Battle of the Atlantic'; the fall of Singapore, probably the greatest single disaster and disappointment of Churchill's wartime Premiership; and the inside story of the Darlan episode in North Africa. Most fascinating is the first speech, *The Fall of France*, delivered 20 June 1940, for which there was no complete record. Instead, the book offers the nine pages of typewritten notes and headings, edited and annotated by Churchill, which he actually held in his hand as he spoke. They form a singular example of what Churchill called 'Speech Form', in which the cadence is established by picking out each group of words or sentences and indenting to show where the pauses should be, creating that marvellous sense of timing which was the key to Churchill's oratory.

Churchill's deletions are as fascinating as what he said. After stating, '[In] my view always Govt. strengthened by S[ecret]. S[essions]', he wasn't utterly sure, so he crossed out the following line: 'Quite ready to have others.' His powerful optimism is abundant, even at this depressing time, with France wiped out. 'I hope it is not so', he starts to say of some grim possibility, but then quickly crosses those words out–why suggest unpleasant developments? As always, there are lighter notes: 'Goering. How do you class him? He was an airman turned politician. I like him better as an airman. Not very much anyway.'

Typing the four later speeches for the printer was the first assignment of Elizabeth Gilliatt, a secretary who would serve Churchill for nearly a decade. Conventionally typeset, the four lack the impact and immediacy of the typescript speech, but still constitute important reading: *Parliament in the Air Raids* (17

September 1940), *The Battle of the Atlantic* (25 June 1941), *The Fall of Singapore* (23 April 1942) and *Admiral Darlan and the North Africa Landings* (10 December 1942).

It is not coincidental that the need for Secret Sessions ended in 1943, when the war started to turn in favour of the Allies.

FROM THE REVIEWS

'More representative of the Churchill who will be remembered are the five major addresses he delivered to the House of Commons at secret sessions. Mr. Churchill had no text from what he told the House of Commons on that solemn day in June 1940, when France had fallen; the speech is reproduced only from his notes. It was his conviction that Britain could weather the storm of the next three months, by which time, it is obvious now, Mr. Churchill hoped that Providence in the form of intervention from the New World would help redress the balance of the Old. In September when, with the bombs raining down on London, there was another secret session of the House, the Prime Minister revealed that a vast enemy armada of 1,700 self-propelled barges and 200 oceangoing ships capable of transporting an invading wave of 500,000 men was gathered across the narrow channel awaiting the order to attack. Expressing his confidence in a victory as "sure as the sun will rise", Mr Churchill added, "Anyhow, whatever happens, we will all go down fighting to the end."

'Even then, long before he delivered his radio speech asking for American aid and declaring "give us the tools and we will finish the job", the Prime Minister was hoping for more direct assistance from the United States. Nothing, he declared, would so arouse American opinion as the news of fighting in the British Isles.'

Raymond Daniell, *New York Times Book Review,* 25 August 1946

First Edition: Cohen, ICS A114ab
Publisher: Simon and Schuster, Inc., New York, 1946

Grey cloth blocked gilt. 'WINSTON CHURCHILL'S | Secret Session Speeches' appears on top board, 'Winston Churchill's SECRET SESSION SPEECHES [four spacer dots] and publisher's name appear on spine, reading down. 8vo, 126 pages numbered (i)–(viii) and (1)–113 (+5). Published 22 August 1946 at $2. No illustrations.

IMPRESSIONS AND QUANTITIES
One impression of 5,910 copies.

VARIANTS
None noted.

DUST JACKETS
Jackets are printed rust-red and dark green on white stock with titles on spine and

Secret Session Speeches. Above: the English and American (the latter being the true first). Below: The Canadian (which carries a jacket uniform with previous Little, Brown American war speech volumes) and Australian (with a jacket uniform with previous Cassell English volumes).

front face and promotional blurbs on flaps and back face. On the front face the jacket designer signs his name: 'Woods' (no relation!). No variations noted.

COMMENTS

The arrangements by which Churchill dropped Putnam for Simon and Schuster for this volume are intricate; readers should consult the Cohen Bibliography for more details. While relaxing in Miami before his *Iron Curtain* speech in Fulton, Missouri in March 1946, Churchill had sent Simon and Schuster the typescript, as part of the agreement with Marshall Field, owner of the *Chicago Sun*, who planned to serialise the speeches upon publication. But after Fulton, the *Sun* attacked Churchill with what he viewed as 'stock Communist output', and Churchill withdrew his serialisation offer. This turned out well enough: while Simon and Schuster paid him £1,000 ($4,035), Henry Luce, publisher of *Life*, bought the serialisation rights for £12,500 ($50,000), though only the last two speeches were published. (See Sir Martin Gilbert, *"Never Despair"*, Vol. VIII of the official biography, pages 194, 204–205, 255, 258.)

APPRAISAL

Contrary to Woods, the American Edition preceded the English by over a month and is therefore the true First Edition. Its small press run has rendered it scarce today, and it will soon be quite rare, especially in jacketed form. The gilt lettering was not of good quality and is usually found quite dull. A really fine copy with some sparkle left to the gilt and a clean, unchipped dust jacket is worth up to $150/£90, and is going higher fast. Without the jacket, $50/£30 is a common price, but it may cost more and is rarely seen for less.

First English (Illustrated) Edition: ICS A114b
Publisher: Cassell and Company Ltd., London, 1946

Light blue cloth blocked gilt on spine: '| | CASSELL | | SECRET SESSION SPEECHES | | CHURCHILL | |' (reading up); three vertical gilt rules at left side of top board. 8vo, 96 pages numbered (i)–(v) and 6–96, plus 16 photographs on 16 coated paper leaves inserted between pages 48–49. Published 26 September 1946 at 6s. ($1.50).

IMPRESSIONS AND QUANTITIES
One impression of 48,500 copies.

VARIANTS
The edition exists bound in dark blue leatherette. Publisher's presentation copies bound uniformly with previous such copies of war speech volumes exist, but are very scarce.

Presentation cards: Churchill presented many copies of this work, unsigned but accompanied by a 2¼ x 3¾in white card printed in black, 'WITH THE COMPLIMENTS OF Winston S. Churchill' (name in script), surrounded by a light blue decorative border. Most of these were accompanied by a second card of the same size, reading 'THE REFERENCE to "American Authorities" in the Introduction refers to the United States Government and General Eisenhower' and surrounded by a thin light blue rule. Churchill apparently thought it proper to be more specific on this point than editor Charles Eade, who wrote in the Introduction, 'Acknowledgement is expressed of the courtesy of the American authorities concerned for permission to publish the documents quoted.'

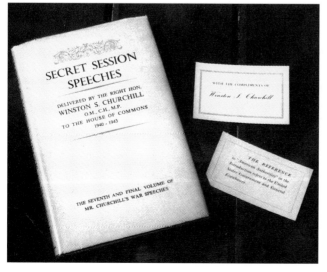

The English Edition *Secret Session Speeches* with the rare presentation cards printed black and light blue in the same style as the dust jacket. The card above presents Churchill's compliments; the one below explains the 'American Authorities' reference in the Introduction.

DUST JACKETS

Jackets, which are not uniform with other Cassell war speech volumes, are printed black and light blue on white paper. On the front flap, each jacket has the original intended price of 7s. 6d. blacked out in two places, and replaced by the 6s. price. No jackets with the 7s. 6d. price have been found.

COMMENTS

Cassell became more generous with photographs with this title, which should be acquired for them alone. Arranged to chronicle the war, most of the photos are rarely seen elsewhere: the PM bidding farewell to French President Reynaud as the Germans closed in; Churchill with troops and defence workers, inspecting Blitz damage, touring warships and working over maps and papers.

APPRAISAL

Although wartime economy standards were still in effect, *Secret Session Speeches* is more uniformly produced and seems to contain slightly better paper. Nevertheless, the truly fine, unspotted copy in bright cloth is a rarity, and can cost up to $80/£48 with a clean jacket. The white jackets soil easily, and bring the price well down when dirty or torn. Unjacketed copies are fairly common and inexpensive. The dark blue binding variant adds 25 per cent to the price. A jacketed copy with both presentation cards laid in is certainly worth up to $250/£150, for these are rare indeed. Still, run-of-the-mill copies without jackets are easy to find and cost little, so there's no excuse for not owning one.

Canadian Edition: ICS A114c

Publisher: McClelland and Stewart Ltd., Toronto, 1946

Red cloth blocked black and gilt. Title and author's name separated by thick rule blocked gilt on black inside thin gilt on top board. 'SECRET SESSION SPEECHES [spacer] CHURCHILL' [smaller type] blocked gilt on black with thin gilt border on spine (reading down); publisher's name toward base and decorative wavy lines at spine ends. 8vo, 112 pages numbered (1)–108 (+4), plus four pages of photographs on coated paper in four leaves inserted between pages 32–33, 48–49, 80–81 and 96–97. Published Autumn 1946 in one impression.

Dust jackets printed red and black on white paper in the style of previous Little, Brown and McClelland and Stewart war speeches. The front face includes title, byline and a silhouetted photo of Churchill working on a train (final photo in the English Edition).

A most interesting production, this work was wholly reset (except for the typescript speech) in Canada and therefore constitutes a separate edition. Unlike its American counterpart, the binding and jacket are uniform with five previous North American war speech volumes. Undoubtedly the American Edition would have looked like this had Little Brown continued as publisher. Highly collectible as a true edition, but quite rare nowadays, it is the hardest Canadian war speech volume to find. Fine jacketed copies command over $100/£60 and can go higher. Unjacketed copies run about 50 per cent lower.

Australian Issue: ICS A114d

Publisher: Cassell and Company Ltd., Melbourne, 1946

Bound in tan, green or pale blue cloth blocked dark blue on spine with publisher's name, title and author's name, reading up. 8vo, 96 pages numbered (1)–96 plus frontispiece and 14 internal photographs on coated stock inserted between pages 16–17, 32–33, 36–37, 48–49, 64–65, 84–85 and 92–93. Offprinted from the English edition by William Brooks & Co. Ltd. All but two photographs from the English Edition are included. Published at A 12s. 6d. The title-page verso contains the line 'First Australian Edition 1946'. Only one impression was published.

DUST JACKETS
While the Canadian Edition shows us the uniform North American jacket style, the Australian Issue displays the uniform British style which Cassell abandoned with this title in Britain. On thin white paper, it is printed black and yellow-orange fading into dark blue on the face only; the spine is blank except for the titles printed black.

VARIANTS
I have seen more tan bindings than green or blue. Unlike previous Australian speech volumes, this was not reset but offprinted from the English edition–a speedier production process, which saw this title appear before the Australian *Victory*.

Bibliophiles are a curious lot. I know one who acquired the Australian Issue instead of an English Edition because in this way he could have a complete set of seven uniform war speech dust jackets! By pointing out that the Australian jacket is not quite uniform, being uncoloured on the spine, and lacking two photographs, succeeded in selling him both editions–as booksellers like to do. Sadly there is not much world demand for this interesting issue. Expect to pay $75/£45 for a fine copy in a near-fine dust jacket, but less for more worn copies and only about $25/£15 for copies without jackets.

TRANSLATIONS

Danish: CHURCHILLS HEMMELIGE TALER
Published by Berlingske· Copenhagen, 1946 (card wrappers, supplied with pages untrimmed).

Foreign translations of *Secret Session Speeches*. Left to right: German, French, Danish, Swedish and Spanish. All carry verbatim transcripts of the first speech in English, which was available only in its original manuscript form.

French: MES DISCOURS SECRETS
Published by DuPont: Paris, 1947.

German: GEHEIMSREDEN/BAND 7
Published by Europa Verlag: Zurich, 1947; bound in coarse and smooth tan cloth with dust jackets.

Italian: I DISCORSI SEGRETI DI CHURCHILL
Published by Edizioni Riunite: Milan 1946, 96 pages in card wrappers, appearance similar to the French edition.

Spanish: LOS SECRETOS DE LA GUERRA
Published by Los Libros de Nuestro Tiempo: Barcelona, 1946.

Swedish: TAL INFÖR LYCKTA DÖRRAR
Published by Skoglund: Stockholm 1946 (soft and clothbound)

THE SECOND WORLD WAR

COHEN A240, WOODS A123

Let us begin by recording all the major criticisms of Winston Churchill's most famous book. 1) It is not history. 2) It is filled with grandiose prose, inflicted on apathetic readers who only want peace and a quiet life. 3) It is highly biased–the author never puts a foot wrong and publishes hundreds of his own memoranda and directives–but few replies to them. 4) It moralises incessantly about dictators and their empires–but not Britain's. 5) The impact of the war on Britain and the details of Cabinet meetings are vague; Churchill alone confronts the French, Hitler, the Soviets, the Americans; one critic says, 'Every instance of adversity becomes an occasion for the narrator's triumph.'

In the words of Arthur Balfour, these indictments contain much that is true and much that is trite, but what's true is trite, and what's not trite is not true.

Professor J. H. Plumb, in *Four Faces and the Man* (London, 1969, published as *Churchill Revised* in New York, 1969), refers to Churchill's work as 'A history of the Second World War' and then says it is not history. The faux title has been oft repeated. Churchill himself insisted that the volumes were memoirs: 'This is not history–this is my case'–his 'life effort', in which he was 'content to be judged'. In other places he calls them 'a contribution to history'. Some of his admirers would say he dissembles and is too modest. Professor John Keegan, in an introduction to a recent new edition, calls *The Second World War* 'a great history' of 'monumental quality...extraordinary in its sweep and comprehensiveness, balance and literary effect; extraordinary in the singularity of its point of view; extraordinary as the labour of a man, already old, who still had ahead of him a career large enough to crown most other statesmen's lives; extraordinary as a contribution to the memorabilia of the English-speaking peoples.'

If that seems too pro-Churchill a view, consider Malcolm Muggeridge's appropriate evaluation: the volumes are 'historic rather than historical'. Or Manfred Weidhorn's: 'a record of history made rather than written ... No other wartime leader in history has given us a work of two million words written only a few years after the events and filled with messages among world potentates which had so recently been heated and secret. Britain was led by a professional writer.'

As a professional writer wishing to build up 'the Churchill Legend', goes another familiar refrain, our author ignored or buried unpleasant facts, or twisted them to suit his purpose. I have yet to read a memoir that didn't. Yet few memoirs are so magnanimous, as illustrated by a principle Churchill adopts in his Preface: 'never criticising any measure of war or policy after the event unless I had before expressed publicly or formally my opinion or warning about it.' The effect, Keegan tells us, 'is to invest the whole history with those qualities of magnanimity and good will by which he set such store, and the more so as it deals with personalities.'

Churchill's prose 'could often be aversive [sic] to modern readers', wrote another recent analyst, and, by the time the books appeared, 'the world had moved on into an exhausted flatness that had little to do with, and little time for, the high-flown attitudes and language of Churchillian rhetoric'. If that's so, why was *The Second World War* able to sell over 300,000 copies of each volume as it was published, millions since, 18 translations into foreign languages, three major serialisations and several million abridgements?

So much for the non-trite and non-true. The other criticisms are mainly valid but hardly crippling. *The Second World War* is indeed intensely personal, considering the war from Churchill's angle not Britain's, and it moralises because the memoir-writer passionately believed in those morals. He even gave the work its own Moral: 'In War: Resolution; In Defeat: Defiance; In Victory: Magnanimity; In Peace: Good Will.' I am not sure what is so wrong about that.

Churchill had a right to make his case. Many times in his career he had been second-guessed or misjudged: over Antwerp and the Dardanelles in the First World War; over how to respond to Bolshevism; over the General Strike of 1926; over India, the Abdication, Franco, Mussolini, Hitler. During the war he had attacked an ally's fleet, fired generals, lost battleships, stalled on launching a second front, argued with Roosevelt and Stalin, engaged in carpet bombing...Perhaps he felt the need to defend his actions, knowing that very soon he would be second-guessed by post-war critics, former colleagues and historians eager to seize on and emphasise his faults and mistakes–which were manifestly there. In fact, 'revisionism' had begun as he worked: 'In view of the many accounts which are extant and multiplying of my supposed aversion from any kind of large-scale opposed-landing, such as took place in Normandy in 1944', Churchill wrote in Volume II, Chapter XII, 'it may be convenient if I make clear that from the very beginning I provided a great deal of the impulse and authority for creating the immense apparatus and armada for the landing of armour on the beaches...'

Australian Prime Minister Robert Menzies (recently named as the should-have-been replacement to Churchill as wartime premier by an eager revisionist) told Churchill in 1948: 'You realize that five years after your death...clever young men will be writing books explaining that you were never right about anything?' Churchill snorted, 'You think so, do you?' 'Yes', Menzies added, 'but not many years later, the clever young men will have been forgotten, and your name will be seen clearly at the pinnacle.' Well, the recent spate of Churchill critiques (some good, some dreadful) are going out of print, and *The Second World War* is still selling.

The merits of our author's six substantial volumes tend rather to eclipse their evident flaws. There is, first, what Robert Pilpel calls 'the warm sense of communion', through which only a great writer can place the reader at his side in the march of events. Those events are conducted like a symphony. 'In the great drama, he was the greatest', said de Gaulle of our author, and *The Second World War* is magnificently dramatic. Manfred Weidhorn compares its greatest scenes with those of a first-class novel: 'Such is the eerie sense of déjà vu and ubi sunt upon his return in 1939, as First Lord [of the Admiralty], to Scapa Flow, exactly a quarter of a century after having, at the start of the other world war, paid the same visit during the same season in the same capacity ... The collapse of the venerable and once mighty France and Churchill's agony are beautifully rendered by the sensuous detail of the old gentlemen industriously carrying French archives on wheelbarrows to bonfires. Another powerful scene is that of the vote of censure, moved by Churchill's critics in the wake of the Singapore and Tobruk disasters, even as the battle rages in the desert. The ensuing debate ... was an "accompaniment to the cannonade"; a climax was being reached in parliamentary and desert fronts simultaneously ... Near the end of the work appears one of the greatest scenes of all. On the way to the Potsdam conference, Churchill flies to Berlin and its "chaos of ruins". Taken to Hitler's chancellery, he walks through its shattered halls for "quite a long time" ... The great duel is over; the victor stands on the site from which so much evil originated ... "We were given the best first-hand accounts available at that time of what had happened in these final scenes."'

Amid the pathos, humour bubbles incessantly to the surface, Pilpel writes, 'as if Puck had escaped from *A Midsummer Night's Dream* and infiltrated *Paradise Lost*'. Few other memoirs, let alone histories, leaven their wisdom with such merry wit. There is Churchill's famous desert conference with his Generals, 'in a tent full of flies and important personages'; an amusing lunch with King Saud of Arabia, whose religion forbids tobacco and alcohol, which Churchill says are mandated by *his* religion; his courtly letter to the Japanese Ambassador, signed 'your obedient servant', announcing 'with highest consideration' that a state of war exists with his country ('When you have to kill a man it costs nothing to be polite'); parties with Stalin where Churchill pooh-poohs the storied drinking bouts ('I had been properly brought up'). All this levity 'somehow sits well with the cataclysmic and lugubrious matter of the story', Weidhorn adds, 'for Churchill does not allow the humor to take the sting out of events or reduce war to a mere game. He simply refuses to overlook the light side ... Such a tone, markedly different from the histrionics of the other side, may well be a secret of survival. As Shaw said, he who laughs lasts.'

It is important to remember that *The Second World War* is not all memoirs. Each volume contains lengthy appendices of personal minutes, telegrams and directives to military and civilian officials which Churchill had secured permission to publish. Here again he has been accused of bias, selectivity and an air of infallibility; some of the documents are trivial even unworthy of him. But in the main they had a powerful effect: they kept everyone's eyes on the prize.

My favourite example appears in Appendix C to Volume III, *The Grand Alliance*, where Churchill responds to General Brooke's report on an invasion exercise called VICTOR, which presupposed that the Germans landed five divisions on the Norfolk coast and established a beachhead within forty-eight hours. Churchill writes:

'I presume the details of this remarkable feat have been worked out by the Staff concerned. Let me see them. For instance, how many ships and transports carried these five Divisions? How many Armoured vehicles did they comprise? How many motor lorries, how many guns, how much ammunition, how many men, how many tons of stores, how far did they advance in the first forty-eight hours, how many men and vehicles were assumed to have landed in the first twelve hours, what percentage of loss were they debited with? What happened to the transports and store-ships while the first forty-eight hours of fighting were going on? Had they completed emptying their cargoes, or were they still lying in shore off the point protected by superior enemy daylight Fighter formations? How many Fighter airplanes did the enemy have to employ, if so, to cover the landing places? ... I should be very glad if the same officers would work out a scheme for our landing an exactly similar force on the French coast at the same extreme range of our Fighter protection and assuming that the Germans have naval superiority in the Channel ...'

Professor Eliot Cohen, citing this memo in a paper on 'The Problems of Supreme Command' at the 1993 Churchill Conference, tells us that 'Brooke replied on April 7th, giving the figures noted by Churchill ... plus the assumption that the Germans would consume petrol and food found on British soil. Churchill responded a few weeks later, noting how much more difficult than this British landings in Greece had proven, and continuing to press his inquiries. He noted that on the last two days of the exercise the British were credited with 432 fighter sorties, and the Germans with 1,500, although the Germans had further to fly ... Gamely enough, Brooke continued to reply, until the exchange petered out.

'What is the signifcance of this episode?', Cohen continued. 'It is noteworthy, first, that the commander in charge of the exercise, Brooke, stood up to Churchill and not only did not suffer by it, but ultimately gained promotion to the post of Chief of Imperial General Staff and chairman of the Chiefs of Staff Committee. But more important is Churchill's observation that "It is of course quite reasonable for assumptions of this character to be made as a foundation for a military exercise. It would be indeed a darkening counsel to make them the foundation of serious military thought." At this very time ... Churchill was arguing–against the position of several of his military advisers–that the risks of invasion were sufficiently low to make the TIGER convoy [of armoured vehicles to the Middle East] worth the attempt. TIGER went through, losing only one ship to a mine and delivering some 250 tanks to the hard-pressed forces in the Middle East.

'By no means did Churchill always have it right, but he often caught his military staff when they had it wrong', Cohen concluded. 'Churchill exercised one of his most important functions as war leader by holding their calculations and assertions up to the standards of a massive common sense, informed by wide reading and experience at war. When his military advisors could not provide plausible answers to these harassing and inconvenient questions, they usually revised their views; when they could, Churchill revised his. In both cases, British strategy benefitted.'

Space is running out and I haven't represented a fraction of this brilliant work. *The Second World War*, a prose epic like *The River War* and *Marlborough*, belongs with them amongst the first rank of Churchill's books. Flaws and all, it is indispensable reading for anyone who seeks a true understanding of the war that made us what we are today. Manfred Weidhorn summarises it better than anyone I've read: 'When viewed beside the achievements of its statesman-narrator [*The Second World War*] remains not just a unique revelation of the exercise of power from atop an empire in duress but also one of the fascinating products of the human spirit, both as an expression of a personality and a somewhat anomalous epic tale filled with the depravities, miseries, and glories of man.'

FROM THE REVIEWS

'Never before, it is safe to say, has the publication of a book in the English language received such widespread acclaim. Newspapers of all political complexions have treated it as a great public event. That the acclamation has been even greater than might have been anticipated is the measure of his unique achievement–to have given the authority and the majesty of history to the stuff of his own times.'

Harold Nicolson in *The Daily Telegraph*, 4 October 1948

'What a theme for a painter in words. It is an incomparable privilege to see the war as Mr. Churchill, directing our herculean effort, saw it then and as he sees it now. Through chapter after chapter one never loses the realisation that here is one of the lasting works of English literature, one of the enduring memorials of our time, one of the noblest tributes to the endurance and resourcefulness of the British people. These memoirs are the master-work of a master-mind. Distinction shines on every page.'

The Yorkshire Post

First Edition: ICS A123aa

Publisher: Houghton Mifflin Co., Boston, 1948–53

Six volumes
Brick-red cloth blocked gilt and black. On cover, facsimile author signature gilt on black panel; on spine, volume title on black panel, 'THE SECOND | WORLD WAR and one to six stars] at head, WINSTON S. | CHURCHILL' below volume title, publisher name at foot. Top page edges usually stained yellow; headbands usually at head and foot. 8vo.

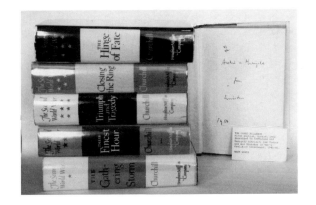

The first edition *The Second World War* (Boston: Houghton Mifflin), with Volume III opened to the first free endpaper, bearing Churchill's inscription 'For Archie & Marigold [Sinclair] from Winston 1950'.

Vol. I published 21 June 1948 at $6, 800 pages numbered (i)–(xvi) and (1)–784. Vol. II published 29 March 1949 at $6, 768 pages numbered (i)–(xvi) and (1)–751 (+1). Vol. III published 24 April 1950 at $6, 928 pages numbered (I)–(xvi), (1)–716 (+2), 717–94 (+2) and 795–903 (+5). Vol. IV published 27 November 1950 at $6, 1,024 pages numbered (i)–(xvi), (1)–20 (+2), 21–222 (+2) and 223–1,000 (+4). Vol. V published 23 November 1951 at $6, 768 pages numbered (i)–(xvi) and (1)–749 (+3). Vol. VI published 30 November 1953 at $6, 816 pages numbered (i)–(xvi) and (1)–800. All volumes illustrated with maps and diagrams.

Most First Editions were printed by The Riverside Press, Cambridge, MA (verso on title page). See 'Variants' for other printers.

Note: The two stars on the title page of Vol. II are inverted. Type on the title pages and spines is hand-drawn.

Front flaps of American dust jackets, if they are not clipped, quickly divulge whether they are from trade (above) or Book-of-the-Month Club (below) editions. All first editions were originally priced at $6.00; BOMC jackets substitute BOOK-OF-THE-MONTH® CLUB SELECTION for the price.

EDITIONS, IMPRESSIONS AND QUANTITIES

The following first impressions were published: Vol. I, 75,000; Vol. II, 35,000; Vol III, 61,000; Vol. IV, 70,000; Vol. V, 60,000; Vol VI, 60,000. The work remained in print hardbound until the late 1980s, when prices had risen to $29.95 per volume; the publisher has since issued the volumes softbound. See Cohen for the publishing history.

Identifying first editions: The most common form of First Edition has yellow stained top page edges, headbands at head and foot of spine, and identifies Riverside Press on title-page verso. (See also 'Variants'.) All First Editions must display date of first publication on title page (1948 for Vol. I, and so on). All reprints omit the title-page date.

DUST JACKETS

First Edition dust jackets all carry the price $6.00 on upper right corner of front flap; the price was quickly raised to $6.50 but any such jacket is not from the First Edition. Jackets printed red, black and yellow (or cream) on white paper, designed by Ronald Murray, who also drew the type for the jackets, spines and title pages. I own a copy of Vol. III inscribed: 'I not only designed this book. I drew the jacket, and shook the hand of the author, Mr. Churchill. –Ronald Murray'.

Murray alternated the colours to make each jacket distinctive: Vol. I yellow, printed red and black, spine panel red; Vol. II red, printed yellow and black, spine panel black; Vol. III black, printed white and yellow, spine panel red; Vol. IV black, printed yellow and red, spine panel yellow; Vol. V red, printed yellow and black, spine panel yellow; Vol VI yellow printed black and red, spine panel black. Note: the three stars on the jacket face and spine of Vol. III are inverted.

VARIANTS

The enormous demand for Churchill's war memoirs in the United States caused both the publisher and the Book-of-the-Month Club (BOMC), who published almost simultaneously, to contract with four different manufacturers–and to use each other's manufacturer during shortages. This created numerous variants and much confusion. In the late Sixties, the London bookseller Harold Mortlake made yeoman-like efforts to sort out what the publisher told him was 'a bibliographic nightmare'; but his list was confusing and the descriptions incomplete. These notes combine and amplify Mortlake's observations. For those who may have his catalogue, his reference letters are mentioned. (See also this section in the following entry on BOMC issues.)

Vol. I. Type 1: the most common form, printed only by Riverside Press, which is named on the title page and verso. Brick red cloth, headbands, yellow top page edges. Title page mentions the firm of Emery Reves, Churchill's literary associate,

The first English edition of Volume II of *The Second World War* (left and centre in jacket), compared with the Australian (right), which is somewhat thicker and bound in textured black cloth.

who placed the work outside the British Empire: 'Published in association with The Cooperation Publishing Company, Inc.' (Mortlake 'C').

Type 2: As above but without yellow page edges or headbands; verso of title page names H. Wolff, New York, as manufacturer (not in Mortlake).

Vol. II. Type 1: Brick red cloth, headbands, yellow top page edges, title page and verso follow the style of 1A (Mortlake 'C').

Type 2: As above, but on third and later impressions the Cooperation Publishing Company line was dropped (Mortlake 'A').

Vol. III. Type 1: Brick red cloth, headbands, yellow top page edges; Riverside Press on title page and verso. (Mortlake 'B').

Type 2: Pink-red cloth (like BOMC), no headbands or yellow top page edges, no BOMC 'dot' on rear board. Title-page names Riverside Press but verso states PRINTED IN THE U.S.A. Probably produced by a BOMC manufacturer to fill a shortage of trade editions. (Not in Mortlake).

Vols. IV–VI. All are found in only one form: brick red cloth, headbands, yellow top page edges, Riverside Press on title-page and verso. (Respectively Mortlake 'A', not listed, and 'D'.)

Vol. VI. Among Churchill's many corrections to the American text was a significant one: omitting, after the First Edition, the name of Averell Harriman from the account of the 9 October 1944 Moscow meeting (Chapter XV, page 226). This is when Churchill made his now-much-criticised 'percentage proposal' dividing Eastern Europe into Russian and British spheres of influence. Harriman's name appears in no American reprints I have examined, nor in any British editions at all (see page 197).

I conclude that sometime after publication of the American Edition, but before the English, Harriman was removed, perhaps on request. In his *Special Envoy* (1975), Harriman writes that he did not attend the Moscow meeting and did not learn of the 'percentage paper' until the 12th.

COMMENTS

The American Edition precedes the English by six months because Houghton Mifflin were less willing than Cassell to wait for the numerous revisions that Churchill was making. To the ire of Cassell he insisted that they all be in the English Edition, which he considered definitive. Therefore, the author's 'final revise' (among first editions) appears in the English, not the First Edition. The American Edition is aesthetically inferior to the English for other reasons: it lacks the latter's many folding maps, and textual maps are printed black instead of two- or three-colour, as in the English.

APPRAISAL

In America this edition is the most common of Churchill's works in bookshops and libraries, but it is not often seen in Britain, where it sometimes commands inflated prices. A fine, bright set in the original dust jackets sells for up to $250/£150, but only if the jackets (which are usually well worn) are in good order. More typical jacketed sets sell for $125/£78 on up, unjacketed sets half that. Sets including later impressions can often be found for as little as $30/£18. Yet cheaper in all these forms is the BOMC Issue (see next entry).

American Book Club Issue: ICS A123aa
Publisher: Houghton Mifflin Company for the Book-of-the-Month Club, Camp Hill, PA, 1948–53

Six volumes
The most common form of Churchill's war memoirs in America, the Book-of-the-Month Club (BOMC) Issue was published virtually simultaneously with the First Edition. Confusingly, BOMC first impressions carry publication dates on their title pages, just like First Editions, but there are other ways quickly to identify them.

Most BOMC issues are bound in a pinkish-red rather than brick red cloth, carry unstained page edges and have no head- or footbands. Most also carry a small debossed blind or black dot on the lower right corner of the rear boards. BOMC dust jacket front flaps do not contain prices but instead contain a line, identifying the work as a selection of the BOMC. Any jacket with the front flap clipped at top or bottom may be strongly suspected to be BOMC's.

VARIANTS
The Haddon Craftsmen, Scranton, Pa. were the chief manufacturers of BOMC volumes, but the huge press runs created variations. Continuing our list expanded from Harold Mortlake's catalogue (see 'Variants' of the First Edition), the following BOMC issues have been encountered. All are as described in the preceding paragraph unless otherwise noted. Where Mortlake assigned an identifying letter, they are indicated:

Vol. I. Type 1: Haddon Craftsmen, Scranton, Pa. named as manufacturers on verso of title page; blind dot on rear board (Mortlake 'E'). Type 2: Kingsport Press, Kingsport, Tenn. on t.p. verso; black dot on rear board (Mortlake 'H'). Type 3: Riverside Press, Cambridge, Ma. on t.p. verso; large blind dot on rear board (often mistaken as a trade edition).

Vol. II. Type 1: Haddon Craftsmen on t.p. verso; blind dot. Type 2: Kingsport Press on t.p. verso; small dot debossed black on rear board (confusingly, also called 'E' by Mortlake). Type 3: Riverside Press on t.p. verso with code letter 'W'; large blind dot on rear board.

Vol. III. Type 1: Haddon Craftsmen on verso; blind dot on rear board. Type 2: As above, later impression with large blind square on rear board. Type 3: Kingsport Press on verso; black dot on rear board (Mortlake 'B'). Type 4: As above, dated 1951 on t.p.; small blind dot on rear board. Type 5: Riverside Press on verso. Type 6: H. Wolff on verso; small blind dot on rear board.

Vol. IV. Type 1: Kingsport Press on verso; black dot on rear board (Mortlake 'B'). Type 2: No manufacturer on verso; large blind square on rear board. Type 3: Both H. Wolff and Riverside Press on verso; large blind dot on rear board.

Vol. V. Type 1: Kingsport Press on verso; small black dot on rear board (Mortlake 'B'). Type 2: H. Wolff and Riverside Press on verso; large blind dot on rear board. Type 3: As above but dot is now embossed; a later Wolff printing.

Vol. VI. Type 1: Haddon Craftsmen and Riverside Press on verso; small blind dot. Type 2: Kingsport Press and Library of Congress catalogue card number on verso; small black dot on rear board (Mortlake 'G'). Type 3: As above but large blind square on rear board. Type 4: Riverside Press and code letter 'W' on verso, no dot or headbands but top page edges stained yellow, bound in BOMC pinkish-red cloth; apparently bound by Riverside to fill a BOMC shortage.

The BOMC issue is readily available in the USA for as little as a dollar a copy. Ultra-fine sets in sparkling jackets sell for up to $50/£30. This is the ideal reading copy.

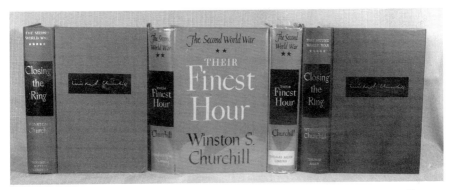

Left to right: American first editions of *Closing the Ring* and *Their Finest Hour*; Canadian firsts of *Their Finest Hour* (spine out, showing the Thomas Allen imprint) and *Closing the Ring*. Just apparent is the darker, burgundy cloth of the Canadian edition, compared to the lighter, brick red cloth of the American.

Canadian Issue: ICS A123ab

Publisher: Thomas Allen Ltd., Toronto, 1948–53

Six volumes
An offprint of the Houghton Mifflin Edition produced in association with them but printed in Canada. Published at $6 (Vols I–IV) and $6.50 (Vols V–VI). Identical to the First Edition except for several distinguishing characteristics: Bound in distinctly darker red cloth, top page edges stained light yellow, white head- and footbands; title page names the American and Canadian publishers, verso notes Canadian origin. Dust jackets are in the Houghton Mifflin style but read 'THOMAS ALLEN | LIMITED' on the spines (in oblong panels on Vols I–III).

The Canadian Issue is bound in a richer red cloth, but complete sets are extremely scarce and hardly ever seen, especially in dust jackets. I have never encountered a set and have had to build mine up from odd volumes. Original Allen dust jackets are even scarcer. Despite this and their handsome appearance, the Canadian issue draws little interest among collectors outside Canada: a shame, since odd volumes can be acquired cheaply, and building a set is a challenge. Most volumes sell for $20/£12 without jackets, double that price with jackets; a complete jacketed set would certainly command the price of a comparable American First Edition.

Note: some dust jackets do not contain prices on front flaps, and some copies originally sold at $6 bear $6.50 jacket prices.

First English Edition: ICS A123ba

Publisher: Cassell & Co. Ltd., London, 1948–54

Six volumes

Black cloth blocked gilt on spine ('WINSTON | CHURCHILL', main title, roman numeral I–VI at head and 'CASSELL' at foot). Top page edges stained dark red; no headbands. 8vo.

Vol. I published 4 October 1948 at 25s. ($4.25), 658 pages numbered (i)–(xvi), (1)–610 (+2) and 611–40. Vol. II published 27 June 1949 at 25s. ($4.25), 704 pages numbered (i)–(xviii), (1)–684 (+2). Vol. III published 20 July 1940 at 25s. ($3.50), 838 pages numbered (i)–(xviii), (1)–819 (+1). Vol. IV published 3 August 1951 at 30s. ($4.20), 936 pages numbered (i)–(xviii), (1)–917 (+1). Vol. V published 3 September 1952 at 30s. ($4.20), 692 pages numbered (i)–(xviii), (1)–673 (+1). Vol. VI published 26 April 1954 at 30s. ($4.20), 736 pages numbered (i)–(xviii), (1)–716 (+2). All volumes variously illustrated with maps and diagrams.

EDITIONS, IMPRESSIONS AND QUANTITIES

The following first impressions were published: Vol. I, 221,000; Vol. II, 276,000; Vol III, 300,000; Vol. IV, 275,000; Vol. V, 275,000; Vol VI, 200,000. Churchill complained about the small type size of Vol. 1; its second edition of 4 November 1949 was entirely reset in two points larger type, which matched the type of Vols. II–VI.

Identifying first editions: Title-page versos state 'first published 1948' [and successive dates] with no indication of successive reprints.

DUST JACKETS

The original, and long-running, dust jacket was printed red and a second colour against a grey background containing alternating rows of rampant lions and the initials 'WSC', the background carrying over both panels and the spine. Printed red were the main title on the jacket face and the volume number and volume title on the spine. Printed in a second colour were the author's name, volume number and subtitle on the face and main title, author's name and CASSELL on the spine. The second colours were as follows: Vols I and V, navy blue; Vol. II, deep purple; Vol. III, dark green; Vol. IV, blue-green, Vol. VI, light green.

First Edition jackets should contain the original price and should not advertise any title which came after them. For example, a Vol. II jacket advertising Vol. III on the rear flap is not from a First Edition. Also, many later impression jackets contain a large spine panel indicating a later impression. More recently, jackets have been laminated on white stock with varying colour panels containing titles.

Jacket variants (first editions): Vol. I jackets of Book Society variant (see below) lack the volume number on the spine. Vol. V jackets exist with back panel overprinted in large black type with a blurb about the contents.

Some jackets (seen on Vols I, V and VI) are wrapped with a red paper promotional band about 2in wide printed white.

VARIANTS

The publisher bound 100 presentation sets in black leather. These are handsomely done and easily distinguishable: plain except for gilt spine lettering, issued without dust jackets. They are hotly desired by collectors.

Among standard bindings, Vols I, V and VI (at least) exist with red wraparound bands. A variant of Vol. I states, on the copyright page: 'THIS EDITION ISSUED ON FIRST PUBLICATION BY THE BOOK SOCIETY, LTD., IN ASSOCIATION WITH CASSELL & CO. LTD. OCTOBER 1948' in place of 'First published 1948'. It is otherwise identical to normal first editions.

Some dust jackets are marked 'OVERSEAS EDITION' at the bottom of the front flap, but the books underneath are conventional editions.

COMMENTS

All of Churchill's revisions and 'overtake corrections' were scrupulously entered by Cassell's which, combined with two- and three-colour textual maps and many finely printed folding maps, make the English Edition more aesthetically pleasing and more definitive than the American/Canadian. But this was not the end, or even the beginning of the end: Churchill kept revising, based on comment from colleagues and readers, through 1955, when the Chartwell Edition proudly produced the absolute final text!

APPRAISAL

Since our author insisted that the English Edition was the definitive version, this is clearly the set to own if you plan to own only one. Fortunately, it is in plentiful supply, though it's best to buy all six volumes as a set rather than try to piece them together: the last volume is considerably harder to find than the others. The enormous press runs make first edition sets relatively inexpensive. For many years $30 or £20 would buy a nice set in jackets, but prices for genuinely fine sets have now risen to as high as $200/£120. To be truly fine, books should display no spotting on page edges, good colour on the top page edges, pristine boards and unspotted contents; jackets should be as bright on their spines as on their faces, and the red spine type, which is liable to fade, should be clean and bright. Scruffier jacketed sets are not worth half the above price, and unjacketed sets or later impressions not more than one-quarter. Jackets with the red and white promotional bands command a premium.

I last saw a presentation set in black leather offered at £1,500 ($2,500) several years ago. That is quite likely to be a low price today.

Australian Issue: ICS A123bb

Publisher: Cassell & Co. Ltd., Melbourne, 1948–54

Six volumes

Volumes I–V printed in Australia by Halsted Press, Sydney, probably by offprinting. Vol. VI is likely to be English sheets bound in Australia. Published at A 30s. (Vols I–IV) and $6.50 (Vols V–VI). Identical to the First Edition except for several distinguishing characteristics: Bound in textured black shiny cloth, top page edges unstained; bulks thicker owing to thicker page stock; verso of title page names the Australian Edition and notes Australian origin. Dust jackets are in the Cassell style but priced in Australian currency. Identifying first impressions: Vol. I had three impressions, the others only one each. Vol. I first impressions state 'First Australian Edition 1948' on the title-page verso, with no indication of later reprints.

The Australian Issue is wholly more satisfying to handle and read than the English because of its superior page stock, although full sets outside Australia are rarities. Not published concurrently with the English edition, it does not carry the same precedence, so prices tend to be lower. Truly fine sets are hardly ever seen; a very good set in lightly worn dust jackets recently sold for $125/£78.

Abridged Edition, Home Issue: ICS A123ca

Publisher: Cassell & Co. Ltd., London, 1959

Black cloth blocked gilt on spine (title: 'THE SECOND | WORLD WAR | ABRIDGED EDITION'), 8vo, 1,056 pages numbered (i)–(xviii), (1)–1,033 (+5), illustrated with maps and diagrams. Published 5 February 1959 at 35s. ($4.90). Seven impressions were published: February 1959, September 1960, September 1961, February 1963, June 1964, June 1965, December 1967. Identifying first impressions: 'First published 1959' with no reprints noted on verso of title page. Dust jackets printed multicolour on white stock including globe of the world artwork.

This edition was prepared by an indefatigable Churchill literary assistant, Denis Kelly, whose acknowledgements appear on page (vi). To it the author added an Epilogue on the years 1945–1957, tracing his personal involvement from the end of his wartime premiership almost to the age of space exploration–Churchill's last

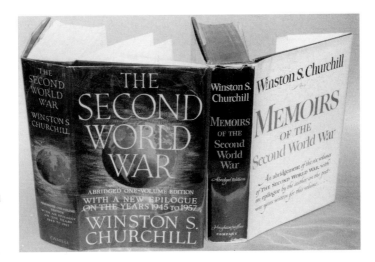

Jacketed abridged editions: the English (left) and American (right).

original writing for book publication. Cassell paid him £20,000 for 10,000 words. Emery Reves wrote Churchill, 'I believe this is the highest amount ever paid for a manuscript, £2 per word.' (Gilbert, *Never Despair'*, London and Boston: 1988).

The Epilogue considers in retrospect Churchill's Fulton speech, the Berlin blockade, the Marshall Plan and NATO, his attempts for a 'summit' with the Russians, the Suez débacle, his hopes for peace in the same first-person narrative as the original six volumes. With so much original material it is highly collectible and belongs in every serious Churchill library. Copies are fairly common but seem always to have gutterbreaks at the title page, probably owing to the many pages and rather loose binding. A fine, unbroken copy in like dust jacket could be worth up to $100/£60, because of its rarity.

Note: this edition is chronologically out of order because Woods assigns it the number A123(c), omitting separate designations for the Reprint Society and Chartwell Editions.

Abridged Edition, American Issue: ICS A123cb
Publisher: Houghton Mifflin Co., Boston, 1959

Green cloth with titles blocked gilt within red boxes on top board and spine. Entirely reset, but retaining English spelling and identical in content to the English Edition except that Denis Kelly's notes are replaced by a 'Publisher's Note' in which he is not mentioned. 16mo, 1,088 pages numbered (i)–(xviii) (+2) and (1)–1,065 (+3). Dust jackets were originally printed red and black on white stock with no artwork. Published 1959 at $8.75.

VARIANTS
There are three binding variants to this issue: First Type: bound as described, red

Two types of the American abridged edition. Left: the first version, bound in green cloth blocked red and gilt. Right: the second version, bound in red cloth blocked black and gilt. A third type is identical to the second but lacks head- and footbands. Despite these differences, all types are the same internally.

top page edges, headbands at spine ends; Second Type: red cloth with black title boxes, plain top page edges, headbands. Third Type: like Second but no headbands, with a jacket marked $9. All three volumes carry the 1959 date on the title page which normally signifies a Houghton Mifflin first edition. There appears no difference in value, about $50/£30 for a fine jacketed copy, but most collectors will want the First Version. This issue has been almost continually in print, the last form issued by Bonanza in 1990 as a large paperback.

Reprint Society Edition: ICS A123d
Publisher: Reprint Society/World Books, London, 1950–56

Six volumes

Smaller (5¼ x 8in) than the First English Edition, this set was issued a volume at a time by the book club, each with reset text incorporating all of the author's corrections. Bound in ivory or white cloth with author's facsimile signature blocked maroon on top board and in block type on spine; also on spine: titles and Reprint Society logo, gilt on maroon panels. Issue dates: Vol. I 1950, 14 impressions; Vol. II 1951, nine impressions; Vol. III 1952, ten impressions; Vol. IV 1953, six impressions; Vol. V 1954, six impressions; Vol. VI 1956, two impressions. The member price was 7s. 6d. (91¢) per volume; in 1952 the first three volumes were offered for only 22s. 6d. ($3.15).

VARIANTS

Top page edges are found plain, stained yellow and (rarely) stained dark red.

Completion of this set in 1956 occasioned issue of a large-scale folding map, boxed and entitled 'Dunkirk to Berlin', showing Churchill's wartime journeys in four-colour on heavy art paper. No jackets. The sets are of incidental value today

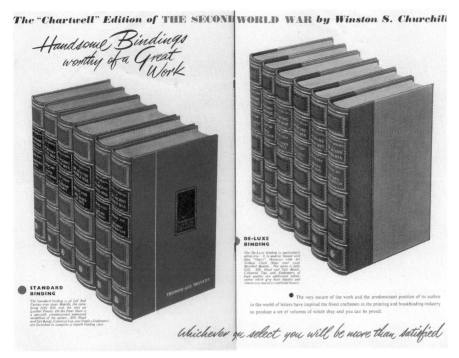

The standard and deluxe bindings of the beautiful Chartwell Edition, published 1956, taken from the publisher's brochure.

(the map is worth at least $50/£30, however!). They certainly were a bargain in their day. A three-volume set (vols. 1/2, 3/4, 5/6) was issued in blue cloth.

Chartwell (First Illustrated) Edition: ICS A123e
Publisher: Educational Book Co. Ltd., London, 1955

Six Volumes
In a special note to this edition dated 1 October 1954, the author writes: 'Now a special edition is being published illustrated for the first time, in which all those first minor errors have been corrected.' Thus this beautiful edition produces an entirely new text in fine readable large type, along with hundreds of illustrations on coated paper–interspersed not in thick 16-page sections but spread around in two- or four-page inserts. Each volume contains a colour frontispiece and three-colour maps, silk head and foot bands and duplex endpapers, although the folding maps of the First English Edition are eliminated. There were no dust jackets; the volumes instead carried plain glassine wrappers.

VARIANTS
The books were offered by mail order in early 1955 in thick, stout boards bound in

two versions by 'Britain's finest craftsmen', and were rightly described as 'beautiful examples of the Bookbinders' art'. Standard: red canvas, titles on brown leather spine panels; on top boards the volume title gilt with a specially commissioned embossed medallion of Churchill on a leather label, £12. 19s. 6d. ($35.93) or £13. 13s. by monthly subscription (20s. on delivery, twelve further 20s. monthly payments). Deluxe: quarter blue 'Oasis' morocco leather with art vellum cloth, bevelled boards, spine blocked gilt, £19. 19s. ($55.86) or £21 by subscription (20s. on delivery, twenty further 20s. monthly payments).

APPRAISAL

This beautiful edition is in my opinion the most elaborate and luxurious rendering of Churchill's war memoirs, and would be the second set I would add after a First English Edition–which it complements nicely, being not only profusely illustrated but fully corrected with all of Churchill's revisions since the original volumes. The Standard binding has lately become scarce in truly fine condition (perfect spine labels, bright colours, no interior gutterbreak) and has risen to as much as $500/£300. The Deluxe binding (of which I encounter about one to every ten standards) can command up to $750/£450 in the same pristine condition. Gutterbreaks are common on these large, thick volumes, and the leather spine labels of Standard bindings are often chipped; such sets sell for half these prices, but even then, they are worth it; this is a truly desirable edition.

Specimen Sample: One function of the Educational Book Company was the support of students, who sold Chartwell Editions door to door. The young sellers usually carried a 'sample' bound in black leatherette, blocked 'SPECIMEN' in gilt on the top board. The boards fold back to reveal the two bindings, the colour frontispiece and title page of Vol. I, excerpted textual pages including 12 maps from Vol. II, and 24 pages of photographs plus four colour plates. I acquired my copy for £125 ($200) and was very glad to obtain this rare souvenir.

Time-Life Illustrated Abridged Edition: ICS A123f
Publisher: Time-Life Inc., New York, 1959

Two volumes

Taking its text from the First Abridged Edition, this elaborate folio set is illustrated by photographs and paintings from the files of *Life* magazine, many published for the first time, and unique maps specially drawn for this edition. Bound in half blue (Vol. I) or half green (Vol. 2) and black leatherette, blocked gilt on spine and top boards, it was published in two formats: Standard: in dust jackets (blue and green respectively), published at $25. Deluxe: slipcased with a 33 1/3 rpm record containing excerpts from Churchill's wartime speeches, published at $39.95. (The record came in a glassine envelope; the volumes were not jacketed in this format).

The *Time-Life* Edition is unique and very attractive, but dealers tend to think it's worth more than it is. It had a huge sale (the Standard version is rather scarcer than the Deluxe), and copies are not difficult to come by. I would certainly not suggest paying more than $75/£45 for the Deluxe or half as much for the Standard, and then only if the slipcase and record are pristine–the books themselves usually are. My own copy is signed over his photo by one of the embattled American soldiers pictured in these dramatic pages, who came to visit me one day and took home two sets with my compliments; he'd earned them.

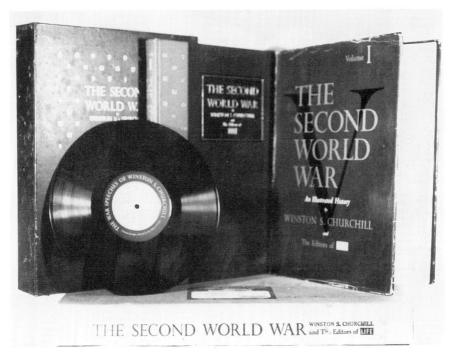

Time-Life illustrated editions in slipcase with record (left), and as issued without slipcase but in dust jackets (right). Underneath is the shipping box of the slipcased set, bearing Houghton Mifflin's address label, suggesting that the Boston publisher produced and shipped these volumes for Time-Life.

The Gathering Storm First Penguin Edition: ICS A123g
Publisher: Penguin Paperbacks, 1960

This paperback was the only volume published of an intended six-volume series which was forestalled by copyright negotiations. Reprinted 1962.

Golden Press Edition: ICS A123h
Publisher: Golden Press, New York, 1960

A one-volume adaptation of the *Time-Life* edition, abridged for young readers by Fred

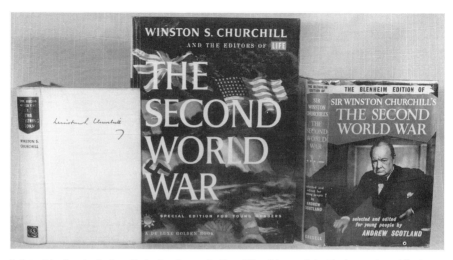

Left to right: Reprint Society *Gathering Storm*; the Time-Life edition; and the Blenheim edition. The latter two were specially selected and annotated for young people.

Cook. 'Certain passages have been paraphrased by him for the purpose of condensation' (but *Time-Life* carefully sets these off in small type and daggers). Quarto, 384 pages, profusely illustrated, this work is easily recognised by pictorial boards, the top board illustrating the national flags of Britain, USSR, USA, Germany, France, China and the Japanese naval ensign. This design is repeated in the dust jacket. Endpapers are multicoloured maps of the European and Asia-Pacific theatres. Published 1960 at $7.95; at least two impressions, 1960 and 1961. Not often seen but never expensive, this is still the ideal introduction to Churchill's war memoirs for young people under the age of 12. Fine jacketed copies are worth no more than $25/£15.

School Edition: ICS A132i
Publisher: Cassell & Co. Ltd., London, 1960

Black, red and white boards with abstract art of ships, planes, world globe and London Blitz. No dust jacket. An abridgement compiled by Dr Andrew Scotland, without illustrations. A set of student questions and assignments, entitled 'For Second Thoughts,' appears on pages 327–333. Quite rare, this edition apparently had only one impression, published 21 January 1960. Value $100/£60.

Blenheim Edition: ICS A132j
Publisher: Cassell & Co. Ltd., London, 1960

Red boards blocked gilt on spine, 334 pages. A rework of the School Edition adding eight pages of coated stock with photos inserted between plates 6/7, 38/9, 70/1, 102/3, 166/7, 198/9, 230/1 and 262/3. In place of 'For Second Thoughts' is an index, which appears on pages 327–334. Published at 12s. 6d. ($1.75). Dust jacket printed black, yellow and red with Karsh 1941 photo of Churchill. Three impressions, April 1960, August 1961, March 1965. Today's value about $35/£22.

Bantam Edition: ICS A123k
Publisher: Bantam Books Inc., New York, 1962

The first American paperback edition, sold initially as a boxed set, has had numerous impressions to date. Originally published at $2.50 each. Boxed sets were later offered for $25.

Second Illustrated (Paperback) Edition: ICS A123L
Publisher: Cassell & Co. Ltd., London, 1964

Twelve volumes

The second full edition to be illustrated, this paperback broke the original 12 'books' of the work (two per volume) into 12 individual volumes. The volume titles are those of Churchill's 'books', e.g. Vol. 5 is 'Germany Drives East'. The text was reset for this edition, and each volume contains an eight-page signature of photographs on coated paper. Wrappers are printed red-orange and black on white, each illustrated with a photograph. Originally published at 6s. 6d. (91¢) for Vols 1–6, but these almost always have their price obliterated by stamps or sticky labels; Vols 7–12 are marked 5s. (70¢). Easily found in Britain, this set is chiefly valued for its photographs; the page stock was pulpy and is almost always yellow and brittle. There were several impressions.

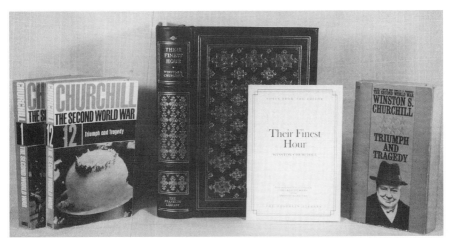

Left to right: two of the Cassell paperbacks; the Franklin Library limited edition of *Their Finest Hour* with explanatory booklet; and one of Bantam's six-volumes.

Heron (Third Illustrated) Edition: ICS A123m

Publisher: Heron Books Ltd., London, 1974

Twelve volumes

This novel edition issued to mark the Churchill Centenary was described by the publisher as 'quarter brown morocco and olive Kivar' (a kind of imitation kidskin) with a gilt Churchill medallion on the cover; much rarer is the variant binding in full blue leatherette, blocked silver. Profusely illustrated (Vol. I contains eight groups of four-page photo sections), head and foot bands, yellow cloth page markers, decorative endpapers. The text was reset for this edition; maps and charts were redrawn and printed in halftone rather than two- or three-colour. The setting is shared with the Diner's Club 'Major Works' edition of *The Second World War* (see Appendix).

Sold via mail order by the Heron Books firm at £2.75 ($7.70) each plus post, the volumes were advertised as offering 'the luxury of real leather' and 'the grandeur of 23 carat gold'. The textual history of the Heron books is interesting. As with previous twelve-volume works, they break the original six volumes into Churchill's

the luxury of real leather
the grandeur of 23 carat gold

to honour Sir Winston Churchill in this Centennial Year of his birth

What more fitting tribute in this Centennial Year of his birth to one of the greatest men in the history of our nation - the man who became the living symbol of freedom to the people of all nations - could there be than his own immortal words magnificently bound into a family heirloom edition . . . to keep alive the values and freedoms for which he so indomitably fought . . . to be an inspiration to our children and their children.

It was this thought that inspired our Swiss craftsmen to create the truly noble volumes we offer here.

READ the first magnificent volume

FREE

FOR 10 DAYS

AND

as an introductory gift take this beautiful volume

SIR WINSTON CHURCHILL HIS WIT AND WISDOM

FREE

Bound with real leather embossed with gleaming golden tooling.

DE-LUXE HEIRLOOM EDITION
Complete in 12 matching volumes most handsomely bound with richly-grained leather, tan marbled Kidron and 23 carat gold.

HERON BOOKS

Publisher's advert for the Heron 12-volume edition, published 1974, which was offered with a nicely bound copy of Jack House's *Sir Winston Churchill: His Wit and Wisdom*. Described as the 'deluxe heirloom edition', these volumes were offered in instalments at £2.75 each.

'books'. The text of Volumes I–IV was offprinted from the considerably revised Second Editions of *Gathering Storm* and *Finest Hour* (1949, 1950). Volumes V–VII appear to be offprinted from First English Editions, but Volume VIII ('Book Two' of *The Hinge of Fate*) comes from the 1968 Fourth Edition, second impression. Volumes IX–X are from the 1966 Fourth Edition of *Closing the Ring*, while Volumes XI–XII are from the 1954 Second Edition of *Triumph and Tragedy*. Evidently all these were the current trade editions in 1974.

Heron Editions have been selling for about $150–250/£90–150 for as long as I can remember, and pop up in general bookshops at much less than that; but as the Chartwell Editions get scarcer, more people turn to this illustrated alternative for gift giving and presentations, so the value is rising. The text contains most of Churchill's final revisions.

Their Finest Hour FRANKLIN LIBRARY EDITION: ICS A123n
Publisher: The Franklin Mint Corp., Franklin Center, Pennsylvania, 1978

A completely reset edition (but with maps offprinted from the American trade edition), this handsome single volume is printed in two-colour (dark blue and black) and contains reportorial sketches by Capt. Bryan de Grineau, M.C. 8vo, bound in full navy morocco, decoratively blocked gilt on boards and spine, with two raised spine bands, all edges gilt, grey silk pagemarker, grey moiré endpapers; issued with a 24-page illustrated booklet entitled 'NOTES FROM THE EDITOR', in the Limited Edition Collection, *The Greatest Books of the Twentieth Century*.

The Franklin Mint produced a magnificent volume here, and it is only a shame that the other five volumes were not included. The most distinctive feature is de Grineau's 16-page collection of sketches of the Battles of France and Britain, which convincingly invoke the feeling of those terrible, glorious times. Copies of this volume are extremely scarce, even in the US. I have seen few for sale, all priced between $150/£90 and $200/£120.

AMERICAN CHARTWELL ISSUE: ICS A123o
Publisher: Houghton Mifflin Co., Boston, 1983

Nicely bound in half navy leather and tan linen cloth, with a Churchill painting of Chartwell tipped onto the front boards, this work was undertaken as a premium for the Book-of-the-Month Club, which offered the set for only $35 to newly joining BOMC members. To justify a book club edition, however, Houghton Mifflin decided to produce 200 sets of a trade edition, priced at a staggering $295. Accordingly, there are two distinct bindings: BOMC Binding: rust stained top page edges and prominent debossed dot on lower right corner of rear boards. Trade Binding: yellow stained top page edges and no debossed 'dot' on rear boards. Endpapers contain excellent three-colour maps relevant to each volume. Note: some BOMC members

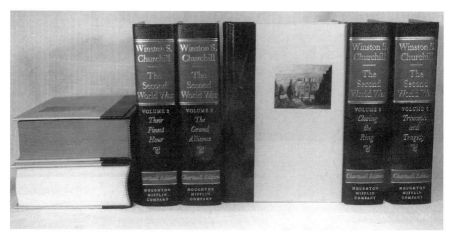

The American Chartwell Edition, produced mainly for the Book-of-the-Month Club. The two copies lying flat at left show the chief identifying characteristic: BOMC issues (top) have rust stained top page ends, while the few trade editions are stained yellow instead.

who ordered this work received the trade binding, probably to cover a shortage in BOMC bindings. Houghton Mifflin undoubtedly had some trade bindings to spare, their sales people told this writer, because at $295 they didn't sell many.

The trade binding is far scarcer than the book club version, and has thus far commanded a healthy premium on the secondhand market. Typical prices are $250/£150 for the trade binding, $150/£90 for the book club. It bears mentioning, however, that the text is a direct offprint from the First American Edition, and contains none of the many changes Churchill rendered through 1955.

PENGUIN EDITION: ICS A123p

Publisher: Penguin Books, London, 1985

Volume I carries a new introduction by John Keegan. Issued in paperback as boxed sets, in both trade and book club varieties. Book club variants do not display prices on the book wrappers.

EASTON PRESS ISSUE: ICS A123q

Publisher: Easton Press, Norwalk, CT, 1989

Another offprint taken from Houghton Mifflin first edition sheets with no textual alterations save for reset title pages. Bound in black pigskin, decorated gilt on boards; five raised spine bands with titles gilt on two red leather labels. Gold moiré endpages, yellow cloth pagemarker, all edges gilt. Offered by mail order at $260/£156. Still available at this writing.

Like all 'limited editions', this is nothing more than a fancy reprint, and because

The pigskin-bound Easton Press limited edition of *The Second World War*.

so many cheaper sets are around, it is no bargain. Textually it retains all the drawbacks of the First American Edition from which it is taken; what a shame Easton Press, which is capable of highly professional reprints, did not print from the English Edition instead! The pigskin binding is heavily dyed, carries no aroma and cracks audibly when the stiff boards are opened. Although it has appeal to collectors of leather-lined libraries, there is really nothing to recommend it over the many other fine editions described above–and much to condemn it. I have not seen the set on the secondhand market. I do not think it will hold its original price.

Taiwan Issues

Both the six-volume original and the 1959 Abridgement were published in Taiwan on cheap page stock, reproducing from the Cassell English editions. Whether or not these are 'pirated' I leave to the Bibliographers, but that is the general impression in the book trade, where they command very low prices.

Six-volumes Unabridged: Offprinted from the English Edition, possibly a later edition, since the title pages are not from the English first. On rear free endpapers of each volume is a Chinese inscription rubber stamped in purple ink (2 x 1⅛in). Measuring 5½ x 8¼in, the books are smaller than the English Edition, but similarly bound. Dust jackets also mimic the English but with different printing: Vol. I, black and red; Vol. II, dark purple and red; Vols III, IV and VI, dark green and red; Vol. VI, dark blue and red. The Vol. VI dust jacket states 'Overseas Edition' in red on front inside flap; none of the others do.

One-volume Abridged: Offprinted from the English Edition, with a Chinese inscription printed on page (iv). Bound in beige cloth blocked silver on spine only.

FOREIGN TRANSLATIONS

Arabic: [MEMOIRS OF WINSTON CHURCHILL]
Published by Political Books, Cairo, 1962; and by General Egyptian Org., 1970.

Bulgarian [title in Bulgarian]: MEMOAPU (6 Vols.)

Danish: DEN ANDEN VERDENSKRIG (6 Vols.)
Published by Hasselbalch, Copenhagen, 1948–1954. Published in brown wrappers or dark brown leather, both with brown dust jackets; blue or black leatherette with pictorial dust jackets; and full red leather (publisher's presentation binding).

Dutch: MEMOIRES (10 vols)
Published by Elsevier, Amsterdam, 1948–1954; Volumes I and VIII, at least, were reprinted. Bound in dark green cloth; black cloth blocked gilt on red panels; quarter red-orange leather over grey cloth (limited edition of 750). Later issued in paperback.

Republished as DE TWEEDE WERELDOORLOG (12 vols) by De Boekenschat, Amsterdam, c. 1974; red leatherette, produced by Edito (Geneva) in the style of the Heron Edition (ICS A123m). Also published by Elsevier, Amsterdam, 1979: navy cloth and silver dust jackets with author's portrait spread across the composite jacket spines. Reissued by Tirion-Baarn, 1989, in yellow-green boards with the same spread-out portrait.

Certainly the most elegant presentation of *The Second World War* in a foreign language is the Belgian *Mémoires*, usually found in three volumes. Volume I contains a tipped-in colour reproduction of the Frank Salisbury portrait, which hangs in Chartwell.

French:

MÉMOIRES SUR LA DEUXIÈME GUERRE MONDIALE (12 vols)

Published by Librairie Plon, Paris, 1948–1954; notable for Churchill's additional remarks in the foreword to Vol. 1, exonerating the French *poilu* from the débacle of 1940. The true 'Edition Originale' was printed on Lafuma paper with cream wrappers (320 copies) or on Aussedat paper in pale blue wrappers (1,800 copies). Standard editions used the same pale blue wrappers fitted with dust jackets and had many impressions. Republished 1964-1966 by Le Cercle du Bibliophile Edition, produced by Edito (Geneva) in the style of the Heron Edition (ICS A123m), hardbound in red leatherette.

TRIOMPHE ET TRAGEDIE was published in two volumes in 1954 by Editions Romaldi: a special limited edition to mark Churchill's Nobel Prize for Literature, with special colour illustrations; limited to 2,500 copies plus a special edition of 80.

French (Belgian): MÉMOIRES SUR LA DEUXIÈME GUERRE MONDIALE

(3 vols.; a variant bound in 4 vols also exists)

Published by Editions Sphinx, Brussels, 1951–1953 in three enormous (9½ x 12in) illustrated volumes elaborately bound in deep maroon leatherette, with an artwork portrait of Churchill on the covers. The variant uses the same binding but divides the work into four volumes.

This is the most luxurious and desirable foreign language edition, printed two-colour and replete with specially drawn maps. Many photographs are unique, including a rare photo of Churchill orating in the well of the House of Commons and a beautiful photo of Roosevelt inscribed in 1942 to Churchill ('with the affectionate regards of his old friend'). Scores of other photos repeatedly depict the Prime Minister and virtually every significant military and political figure of the Second World War. The frontispiece (Vol. I only) is a colour reproduction of the Salisbury portrait of WSC which now hangs at Chartwell. I strongly recommend these volumes. Whether or not one reads French, the captions are brief and easily understood; it is really a scrapbook of 'Who Was Who'. Low demand for foreign translations means that these sets are affordable, though they are not common outside Belgium.

French (Swiss): MÉMOIRES SUR LA DEUXIÈME GUERRE MONDIALE (12 vols)

Published by La Palatine, Geneva, 1948–1954 using Plon sheets, bound in brown and black wrappers with red, black and white dust jackets.

German: DER ZWEITE WELTKRIEG (12 vols)

Published by Scherz: Bern, 1948–1953, in blue cloth. The first two volumes were first published by Toth, Hamburg, then Parnass, Stuttgart for Vol. III, Book One; then Scherz & Govert, Stuttgart for the rest. Finally, Scherz & Govert republished

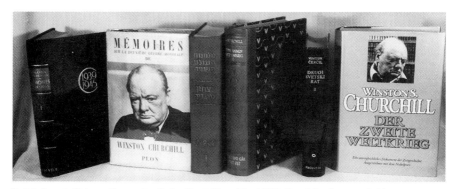

Dutch, French, Hebrew, Norwegian, Serbo-Croat *(Drugi Svetski Rat)* and the German abridgement,.

the earlier volumes in finer black cloth. Still in print in 1992.

Republished in six volumes by Toth, Hamburg (date unknown) and Ullstein (1985, boxed paperbacks). The one-volume Abridged Edition was published by Scherz, Berlin, 1960 (grey cloth, blue and white jacket); Deutsche Buch Gemeinschaft: Berlin–Darmstadt–Vienna 1962 (quarter black leather and dark red paper boards); and Scherz, Berlin, 1985 (grey cloth, silver jacket).

German (Swiss): DER ZWEITE WELTKRIEG (6 vols)
Published by NSB (Neue Schweizer Bibliothek), c. 1960s in white paper boards blocked maroon and gold, white dust jackets.

Greek: [THE SECOND WORLD WAR] (12 vols.)
Published Athens, 1948–1954.

Hebrew: [THE SECOND WORLD WAR] (6 vols.)
Published by Am Hasefer ('People of the Book') jointly with A. Naoz, Tel-Aviv, 1959–1960, illustrated. Bound in red cloth with solid colour dust jackets, the colour varying with the edition. A most novel edition, nicely illustrated and reading back-to-front, the standard Hebrew format. Later bound in red-orange cloth.

Hungarian: A MÁSODIK VILÁGHÁBORU (2 Vols. abridged)
Published by Europa Konyvkiado: Budapest, 1989.

Italian: LA SECONDA GUERRA MONDIALE (12 vols)
Published by Mondadori, Rome, 1948–1953 as large-format paperbacks (L1,400 per volume); white cloth in white and gold dust jackets (L2,000 per volume); or a numbered limited edition signed by the publisher. The latter was issued in dark blue leather or dark blue textured paper covered boards with an elaborate 'WINSTON CHURCHILL' blocked blind on the full height of the top boards. Some of these were numbered, some not; the colophon mentions 1,030 examples, perhaps 30 of

which were numbered.

This was followed by several six-volume hardbound printings, the first in white cloth, slipcased, the ninth published in 1966. Later published by Oscar, 1970 in a boxed 12-volume paperback set.

Japanese: [THE SECOND WORLD WAR] (24 vols)
Published by Mainichi Newspapers, undated. Bound in deep red cloth with glassine dust jackets, each volume in a uniquely printed cardboard box. A new edition has recently been published.

Korean: [MEMOIRS OF WORLD WAR II] (8 vols)
Published by Pak moon, Seoul, 1970 with the volumes arranged as follows: *1. The Gathering Storm, 2. Their Finest Hour, 3. The Sound of Firing in the Balkans, 4. The Grand Alliance, 5. A Dinosaur in the Pacific, 6. The Hinge of Fate, 7. Closing the Ring, 8. Triumph and Tragedy.*

Although this was the first Korean appearance of the full text, there were at least two previous appearances of individual volumes: *Memoirs of World War II*, published by the International Culture Association, Seoul, 1949 (probably *Their Finest Hour*); and SEUNG REE HWA (*Triumph and Tragedy*) published (for obvious political reasons) by Minjung su kwan, Seoul, 1954.

The Abridged Edition was published in two volumes as *Churchill's Memories* by Ham rim Chulpan, Seoul, 1971. Finally, the full work was republished in 12 volumes as *Memoirs of World War II* by Hyang woo, Seoul, 1983 (misdated '1900' in the volumes).

Norwegian: DEN ANNEN VERDENSKRIG (12 vols)
Published by Cappelens, Oslo, 1948–1955 in paper wraps, half cream cloth over red patterned paper boards and red-orange half leather with grey and red paper boards, all in green dust jackets. Also known in quarter black leather with red spine panels and smooth dark blue paper covered boards.

Polish: DRUGA SVETOVNA VOJNA
The Abridged Edition text, published by Z. A. Lozil Zavod, Lublin, 1964.

Portuguese: LA SEGUNDA GUERRA MONDIALE (6 vols)
Published by Centro Ed., Rio de Janeiro, 1948–1953, bound in blue cloth in the style of the Houghton Mifflin American Edition.

Russian: [THE SECOND WORLD WAR] (6 vols)
Published by Chekhov, New York, 1954–1955 in brown wrappers. This was intended to be a 12-volume work, but progressed only through Vol. III, Book Two. Republished in the 1990s in six volumes with colourful dust jackets.

Serbo-Croat: DRUGI SVETSKI RAT (6 vols)
Published by Prosveta, Belgrade in the 1960s. Careful examination suggests that the Yugoslavs left nothing out, including criticism of the Soviets.

Spanish: LA SEGUNDA GUERRA MONDIAL (6 vols)
Published in Barcelona during 1948–1953. Reissued in Barcelona, 1960 in distinctive tan leatherette blocked red, white and blue.

Swedish: ANDRA VARLDSKRIGET (12 vols)
First published in 12 jacketed paperbacks by Skoglund, Stockholm, 1948–1953. Republished by Skoglund in six volumes in grey cloth with dust jackets and two varieties of leather bindings. Also published in Swedish by Holger Schildts, Helsinki.

Turkish: CORCIL ANLYATIYOS (4 vols)
Published by Vatan, Istanbul, 1949–1950. Intended to be 12 volumes, the Turkish Edition progressed only through Vol. II, Book Two. Emery Reves licensed all publication outside the British Empire, and Mrs Wendy Reves has this amusing comment: 'Emery took it away from them–they refused to pay!'

Combined Work: SEKYE INMOOL TAE HOI KOROK (Korean)
Literally 'The Great Memoirs of Our World'. Taken from the abridged texts of *The World Crisis* and *The Second World War*. Published by Korean Publishing Corp., Seoul, 1989, 325 pages.

THE SINEWS OF PEACE

COHEN A241, WOODS A124

After the war was over, Randolph Churchill reassumed the editorship of his father's speeches, which were published over the years in five separate volumes, of which this collection of orations from October 1945 to the end of 1946 is the first. The faithful Desmond Flower, at Cassell's, immediately arranged to publish *The Sinews of Peace* in Britain, but the Americans took more convincing, and it was almost a year after its UK appearance that Houghton Mifflin agreed to issue an American Edition. For years I owned a First English Edition which Randolph took to America in order to sell the project, with editorial notes in his hand (although the American text was unaltered when published).

The volume is named for one of two dominant themes in the speeches within, namely the title Churchill gave to his March 1946 address at Westminster College in Fulton, Missouri, better known as the *Iron Curtain* speech. At Fulton in the presence of President Truman, Churchill had urged a 'fraternal association' of the English-speaking peoples to maintain the forms of cooperation, military and political, that they had established in the war, but critics took this to mean that he was proposing a formal alliance. 'The Fulton speech drew cries of horrified alarm, not only from Communists and their dupes, but from many usually right-minded and sensible politicians and journalists', writes Randolph in the Introduction. 'Re-reading that speech in the light of after-knowledge, many people may wonder what the fuss was all about. They may perhaps conclude that one of the most dangerous and thankless tasks in politics is to tell the truth and to give warning of danger in good time instead of late in the day.' A year after the First Edition of this book was published, NATO was founded, and America and Britain found themselves in an alliance along the lines Churchill proposed at Fulton, along with Canada and a number of non-English-speaking, democratic states of Europe.

Six months after Fulton, Churchill spoke at Zurich University, voicing the second major theme of this volume: European Unity. 'I am now going to say something that will astonish you', he said. 'The first step in the recreation of the European family must be a partnership between France and Germany. In this way only can France recover the moral leadership of Europe. There can be no revival of Europe without a spiritually great France and a spiritually great Germany.' Thus it was Churchill, so often first to recognise compelling truths, who first voiced the advice Europe needed to hear. The results in due course were the European Coal and Steel Community, the European Economic Community, and the Council of Europe. Like Fulton, the truths Churchill uttered at Zurich are now taken for granted.

FROM THE REVIEWS

'The prize for moral leadership should surely go to Mr. Churchill, rather than to any of the official leaders. That is the recognition which fairness demands should be given ... Who in this country–and indeed in the world–could more legitimately claim to have displayed these virtues, at Fulton and after, than Mr. Winston Churchill? Who had enough faith in the Western way of life, not merely to proclaim its superior merits, but to propose that something should be done to safeguard it, regardless of the threats and censure such self-protective measures would evoke from the enemies of liberty? Who showed enough originality of mind to break with the traditional conception of the "quivering, precarious balance of power" and to plead for the replacement of "such narrow margins offering temptations to a trial of strength" [quotes from Fulton] by a new and infinitely more stable system of retaining a balance of power in hand? Who had enough vision, imagination and insight to realise as early as the beginning of 1946 that it was practical politics to count on the Americans making such a system possible? Who was not afraid to confront the British public as early as November, 1945, when it was still flushed with the pride of victory, with the extremely unpalatable fact–surely to none more unpalatable than to this proudest of Britons himself–that the leadership in such a novel system would inevitably pass to the Americans? ... In short, who has led and who has followed?'

H. J. Huizinga, a Dutch journalist, in *Time and Tide,* 1946

First Edition: ICS A124a
Publisher: Cassell and Co. Ltd., London, 1948

Orange-tan cloth blocked gilt with title, author's name and CASSELL on spine. 8vo, 260 pages numbered (i)–(xii) and 9–256. Page (ii) lists 26 other works by the author. Dust jackets were printed black, maroon and light green on white paper. Published 19 August 1948 at 16s. ($3.20) in a single impression of 10,000 copies.

VARIANTS
Publisher's presentation copies were bound in full black pebble grain morocco. A minor point of interest: this edition was printed in Luxembourg.

APPRAISAL
The first and most important collection of Churchill's post-war speeches, the *Sinews* assembles the key speeches surrounding the author's early post-war political themes. The supply has thus far been ample, and copies are available for as little as a few pounds or dollars. Copies without jackets quickly become dull and faded, and the

pulpy paper is inclined to slight yellowing. A fine copy with bright gilt in an unmarked, unchipped dust jacket is fairly uncommon; $75/£45 would not be too much to pay for such an example.

American Issue: ICS A124b

Publisher: Houghton Mifflin Co., Boston, 1949

Medium blue cloth blocked dark blue on spine: 'Sinews of Peace | [star] | CHURCHILL' (reading down) and 'H.M. Co.' at the foot (reading across). 8vo, 256 pages numbered (1)–256. The title-page and verso are reset and the latter mentions the American publication date. Four preliminary leaves have been eliminated by deleting blank leaves and a half-title before the speeches. Dust jackets are printed black, blue and grey-blue on white paper. Published 1949 at $3 in a single impression of 3,000 copies.

APPRAISAL

An altogether more satisfying production than the First Edition, printed on better paper and bound in finer cloth, this issue is never found spotted. In America it remains in good supply, fine copies in clean jackets selling for up to $75/£45, but it commands a higher price elsewhere; unjacketed copies start around $30/£18 in USA. A short press run means low prices won't last, so this edition is best acquired soon.

English (left) and American first editions of *The Sinews of Peace*, shown with spines facing out and with dust jackets.

FOREIGN TRANSLATIONS

Swedish: ATT VINNA FREDEN

Published by Skoglund, Stockholm, 1949, in both card wrappers and blue cloth with the same dust jacket on either version. Later included in a four-volume set of war and post-war speeches. The Swedes were the only translators of the post-war speech volumes; Europe hungered for peace and quiet, and few wanted to hear, or heed, Churchillian oratory.

PIRATED EDITION

A smaller-format, hardbound pirated edition is known to exist. See note under *In the Balance* on page 302.

PAINTING AS A PASTIME

COHEN A242, WOODS A125

Churchill's charming essay about his painting hobby first appeared in *The Strand Magazine* in two parts: *Hobbies* (December 1921) and *Painting as a Pastime* (January 1922). He had been offered £1,000 to write it, though his wife tried to torpedo the project. In her magnificent survey, *Winston Churchill: His Life as a Painter* (1990) their daughter Mary records that Clementine 'was in principle opposed to Winston's writing what she regarded as "pot-boilers" to boost their domestic economy'. Clemmie protested that writing about his painting would vex professional painters and 'cause you to be discussed trivially'. Winston often took his wife's advice, but on this occasion we may be glad he didn't. *Painting as a Pastime* 'is pure enchantment to read', his daughter continues, 'throbbing as it does with enthusiasm and encouragement to others to seize brush and canvas and "have a go", as Winston himself had done before, when, under the flail of misfortune, he had discovered in painting a companion with whom he was to walk for the greater part of the long years which remained to him.'

There was nothing avant-garde about Churchill the artist. He worked in traditional oil-on-canvas, and he painted mainly landscapes–'Trees don't complain', he was wont to say about his subjects. Yet he was not untalented at still life and even at portraiture. He had lessons from accomplished painters like Sir John and Lady Lavery, Richard Sickert and Paul Maze, and he effected a somewhat impressionistic style, though he 'threw in plenty of my own', as he said of his writing. Although he produced well over 500 paintings he was consistently modest about them, at first exhibiting under a pseudonym and putting none up for sale, though he did allow one to be auctioned for charity. Such shyness seems peculiar for a man described by so many as a towering egotist.

He loved to give paintings away, but would carefully consider any potential beneficiaries, and which paintings they might receive. Those who wanted one did best not to ask, but trust that a proper expression of enthusiasm for his 'daubs' would result in a presentation. Winston couldn't bear to part with most of his works: the largest collection remains in his studio at Chartwell, where they may be admired at leisure by the visitor. Most experts agree that Churchill had real talent and could easily have developed into a professional, if only he had had the time.

The development of the text as it appears in this book was gradual. The 'Hobbies' article appeared again in Nash's *Pall Mall* (December 1925) and the *Sunday Chronicle* (*A Man's Hobbies*, 20 April 1930); the two articles were excerpted as *I Ride My Hobby* in America's *Cosmopolitan* (February 1926, reprinted March

1961). But complete, connected text was not published until Churchill's friend Lord Birkenhead did so in *The Hundred Best English Essays* (Cassell, 1929). The two articles were split again in *Thoughts and Adventures* (1932). In 1965, the complete essay was republished in *Country Beautiful* magazine (Vol. 4, No. 2).

By the end of the Second World War his hobby was well known and of considerable public fascination, so Odhams Press persuaded him to issue his painting essay in book form, incorporating 18 colour plates of his works to date, mostly recent ones. Publication was timely, since Churchill had just been elected 'Honorary Academician Extraordinary' by the Royal Academy, and his paintings had been on display at the Academy's 1948 summer exhibitions. Thus the little book was an instant success, and had the widest circulation of any of his post-war single volume works.

FROM THE REVIEWS

'Birkenhead's inclusion of this text in *The Hundred Best English Essays* was ridiculous; *Painting as a Pastime* has its merits, and is certainly pleasant reading, but by no stretch of the imagination can it rank among the great essays. One can only suppose its inclusion was a triumph of friendship over judgement; it was thus, however, that the book text was established, enabling Churchill in later years to offer art among his many talents. Its publication also produced a curious trend: quite suddenly prominent people became artists, including many wartime generals, admirals and ministers; and the rush for paints and easels became universal. Those who were not so successful were soon able to "paint by numbers". No one will blame Churchill for this, but alas he has a lot to answer for.

'The real interest of the book lies in the reason given by Churchill for taking up this pastime. After leaving the Admiralty in shame and despair in 1915, he writes, "the change from the intense executive activities of each day's work at the Admiralty to the narrowly measured duties of a counsellor left me gasping. Like a sea-beast fished up from the depths, or a diver too suddenly hoisted, my veins threatened to burst from the fall in pressure...And then it was that the Muse of Painting came to my rescue–out of charity and out of chivalry, because after all she had nothing to do with me–and said, 'Are these toys any good to you? They amuse some people.'"

'In mythology there never was a Muse of Painting; perhaps it was some unknown, kindly goddess who offered him the "toys" of his new trade. It hardly matters, for he accepted them with joy, and a new Corregio burst upon the world.'

Henry Fearon (privately published)

First Edition: ICS A125a
Publisher: Odhams Press Ltd. / Ernest Benn Ltd., London, 1948

Ivory cloth blocked gilt with title and author's name top board and (reading up) on spine. 8vo, 66 pages numbered (i)–(ii) (+2), (iii)–(vi) and 7–32 plus frontispiece and 32 pages of colour plates on coated stock. Published December 1948 at 10s. 6d. ($2.10). Price in 1965 12s. 6d. ($1.75).

IMPRESSIONS AND QUANTITIES

At least seven impressions: 1948 (25,000 copies), June 1949 (12,000), October 1949 (20,000), 1962, 1965 (twice), 1966. The 1962–1965 impressions were bound in red leatherette with dark red round Churchill artwork on top board and blocked gilt and black on the spine. Some 1965 impressions were sold individually; some 1965 and all 1966 impressions were sold in sets of three with other Churchill or related books, similarly bound. The 1966 impression was in the Odhams Bookplan club series, maroon boards blocked black. Identifying first editions: verso of title-page states, 'First published in Volume Form. 1948'.

VARIANTS

No variants of the First Edition are reported.

DUST JACKETS

First Edition jackets are printed maroon with a black halftone photograph of Churchill at his easel (same as frontispiece) on top face.

The 1965 jacket, printed red and halftone, retains the original front face format and repeats it on the back face. The 1966 Bookplan jacket is blank on spine and rear face; front face carries a halftone photo bust of the author with 'CHURCHILL' printed black, 'Painting as a Pastime' red and a line stating, 'A Part of a collection of three illustrated volumes'. Rear flap is blank, front flap lists the three volumes: this one, Thomson's *Life and Times* and Heath's *Churchill Anthology*.

COMMENTS AND APPRAISAL

The First Edition is always needed to make collections complete, but fine copies

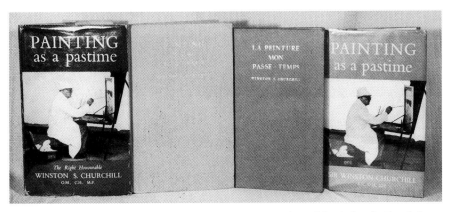

Painting as a Pastime. Left to right: the first (English) edition in and out of dust jacket; the French *La Peinture mon Passe Temps*, bound similarly to the English; and an Odhams reprint from the 1960s.

are in short supply: the ivory cloth soils as easily as the thin dust jacket tears or chips. Top boards often contain an offset jacket pattern. Brilliant copies are rarities. Expect to pay up to $150/£90 for these, but much less, of course, for poorer copies–down to just a few pounds or dollars.

American Issue: ICS A125b

Publisher: McGraw-Hill / Whittlesey House, New York, 1950

Bluish-green cloth blocked gilt on spine: 'WINSTON S. CHURCHILL ... PAINTING AS A PASTIME' and publisher's name, reading down. 8vo, 66 pages numbered (i)– (ii) (+2), (iii)–(vi) and 7–32 plus frontispiece and 32 pages of colour plates on coated stock. Published 1950 at $3.

IMPRESSIONS AND QUANTITIES
There were at least three impressions, the first being of 20,000 copies. Sheets were supplied by the British printers, Hazell, Watson and Viney, Ltd.; the title-page is altered only for the US publisher's name and its verso credits *Amid These Storms* (instead of *Thoughts and Adventures*) for the essay's first appearance in volume form. Identifying first editions: title-page verso lists first publication in USA (1950) with no notice of subsequent impressions.

VARIANTS AND DUST JACKETS
There are three distinct variants of this issue: 1) Whittlesey House: bluish-green cloth, reading 'Whittlesey House' on the jacket spine and 'WHITTLESEY HOUSE | McGraw-Hill Book Co. Inc. ... New York 18, N.Y.' on the back face. 2) As above but in medium blue cloth binding. 3) McGraw-Hill: dark blue cloth; 'McGraw-Hill' on the jacket spine and 'McGRAW-HILL BOOK COMPANY, INC. | 330 West 42nd

American editions and issues. Left to right: first American in two bindings, Whittlesey House and McGraw Hill; one of the former in its dust jacket; a first and second impression of the paperback; and the Cornerstone Library hardback.

Street ... New York 36, N.Y.' on the back face. (All variants carry 'Whittlesey House' on the spine). The jackets are otherwise identical, containing a colour drawing taken from the frontispiece photo on the front face and the painting 'Near Antibes' in colour on the back face.

COMMENTS AND APPRAISAL

American Issues are of superior quality to the English and the Whittlesey House version is often found in bright condition with clean dust jackets. The McGraw-Hill version is extremely rare; I have only encountered one (a first impression) in 15 years. Whittlesey was a specialty subdivision of McGraw-Hill, so I believe that the latter imprint was produced as the official trade edition, while high production went to Whittlesey. A truly fine Whittlesey House issue in like dust jacket is worth up to $100/£60; the same in McGraw-Hill format is probably worth double that. Run-of-the-mill unjacketed copies are of trifling value.

Cornerstone Library Issue: ICS A125c
Publisher: Pocket Books, Inc., New York, 1961

This offprint from the First American Edition, subtitled *An instructive and inspiring invitation to the joy of painting,* was first published in 1961. It was reprinted twice in 1965 and once in 1966; the 1965 reprint was also offered in hardcover. All four paperbacks known carry a halftone cover photo of Churchill by Philippe Halsman and a price of $1.

VARIANTS

Paperback variants: First impression: uncoated wrappers, black spine, blank on the insides; verso of title-page states, 'Reprinted, 1961'. Second impression: coated wrappers, black spine, book lists inside both covers; verso notes 'Reprinted 1965'. Third impression: coated wrappers, solid black panels above and below cover photo with extra type ('Includes 16 full color reproductions of Churchill's paintings'), white spine, book lists inside both covers. (The second impression publisher's address on inside back cover is 'New York 20'; on the third impression this is updated to the new postal 'Zip' code: '10020'.) Verso notes 'Reprinted 1965.' Fourth impression: as the third, but 'Reprinted 1966' on title-page verso.

Hardback variant: bound in laid white paper printed brown, green and red with repeat oak leaf design on boards and spine; on top board the title, author name and a drawing of brushes and oil tube are printed red and green on white panel.

APPRAISAL

I sometimes see the hardback offered at shocking prices. For years I've sold this very common issue for $7 (£4.38) and the paperbacks for $3 (£1.88)!

English Paperback Edition: ICS A125d
Publisher: Penguin Books Ltd., Harmondsworth, Middlesex, 1964

The text was completely reset for this paperback, Penguin Book number 2169, though the trimmed 32-page coated paper section contained the same plates as the original. Published 1964 at 6s. (84¢). At least three impressions, the second in 1965, the third 1968. Wrappers printed orange and mauve. The front wrap contains a colour picture by Leif Frimann Anisdahl of an artist's palette complete with cigar, the back a photograph of a very old Churchill and quotes from the book. Trifling value, although I know of one of these inscribed by Churchill in late 1964– undoubtedly one of the last books, if not the last, he ever signed.

Limited Edition: Not in ICS or Woods
Publisher: Gump's, San Francisco, 1985

This odd little edition of 500 copies uses the same cover titles (reset) and artwork as the hardbound Cornerstone, but is otherwise very different. Boards are printed red and silver with a repeat oak leaf and acorn design; the frontispiece is the author's painting, 'Lady Churchill at the Launching of HMS Indomitable'; the cover title box and 'GUMP'S | SINCE 1861' appears on the title-page. An acknowledgement to *Amid These Storms* on the verso is followed by a new introduction by Winston S. Churchill, M.P. (the author's grandson). Another sheet contains a handwritten number (1–500) and note: 'This book was printed at the Feathered Serpent Press, from type set by Anchor & Acorn, and bound by Cardoza-James in an edition of 500 copies.' Textual pages are numbered (i)–(viii) and (1)–25 (+3).

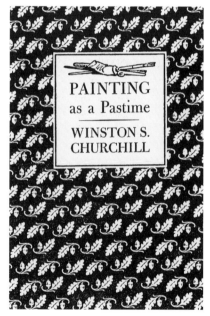

Cover of the limited edition of 500, produced by the San Francisco department store Gump's in 1985. The cover bears the same label as the Cornerstone hardback, but the background is distinct. Many copies were inscribed by Churchill's grandson.

This work was produced by the famous San Francisco department store and many if not all copies were inscribed by Mr Churchill. I have seen only one copy, offered at $200/£120. Considering the size of the edition I expect this was a fair price.

More *Painting as a Pastime*. Left to right: the Odhams Bookplan, Penguin paperback, and German edition.

FOREIGN TRANSLATIONS

Finnish: MAALAUS AJANVIETTEENA
Published by K. J. Gummerus Dsakeyhitö: Jyväskylä, 1950 in blue cloth; republished 1966 in bright green cloth with white dust jacket.

French: LA PEINTURE MON PASSE-TEMPS
Published by Editions de la Paix, Paris, 1949, in pale green paper boards with photo of the author painting and a white dust jacket printed brown. A limited, numbered edition (1–3,000, the first 20 'hors commerce') was published in ivory cloth in the style of the English first edition.

German: PINSEL UND PALETTE ALS ZEITVERTREIB
Published by Hallwag: Bern, n.d., in dark green cloth; dust jacket black with red and white type and painting of 'Near Antibes' in colour.

Japanese: EGAKU TANOSHISHA
Published at 280 yen by Bijutsu Shuppansha, 1951, in dark grey green cloth; white dust jacket printed brown.

EUROPE UNITE

COHEN A246, WOODS A128

Not enough has been written about Churchill's period as Leader of the Opposition (1945–1951), a new and unique role for him: for ten years before the war he had been denied even a supporting role, and he had been too junior to lead in earlier years. Those chroniclers who represent this as a grim and ignominious time for the old lion have not read *Europe Unite*, which publishes 52 speeches and broadcasts delivered in 1947–1948. The galleries still filled when Churchill rose to speak, and his wit crackled across the House in some of the most riveting and heated debates of modern times.

As always he defied the Socialists, who now commanded a huge majority, but in the good-natured way that was then accepted practice, and of which he was a master. 'How nice to see the Hon. Member climb off his perch', Churchill would say when little Sidney Silverman, a feisty but diminutive Labour Member whose legs didn't reach the floor from the bench, would stand to challenge him. Or, when another MP rose to object to something he was saying: 'The Rt. Hon. Member may catch Mr. Speaker's eye. He will not catch mine.' (He didn't catch Mr Speaker's eye, either.)

My favourite amusement in this book comes in the debate of 28 October 1947, as Churchill offers a *tour d'horizon* on behalf of the Opposition, criticising Labour across the board. The Minister of Fuel and Power, Hugh Gaitskell, had earlier suggested people economise by taking fewer baths, saying, 'I have never had a great many baths myself.' Churchill, a noted bather, responds: 'When Ministers of the Crown speak like this on behalf of His Majesty's Government, the Prime Minister and his friends have no need to wonder why they are getting increasingly into bad odour. I have even asked myself, when meditating upon these points whether you, Mr. Speaker, would admit the word "lousy" as a Parliamentary expression in referring to the Administration, provided, of course, it was not intended in a contemptuous sense but purely as one of factual narration.'

Of course there are far weightier matters to occupy us in *Europe Unite*, including the subject of the book's title, embodied in another moving address to the Congress of Europe at The Hague in 1948. There is the escalating violence in Palestine, up and down relations with America and the Soviets, conscription, nationalisation, the grim economy, and above all Britain's precipitate post-war decline.

Nothing more typifies the last than India, for which Churchill has often been excoriated as a die-hard imperialist, determined to preserve the Raj. How much more reasonable his own words sound: 'Great Britain had for many years been committed to handing over responsibility for the government of India to the representatives of the Indian people. There was the promise of Dominion status implicit in the declaration of August 1917. There was the expansion and definition of Dominion status by the Statute of Westminster. There was the Simon Commission Report of 1930, followed by the Hoare-Linlithgow Reforms of 1935. There was the Linlithgow offer of 1940 [that Indians frame a self-governing constitution], for which, as head of the Government in those days, I took my share of responsibility.' The Government had proposed to give the new Viceroy [Louis Mountbatten] fourteen months to organise Indian independence. 'I do not think that ... gives the new Viceroy a fair chance', Churchill continued. 'Everyone knows that the fourteen months' time limit is fatal to any orderly transference of power.' Later, quite arbitrarily, Mountbatten had decided to transfer power only five months after this speech. The result was a bloodbath in which millions died.

Undoubtedly by plan, Churchill published *Europe Unite* in time for the General Election of 1950, where it probably had some influence. The Labour majority of 140 was reduced to six, and that led inevitably to another election in 1951, which restored our author to power.

FROM THE REVIEWS

'Nothing in this series of speeches indicates that Churchill is losing ground, or that his powers are diminishing, in spite of his half-century in political harness. He continues to stress what are for him familiar themes. One of these is the preservation of Great Britain and her interests: "...it never was more needful that we should labour body and soul to preserve and unify whatever is left of our Empire and Commonwealth..." Another is cultivation of U.S. friendship. As a political realist, Churchill hopes that Germany and Italy will be welcomed back into "the European family". He urges European unity so that Europe may form a "sphere of interest and influence" alongside Russia, the United States and the British Commonwealth. All of these spheres of power, of course, are to be only "the massive pillars upon which the world organization would be founded in majesty and calm". In these speeches, Churchill presents his views on a wide variety of subjects, ranging from capital punishment (15 July 1948) to general education (12 May 1948): "...a university training should not be too practical in its aims. Young people study at universities to achieve knowledge, and not to learn a trade".

'This book is worth reading, because Churchill is readable and because he is a speaker worthy of careful study. The jacket of one of his recent volumes calls him "the most eloquent statesman of our time". It is not easy to quarrel with this judgment.'

Halbert E. Gulley, *The Quarterly Review of Speech,* April 1951.

First Edition: ICS A128a
Publisher: Cassell and Co. Ltd., London, 1950

Green cloth blocked gilt with title, author's name and 'CASSELL' on spine. 8vo, 518 pages numbered (i)–(x) (+2) and (1)–506. Page (ii) lists 28 other works by the author.

DUST JACKETS
Dust jackets printed black, green and yellow on white paper. Published 3 February 1950 at 18s. ($2.52) in a single impression of 12,000 copies. Though bound in England, sheets for this edition and the American issue were printed in the Netherlands.

VARIANTS
Publisher's presentation copies were bound in full black pebble grain morocco.

APPRAISAL
Showing Churchill at the height of his powers during his only term as Leader of the Opposition, *Europe Unite* has many powerful, moving and humorous speeches to offer. The supply of run-of-the-mill copies is reasonably good and these are not expensive. The green cloth is subject to splotching and the page stock spots, so a really pristine copy in an undamaged dust jacket is a rarity today. These cost up to $100/£60

All the editions of *Europe Unite*. Left to right: English (in and out of jacket), Swedish and American (out of and in jacket).

American Issue: ICS A128b

Publisher: Houghton Mifflin Co., Boston, 1950

Greenish-blue rough cloth blocked on spine with dark blue-green decorations and in black: 'Europe | Unite | [blue-green star] | CHURCHILL' and 'HOUGHTON | MIFFLIN CO.' (all reading across). Pagination identical to the First Edition although the US publisher's name and date are substituted for Cassell on the title-page. Dust jacket printed black, green and blue-green on white paper. Published 1950 at $5 in a single impression of 2,500 copies, using sheets supplied by the Dutch printer.

APPRAISAL

Again, this is a higher quality production than the English Edition, but with only a quarter the press run of *Sinews of Peace* it is extremely scarce today, and jacketed copies are a rarity. Collectors anxious to complete their sets of American post-war speech volumes have been known to pay $200/£120 for a jacketed copy. Even unjacketed ones are rarely seen, and command prices up to $100/£60 depending on condition. Even though two other American post-war speech volumes saw even fewer copies produced, this is the one I encounter least frequently.

FOREIGN TRANSLATIONS

Swedish: FÖRENADE EUROPA
Published by Skoglund, Stockholm, 1950, in cloth and card wrappers. Later included in a four-volume set of war and post-war speeches.

PIRATED EDITION
A smaller-format, hardbound pirated edition is known to exist. See note under *In the Balance* on page 304.

TALER I DANMARK

ICS A129/4 (NOT IN WOODS)
Publisher: Hasselbalch, Copenhagen, 1950

Greyish-green laid paper wrappers printed maroon on face and spine. 8vo, 42 pages numbered (1)–36 plus four coated paper sheets comprising frontispiece and photographs facing pages 14, 26 and 34. Page 7 reproduces a handwritten note from 28 Hyde Park Gate: 'I have a glowing memory of my visit to Denmark.' Winston S. Churchill | November 1950'. Published in a white folding cardboard case, December 1950. Text in Danish.

VARIANTS
The colophon notes 500 numbered copies for sale to the public; others were gifts from the publisher (one such has a blue on white 'with compliments' card). The press run was much larger, however, because most copies are not numbered. A second variant was published by Langkjërs Bogtrykkeri: Copenhagen 1950, carrying that name on the front wrapper and title page and an altered colophon.

During 9–11 October 1950 Churchill visited Denmark, where he received the Sonning Prize ('Sonning-price'), a Danish European culture award. He delivered four broadcasts and two speeches: one after receiving an honorary degree at Copenhagen University, another to the Danish Students Association. This softbound book collects all four, only one of which was published elsewhere (*In the Balance* a year later; the *Complete Speeches* in 1974). The visit had many moving moments. After being praised as the architect of victory this man so often described as besotted with self replied, 'I was only the servant of my country and had I, at any moment, failed to express her unflinching resolve to fight and conquer, I should at once have been rightly cast aside.' The Danes' praise was 'far too complimentary', he added, with many words 'that no man should hear till dead'.

Although there are several individual and collected speeches presented in book form–I have noted four of these following the 1945 collected *War Speeches*– this work collects three more into what some might consider a legitimate, separate Churchill book. It is the only collection of post-war speeches, other than the five book-length works, that I know to be 100 per cent Churchill. *Churchill's Visit to*

Norway (Oslo, 1949) contains his speeches, but also material not by him. *Taler I Danmark* is the first, and in part only, publication of the Denmark speeches in volume form. Though not often seen outside Denmark it is not expensive, fine copies selling for about $50/£30.

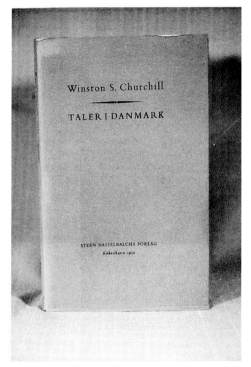

Only published in Denmark, *Taler I Danmark* stands as a unique Churchill work, never published in English.

IN THE BALANCE

COHEN A254, WOODS A130

Like *Europe Unite*, the 1949–1950 speeches had political implications, and fortunately, or by timing, the book arrived just as another General Election loomed. In America, Houghton Mifflin expressed little interest until Churchill won that election, publishing in early 1952. 'Now that Churchill is once more at the helm of the British Government, [his speeches are] more than ever significant', they commented. The chief subjects here are the Council of the European Movement, party political broadcasts and addresses, criticism of Labour's foreign affairs and defence management, and fascinating speeches abroad–at Brussels, Strasbourg, Copenhagen, Boston and New York.

By far the greatest speech in this period, alone worth the price of the book, was one that deserved a much wider circulation in America: 'The Twentieth Century– its Promise and its Realization', delivered at the Massachusetts Institute of Technology's Mid-Century Conference in March 1949. After a dramatic review of the triumphs and tragedies of 1900 to 1945, Churchill added: 'We are now confronted with something quite as wicked but in some ways more formidable than Hitler, because Hitler had only the Herrenvolk pride and anti-Semitic hatred to exploit. He had no fundamental theme. But these thirteen men in the Kremlin have their hierarchy and a church of Communist adepts ... They have their anti-God religion and their Communist doctrine of the entire subjugation of the individual to the State.' His prescription to the West was to hold the line, so that one day 'Russians everywhere would be received as brothers in the human family'.

He ended with his Fulton theme of fraternal association. 'Do not, my friends, I beg of you, underrate the strength of Britain. As I said at Fulton, Do not suppose that half a century from now you will not see 70,000,000 or 80,000,000 of Britons spread about the world and united in defence of our traditions, our way of life, and the world causes which you and we espouse. United we stand secure. Let us then move forward together in discharge of our mission and our duty, fearing God and nothing else.'

FROM THE REVIEWS

'Here again is that sonorous roll, that matchless polish, that hammerlike impact and that bird-winged wit, which make him the greatest living orator. To sit with this book for an evening is to share in the making of history.'

Christian Science Monitor, 1951

FROM THE INTRODUCTION
'The speeches cover a wide range of topics, both domestic and foreign, and, as in previous volumes, provide a running commentary on political events in the age in which we live. The outstanding events of this two-year period were the devaluation of the £ sterling, the General Election of February 1950, the outbreak of the Korean war, the establishment of the North Atlantic Treaty Organization, and the immense rearmament programmes of the United States ... While during these two years dangers have grown, the Western Powers have made steady if belated progress along the paths of safety which Mr. Churchill has persistently sign-posted ... Though the peace of the world is far from assured there is an increasingly wide acceptance of the view that time may yet be allowed in which perseverance with these policies may achieve the safety of Western Civilization.'

Randolph S. Churchill

First Edition: ICS A130a
Publisher: Cassell and Co. Ltd., London, 1951

Dark blue cloth blocked gilt with title, author's name and CASSELL on spine. 8vo, 468 pages numbered (2+) (i)–(x) and (1)–456. Page (ii) lists 31 other works by the author. Dust jackets printed black, blue and red on white paper. Published 1 October 1951 at 25s. ($3.50) in a single impression of 8,200 copies. This was the first post-war speech volume printed in England.

APPRAISAL
Third of five English post-war speech volumes, this one deals often with duller and more domestic subjects, but is essential for completeness. Considerably scarcer than its predecessors, it has become quite pricey, especially for fine jacketed copies,

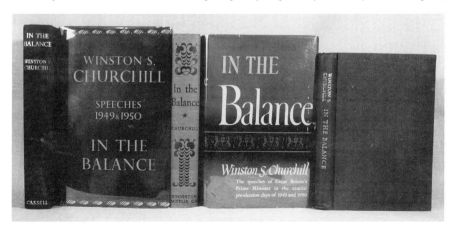

In the Balance in three variations: English first (left), American (centre) and the unlabelled pirated edition in dark blue cloth (right).

which often cost $150/£90, and perhaps more. Even 'very good' copies tend to cost over $100/£60; the only way to get one for less than that, besides a lucky discovery in a general bookshop, would be to settle for a copy without the jacket. The spine gilt on this edition is prone to fading and is often unreadable on unjacketed copies.

American Issue: ICS A130b
Publisher: Houghton Mifflin Co., Boston, 1952

Dark tan cloth blocked on spine with brown decorations and in black: '*In the* | *Balance* | [brown star] | CHURCHILL' and 'HOUGHTON | MIFFLIN CO.' (all reading across). Pagination identical to the First Edition, but the title-page is completely reset, substituting the US publisher's name and the date of US publication plus Library of Congress card number on the title-page verso.

DUST JACKET
Dust jacket printed red, black and dull yellow on white paper, with an abstract design of repeat British Arms on front face and spine. Published 1952 at $5 in a single impression of 2,000 copies, using sheets supplied by the English printer.

APPRAISAL
Churchill's speeches seemed to be losing their appeal to Americans and Houghton Mifflin again reduced their order, with the result that the American issue is rare today, though not so long ago it sold for only around $25/£15. Nowadays a fine jacketed copy will run to around $150/£90, and few if any jacketed copies sell for under $100/£60. The binding is of good quality and holds up well without the dust jacket; expect to pay upwards of $75/£45 for these. Jacket spines fade easily; expect to pay a premium for an unfaded example.

Pirated edition

Blue cloth blocked silver on spine only: 'WINSTON S.' over 'CHURCHILL' and 'IN THE BALANCE' (reading down). 16mo (5¼ x 7⅝in), 466 pages numbered (i)–(x) and (1)–456. Offprinted and very slightly reduced from the English Edition. No publisher's imprints inside or out. Although it lacks the usual Chinese characters or Taipei imprints, the thin page stock suggests another in a long line of oriental pirate editions.

FOREIGN TRANSLATIONS

Swedish: I VÅGSKÅLEN
Published by Skoglund, Stockholm, 1952, in cloth and card wrappers. Later included in a four-volume set of war and post-war speeches.

THE WAR SPEECHES

(DEFINITIVE EDITION)

COHEN A263, WOODS A136

Churchill's return to the Premiership reconcentrated attention on him wonderfully, renewing interest in his war speeches. Produced to cheap standards owing to wartime shortages and restrictions, the original volumes were all out of print by 1952. Cassell decided to reissue the war speeches in a new, expansive and comprehensive edition of three tall, elegant volumes printed in large type with generous margins on quality stock.

Collectors often ask whether this edition contains something different from the seven war speech volumes. The answer is yes. Charles Eade, who had edited all the war volumes save *Into Battle*, eliminated quite a number of the original speeches he considered peripheral, and retitled many others. He also replaced the chronological dates with brief notes where necessary, to form transitions or introductions to various sections. More important is that Eade added five new entries, establishing a new text. Added in Volume I were 'Our Consciences are at Rest' (3 September 1939) and 'The News is Very Bad' (17 June 1940). Added in Volume III were 'The Beast is Cornered' (Message to Danish Resistance Groups 1 Jan 1945), 'Warships for Russia' (5 June 1945) and 'A Threat to Freedom' (21 June 1945).

But the best reason to acquire this new edition is that it provides an index– never present in the original volumes–which makes it the most readable and useful version of the war speeches.

First Edition: ICS A136a

Publisher: Cassell and Co. Ltd., London, 1951-52

Three volumes

8vo, dark navy cloth blocked gilt on spine: author's name, 'WAR | SPEECHES | 1939–45 | [one to three stars] | COMPILED BY | CHARLES EADE' at the top, 'CASSELL' at the foot. Title-page printed two-colour. Page edges unstained, no head or foot bands. Published 1951 (Vol. I) and 1952 (Vols II and III) at 21s. ($2.94) per volume, 63s. ($8.82) the set. Later priced at 70s. ($9.80), revised to £3.75 ($10.50) post-1971. Stars designate volume number.

Vol. I: 500 pages numbered (i)–(xvi) and (1)–484. Vol. II: 578 pages numbered (i)–(xvi) and (1)–560. Vol. III: 596 pages numbered (i)–(xvi), (1)–578 (+2). On page

(vii) of each volume is a subtitle: Vol. I: *From the Rise of Hitler to the Invasion of Russia, June 22, 1941*; Vol. II: *June 25, 1941–September 6, 1943*; Vol. III: *September 11, 1943–August 16, 1945*.

Note: 'Man-Power and Woman-Power' was delivered 2 December 1941, not December 10th as stated in Vol. II, page (xi).

EDITIONS, IMPRESSIONS AND QUANTITIES

The first impression numbered 4,700 sets. Each volume had a second impression (identified as 'edition' on verso of title-page): respectively these were March 1963, February 1965 and July 1964. Volume I only had a third impression ('edition') in September 1967. Identifying first editions: Verso of title-page reads 'THIS EDITION FIRST PUBLISHED 1951' [or '1952' on Vols II and III], with no mention of later 'editions'.

DUST JACKETS

Jackets are printed black and rose on buff paper. The back flap of first impression jackets advertises *The Sinews of Peace, Europe Unite* and *In the Balance*; the back face advertises Vols I–V of *The Second World War*. There is no variation between jackets for the three volumes. Later impression jackets vary, notably by identifying the author as 'Sir Winston S. Churchill'.

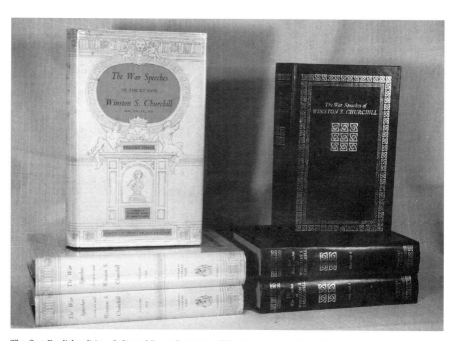

The first English edition (left) and Purnell reprint of the three-volume *War Speeches*.

COMMENTS AND APPRAISAL

This handsome trio is easily the most luxurious and durable rendering of the *War Speeches* and possesses the huge advantage of an index. It adds some new material but, unfortunately, excises much more that appeared in the original volumes; therefore, the fastidious collector requires both. For years the going price of a fine-jacketed first edition set was $250/£150, but these are getting in short supply and the price may be rising soon. Later impressions in jackets, and unjacketed firsts, sell for up to $200/£120; unjacketed later impressions cost up to $125/£78.

American Issue: ICS A136b
Publisher: Houghton Mifflin Co., Boston

Three volumes

8vo, half black cloth and red buckram, blocked gilt on spine with decorative panels and more elaborate titles: 'THE | WAR | SPEECHES | OF THE | RT HON | WINSTON S. | CHURCHILL' plus boxes for Eade's name, volume number and publisher. Title-page printed two-colour. Top page edges stained dark yellow, cloth head and foot bands. Published 1953 in a plain navy leatherette box, priced $25 the set.

For this issue, only 500 sheets were exported from England to Houghton

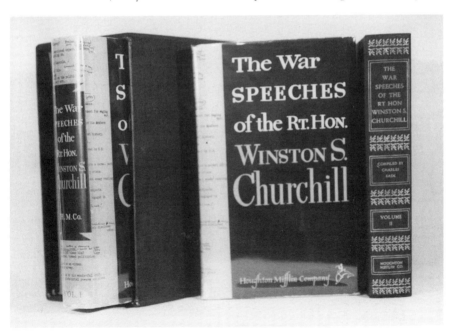

Extremely rare, the American three-volume *War Speeches* had a press run of only 500 copies. Books were bound in half black cloth, jacketed and sold boxed in a slipcase.

Mifflin, who changed only the title-page and verso. American publishers of the individual speech volumes, Putnam, Little, Brown and Simon and Schuster, are acknowledged on the verso.

DUST JACKETS
Dust jackets are printed black and light blue on white coated stock; around the spine is wrapped a reproduction from Churchill's hand-corrected typescript of the first *Secret Session* speech, photographically reproduced in Vol. I.

APPRAISAL
The publisher adopted a particularly ugly binding and a lurid jacket design, and the gilt spine blocking is almost always dull; but none of this matters because of the extreme rarity. There are plenty of collectors who strive to acquire both the British and American issues of everything that Churchill wrote. Thus $500/£300 is a more than fair price for a near-fine set in jackets. If the slipcase is also present, one might have to pay even more. To acquire my own slipcased set I traded a first edition of *My African Journey,* which was quite a deal–for the other collector.

Great War Speeches (Abridged): Cohen A256.3, ICS A136ca

Publisher: Corgi Books, London, 1957

A paperback abridgement from the Definitive Edition, issued as a 'Corgi Giant' paperback at 3s. 6d. (49¢). At least seven impressions: 1957-58-59 (384pp.); 1963-65-65 (288pp.); 1978 (352 pp.).

Great War Speeches (Abridged): Cohen A256.3, ICS A136cb

Publisher: Transworld Paperbacks, New York, 1957

The American version of the above had at least four impressions through 1963.

LIBRARY EDITION OF 3 SUPERBLY BOUND BOOKS–1,600 pages 240 speeches Books which you will read like novels from cover to cover. Once you begin, you will not be able to put them down. You and your children will cherish them as part of a great heritage for many years.

The Purnell *War Speeches,* from a brochure advertising this reprint at 9 gns. for the three volumes, circa 1970.

PURNELL ISSUE: ICS A136d

Publisher: Purnell & Sons Ltd., London, c. 1970 (n.d.)

Three volumes

Reprinted from the Cassell edition ('in Association with Cassell'), this work was trimmed to 5⅝ x 8⅝in and bound in blue leatherette blocked silvery-gilt, carrying the name 'PURNELL/CASSELL' at the foot of the spine. The title-pages were printed black only. The type size shrank very slightly, but trimming reduced the former generous margins. The indexes were retained in each volume.

The set was advertised by mail order as an 'exclusive offer for readers of Purnell's history of the *Second World War*', who were offered the volumes at 3gns. ($8.80) each, 9gns. ($26.40) the set. Purnell must have sold plenty of copies, because they are still easily found. Sets should not exceed $100/£60 on the present-day market and may well cost half that much; this is a best buy if one requires a reading copy only. Most sets remain in nice condition although the spines are inclined to discoloration.

STEMMING THE TIDE

COHEN A264, WOODS A137

The Official Biography tells us that editor Randolph Churchill proposed numerous titles for this work, including *Fight for Survival, Against the Stream, Shouldering the Burden* and *Uphill All The Way*, as well as the one chosen. His father, as usual, favoured the more upbeat titles: 'I rather think *Stemming the Tide* is the best, but *Shouldering the Burden* is a good second.' (Gilbert, *'Never Despair'*, page 784).

The speeches, covering 1951–1952, are of particular importance to students of Churchill's second premiership. Notable in the period were the death of George VI, the triumph of Eisenhower in the United States, and Churchill's own return to power, only to find himself too tired, or too unwilling, to alter many of the Attlee policies he had so excoriated over the past half decade. He was old, and indeed exhausted; to him one great prize remained: peace itself. To his lasting regret, the 'settlement' with Russia that he would try so hard to engineer continued to elude the world.

Churchill was still full of regrets over India: '... three or four times as many lives were destroyed by violent and avoidable butchery in India as were lost by the whole British Empire in the Second World War', he said in October 1951. 'I am astonished that this should be treated as a mere incident in the progress of Oriental liberation and self-government. I am sure that it would have been possible to maintain law and order in India as we did in the face of the armed revolt of the Congress Party at the time of the attempted Japanese invasion without any serious difficulty or bloodshed; and that a Constituent Assembly far more representative of all the real forces of Indian life than the Congress Party could have shaped an Indian constitution and transferred the power to the new rulers of India in an orderly manner ... The vast human tragedy which occurred in the process of handing over is a fact for which I thank God I had no responsibility.'

Randolph in his Introduction states that his father in these years was still 'in the fullest flower ... opening another great chapter in a political career', having outlived all his contemporaries: from Rosebery, Balfour and Asquith to Lloyd George, the Chamberlains, Baldwin, MacDonald, Bevin and Cripps, and all the Second World War leaders. This was overly sentimental: Churchill experienced a mild stroke in July 1952 and would suffer a serious one a year later; few colleagues thought that the Prime Minister of 1951 was the man he had been in the war. In Churchill's own words, 'time ends all things'.

Yet the course of his life and career was astonishing. Among these pages is a speech at a banquet to honour the new Lord Mayor of London; Churchill here admits that he has attended such Guildhall ceremonies for over forty years! But: '...this is the first occasion when I have addressed this assembly here as Prime Minister. The explanation is convincing. When I should have come here as Prime Minister the Guildhall was blown up and before it was repaired I was blown out! I thought at the time they were both disasters.'

Upon the death of the King he recalls his own youth, 'passed in the august, unchallenged and tranquil glories of the Victorian Era', and feels 'a thrill in invoking once more, the prayer and the Anthem, GOD SAVE THE QUEEN.' And he reaches 400 years back in his mind's eye to recall the first Elizabeth, hoping for a new Elizabethan Age.

FROM THE REVIEWS

'It is only when Sir Winston speaks for himself that the full flavor of the great Englishman is evoked. These fifty speeches in 1951 and 1952 reflect the Prime Minister as no leisurely, respectful monographs can ever do. Here he is, the real, the irrepressible Winston: bouncing, determined, magnanimous, shrewd and emotional.

'Not long ago a Tory bewailed the description of Sir Winston as a "politician". The tendency in his own party to regard him as a relic in the National Trust is strong. *Stemming the Tide,* however, shows him as a politician, a great politician in the tradition of Pitt, Lincoln and Gladstone. It also reveals a more human, more likable person than the venerated national hero pictured by some of his contemporaries.

'"I will give way in a moment", he said in the course of a debate in 1951. "I was giving the right honourable gentleman [Aneurin Bevan] an honourable mention for having, it appears by accident, perhaps not from the best of motives, happened to be right."

'Those who advocate keeping Sir Winston in cotton wool might ponder this retort to the most feared of Labour speakers.'

Drew Middleton, *New York Times Book Review,* 28 February 1954

First Edition: ICS A137a
Publisher: Cassell and Co. Ltd., London, 1953

Maroon cloth blocked gilt with title, author's name and CASSELL on spine. 8vo, 390 pages numbered (i)–(x) and (1)–379 (+1). Page (ii) lists 34 other works by the author. Dust jackets are printed black, maroon and light green on white paper and advertise the three previous post-war speech volumes on the front flap and Volumes I–V of *The Second World War* on the back flap. Published 25 June 1953 at 30s. ($4.20) in a single impression of 5,500.

Variant: Cassell did not bind all 5,500 sheets in 1953. In 1961 a remainder binding in a distinctly tighter, smoother maroon cloth was issued which used up the leftover sheets. The dust jacket is quite distinct, printed black on pale green and without the oak leaf repeat border design Cassell used on all the other post-war speech volumes (the front face is entirely black except for lettering). This remainder jacket omits *The Sinews of Peace,* while adding *The Unwritten Alliance* to the front flap, and advertises all six volumes of *The Second World War* on the back flap.

APPRAISAL

A pristine, as-new copy of the original issue in a perfect dust jacket has changed hands for $250/£150, and this will probably be a low price in a few years; there just aren't enough of these to go round. The remainder binding costs less, although it too is not common: about $150/£90 is today's high end for a fine copy in jacket.

American Issue: ICS A137b

Publisher: Houghton Mifflin Co., Boston, 1954

Green cloth blocked on spine with green decorations and in black: 'Stemming | the Tide | [green design] | CHURCHILL' and 'HOUGHTON | MIFFLIN CO.' (all reading across). Pagination identical to the First Edition, but the title-page contains the US publisher's name and 1954 date, its verso the Library of Congress card number and note of first US publication. Dust jacket printed red-orange, navy blue and dull gold on white paper, with a stylised crown on face and spine. Published 1954 at $5 in a single impression of 1,850 copies, using sheets supplied by the English printer.

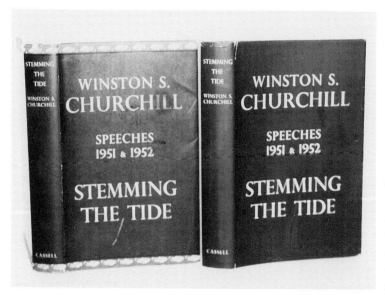

Stemming the Tide in its first edition (left) and remainder (right) dust jackets.

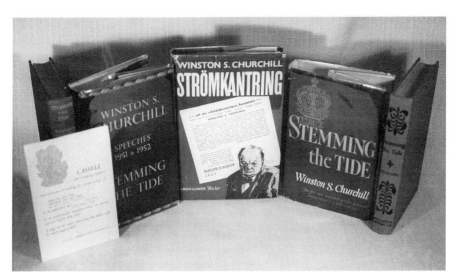

All the editions of *Stemming the Tide*. Left to right: the English (with reviewer's slip), Swedish and American editions.

APPRAISAL
This was the last speech volume the Americans chose to publish. Although it had the lowest press run, I seem to encounter it more than the American *Europe Unite*. But it is hardly common. An ultra-fine copy in unmarked jacket may approach $200/£120 nowadays; lesser jacketed copies cost over $100/£60, and even unjacketed examples are not cheap.

FOREIGN TRANSLATIONS

Swedish: STRÖMKANTRING
Published by Skoglund, Stockholm, 1953, in cloth and wrappers.

PIRATED EDITION
A smaller-format, hardbound pirated edition is known to exist. See note under *In the Balance* on page 302.

A HISTORY OF THE
ENGLISH-SPEAKING PEOPLES

COHEN A267, WOODS A138

Churchill's last great work was published nearly twenty years after he penned its first draft in the late 1930s, just after wrapping up *Marlborough*. This enabled him to utilise the literary team he had assembled for the biography, to which he added dozens of outlines he had solicited from scholars. In his Preface he remarks that the book 'slumbered peacefully' until 1956, 'when things have quietened down'. They had certainly quietened for him; for the first time since 1922–1923, when he was briefly out of Parliament, his voice no longer counted at the summit of affairs. Reading reports of the last decade of his life, one is struck by the central interest his *History* represented in his final years, how rapidly he sank into decline and depression after the final volume was published. His pre-war contract with Cassell called for him to be paid £20,000; the work eventually earned millions, was repeatedly reprinted, and remains in print today.

In its final form the original single volume evolved to four, each of which was published simultaneously in Britain, the USA and Canada–a first for Churchill's works. Each volume is divided into three 'books'. Volume I, *The Birth of Britain*, takes us from the primitive tribes who formed the 'Island Race' to the development of the nation through the Feudal Age, ending with the reign of Richard III. Volume II, *The New World,* spans the period from the consolidation of the Tudor dynasty in 1485 to the 'great and glorious' Revolution of 1688, the emergence of England as a great power, and the establishment in North America of 'lively and assertive communities' of English-speaking peoples. Volume III, *The Age of Revolution*, was perhaps Churchill's favourite, covering as it does the 1668–1815 period· from William III through the age of Marlborough and Queen Anne and the American War of Independence, to Trafalgar, Waterloo and the defeat of Napoleon. Our author reminds us that this critical period produced three revolutions which 'profoundly influenced mankind. They occurred within the space of a hundred years, and all of them led to war between the English and the French.' Volume IV, *The Great Democracies,* is more detailed, covering only 85 years of nineteenth-century history: recovery after the Treaty of Vienna, the mid-century reforms, the development of the United States, Victorian Britain, the modern Empire. There it stops. 'I could not write about the woe and ruin of the terrible twentieth century', Churchill told his doctor, Lord Moran, exhibiting a foretaste of his old age ennui: 'We answered all the tests. But it was useless.' (Diary of 19 June 1956, Moran, *Churchill: The Struggle for Survival*, London and Boston, 1966).

The *History* was roundly hailed in almost sycophantic terms by contemporary reviewers, for Churchill had by now reached the mellow status of a living legend– and deservedly so. He had not yet been subject to the historical reconsideration all legends receive sooner or later (equally deservedly). For the purposes of this book, I find latter-day analyses more interesting, and here offer some dramatically different viewpoints for the usual contemporary book reviews.

This work has been roundly criticised for the same fault as *The Second World War*, that it is 'not history'. It is certainly less an original contribution to history than *Marlborough*. Yet, as with his memoirs of the two World Wars, Churchill himself never claimed that it was history: 'This book does not seek to rival the works of professional historians. It aims rather to present a personal view on the processes whereby English-speaking peoples throughout the world have achieved their distinctive position and character ... If there was a need for it before, that has certainly not passed away ... Language, law, and the processes by which we have come into being [afford] a unique foundation for drawing together and portraying a concerted task.'

Here again Churchill leaves himself open to critics: his work is Atlantic-centric. Australia and New Zealand get only a few paragraphs of boilerplate. Moreover, it is Anglo-centric. Reading it, the proverbial man from Mars would scarcely realise that the United States and Canada were built by many besides Englishmen; that the Industrial Revolution was not entirely beneficent; that labour unions were necessary to stem the excesses of *laissez-faire*; that all wars were not glorious (although the American Civil War gets its share of gravitas); that America and the Great Dominions evolved a new aristocracy based on merit, not birth like the old one–and as such express vastly different cultures from that of the Mother Country. Clearly this complaint about the *History* is valid–but Churchill himself would probably not have contested it. Clement Attlee perhaps had the best one-line description of the work when he suggested that it might have been entitled, *Things in History Which Interested Me*.

Churchill's aristocratic breeding may be his greatest failure as a writer of what might be called (though he didn't use this term) popular history. The great climacterics in democracy's evolution, for example, did not usually lead directly to power of, by and for the people; Magna Charta's immediate effect was privilege for the aristocracy versus the State. But where would the English and American Democracies be without Magna Charta? Is Churchill wrong to emphasise that great piece in democracy's mosaic, even if he doesn't bother equally to limn the influence of Rousseau and Montesquieu on the American Constitution?

Another criticism of the work is our author's 'smug satisfaction' over the 'perfection' of the British and American systems, but this is a sweeping overstatement. Recall if you will his 1954 response to a churlish letter from Eisenhower, suggesting that he make a speech about 'the rights to self-government', since 'Colonialism is on the way out'. Churchill's reply displays remarkable frankness for a statesman so often regarded as a devious Machiavellian: 'In this I must admit I am a laggard. I am a bit sceptical about universal suffrage for the Hottentots even if refined by proportional representation. The British and American Democracies were slowly and painfully forged and even they are not perfect yet.' (Boyle (ed), *The Churchill–Eisenhower Correspondence, 1953–1955* (University of North Carolina Press, 1990)).

Not much smug satisfaction there. And how much better it would have been had Eisenhower and Eden heeded Churchill's strictures over Suez two years later–not to mention the Somalis, Rwandans and Congolese of the 1990s, and maybe even the Indians and Pakistanis of the 1940s? How much better would it have been for all the British colonial peoples if the end of Empire had been pursued with less of what Churchill described as 'unseemly scuttle'?

To other modern analysts of Churchill's literary output, the standard complaints about his *History* miss a fairly broad point. Professor James W. Muller, one of America's leading Churchill scholars, sums it up this way: 'This is a magnificent interpretation of British history from a man who had as good a claim to a practical grasp of statesmanship as any writer who ever described it. One can learn a great deal about how Churchill interpreted his own regime by reading this book–what he thought important, and why. The idea that it is a merely personal view is like the idea that his prime ministry was merely personal: in a sense, quite true, but in a more important sense, beside the point, which is that the views of this person, because of his experience and grasp of politics, are more deserving of our attention than those of any number of conventionally educated Ph.D.s.'

FROM THE REVIEWS

'How, now that we have these four fat volumes before us, can Churchill's value as an historian be assessed? The modern schools of history, composed of serious and pessimistic scholars, do not appreciate the dramatic or romantic representation of events and prefer to analyse human fortunes in social or economic terms. Churchill is, of course, well aware of the alterations occasioned in human thoughts and wishes by such factors as mass immigration, religious enthusiasms, the rivalry between urban and rural communities and the varying demands for spices, sugar, cotton, tar or timber. He adheres, however, to the old-fashioned view that national destiny is most often marred or furthered by the action upon the contemporary environment of men of willpower and genius. "The fortunes of mankind", he writes, "are largely the result of the impact upon events of superior beings". To the scientific historian this may seem an oversimplification of the pattern or circumstance. To the ordinary person the flash and dash of Churchill's zest will render these four volumes readable, humane, exhilarating, memorable and exemplary ... Few historians, moreover, have been gifted with a style of equal subtlety and vigour, a style at once classical and romantic, precise and imaginative, tolerant yet gently ironical, deeply sensitive to the tragedy of human failure and scornful only of those who are faithless to the virtue within them. These four volumes leave us with enhanced admiration for human character, and an added compassion for human fallibility. They are the legacy of a man of superhuman energy, great intellectual powers and utmost simplicity of soul.'

Harold Nicolson, *The New York Times Book Review*, 16 March, 1958

First Edition: Woods A138(a)

Publisher: Cassell & Co. Ltd., London, 1956–58

Four volumes

Dark red cloth, blocked gilt on spine (author's name, title, volume number and 'CASSELL' with red stained top page edges, 8vo. Vol. I published 23 April 1956 at 30s. ($4.20); 440 pages numbered (2+) (i)–(xxii) and (1)–416. Vol. II published 26 November 1956 at 30s., 350 pages numbered (2+) (i)–(xxii) and (1)–334 (+2). Vol. III published 14 October 1957 at 30s., 352 pages numbered (2+) (i)–(xxii) and (1)–332 (+6). Vol. IV published 14 March 1958 at 30s., 346 pages numbered (2+) (i)–(xxii) and (1)–322. All volumes variously illustrated with maps and tables.

Beautifully jacketed, the first English edition of *A History of the English Speaking Peoples* was a classic piece of book design. Above the books are advance publisher's blurbs for Volume I, *The Birth of Britain*.

EDITIONS, IMPRESSIONS AND QUANTITIES

The following impressions are reported: Vol. I, April (130,000) and May (30,000) 1956; January (20,000) and August 1957 (10,000); January 1958 (9,750); February 1959 (5,000); August 1960 (4,375); April 1962, October 1964 and February 1965 (5,000 each). Vol. II, November 1956 (150,000); February 1957 (25,000), June 1963 (5,000), March 1965 (5,400) and November 1966 (3,000). Vol. III, October 1957 (150,000); March 1965 (5,400) and January 1966 (3,325). Vol. IV, 150,000 (March 1958). Further pressings have occurred since. Identifying first editions: The verso of the title-page reads 'First Published 1956 [or 1957 or 1958]' with no notice of later impressions or editions. Paperbacks have been issued since at least 1974, most recently issued in large size, some boxed as a set, sometimes with wrapper designs similar to first edition dust jackets.

DUST JACKETS

These are the most attractive trade dust jackets ever to appear on Churchill's works, beautifully illustrated in four-colour: Vol. I, *The Bayeaux Tapestry*; Vol. II, *The Woburn Abbey portrait of Elizabeth I* and an early map of the world; Vol. III, Stanfield's *Battle of Trafalgar* and Trumbull's *Declaration of Independence*; Vol. IV, Winterhalter's *Queen Victoria and the Royal Family* and Healy's *The Peacemakers* (Lincoln and his military commanders). From the mid-1960s, jackets were varnished and printed in brighter colours. First Edition jackets are all printed on uncoated paper and contain the price '30s. NET' on the lower corner of the front flaps; they promote no other Churchill works although from Volume II on, each jacket contains review excerpts of the previous volume(s).

VARIANTS

Later editions may vary slightly in the cloth binding, all however remaining essentially dark red. A set (not first impressions) was issued in a dark red box with a gold label referring to 'Churchill's People'.

COMMENTS

This is a physically beautiful edition. Churchill told his doctor, Lord Moran, '... it is not necessary to break the back of the book to keep it open. I made them take away a quarter of an inch from the outer margins of the two pages and then add the half-inch so gained to the inner margin. Look at it, Charles. It opens like an angel's wings.' (Diary for 29 February 1956, Moran, *Churchill: The Struggle for Survival*, London and Boston: 1966). The dust jackets are equally magnificent. All this, plus its priority as the First Edition, make this the one to own if you own only one.

APPRAISAL

All volumes are more than usually susceptible to spotting of the page edges and dulling of gilt spines; jackets hold up much better than the books beneath. Clean sets bearing some spotting and dulled gilt, in clean dust jackets, sell for $100/£60 and less, but truly fine sets are at a premium, and may easily clear $250/£150. The latter are good investments, but be sure the stained top page edges haven't faded and that there is no trace of page edge spotting, and store them in a dry place.

Chartwell (First Illustrated) Edition: ICS A138d

Publisher: Educational Book Co. Ltd., London, 1956–58

Four volumes

Navy blue leatherette blocked gilt on top board (volume title and vertical rule); spines decoratively blocked gilt with main and volume titles and author's name gilt on red leather labels. Individually typeset in a slightly larger, more readable face running to slightly more pages than the Trade Edition: respectively 486, 400, 382 and 378 for the four volumes. Blue and white head- and footbands, title-page printed two-colour, no frontispiece. Internal signatures of photographs located between the following pages: Vol. I, 64–65, 208–209, 400–401; Vol. II, 96–97, 160–161, 256–257; Vol. III, 80–81*, 144–145*, 176–177, 272–273; Vol. IV, 48–49*, 64–65*, 96–97, 160–161*, 192–193* and 288–289. (*four-page signatures; all others are eight pages).

Published simultaneously with the First Trade Edition, this beautiful set has a higher priority than ICS assigns it; Ronald Cohen lists it second only to the latter. As with the Chartwell *Second World War*, its obvious differences from the Trade Edition are its fine binding, extra-heavy page stock and internal illustrations; like the former, it was sold by mail order and came only with plain glassine dust jackets. However,

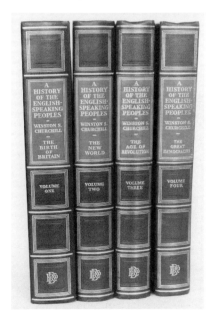

The Chartwell Edition of the *English Speaking Peoples* was beautifully bound in blue leatherette with red spine labels and blocked gilt. Each volume was profusely illustrated; published concurrently with the first edition, this remains the most aesthetically beautiful rendering of the work.

there are no frontispieces and no colour plates. One function of the Educational Book Company was the support of students, who sold Chartwell Editions door to door. For this purpose 'samples' may have been created along the lines of the Chartwell *Second World War* (q.v.).

APPRAISAL

Durably made, these books are almost always found with clean, tight, unyellowed inner pages, but the bindings are subject to wear, most of it on the spines, where exposure causes discoloration and careless handling often produces chipped red leather title labels. Pristine, as-new sets have become rarities, and may reach or exceed $500/£300–add 50 per cent to that if the set is in its original glassine wrappers. For 'very good' sets showing minor external wear, much less is demanded; $150/£90 should buy one of these. Even worn sets are worth owning for the illustrations, fine print and bindings.

American Edition: ICS A138ab

Publisher: Dodd, Mead & Company, New York, 1956–58
Reprinted periodically by Barnes & Noble, New York, 1990s

Four volumes

Quarter navy cloth and grey cloth, blocked gilt on top board (facsimile author signature); on spine are main title; volume title and author name with one to four stars; and publisher's name, gilt on three red panels separated by thin gilt rules. Red stained top page edges, head- and footbands, title-pages printed two-colour, 8vo. Vol. I published 23 April 1956 at $6; 544 pages numbered (i)–(xxii) and (1)–522. Vol. II published 26 November 1956 at $6, 448 pages numbered (i)–(xxii) and (1)–436. Vol. III published 14 October 1957 at $6, 414 pages numbered (i)–(xiv)

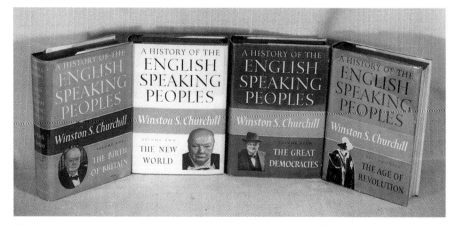

The American *English Speaking Peoples* is aesthetically much less pleasing, shorter, squatter and with unattractive dust jackets. A fine jacketed set like this is, however, quite scarce nowadays.

and (1)–402. Vol. IV published 14 March 1958 at $6, 416 pages numbered (i)–(xiv) and (1)–404. All volumes variously illustrated with maps and tables. The text was separately set for this Edition.

EDITIONS, IMPRESSIONS AND QUANTITIES

The following impressions were reported as of 1962: Vol. I, April 1956 (three), February and September 1958, May 1959, January 1961, September 1962; Vol. II, September 1956, December 1956, March and December 1958, October 1960, June 1961, April 1962; Vol. III, September 1957 (two, both pre-publication), October 1957, September 1962; Vol. IV, November 1957. There have been additional impressions in the years since, and in the 1980s the publisher reissued the work in large format paperbacks. Identifying first editions: The verso of the title-page reads 'FIRST EDITION' just under the copyright line.

DUST JACKETS

Collectors commonly believe the line on all early jacket flaps, 'BOOK-OF-THE-MONTH CLUB SELECTION' means the jacket is from a Book Club Edition. Not so; all trade editions advertised this fact. The real key to a trade edition jacket is the $6 price, located at upper right of the front flap. This has often been clipped, but beware: BOMC jackets also state 'BOOK-OF-THE-MONTH CLUB SELECTION' in this place, and an unscrupulous seller may have clipped it off.

VARIANTS

A publisher's presentation set exists in a light red buckram slipcase with a label containing the title and a photograph of the author. The books inside state on the title-page verso, 'PRESENTATION EDITION NOT FOR SALE' below a line containing the exact publication date. The books carry normal dust jackets with the $6 price on front flaps.

Some first editions were printed on much thinner paper to meet demand; invariably, these are found with very dark red, that is, maroon, spine panels instead of the normal bright red. Easily spotted because of their thinner bulk, these are nevertheless true First Editions.

COMMENTS

Squat and ugly, except for the fancy spinework, the American Edition is one of the least desired Churchill titles, even though it was apparently issued simultaneously with the English Edition. Of course these are much scarcer outside the USA, where they are often offered at inflated prices; but buyers abroad should not pay premiums for them.

APPRAISAL

Prices have been depressed for years, although condition makes a difference. Dust jackets fade easily, and a set in pristine unfaded jackets is worth up to $150/£90. Ordinary jacketed sets sell for $50/£30 or less; unjacketed copies can be had for a few dollars.

Book Club Issue: ICS A138ac
Publisher: Book-of-the-Month Club, Camp Hill, PA.

Four volumes
Published in association with Dodd, Mead, the BOMC Issue had an enormous sale and quickly outstripped all rivals as the largest selling version of Churchill's *History*. Through 1962, BOMC Issues had enjoyed 22, 14, 12 and 10 impressions of the four volumes respectively.

Although at first glance they appear to be twins of the American Edition, BOMC issues are usually easily identified. Most lack head- and footbands, stained top page edges and the words 'FIRST EDITION' on the versos of title-pages; all carry a BOMC embossed 'dot' or 'square' at the lower righthand corner of the back boards. But as usual there are exceptions to the rule: some BOMC copies do state 'FIRST EDITION' on the verso ... but even these carry the 'dot' on rear boards and their jackets are uniform BOMC jackets.

BOMC dust jackets carry a line of small type, 'BOOK-OF-THE-MONTH CLUB* SELECTION' in place of the $6 price of Trade Editions. (The asterisk is footnoted as

$6.00

For American readers this final volume of Churchill's HISTORY will undoubtedly have a larger interest than any of the others because more than a third of the book is devoted to our Civil War and to American affairs generally. Sir Winston is in his element when describing issues and battles and personalities — to them he brings a perspective and interpretations which are refreshingly new to American readers. Lee is his military and Lincoln his political hero, and his grasp of minute detail as well as of the broad sweep of events will astonish even those who have come to expect this of him.

BOOK-OF-THE-MONTH CLUB* SELECTION

For American readers this final volume of Churchill's HISTORY will undoubtedly have a larger interest than any of the others because more than a third of the book is devoted to our Civil War and to American affairs generally. Sir Winston is in his element when describing issues and battles and personalities — to them he brings a perspective and interpretations which are refreshingly new to American readers. Lee is his military and Lincoln his political hero, and his grasp of minute detail as well as of the broad sweep of events will astonish even those who have come to expect this of him.

Whilst all jacket flaps of American *English Speaking Peoples* state BOOK-OF-THE-MONTH CLUB SELECTION at the bottom, the top corners (if they are not clipped) distinguish the trade edition (priced $6.00, above) from the book club jacket (below).

a trademark on the lower right corner of the flap). Later printings have dark instead of bright red spine panels; later dust jackets carry BOMC stock numbers (0061 through 0064 respectively) above the Dodd, Mead name on spines.

Today these volumes are common in almost all American secondhand bookshops, where they sell for just a few dollars. A fine set in dust jackets is worth no more than $50/£30.

Canadian Issue: ICS A138ad
Publisher: McClelland & Stewart Ltd., Toronto, 1956–58

Four volumes
Bound in navy cloth with facsimile author's signature blocked blind on top board; spine printed like the American Issue except for the publisher's name. The volumes carry cloth head- and footbands, but top page edges are unstained and title-pages are printed in black only. Pagination as per the American Issue; title-pages changed to state Canadian publisher. Dust jackets as per the American Issue, but no prices or BOMC mentions on front jacket flaps.

Offprinted from the American Edition, the Canadian Issue was published simultaneously with it and the English Edition, according to publisher's slips laid into the volumes, making it, like them, a true First Edition. Identifying first editions: only the blue binding appears to be the true first (see 'Book Club Issue' below), but there is no indication to this effect on the title-page or verso; unless a verso contains notice of reprinting, it may be assumed to be a First Edition.

A Canadian reprint (left; red and light blue cloth) with two varieties of American first editions. Centre: the standard type; right: the variant, printed on thinner paper with very dark red spine panels.

Presentation Variant: A limited run of 350 presentation copies of each volume was created by inserting an extra leaf before the title-page, with a few lines praising the work (or preceding volumes) and presenting the current volume 'with the best wishes and compliments of the season from myself and my associates', hand-signed 'John McClelland' for the company. The name of the recipient was written in a line reserved for that purpose. Such a set, inscribed to Churchill, was auctioned by Sotheby's in 1976.

Book Club Issue: A reprint was bound in red cloth with blue spine panels and no head- and footbands for the Canadian Book-of-the-Month Club. A jacket found on Volume I of this issue indicates its BOMC relationship.

APPRAISAL

The Canadian Issue is rare outside Canada, and preferred by some to the American for its rarity and richer navy blue binding. But no premium attaches to ordinary copies, which sell for the same modest prices as the American versions—except, of course for the presentation variant. I have never seen a complete set of the latter, but individual volumes have changed hands for up to $100/£60 each. It would not be extraordinary to encounter a full presentation set at $500/£300, since putting one together is not easy.

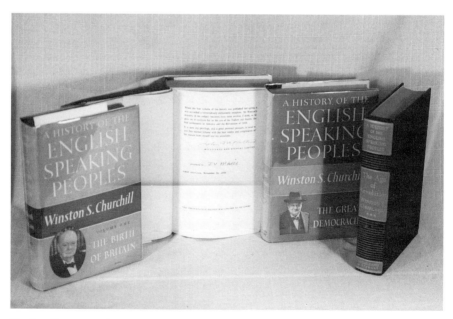

The Canadian issue, with one volume opened to show the extra leaf inserted in 350 publisher's presentation copies. Canadian issues are bound in dark blue (as at right), which many collectors find more satisfying than the grey binding of the American version.

FIRST PAPERBACK EDITION: ICS A138ea
Publisher: Cassell & Co. Ltd, London, 1962

Published in large format (5 x 7½in) with unillustrated wrappers, completely reset. Later wrappers were illustrated. Still in print, it has had a huge press run. In the mid-1980s it had reached the fourth or fifth printings of a fourth distinct paperback edition. Originally 10s. ($1.40) per volume, it had risen to £3.50 per volume by the 1980s. In 1974 the work was also published in conventional small paperback size with the additional title, 'Churchill's People', the wrappers bearing illustrations of the BBC Television series by that name. Trifling value today, although some collectors might pay up to $40/£24 for a clean set of first impressions (labelled 'first impression 1962' on title-page verso).

BANTAM PAPERBACK EDITION: ICS A138eb
Publisher: Bantam Books Inc., New York, 1963

Four volumes
Another resetting, the Bantam Edition was published in July 1963 at $1.25 per volume, or $5 for the 'Deluxe Gift-Box Edition'. Numerous reprints since; consult Cohen for details. Trifling value, except for the (rare) first impression of 1963, but even this is not worth more than $25/£15 in the original box.

FIRST ABRIDGED EDITION: ICS A138f
Publisher: Dodd, Mead & Co., New York, 1965

Bound in blue cloth blocked gilt with facsimile author signature on top board and titles gilt on dark blue panels on spine. 8vo, 496 pages numbered (i)–(xvi) and (1)–475 (+5) plus colour frontispiece (1954 photo of author by Karsh) and 16 unnumbered heavier paper sheets containing photographs; also illustrated with maps and tables. Dust jacket printed red, blue and black on white stock with the Karsh frontispiece photo printed multicolour. Published at $7.95.

Henry Steele Commager's preface notes that he has reduced the text to half its original size, with the remainder just as Churchill wrote it. Stating that it was 'a grave responsibility to cut and trim and arrange a classic', he explains that the abridged work is meant 'for the large reading public which Churchill himself most wanted to reach ... While Churchill was incapable of writing a dull paragraph, I have attempted to keep those chapters and passages which seem to have the greatest literary vigor and beauty. And as this book is designed primarily for American readers, I have given proportionately larger space to the story of the expansion of England, to the Empire, the Commonwealth, and the United States, than Churchill gave them in the four volumes of the *History*.'

This work has had numerous reprints; the description above applies to the

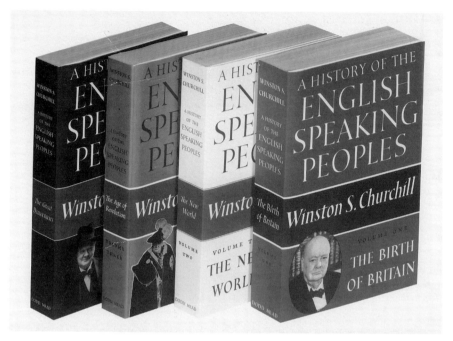

The last issues of *English Speaking Peoples* from Dodd, Mead before they closed were large format paperbacks with wrappers in the design of the original dust jackets.

First Edition, which is the only one with significant value on the antiquarian market, where it is worth up to $75/£45 in perfect condition with dust jacket.

SUBSEQUENT ABRIDGEMENTS

English Abridged Issue
Publisher: Cassell & Co. Ltd., London, 1965

Offprinted from the First American Edition.

Canadian Abridged Issue: ICS A138fb
Publisher: McClelland & Stewart Ltd., Toronto, 1965

Offprinted from the First American Edition.

Paperback Abridged Edition: ICS A138fc
Publisher: Pocketbooks, New York, 1966

Reset for small paperback format, published July 1966 at $1.95.

Second American Issue: ICS A138fd
Publisher: Greenwich House, New York, 1983

Offprinted from the American Edition by a division of Crown Publishers for the mail order trade. Shiny navy cloth blocked gilt on spine; dust jacket with colour Karsh photo similar to the First American but with reset type.

Third American Issue: ICS A138fe
Publisher: Barnes & Noble Books, New York, 1994

Offprinted from a First American Edition furnished by the International Churchill Societies, who received a blurb on page (476) by way of thanks. Bound in half maroon cloth and rose paper-covered boards, dust jacket predominately brown. Still in print at this writing, $7.95.

Fourth American Issue: ICS A138ff
Publisher: Wing Books, NJ, 1994

Apparently offprinted from the Barnes & Noble issue. Bound in quarter red cloth on black boards, spine blocked gilt. The dust jacket is printed in gold, red and white with a black and white photo of the author. Distributed by Random House Value Publishing, Inc.

Blenheim/School Edition: ICS A138g
Publisher: Cassel & Co. Ltd., London, 1965–66

Twelve volumes
An abridgement of the original text specially developed for young people, this work was issued in two versions. Blenheim Edition: bound in plain green boards with colour illustrated dust jackets. School Edition: bound in colour printed boards to the same designs as the dust jackets. The contents of each version were identical. Though of incidental value on the secondhand book market, this work deserves to be reprinted; it is the best adaptation of the larger work for children ages 10–15.

Easton Press Edition: ICS A138k
Publisher: Easton Press Inc., Norwalk, CT, 1992

Four volumes
Another of Easton Press's leatherbound 'collector's editions', this one handsomely offprinted from the English Chartwell Edition of 1956–1958. 8vo, bound in dark blue pigskin, decoratively blocked gilt on boards and spine, five raised spine bands, volume title and author's name gilt on separate red leather spine panels; gold

The Blenheim 12-volume edition for young people, which can be distinguished from the look-alike School Edition by its green boards and dust jackets. (The School Edition carries multicolour boards printed in the dust jacket design.)

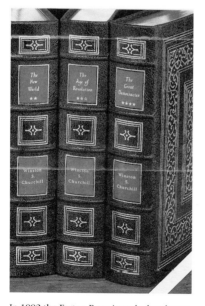

In 1992 the Easton Press issued a handsome set offprinted from, and bound similarly to, the English Chartwell Edition. The binding is dark blue pigskin with red leather spine labels blocked gilt.

moiré cloth endpapers, all edges gilt, gold cloth pagemarker. Pagination essentially the same as the Chartwell Edition, but the title-page is reset. In place of the author's note about the Chartwell Edition on page (xix) is a 'Bibliographic Note' by this writer, extending to page (xx), while page (xxi) contains a note about the International Churchill Societies. The Societies provided the Chartwell Edition from which this edition is offprinted. Published at $260.

The blue, red and gilt binding and offprinted contents make this a modern version of the fine Chartwell Edition. Given the recent rise in price of the latter, this may soon become a bargain alternative. Still in print at this writing, the Easton Edition is a handsome presentation. Its faults are a fairly low grade of leather with no aroma, and garish peel-'n'-stick bookplates laid into the volumes. The plates might be kept for the record, but definitely should not be pasted over those lovely moiré endpapers.

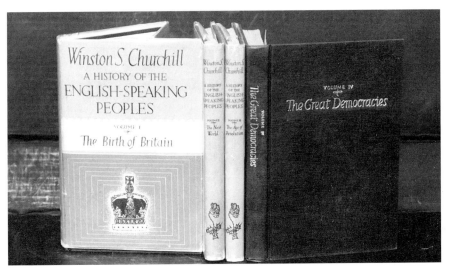

Book World in Taiwan may have pirated this interesting offprint of the English edition, which is undated. Printed on thinner paper, the books are nicely bound with cloth page markers and attractive dust jackets.

Taiwan Edition
Publisher: Book World Company, Taipei (n.d.)

Four volumes; later bound in one volume
Offprinted from the original four volumes on thin paper, these are generally considered to be pirated volumes. 8vo, bound in brown cloth blocked silver on top board and spine; head- and footbands, brown cloth page marker; pagination as per the First Edition. A purple rubber stamped message in Chinese (1 x 2in) is found on the lower lefthand corner of the rear free endpaper. Dust jackets printed light purple, red and black on white stock with a crown design on the top face and a rose design on the spine later bound in a single red cloth volume.

Though rather more handsome than the usual Asian reproductions, no particular value attaches to these volumes; I acquired my fine jacketed set for $40/ £24.

EXCERPTED WORKS

THE AMERICAN CIVIL WAR: Cohen A272, Woods A138(b)

The first of many spin-offs from Churchill's *History*, this fine little work captures his marvellous and detailed description of America's greatest domestic convulsion, coupling his text with excellent Civil War photographs by Matthew Brady and others. Churchill had explored the Battlefields of Virginia with none other than

Douglas Southall Freeman, the great American Civil War historian; and he had toured Gettysburg with a local resident of some experience at war, Dwight Eisenhower. His fine if brief account of the War Between the States has been admired by historians and students alike.

First Edition: ICS A138ba
Publisher: Cassell and Co. Ltd., London, 1961

Bound in red cloth blocked gilt on spine only with 'WINSTON | SPENCER | CHURCHILL' at head, Cassell at foot, and The American Civil War centred, reading up. 8vo, 128 pages numbered (i)–(xiv) and (1)–111 (+1), plus 32 pages of photos on coated paper arranged as follows: four each between pages 16–17, 32–33; eight each between pages 24–25, 64–65 and 80–81. Also illustrated with maps. Published 23 March 1961 at 12s. 6d. ($1.75). Two impressions of 10,000 in March and 5,000 in April (not May as per Woods). Dust jacket printed black and red on white paper with photograph of two soldiers on top face.

Printed on thick, rather pulpy paper, this edition does not hold up well, and is given to yellowing and spotting. Genuinely fine copies in crisp dust jackets are rare, and certainly worth $100/£60 or more nowadays, mundane worn copies half as much or less.

American Edition: ICS A138bb
Publisher: Dodd, Mead & Co., New York, 1961

Wholly set up and printed in the United States. Bound in bluish-green cloth blocked

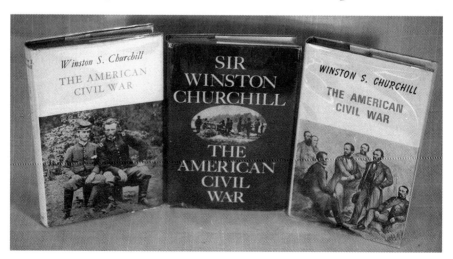

The American Civil War. Left to right: the First (English), American edition and Indian issue. (For details on the latter, see page 330.)

gilt on spine (all type reading down); title in a black panel with gilt border. 8vo, 160 pages numbered (i)–(xiv) and (1)–145 (+1), with the same 32 coated paper photo pages as above, inserted between pages 18–19, 34–35, 50–51, 82–84 and 114–115. Also illustrated with maps. Published 1961 at $3.

Less often seen than the First Edition, but printed on far superior paper and rather more attractively bound, this is a handsome addition to the Churchill library. Prices as per the First Edition.

First Paperback Issue: ICS A138bc
Publisher: Apollo Books, New York, 1966

The first paperback version of the work was offprinted from the Dodd, Mead American Edition. Pagination is the same, but the 32 pages of photos (on heavy uncoated bright white paper) are inserted in a single unnumbered signature between pages 50–51. Published at $1.95.

Corgi Edition: ICS A138bd
Publisher: Corgi Books, London, 1970

The size of a paperback but bound in illustrated wrappers with a photo from the original dust jacket and a superimposed photo of Lincoln on an olive background. 144 pages numbered (1)–144 plus 16 pages of photographs on coated paper. Published at 7s. (50¢).

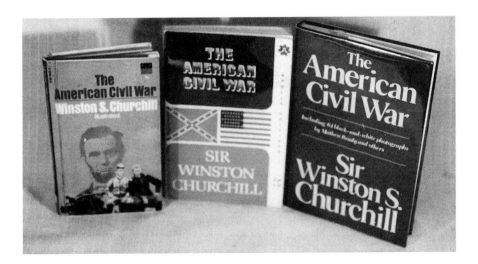

Later impressions of *The American Civil War*. Left to right: Corgi (1970), Apollo (1966) and Fairfax Press (1984).

Indian Issue: ICS A138be

Publisher: Upendra Arora for Natraj Publishers, Dehra Dun, 1978

An offprint of the First Edition bound in similar red cloth blocked gilt on spine (author's name and title reading down), 'NATRAJ' reading across at foot). The dust jacket is similar in format to the First Edition but the top face illustration is of Lincoln and his generals. This is a rare item, hardly ever seen. I cheerfully paid $100/£60 for my copy, which is barely 'very good', though in quite a decent dust jacket.

Second American Issue: ICS A138bf

Publisher: Fairfax Press, New York, 1985

Offprinted from the Dodd, Mead Edition, with photographs included (but not on coated paper). Navy cloth blocked gilt on spine; dust jacket printed purple, red and tan on white stock, without illustrations. Distributed by Crown Publishers, the discount remainder house, and also sold by Barnes & Noble Bookstores at $7.

THE ISLAND RACE: Cohen A272, Woods A138(c)

Originally published as a large format, coffee table book, elaborately illustrated with much colour, this excerpted work saw several forms and was occasionally used as a corporate gift item. '*The Island Race* has been designed as a majestic volume to present, in impressive array, the hundreds of reproductions in colour and monochrome of those historic paintings which have preserved for all time a contemporary view of the great events and the outstanding figures of this country's history. No more fitting setting could be devised for the story of his own people told by the greatest Briton of our age.' (Publisher's blurb)

First Edition: ICS A138ca

Publisher: Cassell and Co. Ltd., London, 1964

Bound in quarter dark green leatherette and bright green canvas cloth blocked gilt on top board (vertical rule) and spine 'WINSTON S. | CHURCHILL' at head, 'CASSELL' at foot, and 'The | Island | Race' toward the top. 4to (9¾ x 12¼in), 320 pages numbered (i)–(viii) and (1)–312, printed on satin-coated page stock and profusely illustrated throughout. Published 23 November 1964 at £6. 6s. ($17.64). Three impressions (designated 'editions') of 42,500, 10,290 (December 1964), May 1966 (5,000). Dust jacket printed multicolour on a bright green background.

VARIANTS

Third and Popular eds. exist with 'The Swedish American Line' on title pages, and a colour print of the MV Stockholm tipped onto the half title, which is imprinted, 'Pleasant Memories of My Cruise with | the Swedish American Line'. A 'Popular Edition' measuring 8 x 10½in and printed on cheaper stock was produced in 1968. A 1985 edition was published by Webb & Bower, printed in Italy by Padane.

The huge press run renders this edition very common and prices of First Editions have never risen significantly. Today, a fine example in like dust jacket costs under $100/£60, sometimes substantially under; reprints in like condition are not worth more than $50/£30. The Swedish American Line variant is interesting, but as a reprint it does not sell for much more than ordinary reprints.

'The Island Race' Reprint Society Issue: ICS 138ca/1
Publisher: Reprint Society, London, 1966

Marked 'third edition 1966', same as first edition but 'Cassell World Books' on spine and 'Reprint Society' on title page.

American Issue: ICS A138cb
Publisher: Dodd, Mead & Company, New York, 1964

Similar to the First Edition, printed in England for Dodd, Mead and differing only through their name on the jacket and book spine and title-page, and Library of Congress details on title-page verso. They are also slightly thinner, Woods records that 7,500 copies were printed for Dodd, Mead, but a second impression (also 1964) has been reported as well.

Left to right: the first edition *Island Race*; a third impression imprinted by the Swedish-American Line for cruise participants; and the 1968 Popular Edition, which was substantially smaller in size.

Presentation variant: An elegant binding in full dark red leather with tooled gilt title between horizontal rules on cover, with title, author and 'NELSON' blocked gilt on spine, was printed and bound in Italy by Grafiche Editoriali Padane.

In 1987 the work was again reprinted and bound by Grafiche Editoriali Padane, but this time in conventional format, and offered by Dodd, Mead in the USA at $24.95. The binding is similar to the original trade edition but the colours of the two halves are almost uniform olive green and the volume bulks thinner because of thinner page stock.

Popular Edition: ICS A138cc

Publisher: Cassell and Co. Ltd., London, 1968

Substantially reduced (8 x 10½in), this cheap edition was printed on uncoated page stock although pagination was unaltered and all colour and monochrome illustrations were retained. Published at 63s. ($8.62) in cloth; also known in illustrated card covers. A much less impressive affair than the magisterial First Edition, this book has incidental value on the secondhand market.

Corgi Paperback Edition: ICS A138cd

Publisher: Corgi Books, London 1968

One and Two volumes
Originally published in large format (7½ x 10") single volume with top board printed like the first edition dust jacket. Reprinted 1972 in two volumes in new multicolour wrappers (Vol. 1 blue background, Vol. 2 purple), in a dark blue slipcase decorated with a Union Flag. A later slipcase was silver with a stylised Royal Arms. The 1972 price was £2.50 ($7) for the slipcased set.

A Corgi two-volume wrapper edition of *The Island Race* in its second variant (second version silver slipcase with Royal Arms).

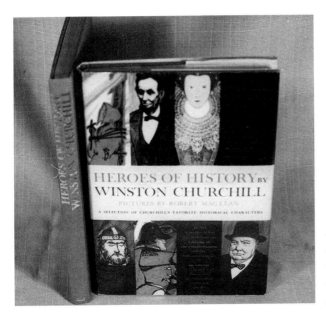

Heroes of History, another excerpted work, which has the distinction of possessing the ugliest dust jacket on any of Churchill's works.

HEROES OF HISTORY: Cohen A278, ICS A138h

An interesting extract from Churchill's original text, this work contains his words on 16 of what the publisher calls his 'favourite characters': Kings Alfred and Harold, William the Conqueror, Henry Plantagenet, Thomas Becket, Richard II, Henry V, Joan of Arc, Henry VIII, Elizabeth I, Washington, Nelson, Wellington, Lincoln, Robert E. Lee and Queen Victoria. A seventeenth chapter is on Churchill himself, comprising his words from *My Early Life* and various speeches in the Commons from the Boer War through the Second World War. All versions of this work contain 192 pages numbered (1)–192, sprinkled with illustrations in colour by Robert Maclean. Dust jackets printed multicolour on white stock with black spine panel containing title and author printed red and white respectively. The title is fairly uncommon, but no great value attaches to any of the various issues: $50/£30 usually secures a fine jacketed copy. All were published in 1968; the three different issues are identified by the publisher's name on the spine and jacket spine:

FIRST EDITION: ICS A138ha (Cassell)

Published at 30s. ($4.20). Jacket spine type reads down.

AMERICAN ISSUE: ICS A138hb (Dodd, Mead)

Published at $4.95. Jacket spine type reads up.

CANADIAN ISSUE: ICS A138hc (McClelland and Stewart)

Published at C$4.95. Jacket spine type reads up.

Purnell Magazine Edition: ICS A138i
Publisher: BPC-Purnell Ltd., 1968

Twenty-three volumes

Initially published serially in magazine format, this work is not 100 per cent by Churchill and is relegated to a later section of Ronald Cohen's Bibliography. It is mentioned here for those who may have encountered it. The text consists partially of excerpts from Churchill's *History*, and partially of additional notes, treatises and sidebars by other authors. The pages are profusely illustrated in colour and monochrome.

Binders: After all volumes were issued, BPC offered thick blue vinyl binders to house them. Binders were blocked dull gold, numbered (1)–7, and were accompanied by two guidebooks containing supplemental material.

Variant binding: The publisher also offered the complete set of 23 volumes bound in red leatherette blocked gilt (rampant lion on top board, type on spine). Sets are also known in dark blue leatherette blocked gilt and red.

There is little demand for the volumes in binders, probably because they are unwieldy and take up so much space. Occasionally one of the bound sets sells for up to $100/£60, but as a bookseller I have often given away odd volumes.

JOAN OF ARC: Cohen A279, ICS A138j
Publisher: Dodd, Mead & Co., New York, 1969

Subtitled, *Her Life as Told by WINSTON CHURCHILL*. Bound in white cloth blocked gilt (fleur de lis on top board, titles on spine). 16mo, 48 pages numbered (1)–48 including 17 colour illustrations by Lauren Ford. Dust jacket printed light blue and red–brown with two Ford illustrations printed multicolour.

This sweet little book (4¾ x 7in) excerpts Churchill's words from Vol. I of his *History* on the French heroine, which the publishers rather optimistically call 'perhaps the finest prose that England's great hero has ever written'. The publishers also feel obligated to explain in a note that the text opens shortly before the end of the Hundred Years' War, and that 'the events which are recounted were to lead at last to the breaking forever of England's hold over France'.

This work enjoyed a very limited run and is the scarcest of all extracts from Churchill's *History*. In 15 years of bookselling I have encountered three copies, all as-new in dust jackets–people tend to take care of them. Two copies were inscribed by the illustrator. My own contains a charming drawing of a girl and two sheep and

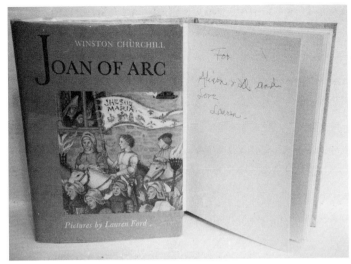

Joan of Arc is the rarest spin-off of the *English Speaking Peoples*, published by Dodd, Mead in 1969 in white cloth with pretty illustrations, one shown on the dust jacket, by Lauren Ford. Mrs Ford has inscribed this copy.

is inscribed 'To Linda | do you remember the sheep | Love Lauren -Lauren Ford'. Linda and the sheep may well have been her model for Ford's illustration of Joan with sheep on page 9. Serious collectors want this interesting extract badly, and the only one I've sold (the other inscribed copy) went for $250/£150.

FOREIGN TRANSLATIONS

French: HISTOIRE (4 vols)
Published by Plon, Paris, 1956–1959. The 'édition originale' is limited to 87 copies on Lafuma paper and 330 copies on Roto Blanc Aussedat paper bound in pale blue wrappers. The trade edition has brightly coloured card wrappers.

German: GESCHICHTE (4 vols)
Published by Scherz, Zurich, 1956–1958 in deep red-brown cloth and colourful dust jackets. Republished 1990 by Weltbild: Augsberg in red cloth blocked yellow.

Hebrew: (4 vols)
Published 1958–1959 (two volumes each year) in dark blue cloth with dust jackets.

Italian: STORIA (4 vols)
Published by Mondadori, Rome 1956–1959 in cloth, each volume in an individual orange cardboard slipcase.

Norwegian: HISTOIRIE SAGAEN OM DE ENGELSKTALEND NASJONER (4 vols)
Published by Cappelens, Oslo, 1956–1961: a beautiful set in quarter dark green leather and red cloth, spines elaborately blocked with gilt lions, red and black title panels. Multicolour dust jackets.

Portuguese: HISTÓRIA DOS POVOS DE LINGUA INGLÊSA (4 vols)
Published by Instituicao Brasilieira de Difusao Cultural SA, Sao Paulo, 1960. Pale green cloth or card wrappers in various colours, photo of the author on rear boards.

Spanish: HISTORIA
Confirmation needed.

Swedish: HISTORIA (4 vols)
Published by Skoglund, Stockholm, 1956–1958, in wrappers, blue cloth and natural or dark red leather, all with dust jackets.

THE UNWRITTEN ALLIANCE

COHEN A273, WOODS A142

The last of Churchill's books published in his lifetime, this compilation of 1953–1959 speeches appeared only in England, and is the rarest of his post-war speech volumes. The bulk of the speeches occur in the last two years of his Premiership, for after 1955 he spoke rarely, and usually only during election campaigns.

Churchill in his eighties was still capable of the memorable phrase. In a 29 September 1959 election address to his Woodford constituency, approaching his 85th birthday, he spoke about capitalism: 'Some of [our opponents] regard private enterprise as a predatory tiger to be shot. Others look on it as a cow they can milk [here his hands imitated the act of milking!]. Only a handful see it for what it really is–the strong and willing horse that pulls the whole cart along.'

This was, as it proved, our author's last political speech. Re-elected in 1959, he attended Parliament for its five-year lifetime, choosing, with some reluctance, not to run again in 1964. People would crowd the House chamber when he would arrive to take his accustomed seat in the first row below the gangway, hoping for a sudden re-emergence of the voice that had dominated the House for half a century. But Churchill disappointed them. 'Time', as he once said to a former enemy who had saluted him, 'ends all things'. Still it was a thrill to know he was yet among them, for he had indeed passed into legend.

The Unwritten Alliance is nevertheless a remarkable coda to a singular, poignant career. It contains Churchill's words at dinners and banquets, and to the Primrose League, whose meeting had been the occasion of his maiden political speech in 1897. Here too is his speech at Aachen ('which some call Aix-la-Chapelle', he bravely reminded them), upon receiving the Charlemagne Prize on 10 May 1956: 'It may well be that the great issues which perplex us, of which one of the gravest is the reunification of Germany, could be solved more easily than they can by rival blocks confronting each other with suspicion and hostility. That is for the future.' As in so many things, his hopes came true 35 years later.

His son and editor selected the title of this book from the many speeches it contains on the Anglo-American 'special relationship', which had survived Eisenhower's rejection of Churchill's efforts on détente, and American opposition to the Anglo-French action over Suez in 1956. Randolph Churchill writes in the preface of 'an alliance far closer in fact than many which exist in writing...a treaty with more enduring elements than clauses and protocols. We have history, law, philosophy and literature; we have sentiment and common interest; we have language. We are often in agreement on current events and we stand on the same foundation of the supreme realities of the modern world.' Watching as I read these words the funeral of the Princess of Wales, I am struck by the continuing relevance of Randolph's words.

FROM THE REVIEWS

'This is a wonderful book, showing all the vigour of a long, hard life, filled with many prizes, acclamations and fulfillment–and a large number of heartbreaking setbacks. It is a sad book, for we know it to be the end; and Churchill, too, must have known it. One cannot help wishing that some happy illustrations might be found among the pages, embellishing the text; but the book is purely a record, a collection of things said during the last working years of his life. It is a practical monument.

'Let us end this series of the great speeches with one which all who heard it will remember forever, on 2 June 1953 when a young Queen was crowned at Westminster: "We have had a day which the oldest are proud to have lived to see and the youngest will remember all their lives ... Here at the summit of our world-wide community is a lady whom we respect because she is our Queen and whom we love because she is herself. 'Gracious' and 'Noble' are words familiar to us all in courtly phrasing. Tonight they have a new ring in them because we know that they are true about the gleaming figure whom Providence has brought to us in times where the present is hard and the future veiled ... We pray to have rulers who serve, for nations who comfort each other, and for peoples who thrive and prosper free from fear. May God grant us these blessings."'

Henry Fearon (unpublished catalogue)

First Edition: Woods A142
Publisher: Cassell and Co. Ltd., London, 1961

Bright red cloth blocked gilt on spine with title, author's name and CASSELL. 8vo, 344 pages numbered (i)–(xii) and (1)–332. Page (ii) lists 27 works by the author. Dust jackets are printed black, blue and orange. Published 27 April 1961 at 35s. ($4.90) in a single impression of 5,000.

APPRAISAL

Nearly twenty years ago when I became a Churchill bookseller, nice jacketed copies of this work were selling for as little as $25/£15; today they are fast approaching $250/£150, a compound rate of return as good as many mutual funds. It is not so much that *The Unwritten Alliance* is rare, but that so few come up for sale anymore. So many have now gone into private libraries that the supply is truly small. Most that we do see are in excellent condition, though the dust jacket was poorly printed and is almost always rubbed or streaked. A fine copy in a perfect dust jacket is certainly worth the figure mentioned above. Occasionally I see scruffy copies without jackets, but even these usually top $100/£60.

PIRATED EDITION
A smaller-format, hardbound pirated edition is known to exist. See note under *In the Balance* on page 302.

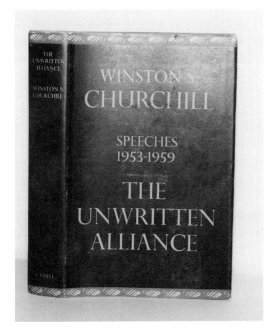

The first and only edition of *The Unwritten Alliance*, jacketed uniformly with the previous English post-war speech volumes. This work was not published in the United States.

FRONTIERS AND WARS

COHEN A274, ICS A142/1

Although this work appeared in Churchill's lifetime he had nothing to do with its preparation, nor does it contain new material. It was an extraction of his first four war books, the *Malakand, River War, Ladysmith* and *Hamilton*, compiled in a single volume by Eyre and Spottiswoode, publishers of Churchill's own abridged *River War* since 1933. In the jacket blurb for this work, E&S are careful to note that *The River War* is still available (from them), though the other three works have 'been out of print since before the first World War.'

The abridging is ruthless but effective. What remains are the backgrounds to the wars and the chief features of them, culled and packaged to fit a volume of fewer than 600 pages. As such it constitutes a new text, which most Churchill collectors are anxious to own. As a bonus, the book is generously illustrated with the main characters in the stories, along with contemporary drawings and photographs of famous places and things: the Malakand Field Force on the march, the Charge of the 21st Lancers at Omdurman, Boer fighters in the field, an armoured train 'similar to the one on which Churchill was captured'. The books are tall and elegantly produced, with fine large type and ample margins. *Frontiers and Wars* is the ideal introduction to Churchill the Victorian war historian, and I often recommend it to readers who have never before dipped into this portion of the canon. Most of them soon end up reading the original texts–which is all to the good.

First Edition: ICS A142/1a
Publisher: Eyre & Spottiswoode, London, 1962

Bluish-grey cloth blocked gilt on spine with author's name, title (on maroon panel) and 'E&S' at the foot. 8vo, 568 pages numbered (1)–568 plus frontispiece and 15 pages of illustrations on coated stock, interspersed throughout. Dust jackets are printed black, red and olive on coated white paper and illustrated with a silhouetted black and white photo of our author (from frontispiece) on the front face and an illustration of the charge at Omdurman on the back face, wrapping around the spine. Published at 42s. ($5.88); two impressions. Identifying first editions: no mention of a second impression on verso of title page.

APPRAISAL

Although plenty of copies are around, fine ones are scarce; and fine dust jackets

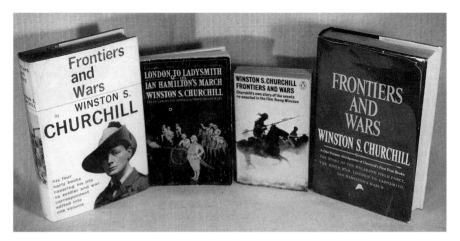

Frontiers and Wars. Left to right: the first English edition, the Harvest paperback abridgement of the *Ladysmith* and *Ian Hamilton's*, the Penguin paperback and the first American edition.

scarcer. The latter are prone to chipping and tearing. For a fine first in clean untorn jacket, $100/£60 is not too much to pay, but copies in poorer condition cost much less; and the second impression is worth only half the price of a first, conditions being equal.

American Issue: ICS A142/1b
Publisher: Harcourt, Brace & World, Inc., New York, 1962

Bound in black cloth blocked gold and red on spine with sheets supplied by the English printers. Pagination identical to the First Edition. Dust jacket printed red and black on white paper and illustrated only with a subaltern's helmet on front face and spine; one impression, no variants.
    Published at $8.75.

APPRAISAL
Not the true first, this issue tends to cost less than the English Edition, although it is much scarcer. Fine copies in clean, untorn dust jackets cost around $75/£45.

First Paperback Edition: ICS A142/1c
Publisher: Penguin Books, Harmondsworth, Middlesex, 1972

A thick, 608-page paperback with 16 pages of illustrations on coated paper, this reset work was published to coincide with the release of the Columbia Pictures film 'Young Winston', and contains the Omdurman scene from that film on its wrappers. Published at 60p ($1.68).

Second American Issue: ICS A142/1d
Publisher: Konecky and Konecky, New York, c.1990

Offprinted from the first American issue, produced for the bargain books counters.

EXTRACTED WORKS

LONDON TO LADYSMITH AND IAN HAMILTON'S MARCH
Publisher: Harcourt, Brace & World, Inc., New York [n.d.]

An 'abridgement of the abridgement', this 214-page, 5¼ x 8in paperback is in the publisher's 'Harvest Book' series, numbered 'HB 98'. Published at $1.75, it contains no date. The text covers the Boer War sections of *Frontiers and Wars* but leaves out the illustrations. The cover is printed black with an illustration by John Sposato: British colonial troops firing a cannon.

'The River War' Prion Edition
Publisher: Prion, London, 1997

Completely reset and published at £9.99 in the Prion 'Lost Treasures' series, this edition carries a new foreword by Winston Churchill, our author's grandson. Unfortunately, its text is not from any previous edition of *The River War*. Instead it is taken from *Frontiers and Wars* (see page 340), a severely truncated sampler of Churchill's first four war books, in which Churchill's 1902–1987 *River War* abridgement was chopped by about 40 per cent. Oddly, the title page is lifted from a First edtion of *The River War*, announcing illustrations and two volumes, which aren't present. The Lost Treasure remains lost.

YOUNG WINSTON'S WARS

COHEN A282, WOODS A143

Sometimes thought to be an extracted work like *Frontiers and Wars*, this book presents entirely new material and marks Churchill's posthumous return to the ranks of current authors, which continues to the present day. Undoubtedly its publication was influenced by the appearance of the film 'Young Winston', starring Simon Ward. (*The Times Literary Supplement* called it the 'Book of the Film'.) Compiled by bibliographer Frederick Woods, *Young Winston's Wars* comprises Churchill's original despatches as a war correspondent covering the same three military campaigns as his first four war books: the Northwest Frontier of India, the Sudan and South Africa.

Naming Churchill (along with Steevens and Russell) 'among the most brilliant, involved and fluent' war correspondents, Woods's Introduction is critical but not unadmiring: 'Churchill's war despatches were very much of their time. He wrote passionately of the Queen, the Empire and the Flag; yet he rarely wrote jingoistically. His writing was informed with humanity and charity (except when he was attacking hypocrisy or what he considered to be official ineptitude) and he displayed that respect–even admiration–for a good enemy that characterised the days when chivalry

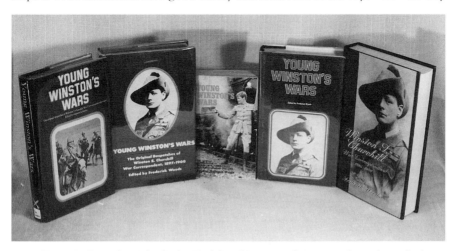

Young Winston's Wars. Left to right: the first English and American editions; one of several paperbacks; the Reader's Union issue, and the most recent Brassey's edition, *Winston S. Churchill: War Correspondent 1895-1900*, which adds the Cuban despatches that were omitted from the earlier appearances.

and cavalry were synonymous ... After the battle of Omdurman he visited the field and saw the thousands of Dervish dead. While relishing the victory over what he saw as feudal tyranny, he nevertheless paid tribute to the twisted corpses ... Emotions about Churchill can still run high ... but on an objective basis, it must be conceded that his war despatches during this limited period rank among his greatest writings. When it is considered that he was still in his early twenties when he wrote them, the achievement should be seen in true perspective.'

FROM THE REVIEWS

'It is well to be reminded that the future winner of a Nobel Prize for literature began by writing for the papers. He laid thereby the foundations of his literary style, his political career and his fortune. Within six months of the date of the last despatch printed here he was MP for Oldham and was able to write to his mother, on the first day of the new century, "I am very proud of the fact that there is not one person in a million who at my age could have earned £10,000 without any capital in less than two years."

'In return his editors received a series of remarkable documents, quite out of the ordinary run of correspondence, which can be read with pleasure today even by those who care little for their subjects. The Churchillian style was already well developed. He cared about good writing and would never give less than his best even when he was writing "on the ground in a tent temperature of 115 degrees" ... Perhaps the most memorable passages in this collection are those in which he celebrates the courage and deplores the losses of the Sudanese at Omdurman and applauds the skill and resolution of the Afrikaners. Already in his youth he was preaching the virtues of resolution in war and magnanimity in victory.'

The Times Literary Supplement, 15 September 1972

First Edition: ICS A143a
Publisher: Leo Cooper Ltd., London, 1972

Dark blue cloth blocked gilt on spine with title, publisher's logo and name. 8vo, 384 pages numbered (i)–(xxx) and (1)–350 (+4) plus two sheets of illustrations printed on coated paper between pages 130–131 and 160–161. Seven maps, integral with the pages. Dust jackets are printed black, red and yellow with multicolour illustration of the Omdurman charge from 'Young Winston' starring Simon Ward. Published 20 July 1972 at £3.50 ($9.80). Two impressions, the first of 5,000 copies. Identifying First Editions: no mention of a reprint on the verso of the title-page; the reprint states, 'Reprinted September 1972'.

APPRAISAL
Leo Cooper's military books are avidly sought by collectors of militaria as well as of Churchill, and demand has begun rapidly to raise the price of first editions. Today's

collectors may have to pay up to $75/£45 for a fine copy in dust jacket (which most of them are). The alternative is the second impression, which should cost as little as $25/£15.

American Issue: ICS A143b
Publisher: The Viking Press, Inc., New York, 1972

Offprinted (or printed from English plates) in the United States, this volume's pagination matches that of the English Edition, but it is slightly wider thanks to more generous page margins. Bound in olive cloth blocked gilt and black on spine. Dust jackets are printed blue, black and red with a black and white photograph of Churchill in the South Africa Light Horse uniform on the front face. One impression, published at $8.95.

APPRAISAL
This volume is common in America and tends to cost less than the Cooper Edition. A high price for a fine jacketed copy would be $50/£30; it is usually found for less.

First Paperback Edition: ICS A143c
Publisher: Sphere Books Ltd., London, 1972

A paperback of 440 pages plus four pages of illustrations on coated paper, first published at 50p ($1.40) to coincide with the release of the film 'Young Winston'. Identifying first editions: the first edition is printed in shades of brown with scenes from 'Young Winston' superimposed on a photograph of Churchill c.1900; the spine is predominately tan and the UK price (back wrapper) is 50p. A later, slightly larger issue has a multicolour film still (Young Winston firing at the armoured train ambush) with the title printed red, the spine mainly red, and the UK price (back wrapper) of 60p. Despite its obviously later appearance, this second issue is labelled 'First Sphere Edition' on the title-page verso, like its predecessor.

Readers Union Issue: ICS A143d
Publisher: Readers Union Ltd., Newton Abbot, Devon, 1975

A book club issue offprinted from the Cooper Edition; the only change aside from the title-page and verso is the location of the photo pages: all between pages 66–67. Bound in black paper-covered boards blocked silver on spine (running down). A curious error: the byline at the spine top reads 'Kenneth Warren'. The dust jacket is printed brown and turquoise on white stock with the Light Horse photo of Churchill on the front face. Of fairly low value, this is a good edition for the reader who is not a collector.

New Revised Edition: ICS A143e

WINSTON S. CHURCHILL WAR CORRESPONDENT 1895–1900

Publisher: Brassey's (UK) Ltd., London, 1992

Bound in black cloth blocked gilt on spine ('Woods', title and 'Brassey's', reading down. 8vo, 388 pages numbered (i)–(xxxii) and (1)–355 (+1). Dust jacket printed turquoise and sepia on white stock; the Light Horse photograph takes up most of the front face. Published at £17.95, simultaneously published in the United States at $29.95. One impression.

Entirely reset, this important new edition adds Churchill's five despatches from Cuba in 1895, which Woods omitted from the First Edition because Randolph Churchill had recently included them in the proximate Companion Volume to the Official Biography. There is also a new foreword by our author's grandson, Winston S. Churchill. There are two new maps but illustrations are omitted.

APPRAISAL

Fine copies are certainly worth 50 per cent more than the original price today. This edition is much in demand for its superior appearance and the additional despatches on Cuba. Although the latter are available in the Companion Volumes to the Official Biography, and copies of the earlier editions are plentiful, this is the only really complete collection of our author's war despatches, and I wish the publishers would put it back in print.

IF I LIVED MY LIFE AGAIN

COHEN A283, ICS A144

Little known, except to collectors of Churchilliana, this work was compiled from Churchill's writings and speeches by Jack Fishman, the journalist who had published the first biography of our author's wife, *My Darling Clementine*, in 1963. Lady Churchill herself contributes a note stating that proceeds of sales will go to Churchill College, Cambridge and the Winston Churchill Memorial Trust, the two principal British national memorials to Sir Winston. Longtime friend Jock Colville adds a note about these two entities.

Fishman was a skilled journalist and friend of Sir Winston, but he did us no scholarly favours with this work, which is rambling, disconnected, without an index and almost without references to the material. A three-page essay on 'sources' lists where Fishman obtained the material, but nothing more specific. Many of the titles are familiar to collectors of Churchill's periodical articles, but careful readers will find their texts polluted by omissions, and additions from other sources. In his Preface, Fishman says he produced the book out of a vast archive on the Churchills

Jack Fishman compiled *If I Lived My Life Again* from a variety of Churchill sources both in books and periodicals. Although poorly annotated and heavily edited, it nevertheless constitutes a genuine Churchill work in its own right.

that he had compiled over 30 years and over 600,000 words of notes, only a third of which he referred to in the Clementine biography. Perhaps he did not realise how diligently scholars would be researching the canon a quarter of a century and more after his book was published. That said, Fishman's work comprises a marvellous read for people who just want to get a grasp of Churchill as journalist, as opposed to a writer of histories, memoirs and speeches.

Fishman begins with a highly readable and instructive nine-page appreciation of Churchill from the perspective of a fellow journalist. From there on, Fishman scrupulously provides a text that is all Churchill (wherever it comes from). Some of the chapters are vintage Winston: 'The Truth About Myself', 'It's No Good Arguing With A Communist', 'I'd Sooner Be Right Than Consistent', 'America! America!', 'Why Are We Here?' and, of course, 'If I Lived My Life Again.' The penultimate chapter, 'We Miss Our Giants', is as much an ode to Churchill as to those he wrote about–knowing him, we may imagine he had exactly that purpose in mind.

Whatever its faults as a research tool, *If I Lived My Life Again* is quite entertaining stuff. I can't imagine how any serious reader of Churchill can be without it.

First Edition: ICS A144
Publisher: W. H. Allen, London, 1974

Blue-green cloth blocked gilt on spine with title and 'Sir Winston Churchill' reading down and publisher's logo and name reading across at the foot. 8vo, 332 pages numbered (i)–(xx) and (1)–309 (+3). Dust jacket printed three-colour with a photograph of Churchill watching a Second World War II battle on the front face, wrapping around the spine. One impression, without variants, published at £3.95 ($11).

APPRAISAL
This is the only version of the work published, and since its rediscovery by Churchill booksellers in the mid-1980s, it has become a scarce item. Fine jacketed copies now bring up to $50/£35, and will no doubt be going higher in the years ahead.

WINSTON S. CHURCHILL /
HIS COMPLETE SPEECHES
1897-1963

COHEN A284, ICS A145

Prior to this work, four-fifths of Churchill's speeches had never been published in volume form. To correct this, and to coincide with the Centenary of Churchill's birth, a team of Columbia University graduate students spent six months combing Parliamentary records, newspapers, pamphlets, Conservative Party and BBC broadcast transcripts. The result was eight massive volumes totalling nearly 9,000 pages, pulled together by Robert Rhodes James, who had earlier published a biography of Lord Randolph Churchill and the seminal *Churchill: A Study in Failure 1900–1939*. Rhodes James added introductory essays for the four parts of the work and useful prefatory notes before many speeches; the publishers provided two comprehensive indices. The editor was paid £5,000 for his work (55p per page), surely the publisher's bargain of the decade.

Indispensable as it is, *His Complete Speeches* remains a flawed work, primarily

Now bordering on the rare is the mammoth and invaluable *Complete Speeches*, published by Chelsea House and Bowker in 1974. Fine sets like these are appreciating very rapidly, for there are far too few to go round.

because it is not complete. Granted, the editing required difficult judgements. For example, Churchill's speech in defence of Edward VIII in the Albert Hall (3 December 1936) was omitted because he didn't finish it–the audience protested and began walking out! But there are many inexplicable omissions: the final peroration from the post-Munich speech in 1938 ('I have watched this famous Island descending the staircase which leads to a dark gulf...') is nowhere to be found. Some key speeches are wholly absent, for example 28 June 1954, when Churchill called for détente with the Soviet Union at the Washington Press Club, adding coyly that he hoped nobody would think him a Communist for doing so. Churchill's youthful orations were spottily recorded, and many of these were left out. Although Hansard went verbatim in 1911, even it was not reliable, since its reporters said Churchill's remarks were sometimes inaudible.

It is possible that some omissions in this text may not be the fault of the researchers. For example, we know that Churchill edited his speeches in *Arms and the Covenant*. Could he have added the memorable lines about 'this famous island' for the book, but not used them in debate? It would be interesting to run down these possibilities.

FROM THE REVIEWS

'The public Churchill emerges with great clarity ... What an elocutionary feast remains! All the pinnacles of a turbulent career are here: the condemnation of the Munich settlement, the promise of "blood, toil, tears and sweat", and the fateful iron curtain speech at Fulton. Indeed, the parts are engulfed by the whole in what turns out to be a sweeping chronicle of the major events of the first half of the century.

'These speeches do more than remind us that Churchill was a gifted orator and writer. They increase our understanding of a matchlessly dramatic life; we watch its progress or recession in their pages. We learn more about the events that molded Churchill, his world and our own. Appearing in his centenary, these monumental works may even help to make Churchill fashionable again.'

Jon Foreman in *The Nation* (USA), 21 September 1974

First Edition: ICS A145a
Publisher: Chelsea House/Bowker, New York, 1974

Eight volumes
Red cloth blocked gold and black. On cover, author's name, general title and Churchill Arms; on spine, author's name and general title gold on black panel; volume number, years, editor's and publishers' names blocked gold. Red cloth head- and footbands, each volume with frontispiece. The eight volumes published as a set at $185.

Vol. I, 1072 pages numbered (i)–(xvi) and (1)–1,056. Vol. II, 1158 pages numbered (i)–(xii) and 1,057–2,197 (+1). Vol. III, 1,010 pages numbered (i)–(xii) and 2,299–3,296. Vol. IV, 1212 pages numbered (i)–(xii) and 3,297–44/6. Vol. V, 1160 pages numbered (i)–(xiv) and 4,417–5,572. Vol. VI, 1176 pages numbered (i)–xii and 5,573–6,733 (+1). Vol. VII, 1182 pages numbered (i)–(xiv) and 6,735–7,902. Vol. VIII, 1,028 pages numbered (i)–(xii) and 7,903–8,917 (+1).

APPRAISAL

The original price was steep in 1974, but would be a bargain today. Typical sets in fine condition are now selling for up to $1,000/£600 and I've seen them catalogued for double that. Some sets on today's market have come from libraries, with defacing marks on their spines or library stamps on title-pages; these cost less, but not much less. As formidable a job as it seems, the prospective buyer should collate each volume: several volumes exist with missing signatures of 32 pages ... including my own.

Abridged One-Volume Edition: ICS A145b

Publisher: Chelsea House, New York, 1980; Windward, London, 1981; Barnes & Noble, 1998 (hardback entitled Churchill Speaks)

This very thick paperback was published at $25/£15 and, until 1997, I was not aware that it existed. Well put together for a softbound work, it numbers 1,088 pages and contains a good selection of speeches from the original eight volumes. Given the increasing scarcity of the original, it is a good stopgap volume until one can find (or afford) the first edition.

Abridged Edition: ICS A145c

Publisher: Chelsea House, New York, 1983

Eight volumes

A paperback edition, greatly abridged, is the final successor to the original work. It appears infrequently, but should not be looked upon as anything approaching the complete text. A fine set might be worth up to $100/£60, but certainly not more.

The 1980 abridgement is attractively bound in heavy card wrappers.

CHURCHILL CORRESPONDENCE

Correspondence between Stalin and Churchill, Roosevelt, Truman and Attlee was published in Moscow in a two-volume set in 1957 and published in one-volume in New York the same year (Woods B57). Churchill's selected correspondence with Roosevelt, edited by Lowenheim, was published in New York as a single volume in 1975 (Cohen A278). *Churchill and Roosevelt | The Complete Correspondence,* edited by Kimball, was published by Princeton University Press in three volumes in 1984 (Cohen A280). Peter G. Boyle edited *The Churchill-Eisenhower Correspondence 1953-1955,* published by the University of North Carolina Press in 1990. Because these books contain substantial material not by Churchill, they are beyond the purview of this book; consult Cohen for bibliographic details.

THE COLLECTED ESSAYS OF SIR WINSTON CHURCHILL

COHEN A286, ICS A146

Upon publication of the *Collected Works* (see Appendix), it was observed that those 34 volumes did not comprise the complete canon, since Churchill had written hundreds of essays for periodicals which he did not include in compilations such as *Thoughts and Adventures*. Accordingly, the publishers of the *Collected Works* commissioned Michael Wolff, one of Randolph Churchill's former assistants on the Official Biography, to compile all the essays not already contained within the 34 *Collected Works*. The result was four satisfying volumes of material that would cost $20,000/£12,000 or so to acquire in its original form, assuming one could locate all of the many periodicals which had published Churchill for 60 years.

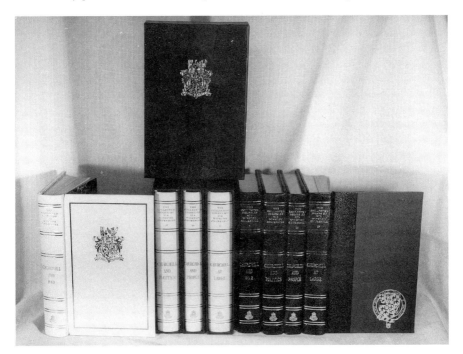

The *Collected Essays* were an afterthought to the *Collected Works*, but a very important one, capturing many of Churchill's periodical articles not published in his books. Originally bound in vellum with slipcases (left) and in half blue morocco (right), they are still being bound today from leftover sheets.

The Collected Essays comprise genuine Churchill material, published for the first time in volume form. Wolff fastidiously grouped the articles into separate volumes for War, Politics and People, with a catch-all *Churchill At Large* volume as the finale. He also provides an erudite and useful foreword to the work in Vol. I. Here Wolff suggests that these articles, written quickly and raced into print, are more a reflection of our author's true opinions than his books, which were exhaustively edited and revised before Churchill released them to publishers. Whether or not that is so, the *Essays* are a stunning and important addition to the Churchill canon, quite indispensable to students of our author.

Centenary Limited Edition: ICS A146a
Publisher: Library of Imperial History, London, 1976

Four volumes
Elaborately bound in full vellum blocked gilt with titles on spine and Churchill arms on cover. All edges gilt, inside edges of boards tooled gilt, silk page markers, marbled endpapers, head- and footbands, and so on. Each volume houses in a dark green leatherette slipcase with the Churchill Arms gilt on top panel.

Vol. I, *Churchill and War*, 510 pages numbered (i)–(xviii) and (1)–492 (+2). Vol. II, *Churchill and Politics*, 494 pages numbered (i)–(xii) and (1)–477 (+5). Vol. III, *Churchill and People*, 362 pages numbered (i)–(xii) and (1)–347 (+3). Vol. IV, *Churchill at Large*, 530 pages numbered (i)–(xii) and (1)–511 (+7).

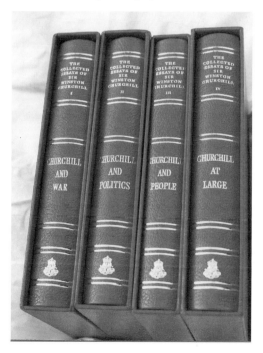

At least 20 sets of the 'Collected Works', including the *Essays* were bound in full red morocco, and ten more sets were bound in dark red goatskin. Another two to four sets were bound individually in red morocco. All were equipped with matching red slipcases. *(Photo: Ray Butterworth)*

VARIANTS

In 1987, I discovered the remaining unbound sheets of this work at the bindery in Cornwall, and a number of sets were made up, bound in materials other than the original vellum. Chief among these are full cream morocco (green slipcases) and full red morocco (red slipcases). Note that this production is distinct from the differently bound variant below, but can be identified by the words 'Centenary Limited Edition' on the half title and title-page.

APPRAISAL

Vellum and full morocco sets were still being bound at this writing at $750/£475 the set.

Centenary Edition: ICS A146b
Publisher: Library of Imperial History, London, 1976

Four volumes

Internally the same as the above, this version is bound differently, and can also be identified by the words 'Centenary Edition' on the half title and title-page. Bound in quarter navy morocco and blue cloth, a circular version of the Churchill Arms blocked gilt on the top board and the titles blocked gilt on the spine. While equipped with page markers and marbled endpapers, the volumes lack the fancy gilt tooling on the inside of the boards and only the top page edges are gilt. Some of the sheets were also later bound in full red morocco (illustration opposite), and in goatskin.

THE DREAM

ICS A147

Churchill wrote *The Dream* just after the Second World War, entitling it 'Private Article' and filing it away. In his will, Sir Winston bequeathed the piece to Lady Churchill; it was finally published in *The Daily Telegraph* (1966) and the *Collected Essays* (1976). Lady Churchill assigned the rights to the work as a donation to Churchill College Cambridge, by whose kind permission it was published for the first time in single volume form by the International Churchill Society 22 years after Sir Winston's death. Though of modest size, it has an important place among his writings.

The story is of the imagined return of Lord Randolph Churchill, 'just as I had seen him in his prime', who finds his son painting in the Chartwell studio. In typical prose Winston recounts all that has happened since his father's death in 1895, without once hinting at the myriad roles Winston himself played in those events. Winston's son Randolph believed that 'the story may have been inspired subconsciously by Churchill's regret that his father would never know what he had achieved. It is part of the artistry of this tale that the inquisitive young father of 37 is not allowed to know the one thing about his 72-year-old son that would have amazed him more than anything else which he had he learned.'

There are many other ironies. Lord Randolph asks if Russia is 'still the danger' and enquires, 'Is there still a Tsar?' Winston replies, 'Yes, but he is not a Romanoff.' India, Winston admits, 'has gone down the drain', but the remaining Dominions 'are our brothers.' Lord Randolph asks if there has been war. Winston replies, 'We have had nothing else but wars since democracy took charge.' But our author remains optimistic: 'Having gone through so much, we do not despair...we are trying to make a world organisation in which we and America will be very important.'

Lord Randolph compliments his son on his grasp of 'these fearful facts ... I never expected that you would develop so far and so fully. Of course you are too old now to think about such things, but when I hear you talk I really wonder you didn't go into politics. You might have done a lot to help. You might even have made a name for yourself.' With that he lights his cigarette, and vanishes.

The attraction of this work is manifest, but one question about it remains. Just how much of it was regarded by Churchill as fiction?

Sir Winston was a man of transcendental, almost supernatural powers. In 1953 he told his private secretary, Jock Colville, that he would die on 24 January, the same day as his father died; twelve years later he lapsed into a coma on 10 January, and Colville was able to assure The Queen's private secretary, that he wouldn't die for a fortnight. Unconscious, Churchill did just that. *The Dream* is said to be fiction; there is no doubt in my mind that it was not entirely a dream to its author.

First Edition: ICS A147a

Publisher: Churchill Literary Foundation, Hopkinton, NH. 1987

Bound in padded red leather, 16mo, blocked gilt with Churchill Arms blocked blind on top board. All edges gilt, head- and footbands, satin pagemarker. 16mo, 48 pages numbered (i)–(xvi) (+2) and (1)–28 (+2), with colour illustration running over two coated paper sheets inserted after page (xvi). A limited edition of 500 individually numbered copies: copies #1–20 (plus one proof copy) carried handmade French marbled endpapers and copies #21–500 (plus ten proof copies) carried red moiré cloth endpapers. Not sold commercially but presented to supporters of the Churchill Literary Foundation (predecessor to The Churchill Center) through donations of $100, £65 or $135 Canadian. Published September 1987.

This extraordinary production was printed by traditional letterpress on 300-year Mohawk Superfine archival paper and bound in padded leather, with many symbolic features. The top board is blocked gilt with Churchill's signature taken from the First Edition of the one-volume abridged *World Crisis,* bordered by a design based on the title-page of David Kirkwood's *My Life of Revolt* (1935), which contains a Churchill introduction and was published by Harrap, publishers of

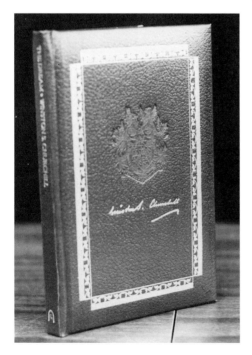

The Dream was published in limited edition by the Churchill Literary Foundation, a predecessor of The Churchill Center.

Variations of *The Dream*. Left to right: the current wrapper copy; the hardbound first edition showing two styles of endpapers (red moiré cloth and marbled paper); the Latvian *Sapnis*, and the limited edition for the Churchill family, produced in celebration of Sir Winston's 120th birthday, 30 November 1994.

Marlborough. French handmade endpapers on copies #1–20 were chosen to denote Churchill's special affection for France; such copies were presented to President Mitterrand, the Pol-Roger family, and the Duff Cooper Library at the British Embassy in Paris, as well as to HM The Queen (copy #1), President Reagan (#2) and Lady Soames (the proof copy). The colour illustration is from an oil painting by Sal Asaro commissioned by the publishers, the original of which was purchased from the artist by Harvey Greisman of Connecticut, USA.

APPRAISAL
The edition was fully subscribed by mid-1988, and the only copies that have come on the secondhand market have appeared through sales of estates and collections, selling for around $500/£350.

Second Edition: ICS A147b
Publisher: International Churchill Society, Hopkinton, NH, 1994

Bound in maroon textured heavy paper wrappers blocked gilt with title, Churchill Arms and author's name on top wrapper. 16mo, 32 pages numbered (1)–32; pages 15–18 on coated paper contain the Asaro painting running as a double page spread on pages 16–17. Published June 1994 in an edition of 1,000 copies. Still in print and available from The Churchill Center's sales department (Churchill Stores) for $15/£9.

VARIANT
Seventy copies of this edition, plus ten proof copies, were specially bound in dark

green leather boards for the Churchill Family, celebrating the 120th birthday of Sir Winston, at the Pinafore Room, Savoy Hotel, London on 30 November 1994. These copies are blocked gilt with the title, Churchill Arms and author's name on top board and the title and author's name (running down) on the spine. They feature light green marbled endpapers and gilt page edges. An extra sheet comprising two leafs and four pages is inserted to fall before the title-page and page 32, the first page of which states 'COMMEMORATIVE EDITION', a note about the occasion for which it was produced, and the number (#1–70) or 'proof copy'.

FOREIGN TRANSLATIONS

Latvian: SAPNIS
Publisher: International Churchill Society, Hopkinton, NH, 1995
Bound in bright red morocco with Churchill Arms, 'SAPNIS' and author's name on top board and 'SAPNIS' and author's name (reading down) on spine. 16mo, 44 pages numbered (4+) (1)–37 (+3); plus four unnumbered coated paper pages containing the Asaro painting as a double page spread.

The first Churchill book published in Latvian, this work consists of the original text plus 22 explanatory notes to Latvians unfamiliar with British terminology or place names. The translation was prepared by the British Embassy in Riga, reproduced by the publisher in New Hampshire, and bound by Robert Hartnoll Ltd. in Cornwall, England. This limited edition of 25 numbered copies was published in May 1995.

Sapnis was produced for Richard Ralph, Her Majesty's Ambassador to Latvia, who had asked this writer for an appropriate gift for the Latvian President, an admirer of Sir Winston. The presentation was made during 'Latviesu Krasts', a commemorative bicycle tour of the Latvian coast in May 1995, marking the 50th anniversary of the continuing struggle of Latvian patriots for freedom after the end of the Second World War. Copy #1 was retained by the publisher; copy #2 was presented in Jūrmala, Latvia on 18 June 1995 to President Guntis Ulmanis by Ambassador Ralph and the bicyclists: Talevaldis Dumpis, Maxim Vickers, Douglas Russell and this writer. Other copies were presented to Latvian dignitaries and Churchill Society Trustees and special friends.

THE CHARTWELL BULLETINS
1935

ICS A148

When his wife was away from home, Churchill often kept her up to date with what he called *Chartwell Bulletins*. Between January and April 1935, Clementine undertook a voyage to the South Seas, and Winston sent her 12 charming bulletins which tell a remarkable and cohesive tale about life at Chartwell and contemporary politics. The 12 are collected here, along with exchanges of telegrams during the period and photographs, some annotated in Churchill's own hand, by courtesy of Lady Soames. The letters had previously been published only in the thick and now-rare Companion Volume V, Part 2 of the official biography. The editor was official biographer Sir Martin Gilbert, who reviewed, amended and amplified his original footnotes to bring them up to date, and to identify every person mentioned.

The dialogue is captivating. Here we meet daughter Mary's pug, committing 'at least three indiscretions a day' on Winston's carpet; Churchill wishing he'd been in the Commons to defend a political foe, Ramsay MacDonald, from 'brutal insults'; son Randolph growing 'a hideous, scrubby beard'; an island in Chartwell's lake being made by a steam shovel always referred to as a living being; the current book project stalled by politics ('Poor Marlborough lingers on the battlefield of

The two variants of *The Chartwell Bulletins*. Left: the standard wrapper copy. Right, one of a handful of hardback copies bound in bright red leather.

both brothers and both sisters ... The Ptolemys always did this and Cleopatra was the result ... I have not thought it my duty to interfere.' Alongside the merriment we read of Churchill's forebodings over Germany: 'I expect in fact [that Hitler] is really much stronger than we are.'

Many writers have tried to relate what life at Chartwell was really like in its prime as Churchill's 'factory'. Some, like William Manchester, have succeeded, while others have only created caricature. In *The Chartwell Bulletins* we are given a true glimpse–by the man who knew Chartwell best.

First Edition: ICS A148
Publisher: International Churchill Society, Hopkinton, NH, 1989

Perfect-bound (square spine) in maroon textured heavy paper wrappers. Title, Churchill Arms and author's, editor's and publisher's names blocked gilt on top wrapper. 16mo, 64 pages numbered (1)–64, illustrated. Published June 1989 at $15 in an edition of 2,000 copies.

VARIANT
Fifty copies were bound in red leather boards blocked gilt.

The Chartwell Bulletins were still available from Churchill Stores (sales department for The Churchill Center) as of this writing. The Bulletins are now reappearing in a volume of Winston–Clementine correspondence, edited by their daughter, Lady Soames.

THE GREAT REPUBLIC

First Edition: ICS A149
Publisher: Random House, New York, 1999

Hardbound, 470 pages numbered (i)-xxii and (1)-(458). Published September 1999 at $25.95.

Edited and arranged by Sir Winston's grandson, this volume distills everything Churchill wrote about America in his *History of the English Speaking Peoples* (about 230 pages) plus all of his major essays on the USA (about 130 pages). Also included are three Churchill essays on English Common Law, Magna Carta and Parliament ("America's English Heritage") and Churchill's famous "what-if" story, "If Lee Had Not Won the Battle of Gettysburg". Greeted enthusiastically on publication, this latest work demonstrates our author's ability to keep on publishing long after he has left this vale of tears.

APPENDIX 1:
THE COLLECTED EDITIONS

THE COLLECTED WORKS, ICS AA1

In 1973 on the eve of the Churchill Centenary, word broke of the first collected edition of Sir Winston's books, edited by Frederick Woods, limited to an edition of 'no more than 3,000 copies', and selling for £945, then about $2,500.

Aesthetically, the set was magnificent: bound in natural calfskin vellum with the titling in 22 ct. gold, the page edges gilt, marbled endpapers, and printed on special 500-year archival paper. Each volume was contained in a dark green slipcase stamped with the Churchill Arms. The specifications were titanic: five million words in 19,000 pages, weighing 90lbs, taking up 4½ft of shelf space. To achieve publication, 11 publishing houses in Great Britain, the United States and Canada released their individual copyrights, in exchange for the promise that no other complete collection of Churchill's works would be published until the expiration of international copyright in 2019.

The *Collected Works* as originally published, in full calfskin vellum blocked 22 ct. gilt, 34 volumes in all. (The handsome bookcase was not part of the publisher's offering.) Four volumes of *Collected Essays* were added later.

The Works were promoted with a set of impressive testimonials. Lady Churchill, who wrote the foreword to Vol. 1, said the books would have given Sir Winston, 'enormous pleasure'. She presented the first set to Prime Minister Edward Heath, who called it 'a great venture which will at once mark the centenary of his birth and preserve the memory of his life and his writing for future generations'.

Opinion among bibliophiles was less uniformly enthusiastic, and not long in coming. Writing in *Finest Hour*, the Churchill Society journal, editor Dalton Newfield termed the announcement 'tragic news. Thousands of Churchillophiles and students of the Great Man's life will never own this wonderful work, indeed few will ever even see it. Few libraries will find $2,500 for an edition so expensive that they cannot give it general circulation. Up to now there has been no library in which one could find all of Sir Winston's works, and this edition bids fair to change the situation hardly at all.' The collection, he said, was 'canted toward the speculator, and even the claim that "a substantial part of the proceeds ... will be used to further the work of the Churchill Centenary Trust, Churchill College Cambridge and the Winston Churchill Foundation in the United States" helps very little. 3,000 x $2,500 = $7,500,000 ... There is no valid reason why the plates could not be used on ordinary paper, in ordinary binding, for an ordinary profit in addition to the deluxe binding, except that the deluxe could not be sold for such an inordinate price if this were done.

'What pains most is that it is all so unChurchillian. Sir Winston was not unconscious of money–quite the contrary–but he did put out abridgements, cheap editions, etc., so that people at all levels could enjoy his works'. Newfield added that the latest *Encyclopaedia Britannica* had three editions from $998 to $5,000, but 'all who want to use this valuable reference will be able to buy it for just under $500, and EB will knock another $100 off if you trade in any old edition. What a contrast!'

To Newfield's question of how much of the proceeds would really go to worthy Churchill institutions, the publishers replied that they 'planned' 20 three-year scholarships and six one-year fellowships from Canada, New Zealand and Australia to Churchill College. But he was not told if those grants would be funded or would be a one-time arrangement. 'Estimating their worth at about, £1,500 per annum', wrote Newfield of the scholarships, 'there is a total of about £100,000, or slightly above 3% of the gross potential of the edition. Funding these grants would require, at 6%, about £650,000, a capital sum clearly beyond the capabilities of this edition even considering the availability of interest above 6%.' So much for "a substantial part of the proceeds".'

Dalton Newfield also raised very real problems of scholarship. Certain works were being reset and reedited. Some volumes were taken from later editions which differed radically from the firsts. The worst offender was *The River War*, which appears in the *Works* only as an abridgement, a far cry from the original text. Even *The World Crisis*, which with its shoulder notes looked at a glance like an offprint of the First English Edition, was reset, re-edited and its maps redrawn.

In all, only eight volumes and half of a ninth, offprinted from first or early impressions, contain the original text and pagination. Seven volumes were offprinted from later editions. The other eighteen and a half volumes, though often improved with uniform type and better maps, bear no resemblance to the originals. They are of limited value for footnotes or references since the *Collected Works* are so rare that few can access them.

The reset works were severely edited (see review below). While this often improved or modernized the text, it created enormous differences from the original. If an editor took the liberty of changing 'Currachee' to 'Karachi', was the editor not also tempted to change the meaning of whole passages? We will not know until the Works are computer-scanned and electronically compared with an original. 'I concede that WSC's works can stand a lot of editing, particularly his maps and quotations', wrote Dalton Newfield, 'but such editing, of course, makes the issue useless for the student and scholar.'

The term *Collected Works* was itself misleading, since only Churchill's books and some of his speeches were included; forewords and contributions to other books, contributions to press and periodicals, and most of Churchill's speeches were omitted. The Library of Imperial History reacted to this criticism when it issued, in 1976, the *Collected Essays of Winston Churchill,* a four-volume compilation of most major forewords and periodical contributions not in the *Works.* This set (see its entry on page 353) was a true contribution to the Churchill canon. Purchasers of the *Works* were duly given the option to add the four volumes of *Essays,* although it was noticed that a less expensive binding of the *Essays* was offered.

Shortly after publication the price went up to £1,060 in Britain and $3,000 in America. This did nothing to encourage sales, and by 1976 all signs pointed to somewhat less than the sell-out the Library of Imperial History had promised. In a much less deluxe prospectus issued that year it was admitted that only 1,750 of the authorized 3,000 sets 'have been published'. I later learned that the actual press run of sheets was never 3,000 but around 2,000, and that books were bound only as orders were taken.

Its high-sounding name notwithstanding, the Library of Imperial History was nothing more than a small office set up for this project. If they did manage to sell 1,750 copies at $3,000, the firm should have grossed over $5 million, which one would suppose was enough to keep it going. But by the late 1970s the Library of Imperial History declared bankruptcy. The receivers relocated from London to Royal Tunbridge Wells, and fitful efforts were made to dispose of further sets, without much success.

By 1982, when I attempted to locate the Tunbridge people, both they and the remaining copies of the *Works* and *Essays* had vanished. I had word that someone unnamed had bought the stock and moved it to New York, but letters to the given address went unanswered, and when a New York bookseller colleague went personally to the location he found it an 'accommodation address'.

For a year or more I tried without success to rediscover the thread of the 'great venture'. Then, suddenly, I found a firm of London solicitors who had been involved in some phase of the firm's liquidation. They had no clue as to the whereabouts, but suggested that the bindery might know. The bindery did. For the past several years they had been warehousing some 200 unbound sheets of *Collected Essays* and about fifty sets of *Collected Works*.

The unknown New York entrepreneur had apparently bought the sheets from the receivers and had persuaded the bindery to make up 20 sets of *Collected Works*–not in vellum but in red morocco. Although the gilt lettering and coat of arms on the books exactly matched the original, the new slipcases were red, not green, and did not carry the gilt Churchill Arms. Still, it was a sensational discovery: there were enough sets of *Essays* to satisfy everyone who needed them, and many collectors thought the morocco-bound *Works* were more handsome and durable than the vellum.

Alas, the process of making them available was a test of will, strength, computer time and patience. The owner of the sheets had disappeared, leaving a huge bindery bill for the 20 sets in red morocco. The law moves slowly, and the bindery was told that seven years must go by before it could consider the books its own to dispose of, without risk of the owner surfacing and accusing them of dealing in stolen property!

I kept at them. 'Isn't there some way you can meet the law and still get rid of the books?', I asked. In the summer of 1987, three years after I had located the trove, they thought of one: sell the books, but keep the proceeds in an escrow account for the prescribed number of years. In this way the bindery would meet the letter of the law while the Churchill world would get the books many were so desperate to own.

Today, all the bindery's copies of the *Works* are sold, though they regularly appear in auction sales, while the *Essays* can still be ordered, in vellum, full or quarter morocco, from my colleague, Mark Weber, and from me. Over the years Mark and I have also sold about twenty sets bound in full cream morocco in the original dark green slipcases, duplicating the colour of the original vellum but substituting a much more satisfying and longer-lived binding. (Vellum is beautiful, but tends to swell and discolour with age.)

APPRAISAL

While they have some importance as the first collected edition, and as beautiful examples of the binder's art, the *Works* remain expensive reprints. Nor do they all contain the original text. Since the true collector likes to hold in his or her hands the work in the form Sir Winston first gave it to the world, these luxurious volumes will never replace the first editions in value or desirability.

It is true that for the price of a set of *Works* and *Essays* today, one cannot buy a complete set of Churchill first editions. But give me $4,000/£2,400 and let me spend it as I wish, on postwar first editions and fine prewar trade editions, and I will create a better, more interesting, more textually correct Churchill library than this made-to-order collector's item.

The Collected Essays are something else entirely: the first publication of Churchill articles in volume form, important books despite their tall price. I hope that some day The Churchill Center may be able to reprint the *Essays* in a form which colleges, students, scholars and libraries everywhere can afford.

FROM THE REVIEWS

'Even the warmest Churchill devotee may shrink from the $2,500 price of the collected works. Some will note that Churchill's books are in print in cheaper editions. Any scholar, however, will approve of the painstaking correction of the stylistic errors that cropped up in the earlier works. Churchill's mastery of English, for example, completely outdistanced his grasp of Latin and Greek, as sometimes is manifest in his inaccurate quotations. And these extend to the English citations as well: in the first volume of *The World Crisis*, Churchill misquotes Housman's "On the idle hill of summer, sleeping with the flow of streams" as "sleepy with the sounds of streams".

'Maps, notably in the fledgling books, tend to confuse rather than clarify. In fact, about 300 maps were remade for the collected works, either because of original geographical inaccuracies or changed spellings of locations. Writing early in the century, Churchill spelled Karachi as Currachee and Chile as Chili. In *The River War,* he writes confidently, "All these positions can be followed on the map." But a place called Selim in the text appears as Esselem in the maps. Churchill took little care in obtaining these, often borrowing from contemporary school atlases or other books of the period ... While revising outmoded or incorrect spelling and obstacles to geographical comprehension, however, the editors wisely retain old-fashioned but characteristic Churchillisms like "I am of the opinion".'

Jon Foreman in *The Nation*, New York, 21 September 1974

The Collected Works of Sir Winston Churchill
Publisher: Library of Imperial History, London, 1974–75

Thirty four volumes
Elaborately bound in full vellum blocked gilt with titles on spine and Churchill arms on cover. All edges gilt, inside edges of boards tooled gilt, silk page markers, marbled endpapers, head- and footbands, and so on. Each volume housed in a dark green leatherette slipcase with the Churchill Arms gilt on top panel.

VARIANTS
Some sets were bound in full red morocco with plain red slipcases; in full cream

Each volume of the *Works* was contained in a dark green slipcase, blocked gilt. Volume I, which was widely distributed as a sample, combined the *Early Life* and *African Journey*, a rather odd duo.

morocco with the original style of slipcases; and in a few other colours on an individual basis (at least one set exists in light blue morocco, and another in full green goatskin).

APPRAISAL

Original worn vellum sets without slipcases have occasionally sold for $3,000/£1800 or slightly less. Fine vellum or morocco bound sets have lately ranged up to $6,000/£3600; an original publisher's numbered set in slipcases, in fine condition, should be expected to sell for the upper figure or more.

For the benefit of scholars and researchers with access to these volumes, I list below the 'true texts' (offprints from trade editions) and 'altered texts' (volumes reset and re-edited, with altered pagination). The second group is almost worthless for citation in footnotes and references, and should be cited only as a supplement to first or trade editions.

TRUE TEXTS

(Pagination coincides with first or early editions.)

XIV–XV.   *Marlborough*: offprinted from the 1947 Harrap two-volume edition, which itself was considerably revised by the author.

XVII.   *Arms and the Covenant*: offprinted from the First Edition.

XVIII.   *Step by Step*: offprinted from a first or early edition.

XIX–XX1.   *The War Speeches*: offprinted from the 1952 Definitive Edition with the same pagination; but this edition omits some speeches published in the original seven volumes.

XXIX. *In the Balance:* offprinted from the First Edition.

XXX. *Stemming the Tide, The Unwritten Alliance:* offprinted from First Editions.

XXI–XXIV. *A History of the English-Speaking Peoples:* offprinted from first or early editions.

ALTERED TEXTS

(Pagination does not coincide with any trade editions except the 1989–1990 reprints by Cooper and Norton (*Malakand Field Force, Savrola, The Boer War, My Early Life, My African Journey, Thoughts and Adventures, Great Contemporaries*) which were themselves offprinted from the *Collected Works.* Reset texts should be assumed to have been re-edited–see 'From the Reviews'.)

I. *My Early Life, My African Journey:* the first title is offprinted from the First Edition, the second title reset from an unknown edition.

About 100 unbound sets of *Collected Works* were discovered by this writer in the mid-1980s. About 20, including the four *Collected Essays,* had been bound in full red morocco, and these are occasionally seen on the secondhand market.

II.	*The Story of the Malakand Field Force:* reset, based on the 1899 Silver Library Edition.
III.	*The River War:* reset using an abridged text (1902 onward).
IV.	*The Boer War:* reset from first editions of *London to Ladysmith via Pretoria* and *Ian Hamilton's March.*
V.	*Savrola:* reset from an unknown edition.
VI.	*Lord Randolph Churchill:* reset from the 1952 Odhams edition.
VII.	*Mr. Brodrick's Army* and *Other Early Speeches:* reset from *Mr. Brodrick's Army, For Free Trade, Liberalism and the Social Problem, The People's Rights* and *India* and entirely repaginated.
VIII–XII.	*The World Crisis:* reset text combining the original two volumes of 1916–1918 into one volume; pagination and shoulder notes do not coincide.
XIII.	*Thoughts and Adventures:* reset, edition unknown.
XVI.	*Great Contemporaries:* reset, based on the 1938 revised edition.
XXII–XXVII.	*The Second World War:* reset; maps and plans redrawn.
XXVIII.	*The Sinews of Peace, Europe Unite:* reset from First Editions.

THE MAJOR WORKS OF SIR WINSTON CHURCHILL, ICS AA2

While the Library of Imperial History was setting about the almost impossible task of finding and publishing Churchill's entire canon, the Diner's Club in association with Fine Art International Ltd. and the Hamlyn Publishing Group began a slightly more modest project to celebrate the Centenary of his birth: a fine edition of 25 'major works' from *Lord Randolph Churchill* through the *History of the English-Speaking Peoples.* The sets were produced and handsomely bound by Edito-Service SA in Geneva. Like the L.I.H. collection they did not sell out, and odd volumes were still on sale at Chartwell in the mid-1980s. Sold on subscription, to which not everyone stuck, they are often encountered individually today. They are the only collected edition besides the *Collected Works.*

Centenary First Edition
Publisher: The Diner's Club, London, 1974

Twenty-five volumes
Bound in full maroon morocco blocked gilt with initials 'WSC' and elaborate border on top board. On spines are three black leather labels for the author, volume title and 'CENTENARY FIRST EDITION'; the 'WSC' is also blocked on the spine along with two empty square panels. All page edges gilt, inside edges of boards tooled gilt, black cloth page markers, maroon moiré cloth endpapers, head- and footbands. Each volume contains an identical frontispiece, the Karsh 'Angry Lion' 1941 photograph, tipped in opposite the title-page.

APPRAISAL

Complete sets have recently sold in the neighbourhood of $800/£480, individual volumes for up to $50/£35 apiece. There is less demand for these than the *Collected Works* because they include fewer volumes of Churchill's books.

Though smaller, the Diner's Club collection is truer to the original texts than the *Collected Works,* since all but *The Second World War* were offprinted from readily available first or early impressions. Even *The Second World War* was derived from a popular current edition, which although reset was based on Churchill's final corrected text. For the benefit of scholars and researchers with access to these volumes, I list the sources of the various texts.

TRUE TEXTS

(Pagination coincides with first or early impressions.)

Lord Randolph Churchill (I–II): offprinted from the First Edition.

My Early Life: offprinted from the First Edition.

The World Crisis (I–V): offprinted from First Editions, but omitting *The Eastern Front.*

Marlborough (I–IV) offprinted from the 1947 Harrap two-volume edition, but redivided back into four volumes.

War Speeches (I–III): offprinted from the 1952 Definitive Edition with the same pagination; but this edition omits many speeches published in the original seven volumes.

History of the English Speaking Peoples (I–IV): offprinted from the First Edition.

ALTERED TEXTS

(Pagination does not coincide with first or early editions.)

The Second World War (I–VI): printed from the same plates as the Heron Edition (ICS A123m), which was also being produced at this time by Edito-Service SA. The Heron illustrations are also included, but in groups of one or two per volume, not interspersed as in the Heron in one signature per volume.

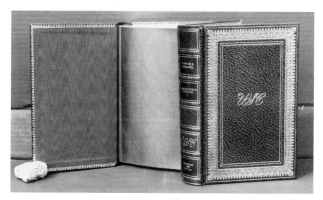

The Diner's Club in London produced the only other collected edition, the 'Major Works', consisting of 25 volumes. The books were produced by Edito-Service SA in Geneva, bound in burgundy morocco with black leather spine labels and cloth moiré pattern endpapers.

APPENDIX 2:
THE CHURCHILL CENTER

The Churchill Center, headquartered in Washington, D.C. but active internationally, has a unique mission: 'To encourage study of the life and thought of Sir Winston Spencer Churchill; to foster research about his speeches, writings and deeds; to advance knowledge of his example as a statesman; and, by programmes of teaching and publishing, to impart that learning to men, women and young people around the world.'

The Churchill Center has an active membership in America, and also in Great Britain, Canada and Australia through its chief affiliates the International Churchill Societies. Together, the Center and Societies publish a quarterly journal, *Finest Hour*, along the biannual *Churchill Proceedings* and other speciality publications; sponsor international conferences and Churchill Tours; hold a variety of local meetings; and offer a constantly expanding Internet website *(www.winstonchurchill.org)*.

The Churchill Center has, over the years, helped bring about republication of over 20 of Churchill's long out of print books and launched the campaign for completion of the Companion Volumes of the official biography, made possible by the generous support of old friend of Sir Winston, Wendy Reves. More recently, the Center has sponsored three academic symposia in the USA and UK, each of which has produced or will produce a book; seminars bringing students and professors together for discussions of Churchill's books; scholarships for students pursuing Churchill Studies at the University of Edinburgh; and publication subventions helping to produce important reference works, including this one.

Today The Churchill Center is embarked on an endowment campaign to raise sufficient capital to allow it to expand and operate forever. Aside from the activities mentioned above are plans for a headquarters building; a standard library of Churchill's books and books about him; computer facilities indexing every word he wrote and spoke, linked to the major Churchill archives; seminars on aspects of Churchill's long and multifaceted career; an annual Winston Churchill lecture by a prominent world leader; video programmes for schoolchildren; college or graduate level courses on the career of Churchill; fellowships to assist graduate students writing dissertations dealing with Churchill or related aspects of 20th century history; visiting professorships and academic chairs. The overall aim is to 'teach statesmanship', using the greatest teacher of that craft the 20th century produced.

Membership in the Churchill Center and Societies is available for a modest subscription, with discounts to students. For further information please contact:

- USA: The Churchill Center, PO Box 385-G, Hopkinton NH 03229
- UK: International Churchill Society, PO Box 1257, Melksham Wilts. SN12 6GQ
- Canada: International Churchill Society, 3256 Rymal Rd., Mississauga Ont. L4Y 3C1
- Australia: International Churchill Society, 181 Jersey Street, Wembley WA 6014

You may also join by downloading membership applications and clicking JOIN US on the Churchill Home Page: www.winstonchurchill.org.

Recent Discoveries

Spanish: *Obasa Escogidas* (Selected Works) including *Pensamientos y Aventuras, Grandes Contemporaneos, La Forza de la Victoria*. Published by Bibliotech, Premios Nobel, Madrid: 1957.